MEDIA ETHICS

Media Ethics
Opening Social Dialogue

Edited by

Bart Pattyn

PEETERS
2000

ISBN 90-429-0902-1
D. 2000/0602/107

© Peeters – Bondgenotenlaan 153 – B-3000 Leuven – Belgium – 2000

TABLE OF CONTENTS

FOREWORD
Professional Ethics and Ethics Education: Vision of the Core Materials Project

Johan Verstraeten

This book is a result of the core materials project for the development of courses in professional ethics initiated by the *European Ethics Network* and subsidized by the European Commission DG XXII.

The project, in which ethicists from all over Europe have participated, is a response to a real need: a better ethical formation and education of students via (1) an improvement of the courses and (2) the development of an integral life-enabling education project of universities and institutions of higher learning.

The project starts from the assumption that the students of today are the professionals of tomorrow. In a world dominated by the power of knowledge, professional experts such as scientists, (bio)engineers, physicians, lawyers, public servants, media experts, economists and business administrators exercise a crucial influence on the lives and the quality of life of millions of citizens. In the future this will increase under the influence of new (bio)technological, biomedical and managerial developments. Their implementation by professionals will affect the human and natural environment, the solution of problems with regard to life and death, employment and the quality of information and public office.

Very often the current and future professionals are not sufficiently prepared to deal with the ethical aspects of their professional decisions and with the social consequences of their work. They need a broader education in which their professional knowledge and expertise is completed with the ability to resolve ethical dilemmas and with the capacity to discern the values that are at stake in every professional decision.

Providing students with greater ethical expertise is necessary but not sufficient, since the tendency to hyperspecialization in already quite specialized disciplines goes together with a loss of the ability to integrate everything into a larger and meaningful whole. In such a context, there is need for a broad education in which space is created for an integral interpretation of reality, for initiation into traditions of thought, for the development of the student's civic sense and the configuration of persons as moral subjects.

1. Learning to Interpret

Before one can ethically reflect about the solution to a problem, one must clarify what the problem means, what meanings are connected with the problem and how the problem fits into the wider social context.[1] It would make little sense to pose questions of business ethics if one does not understand what business as a human activity means. It makes little sense to have a technical discussion about euthanasia without asking oneself about the meaning of human life and death. This is confirmed by the European Commission's white paper on *Teaching and Learning: Towards the Learning Society*, where an argument is made, precisely in the context of policy proposals, for better technical and scientific education. According to this document professional ethics requires more than simply a transfer of ideas from a differentiated ethical discipline or of models of ethical argumentation. It is rather a matter of opening minds and improving the capacity to interpret reality by way of additional education in literature and philosophy. The white paper considers these subjects to be important because, in a world where knowledge is quantitatively increasing, they "arm the individual with powers of discernment and critical sense. This can provide the best protection against manipulation, enabling people to interpret and understand the information they receive."

That a wider and especially a literary education is one of the conditions for acquiring ethical competence has been suggested by Martha Nussbaum, among others. In her book *Poetic Justice* she shows that it is not enough to initiate students into rational ethical argumentation.[2] One must also educate their emotional intelligence

---

[1] P. Van Tongeren, 'Ethiek en traditie' in *Tijdschrift voor Filosofie*, 58(1996), pp. 84-102.
[2] M.C. Nussbaum, *Poetic Justice: The Literary Imagination and Public Life*. Boston, Beacon Press, 1995, pp. 72-78.

and their capacity to put themselves in the place of others. One of the conditions for this is an initiation into the reading of literary texts. Without an activation of their imaginative powers, according to Nussbaum, future professionals will be unable to put themselves as unprejudiced spectators in the situation of the people about whom they will make decisions in their professional life. Initiation into the reading of literary texts is also a way to liberate future professionals from limited or enclosed circles of interpretation. Their situation is sometimes comparable to that of the cave dwellers in Plato's *Republic*, particularly if they consider a severely limited approach to reality to be the only true one. Sometimes they see only those dimensions of a problem that are considered to be relevant according to the premises of a certain scientific discipline. Especially the applied sciences are apt to get stuck in what Weber called the steel cage of bureaucratic or technical rationality, and what MacIntyre described as a kind of thinking permeated by instrumental rationality and a kind of action reduced to manipulative expertise.

By teaching future scientists and professionals how to deal with new, different, even poetic possibilities for interpreting reality, through an introduction to literary and philosophical texts, one provides them with the means of breaking out of their closed or limited hermeneutic circles. This is not to say that scientific interpretations of reality are meaningless or without value. I mean rather that it is necessary, through initiation into literature and philosophy, to give students access to a horizon of interpretation which is different than the scientific one in which they have been trained. Through a creative confrontation between various possibilities of interpretation, their field of vision expands. One might echo Marcel Proust and say that the true voyage of discovery is not to seek out new territory, but to learn to see with new eyes. The most important change that a person can undergo is the change in the way they view reality. One can change studies, job, neighbourhood, country or even continent and yet remain the same. If the fundamental hermeneutic perspective changes, however, then the way in which one experiences reality also changes.

In addition to a specialized course in ethics, something more is needed: the embedding of technical, scientific education within a *universitas* education, a broadly literary, philosophical, and cultural education that provides future professionals with the capacity to 'meaning-fully' interpret the reality in which they live and act.

2. A Purely Neutral Ethics Education is an Illusion

The basic philosophy behind the core materials project is not based on the idea of a value neutral ethical expertise. The project also differs from theories in which it has become almost a dogma that ethics should take a distance from particular moral or philosophical convictions or religious beliefs if it is to remain meaningful in a pluralistic society. In these theories one starts from a 'method of avoidance' or in the best case from the 'thinning out of the conflictuous thickness of moral concepts'. The project texts do not deny that overcoming philosophical and religious differences and achieving a reflexive equilibrium or an overlapping consensus is necessary if we are to achieve a minimum consensus regarding difficult questions. But there are doubts about whether a pedagogical process can work with ethical concepts and models that have been *totally* cut off from their original philosophical or religious frame of reference. People do not merely act on the basis of abstract principles or de-natured rational arguments. In making moral decisions, they make use of a scale of values and this is influenced in part by what Charles Taylor would call fundamental frames of reference, i.e., fundamental principles which are not as such rationally justified, but which determine the perspectives on whose basis one attaches importance to specific values.[3] Ultimate frames of reference and meaning, then, have an enormous influence on action. Like it or not, one always belongs to a tradition of thought or belief or, in a fragmented culture, to various traditions from which one draws inspiration. Even when one tries *a priori* to put the influence of traditions out of play, one belongs to a tradition, namely the tradition that uses this conception. This is the reason why it remains of crucial importance to the educational mission of a university to initiate students into tradition(s) of thought and to show them how different particular convictions have ethical implications. According to some scholars such as Alasdair MacIntyre, to be initiated into a tradition is even a precondition for meeting and understanding other cultures.[4] There exists no Archimedean or neutral point from which one can approach these traditions. On the basis

---

[3] C. TAYLOR, *Sources of the Self: The Making of Modernity.* Cambridge, Harvard University Press, 1989, p. 26.

[4] We adopt here a standpoint based on A. MACINTYRE, *Whose Justice, Which Rationality?* Notre Dame, University of Notre Dame Press, 1989, p. 26.

of a particular rationality, one can also recognize and clarify the reasonableness of other traditions and, where necessary, even critically integrate their incommensurable aspects into one's own tradition.

3. Ethics Education Requires Training in Civic Sense

As a standard-bearer for the knowledge industry, the university is often too one-sidedly oriented towards producing *employable* individuals in the service of the economic system.[5] One then runs the risk of losing sight of an important aspect of education: training in civic sense. Students must also learn to think about their social responsibility and take account of the social consequences of exercising professional power or knowledge power. Training in civic sense requires not only the transfer of knowledge about political and social ethics, but also the formation of social attitudes such as attention for the least advantaged in society. A university as centre of excellence should not only focus on high points of culture and science, but also the depths of suffering into which a society and its citizens can fall.[6] Every society exhibits the face of its victims, and it is certainly not asking too much of students that they learn as professionals how to recognize that face.

4. There is no Ethical Responsibility without Personal Development

> The essential mission of education is to help everyone to develop their own potential and become a complete human being, as opposed to a tool at the service of the economy. The acquisition of knowledge and skills should go hand in hand with building up character (...) and accepting one's responsibility in society.
> White Paper, p. 26

Ethics requires more than just knowledge acquisition. An ethical education implies more than providing future professionals with the

---

[5] Robert BELLAH, Richard MADSEN, William SULLIVAN, Ann SWINDLER, Steven TIPTON, *The Good Society*. New York, Vintage Books, 1992.

[6] D. HOLLENBACH, `Intellectual and Social Solidarity: Comment on J.M Buckley's The Catholic University and the Promise Inherent in its Identity' in J.P. LANGAN, L.J. O'DONNOVAN, *Catholic Universities in Church and Society*, Washington, Georgetown University Press, 1993, pp. 90-94.

means to make a critical judgement about problems through rational argumentation. Traditionally ethics has also been viewed as practical wisdom, aimed at the moral development of the acting person. Such a person is not only responsible for what he or she does in specific situations of choice, but also for the moral quality of his or her life, in other words, for the integration of moral choices and actions into a meaningful life that is configured as a narrative unity.

This development of a moral identity has become exceptionally problematic nowadays. In fact, we currently find ourselves in a tension between a modern, liberal illusion of a completely autonomous and self-affirming subject and the factual break-up of the subject by a fragmented existence.[7] The latter implies not merely that the value and meaning systems outside us are breaking up (what the sociologists refer to as the disappearance of plausibility structures), but also that the inner life of people is falling apart into a multiplicity of experiences and possibilities. Fragmentation is embedded inside us as a cognitive possibility. In order to get around this impasse, it is necessary to once again offer the conditions of possibility for a new personal configuration. According to Ricoeur, this is primarily a matter of integrating the autonomous ego-identity that maintains itself through the course of time (*idem* identity) and the identity that is built up through the encounter with the other (*ipse* identity).[8] This other is not only the concrete other or the community, but also the texts which offer models in which a person can imaginatively recognize his/her conditions of existence as one step in the direction of a reconfiguration of himself (herself). For Ricoeur, understanding oneself is always a *se comprendre devant le texte*. If this conception is correct, then it means, once again, that initiating students into literary, philosophical and religious texts is a *sine qua non* condition for their moral education. Admittedly these texts have no direct influence on the concrete moral choices that a person must make, but they do open up an entire world of meaning that can stimulate the moral imagination with which moral subjects can recognize new ways of acting and being.

In light of these four points the steering committee holds the opinion that ethical education requires a global pedagogical project. A

---

[7] J. MORNY, 'Reflections on Paul Ricoeur's Soi-même comme un autre' in R.C. CULLEY, W. KLEMPA, *The Three Loves: Theology, Philosophy and World Religions*, Essays in Honour of J.C. McLelland in *McGill Studies in Religion* 23(1994), p. 85.

[8] Cf. P. RICOEUR, *Soi-même comme un autre*. Paris, Seuil, 1990, pp. 137-198.

university is more than an institution devoted to scientific research and education, more than a place where knowledge is acquired and transmitted. It is also a community of professors and students in which life-promoting learning processes are inculcated. As a school of life, the university can make a contribution to the education of citizens with a sense of responsibility.[9]

It is in this broader framework that professional ethics gets its necessary place. The participants in the core materials project do not want to relativize the fact that, in an academic environment, characterized by an increasing number of specializations and hyperspecializations, the rapidly evolving scientific and technological innovations require adequate ethical answers and a permanent adaptation of the law.

Before we can even think of excellent courses in professional ethics, we need to consider that first a two-fold expertise is required. On the one hand, there is a need for ethicists with highly specialized knowledge who can function as discussion partners with experts; on the other hand, these experts themselves must learn to discover ethical problems and moral dilemmas in their own field. Ethics is not the application of abstract norms that would be imposed on a discipline like a *deus ex machina*. It begins by uncovering the problems and dilemmas as they present themselves in a specialized domain of knowledge. It is only after an adequate and expert analysis that a reasonably legitimate judgement can be passed. For instance, one cannot say anything meaningful about the ethics of international financial markets without an expert knowledge of derivatives and speculative techniques. It is impossible to pass a legitimate ethical judgement on prenatal diagnosis without a thorough knowledge of the medical aspects of the problem, and the techniques involved. This is why a specialized course in *ethics* for licentiate and postgraduate students is necessary, in addition to training the ethics instructors to be experts in a specific domain. Education in ethics, however, requires more than the introduction of a course in *applied* ethics and a pedagogic relationship between expert ethicists and students. At least as important is dialogue with specialists themselves, not only because ethicists should acquire a better knowledge, but also because the instructors and experts from various disciplines who are

---

[9] J. VERSTRAETEN, 'De spirituele bronnen van burgerzin en de taak van de katholieke universiteit' in *Ethische Perspectieven* 8(1998)2, pp. 59-64.

not ethicists, should themselves learn to pose ethical questions about their own specialized domain. Whenever *ethics* is restricted to a separate discipline, it is easily perceived by the students to be something standing somewhere outside their own discipline or professional training.

In other words, training in the students' ethical competence demands a simultaneous training in the ethical competence of all the instructors. This is the reason why the texts of the *Core Materials Project* are both destined for ethicists and experts in different fields.

INTRODUCTION

Bart Pattyn

All of us form some kind of idea about what we see, hear or read in the media, not only about the content of the reports but also about the way in which they are presented and their relevance. We judge the reports as good or bad for this or that reason. And yet most people remain convinced that 'media ethics' has nothing to do with them. The term 'media ethics' leaves many people with the impression that it refers to an exclusive specialist discipline for professionally trained experts. But ethics is not a field like biochemistry or ancient history: ethics has more to do with the skill of being able to distinguish good institutions, actions and ideas from ones that are not so good. Ethicists — and they are usually philosophers, theologians or social scientists — differ from other people only in that they reflect more often on the arguments and theories underlying the claim that something is praiseworthy, necessary, contestable or beyond the pale. Ethicists are interested in the origin, the authority and the peculiarities of the reasons for calling something good, and they are intent on analyzing motives and decision strategies. Even though this means they can defend themselves against rhetorical violence and ideological obfuscation, they are still participants in a discussion that everyone is ultimately involved in.

Producers, directors, journalists and media magnates are also inveterate critics of the media. Their judgements usually spring from loyalties to a specific set of background ideas. For instance, the argument from circulation or viewer statistics that is often used to evaluate programmes rests on moral ideals such as the freedom of the consumer, the importance of independent decisions and personal preferences, the respectability of popular culture, resistance to political, religious or ideological interference, and an aversion to patronizing elitism. If the managers of a production studio or a publishing house would be unable to justify their strategy by appealing to these kinds of socially prevalent ethical beliefs, their moral integrity would be quickly called into question and legal measures would likely be undertaken to limit their actions.

Yet one can probably devise moral reasons for any sort of decision and someone well versed in communication strategies will have little difficulty in finding convincing justifications. Even though not all moral justifications have the same value, it is often quite difficult to weigh them against one another. The deceptive nature of such justifications results not from what they bring to light but rather from what they tend to obscure. This is no different with the current justification of the commercially oriented media: the manifest content looks acceptable but it must be supplemented and completed. That is the intention of this volume. Here, we pose the question of what 'good media' means, from various perspectives and different points of departure.

The historical survey with which Clifford Christians opens the volume confronts us with a dual idea: in the first place it is certainly not the first time that there is an explicit demand for media ethics, and in the second place, every time that this happened in the past, the response from philosophy was weak. However, Christians is optimistic regarding the current situation because there is more agreement between philosophers and social scientists that dialogue is the cornerstone of social ideas. This strengthens his conviction that a philosophically justified normative foundation exists on the basis of which one can judge the media. Both the producers and the consumers of the media can be referred to their moral responsibility in the process of social dialogue. Christians' idea is further worked out in this volume's first part. There it is argued that the normative character of judgements about the media refer to the ethical importance of an open democratic dialogue, both at the national and the international level (White, Nordenstreng, Nicoletti and Hamelink).

The optimism and hope that is expressed in the first part is slightly tempered in the book's second part. The analysis of the cultural shift from modern to postmodern society (Van Poecke and Lesch), the analysis of the group-dynamic motives for media consumption (Pattyn) and the increasing concentrations of economic power (Van de Bulck) — these are all issues that clarify but at the same time also problematize the development of the modern media. Yet any balanced, long-term view of the media's relation to society cannot dispense with such a reflection.

In the third and fourth parts we move to the level of the individual (such as in the article by Thomass) and examine professional codes (Evers, Barroso) and the moral virtues (White) of the journalist. We direct attention to the practical guidelines for careful decision-making in editorial problem situations (Hamelink), we look at the topics that are offered in journalism education (Thomass), and we learn more about the increasing tendency to mix genres and styles (Geerardijn & Fauconnier). In this part as well, we make room for a consideration of the meaning of the ideals on which the individual guidelines are based. (Becker).

The ethics of the user is something that is undoubtedly significant for the future (Funiok, Hamelink). There are probably many developments within the media that escape the control of individual journalists and producers because the economic and cultural context leaves them with little choice. On the other hand, the moral freedom of the media consumer to make his or her own choices is much greater. The success of a media policy that aims at a high-quality social dialogue will therefore depend to a large extent on the way in which users deal with the media and on their willingness to organize themselves more effectively.

In an ideal world, media ethics would be based on a well-balanced social dialogue in which various actors with various points of view participate. In contrast to traditional ethical frameworks, a dialogue is not a closed and perfect system in which all the aspects have their own logical place. Such systems provide an impression of consistency, but usually have a dogmatic and sterile character. In this book, we have not attempted to develop a global theory or construct a purely logical framework for thought. The intention was rather to breathe new life into a dynamic discussion that can, in principle, always be continued and expanded. Loyalties can shift, power relations change, technologies evolve, public interests alter and functions re-defined. So something that would claim to be a definitive media ethics cannot exist, even though the conditions that have led to a balanced dialogue might be quite durable and long-lived.

I would like to thank all of the authors who contributed to this volume. It was astonishing to experience how efficient and committed they were in working across the borders of various countries and disciplines in bringing this book to life. This strengthens my hope that a balanced dialogue will prevail over rhetorical violence. The idea for this book is in part the result of various meetings and individual discussions with people who visited Leuven as Hoover Fellows under the auspices of the Media Ethics project. Without the support of the Hoover Foundation and the FWO-VL this book would not have been possible. My thanks also to Antonio Calcagno, Ria Vandebeek and Dale Kidd for their devoted efforts in editorial matters.

Bart Pattyn
Leuven, 21 March 2000

PART I

MEDIA ETHICS
History and Foundations

AN INTELLECTUAL HISTORY OF MEDIA ETHICS

Clifford G. Christians

Contemporary philosophical usage normally distinguishes ethics into three parts: descriptive ethics, metaethics, and normative ethics. Descriptive ethics seeks to account for actual moral practices, beliefs and traditions of particular persons or groups. It avoids moral judgments concerning the behaviour or belief system studied. This approach belongs to the social sciences. Metaethics examines the meanings and uses of moral terms such as 'good' or 'right', analyzes moral discourse and reasoning, and establishes the foundations upon which moral judgments are based. Normative ethics studies what instances or classes of conduct are right or wrong, good or bad, worthy of praise or blame. It examines the moral arguments for the justice or injustice of societies and institutions. More broadly, normative ethics concerns those states of affairs which ought to be furthered in society. These three definitions are necessary in accounting for the history of media ethics as an academic enterprise, though moral philosophy only encompasses metaethics and normative ethics.

For various reasons, mass communication ethics first established itself in the decade of the 1890s, and then took a distinct 20th century form in the 1920s. The current period of activism began around 1980. At the turn of the 20th century, as moral issues took root in the communications enterprise, it was left without the needed intellectual tools because of philosophy's preoccupation with metaethics. During the 1920s, utilitarianism was the only normative theory with any impact on communications, and in a weakened form it allowed scientific naturalism to define the issues. The current phase of mass communication ethics, rooted in practical and professional ethics, appears to be following the same trajectories as before, with philosophical ethics not engaged in a definitive manner once again. While appealing to applied ethics as a branch of normative ethics, the results are generally the non-philosophical descriptive ethics of social science.

"Communication ethics has developed with only remote connections to systematic moral philosophies" (White, 1989: 46). This essay documents that conclusion in terms of three critical moments over the last century. The aim of this essay in intellectual history is to identify as precisely as possible the current challenges and opportunities in mass media ethics at a crucial historical juncture. While only those philosophical currents are accounted for that impinge directly on media ethics, this historical framework teaches us to avoid the interminable disputes of a lesser order that a faulty modernist paradigm has overvalued and imposed on us.[1]

1. Foundations in the 1890s

The rights and responsibilities of media use, freedom, regulation and journalistic conduct have been debated in Western societies since the oldest known newspaper was published in Germany in 1609. But the press's harm to society was not explicitly linked to ethical principles until the end of the 19th century. The first time press critics used 'ethics' in a title was July 1889 (Lilly, 1889). Hazel Dicken Garcia (1989) ends her examination of journalistic standards in the US at that date, citing it as the transition from everyday procedures to a more reflective period related to ethical precepts. *Scribner's Magazine* in April 1896 applauded a French critic for finally getting beyond "short and most immediate views" and assessing journalism "philosophically" (Gorren, 1896: 507). Once the press develops into an industrial structure in the 1890s, and the first forays into journalism education appear, an intellectual concern about the press's obligation takes root in a form basically unchanged until now.

---

[1] This survey is the basis of a book length study in collaboration with John Nerone. The focus of this essay is on those areas of philosophical ethics that explicitly intersect with communication ethics. Several important philosophical movements have no discernible influence on the conceptual world of communication ethics, and therefore, are not included. Also there are throughout Europe and North America political and professional debates on media responsibility that have been excluded, since the approach here is an intellectual history of philosophical work. Religious movements and ecclesiastical pronouncements have influenced our understanding of media morality, but are not accounted for in this study of academic ethics.

1.1 *The Press and Utilitarian Ethics*

Several factors congealed in the 1890s to give communication ethics its distinctive shape. The press had become a complex and diversified social institution, with journalists an expert class pursuing specialized tasks. The North American press began understanding itself during this decade not as a political forum or socializing force, but as a corporate economic structure marketing a commodity for consumers. Structural patterns of authority and accountability were utilitarian in form, and utilitarianism characterized its organizational culture, which in turn was rooted in industrial production and market distribution. The industrialization and commercialization of the media displaced an earlier media culture that was primarily organized around politics and that frequently used partisan advantage as its main standard. With the industrialization of the press, media occupations, especially journalism, began to redefine themselves as middle-class professions. They began to seek a place within the rising university system.

In the US, a university education for journalists was first seriously attempted late in the nineteenth century. By 1910 when Abraham Flexner had written his monumental Carnegie Reports on professional training in a university context, journalism education had adopted a functional model for itself compatible with the utility theory that dominated the first debates in ethics. The key impetus behind the creation of these early university programs in journalism was the need for the press to enhance its respectability in the face of heated public criticism. In the early and mid nineteenth century, journalism was a low-prestige occupation in a highly competitive market. Because newspapers and journalists were perceived to have very little power, the public was not impressed by the typical newspaper or journalist, but was not especially alarmed either.

However, the circumstances began to change dramatically as the 19th century neared its end. The press expanded rapidly in all the major urban centers of Britain, with major national newspapers coming into existence (*People*, 1881; *Daily Mail*, 1896; *Daily Express*, 1900; and *Daily Mirror* 1903) and playing a prominent role in British journalism for most of the century following. While multiple ownership of weekly newspapers started early in the 18th century, "press chains created by the press barons in the late 19th and early 20th centuries" began gaining a dominant market position. By 1884, a syndicate headed by the Scots-American, Andrew Carnegie, controlled eight dailies and ten weeklies. Such newspaper chains accelerated rapidly between 1890 and 1920; the "three traditional features of the press — chain ownership, an expanding market, and a tendency for a few papers to become dominant — merely became more accentuated under the press barons" (Curran and Seaton, 1997: 43; cf. 28-29 for data above).

Newspapers in the US grew in circulation, industrialized their production, and introduced economies of scale through modern distribution and through reliance on advertising that led to increasing monopolization of local markets in the later nineteenth and early twentieth centuries. The rising power of the press made lapses that had earlier been colorful now seem dangerous. Newspaper magnates, like railroad magnates, were seen by many as robber barons and anti-democrats. This popular perception of corruption had a significant amount of truth to it. In response, 'respectable' elements of the press sought to develop a more polished public image.

Major new communication technologies between 1837 (telegraph) and World War I (telephone, 1876, and wireless, 1899), gave birth to the modern international communication system. These technologies spawned some of the first transnational companies: Marconi (operating in several countries with the parent company in the United Kingdom); Siemens and Slaby-Arco (Telefunken after 1903) in Germany; Thomson in France; Western Union, AT&T, and United Wireless in the United States; Philips in the Netherlands (Fortner, 1993: 77). The first submarine cable was laid across the Straits of Dover in 1851, with the transatlantic cable in 1866, and Britain completing its first direct cable to Bombay already in 1870 and to Australia in 1872. As international agreements were signed to make technical services more standardized and efficient, "they were complicated by struggles between state administrators and private interests" and among competing inventor-capitalists themselves (Fortner, 1993: 78-79, 92). An example of the intense cross-pressures is the British government's relationship with Marconi.

> The Post Office wanted to extend its telegraph monopoly to wireless; Marconi wanted to break the domestic telegraph monopoly to increase its own business. The newspapers wanted wireless competition to drive down cable rates; the cable companies wanted to protect their monopoly and capital investment. Whose interests, then, were to be represented at international conferences? Could the Post

Office adequately represent interests other than its own, even if instructed to do so by the cabinet? (Fortner, 1993: 79)

With the development of the submarine telegraph, "the turn of the century marked the zenith of the monopolistic power of the great cable companies," to be overturned themselves by Marconi. Monopoly becomes a crucial issue for international communication henceforth, with regulation entangled by domestic and imperial interests. "The period up to World War I was one of rising nationalism, creation and consolidation of empires, and intense commercial rivalry. The tendency was to equate national interests with those of a country's major industrial concerns" (Fortner, 1993: 87). As the long-distance technologies established new centralizations of power, cooperation was necessary for technical reasons. But in these early years of the international communication system, "it was nation against nation, company versus company, suspicion opposing suspicion... [in the] competition to control the means of communication and to establish commercial hegemonies and information monopolies" (Fortner, 1993: 92).

A half dozen issues were primary in these contested and volatile terrains. Sensationalism had been a staple of the entire century, but it took institutional form in the late 1890s from the Hearst and Pulitzer circulation battles during the Spanish-American War. In Virginia Berridge's analysis, as the century turned, the commercialization of the British press relied on "sensationalist manipulation of popular sentiment" and contributed to the decline of the politically committed press (Curran and Seaton, 1997: 29). Invasion of privacy also entered the ethics agenda also. In the US, it spun off from Warren and Brandeis' 'The Right to Privacy' in the *Harvard Law Review* (December 1890). As electronic communication systems were being established, privacy became an urgent issue as sensitive diplomatic, military and commercial information crossed multiple borders, especially in Europe (Fortner, 1993: 88-89). Freebies and junkets, scourged by media critics since 1870, were now treated more systematically in the context of big-business competition. Film censorship was initiated in the UK in 1896. Telling the truth as a moral principle was abstracted for the first time from the practice of accurately reporting facts. And a platform was laid for the free press/fair trial debate, though with virtually no progress beyond insisting on the press's rights. Without exception, as the canon of ethical issues was being established, they were articulated in terms of common-sense utilitarianism.

The rise of this ethical discourse served a variety of purposes. On the one hand, it focused an already existing hostility toward media behaviour. On the other hand, it re-directed this hostility from movements for structural change (limits on newspaper ownership, for instance, or public ownership of 'natural monopoly' media, like telegraph lines) toward individual behaviour. In this way, the rise of ethical discourse mediated between the 'lords of the press' and their critics.

1.2 Moral Philosophy at the Turn of the Century

In the Western tradition, philosophers since the Greeks were concerned with questions of metaethics and of normative ethics. "Until the 20th century, however, the two kinds of questions were often confused" (Taylor, 1963: ix). As their differences were increasingly recognized around the turn of the century, ethical theory received a fresh impetus. New methods of philosophical investigation emerged, and the aims of ethical inquiry were redefined and clarified. Philosophers began searching into the foundations of moral discourse, the criteria of goodness, and the justification of moral judgments. "Professor G.E. Moore's discussion of [these issues] in 1903 was perhaps the single most important stimulus to the development of metaethics in the 20th century" (Taylor, 1963: xvi). From Moore's *Principia Ethica* (1903) to W.D. Ross's work on right acts (1930), to Strawson's ethical intutionism (1949), Westermarck's (1932) subjectivism, and A.J. Ayer's (1936) critique of ethics — debates in metaethics rather than the nature of professional morality animated European philosophical ethics throughout the early decades of the twentieth century.

In institutional terms, the American case is instructive. Throughout the 19th century, moral philosophy was the most important course in the US college curriculum. Taught usually by the president and required of all seniors, moral philosophy provided the capstone for the curriculum. Following a tradition since the medieval university, moral philosophy integrated the students' entire training and aimed to prepare them for benefitting the civic good. Moral philosophy had central importance because it gave intellectual unity to the different branches of knowledge, and was an anchor of stability in a rapidly changing nation still in search of its identity. A main component of the moral philosophy course was the theoretical underpinnings of ethics, based on the assumption that humans were fundamentally moral creatures in a moral universe, and ethical principles could awaken this moral sensibility and provide the best long-term guidance.

As journalism education entered the academy, moral philosophy was in decline. According to a student of 19th-century philosophy, David Meyer, the last North American textbook of the traditional type was *Our Moral Nature*, written by the president of Princeton in 1892. The vision of a unified curriculum and culture of learning was being abandoned as the explosion of knowledge fostered departmentalization and specialization instead. The serious, systematic work in ethics ended up in philosophy departments where it was isolated from the university, and taught to a few majors as metaethics in non-normative terms. There was little incentive to keep pace with the advances of science, technology, and the professions; moral philosophy was measured by scholastic categories instead. A social institution growing in power and complexity arrived in an academic setting at the very time significant moral philosophy was making itself irrelevant. There was no heavyweight philosophical arena to counter journalism's anemic utilitarianism.

The nascent work in journalism ethics took place outside the domain of moral philosophy. Both institutionally and intellectually, philosophical ethics had accepted exile from the increasingly dominant work of the university in the professions, and in the social and natural sciences. As a result, the architects of journalism ethics lacked the conceptual tools with which to build a house that could withstand the hostile elements.

2. The 20th Century Crisis in Communication Ethics, 1920-1950

2.1 *The Flowering of Academic Study in the 1920s*

In the United States, the initial work of the 1890s, though rudimentary in ethics, evolved into a serious effort during the 1920s as journalism education was established within the liberal arts. Four important textbooks in journalism ethics emerged from America's heartland during this period: Nelson Crawford's *Ethics of Journalism* (1924), Leon Flint's *The Conscience of the Newspaper* (1925), William

Gibbons's *Newspaper Ethics* (1926), and Albert Henning's *Ethics and Practices of Journalism* (1932). None recognized the others in quotation or argument, yet they were similar in the topics they considered central: reporters and sources, economic temptations and conflicts of interest, national security, free press/fair trial, deception, fairness, accuracy, sensationalism, and protection of privacy.

Again, this arousal of ethical inquiry followed a period of intense media criticism. Muckrakers like Upton Sinclair (1912) and Will Irwin (1911) exposed the corruptions of the 'money power' in the wire services and in daily newspapers, which were increasingly monopolistic. Thinkers like Walter Lippmann (1922) perceived the fundamental irrationality of public opinion and the failure of journalism to inform it properly. Some professional leaders themselves recognized the perils. Writing in 1924, Lord Reith of the BBC, for example, articulated a strong ethos of public service: "I think it will be admitted by all that to have exploited so great a scientific invention [radio] for the purpose and pursuit of entertainment alone would have been a prostitution of its powers and an insult to the character and intelligence of the people." (MacDonald and Petheram, 1998: 83). Moreover, the experience of propaganda in World War I and the rise of the motion picture in the 1900s and 1910s produced a palpable feeling of cultural peril among both reformers and traditional opinion leaders.

On another level, these books demonstrated a dogged preoccupation with public obligation. For example, in chapters 4 (The Newspaper and the Public), 7 (The Newspaper's Responsibility), and 8 (The Newspaper in a Democracy), Gibbons delineated a social responsibility theory of the press, with every major doctrine the equivalent of the Hutchins Commission's two decades later. Hutchins insisted on news in a context that gave it meaning, and this was likewise the cornerstone of Gibbons's argument when confronting the issues of confidentiality, accuracy, crime reporting, fair trial, and so forth. It was a considerable achievement in one decade. Leaders in ethics identified the crucial issues and the substance of their public service appeal rivaled in quality anything that has appeared subsequently.

2.2 *Scientific Naturalism as Prevailing Worldview*

After Crawford's work in 1932, the term 'ethics' and its cognates disappeared from mass communications book titles for forty years in

North America. This almost certainly indicates that ethical inquiry dropped from the prominent place it had held in journalism education. Perhaps ethics had been incorporated into standard texts; perhaps its place was taken by hortatory courses in journalism history — the example of the great journalists of the past was all the ethical instruction one would need, or in media law — a knowledge of the First Amendment was the alpha and omega of journalism ethics. Perhaps it was thought that codes of ethics had taken care of the problems that had occupied educators in the 1920s. Whatever can be learned from looking further into these questions, the overarching explanation to the passing of this second ethical boom is similar to the first — disconnectedness from and weaknesses in philosophical ethics. The flurry of academic activity in the twenties, the growth of professional societies with codes of ethics, the expansion of curricula into the liberal arts — none of these could prevent the demise of ethics in the face of an antithetical worldview, scientific naturalism.

Scientific naturalism aggressively ordered the structure of knowing during this period — naturalism in the sense that genuine knowledge can be identified only in the natural laws of the hard sciences (cf. Purcell, 1973). For Quine (1953), philosophical inquiry was natural science reflecting on itself and all meaningful knowledge was continuous with the paradigmatic disciplines — physics, chemistry, and biology. Advances in the physical sciences became the applauded ideal as academicians — including those in communications — promoted its methods and principles. As the pacesetter, Lawrence Murphy, concluded already in 1924, "Journalism ... is now emerging from an imaginative type of writing into one governed by basic and scientifically sound principles. We now recognize that the scientific attitude toward news materials is the only safeguard we have against journalism graduates being capricious and emotional" (Murphy, 1924: 31). Emery and Emery (1998) describe the period from the 1930s as the social scientific phase of communications study.

Stretched across the fact-value dichotomy of scientific naturalism, journalistic morality became equivalent to unbiased reporting of neutral data. The seeds of this definition existed already in Henning (1932), though duty to the public realm dominated (as it did with Gibbons, 1926). Presenting unvarnished facts was heralded as the standard of good performance. Objective reporting was not merely a technique, but a moral imperative (cf. Lichtenberg, 1996). The bracketing of value judgments from the transmitting of information was considered virtuous. In C.P. Scott's famous declaration in the *Manchester Guardian* (6 May 1921): A newspaper's "primary office is the gathering of news... The unclouded face of Trust [must not] suffer wrong. Comment is free, but facts are sacred" (MacDonald and Petheram, 1998: 53). Grove Patterson, for example, made an impassioned plea in his Don R. Mellet Memorial Lecture that reporters demonstrate moral leadership in improving democratic life; and the cornerstone of their responsibility he considered "objective reporting and unslanted facts" (Boston University, 1948).

Concern for ethics during the thirties through sixties occurred only on isolated occasions. The Report of the Commission on Freedom of the Press in 1947 was the most famous counterstatement of this period. Occasionally there were pockets of resistance in journalism's intellectual and vocational life, but the professional statistical model prevailed nonetheless. The scientific worldview was the ruling paradigm. A preoccupation with that value-centered enterprise called ethics seemed out of place in an academic and professional environment committed to facticity.

2.3 *Social Responsibility*

In most accounts of press criticism and normative press theory, the work of the Hutchins Commission stands as a major milestone. But in terms of communication ethics its impact was disappointing. Although some members of the Commission, especially William Ernest Hocking, were engaged in a serious rethinking of ethical issues, the ultimate product of the Commission's deliberations was a policy-oriented set of recommendations on ameliorating the worst aspects of the material conditions of the press.

The impetus behind the Hutchins Commission came from a general sense of anxiety over freedom of the press in the shadow of World War II. The world seemed to Americans to present mirror totalitarianisms of the left and the right in the Soviet Union and Nazi Germany; meanwhile, intellectuals and publishers alike wondered just how far the public might condone press regulation, especially in the face of a perception that the power of media operators was growing. Henry Luce, who bankrolled the Commission, obviously wanted its report to be a strong re-affirmation of traditional free market media. He was disappointed. But the Commission did not recommend structural changes in media ownership or federal regulation of the media. Nor did the Commission move ethical thought to a new plane.

As Mark Fackler has argued in his intellectual history of the decades surrounding the Hutchins Commission, a major contingent of the Commission (Robert Hutchins, Reinhold Niebuhr, and William Ernest Hocking) understood the substantive issues in terms of scientific naturalism. As long-time chairman of the Harvard Department of Philosophy, Hocking (1947) provided the conceptual foundation for the Commission's work (published as *Freedom of the Press: A Framework of Principle*). Its overriding themes (positive freedom; intersubjectivity of human experience; freedom of expression as an earned moral right rather than an inalienable natural right) are a sustained argument against the monism of scientific naturalism and its fact-value dichotomy. However, the social scientists and legal theorists on the Commission were more preoccupied with immediate concerns in the free market media (their tendency toward oligopolies and monopolization, lack of diversity in content, self-serving use of First Amendment protection, for instance). Rather than distilling *A Framework of Principle*, the Hutchins Report itself is a compromise, a working document centered on policy and giving the social scientific rationale for a shift to social responsibility. And as most observers have argued, the report's ambiguities about liberalism (that is, its tepid neoliberalism conditioned throughout by libertarian themes) further compromised its distinctiveness (cf. Nerone, 1995).

Although scorned by the press itself, the Hutchins Commission did stimulate a heavy emphasis on professionalism (quality work and integrity), codes of ethics, media councils, better training, and media criticism. The foundation of ethics was oriented to duty rather than rights. However, the precise content of that moral foundation was not articulated, and social responsibility theory has generally allowed utilitarianism to dominate its paradigm in the same way utility has commandeered liberalism as a whole. Hutchins did not serve as a radical alternative to academia's naturalistic worldview and therefore did not establish a distinctive normative base for the media in a democratic society.

Social responsibility is not strictly atomistic, but it shares with classical democracy a contractarian view of the state. Therefore, social democracies are more compatible with the view of positive freedom, fostering more effectively as they do the public conditions under which all citizens can exercise their freedom effectively. Public ownership of the media, natural to democratic socialism, helps ensure that they operate in the public interest. In fact, already in 1916, a Swedish Press Council to provide media accountability was formed. Broadcasting introduced into Britain in the mid-twenties and the Swedish Broadcasting corporation (1928) used the public service model. Lennart Weibull (1991) in Sweden and Claude Jean Bertrand (1999) in France have been on the forefront in applying and refining media accountability systems. Shelton Gunaratne (1998) sees fundamental similarities between social responsibility theory, NWICO and the emerging concept of public journalism. Today, "most of Europe and the rest of the world take social responsibility for granted. It is the dominant, mainstream doctrine in journalism and media policies, including public service broadcasting" (Norden-streng, 1998: 425). When the Summit of the European Union in June 1997 adopted its *Protocol on Public Service Broadcasting*, it reflected the spirit of Hutchins.

2.4 *Utilitarian Rationalism*

The normative ethics with the greatest influence during this period was utilitarian rationalism. Since its origins with John Stuart Mill, neutrality is seen as necessary in this model to promote individual autonomy. This neutrality, based on the supremacy of individual autonomy, is the foundational principle in Mill's *On Liberty* (1859) and in his *Utilitarianism* (1861), as it was in his earlier *A System of Logic* (1843) as well. In addition to bringing classical utilitarianism to its maximum development and establishing with Locke the liberal state, Mill delineated the foundations of inductive inquiry as social scientific method. In terms of the principles of empiricism, he per-fected the inductive techniques of Francis Bacon as a problem-solv-ing methodology to replace Aristotelian deductive logic (Mill, 1843, 1865).

In addition to its this-worldly humanism, utilitarian ethics was attractive for its compatibility with the canons of rational calcula-tion.

> In the utilitarian perspective, one validated an ethical position by hard evidence. You count the consequences for human happiness of

one or another course, and you go with the one with the highest favorable total. What counts as human happiness was thought to be something conceptually unproblematic, a scientifically establishable domain of facts. One could abandon all the metaphysical or theological factors which made ethical questions scientifically undecidable (Taylor, 1982: 129).

Utilitarian ethics replaces metaphysical distinctions with the calculation of empirical quantities. It follows the procedural demand that if "the happiness of each agent counts for one ... the right course of action should be what satisfies all, or the largest number possible" (Taylor, 1982: 131). Autonomous reason is the arbiter of moral disputes.

With moral reasoning equivalent to calculating consequences for human happiness, utilitarianism presumes there is "a single consistent domain of the moral, that there is one set of considerations which determines what we ought morally to do" (Taylor, 1982: 132). This single-consideration theory not only demands that we maximize general happiness, but considers irrelevant other moral imperatives that conflict with it such as equal distribution. One-factor models appeal to the "epistemological squeamishness" of value-neutral social science which "dislikes contrastive languages." Moreover, utilitarianism appealingly offers "the prospect of exact calculation of policy through ... rational choice theory" (Taylor, 1982: 143). "It portrays all moral issues as discrete problems amenable to largely technical solutions" (Euben, 1981: 117). However, to its critics, this kind of exactness represents "a semblance of validity" by leaving out whatever cannot be calculated (Taylor, 1982: 143).

Given its dualism of means and ends, the domain of the good in utilitarian theory is extrinsic. All that is worth valuing is a function of their consequences. *Prima facie* duties are literally inconceivable. "The degree to which my actions and statements" truly express what is important to someone does not count. Ethical and political thinking in consequentialist terms legislate intrinsic value out of existence (Taylor, 1982: 144). The exteriority of ethics is seen to guarantee the value neutrality of experimental procedures.

In value-free communications science, codes of ethics for professional and academic associations are the conventional format for moral principles (cf. White, 1989: 49-56; cf. Cooper, 1989: 273-336). Of the 35 states that signed the Helsinki Act in 1975, professional media organizations in 24 of them had codes of ethics (Juusela, 1991). In

1995, 31 ethical codes of journalists existed in 29 European countries (Nordenstreng, 1995: 85). In terms of media types, virtually every medium is represented with codes of ethics reflecting their techno-logical specifics and institutional structure (cf. Barosso, 1984).

3. The Rise of Practical Philosophy, 1980-Present

In 1980, the so-called 'MacBride Report' was published in book form as *Many Voices, One World: Towards a New More Just and More Efficient World Information and Communication Order*. As president of the International Commission for the Study of Communication Problems, Sean MacBride spearheaded a study for UNESCO on international media policies and practices, communication and human rights, cultural diversity and professional journalism.[2] *Many Voices, One World* serves as a marker for the rapid globalization of media technologies since the 1980s (cf. Ducatel et al., 1999). For the last two decades, our communication agenda has been dominated by massive investment in the global entertainment economy, the consolidation of free trade in audio-visual and telecommunications services under the aegis of the World Trade Organization (Editorial, 1999: 2), the restructuring of democratic political processes through the convergence of digital information systems (Corcoran and Preston, 1995), and the economic concentration of media industries worldwide.[3]

Many of the crucial ethical issues are being identified through debates over public policy, from academic scholarship and conferences, think tanks, religious organizations, and thoughtful professionals (cf. Nordenstreng, 1995; Servaes and Lie, 1997). The Berlin Declaration on 'Communication in Changing Europe' (March 1993) called on the media to promote a multi-lingual, multi-cultural Europe. The 1997 European Union 'Directive on Universal Services and Interoperability in Telecommunications' and its 'Television Without Frontiers Directive' warning against incitement toward

---

[2] Michael Traber's, *The Myth of the Information Revolution* (1986) and the ten MacBride Roundtables held around the world (with the first one in 1989 in Harare, Zimbabwe and the latest in 1998 in Amman, Jordan) have kept the issues alive and developed them further.

[3] For a summary of Armand Mattebart's contributions to our understanding of the globalization of communication, in the context of French communications research generally, see Beaud and Kaufmann (1998: 8-9).

hatred are based on human dignity. The Council of Europe in 1994 issued the 'Prague Resolution' to protect national public service broadcasting for the sake of fruitful democratic citizenship (Porter, 1999: 5-10; cf. Tracey, 1998; cf. Venturelli, 1997). The International Organization of Journalists produced a document called 'International Principles of Professional Ethics in Journalism' at meetings in Prague and Paris in 1983 emphasising the people's right to timely information (Nordenstreng, 1998: 124-134; cf. Weaver, 1998). The European Journalism Centre in Maastricht teaches courses applying ethical principles to European cases (Sonnenberg, 1997a, 1997b).

3.1 Growth in Mass Communication Ethics Since 1980

In these demanding days as a global information order emerges, applied and practical ethics dominate the academy. Applied ethics has sought to develop itself into a field of study with its own identity; this pursuit is still underway and has met with some successes (Almond, 1995). Applied ethics has an interactive view of theory construction, with principles and practice building on one another dialogically (cf. Bowie, 1982). Stephen Toulmin (1988) has assisted the enterprise by his reminder that issues from the bedside, newsroom, and parliament have always dominated the history of philosophy, and applied ethics is happily restoring that vision. In fact, practical and professional ethics has gained at least a modicum of support as a scholarly enterprise with its own logic and subject matter. The reissuing of Henry Sidgwick's 1898 *Practical Ethics*, with an articulate defense of its intellectual significance by Sissela Bok, signals this trend (Sidgwick, 1997).

In 1992, Andrew Belsey and Ruth Chadwick edited an anthology of 11 British authors for the University of Wales professional ethics series. It helped fill the gap in textbook material, with only Wolfgang Wunden's (1989) book of readings and Gudmund Gjelsten's *Møte eller manipulasjon? Om etikk i massemedia* (1988) suitable for classroom use before. Matthew Kieran's *Media Ethics* (1998) is an anthology of essays by largely British contributors on such issues as privacy, truth, objectivity censorship and political journalism.

The trappings of this new field are everywhere outside the classroom. The Association for Practical and Professional Ethics began in 1991. Journals such as *The International Journal of Applied Philosophy* and *Professional Ethics* deal with generic issues, while virtually all the professions now have their own journals, books, and courses on ethics as well. Interest groups within academic associations and centers for ethics and society are commonplace. Vernon Jensen (1997: 191-200) identifies 68 such centers. MacDonald and Petheram (1998: 257-349) list over 200 research centers and academic departments around the world committed to media ethics. Research universities are including practical ethics courses within their general education curriculum; in professional programs such as business, law, medicine, communications, and engineering; in graduate studies such as courses in the ethics of scientific research and ethical standards in social science methodology. Liberal arts colleges reflect similar dynamics, introducing courses in bioethics and ethics of health care, ethics in government, social work ethics, computer ethics, accounting ethics, and so forth. The dramatic growth in research, teaching, and interest among media professionals and academics has been unrelenting, though the methodologies of ethics scholarship are often impressionistic.

There have been intellectual gains in the middle range. We understand more sharply conflict of interest, promisekeeping and contractual obligation, paternalism and client autonomy, indoctrination, reform of institutional structures, and vocation. However, the critics are generally correct — applying ethical principles to particular cases is often busywork, descriptive and functional in character, teaching students to choose from practical alternatives but often without knowing how to consider the right course of action. The intellectual pay-off from applied ethics will be limited until it develops an adequate infrastructure, until its conceptual foundations are built on credible versions of normativity, organizational culture, accountability, loyalty, and moral agency. For mass communication ethics to be taken seriously, it needs to contribute to this broader task, and also make significant progress on its own agenda. Important advances have been made on the ethics of privacy, confidentiality, and deception. But most of the crucial issues (promisekeeping, distributive justice, diversity in popular culture, digital manipulation, and conflict of interest) are still woefully underdeveloped. Even truthtelling — central to information systems as a norm — has been largely neglected.

While applied ethics dominates mass communications at present, non-descriptive normative approaches are appearing along the margins. Matthew Kieran (1997) of Leeds uses the philosophical literature and a dialectical method to analyze such concepts as responsibility, information and news, and to confront such issues as privacy, violence, lies, and impartiality. *Ethical Perspectives* of the European Ethics Network puts applied ethics in dialogue with fundamental ethics. Cees Hamelink's extensive work on global communications and human rights is rooted in an ethics of justice and philosophical anthropology. In *Ethik der Medienkommunikation: Grundlagen* (Holderegger, 1992), eight theological ethicists approach the mass media system from a critical cultural perspective. The Danish philosopher Niels Thomassen (1992) develops a communicative model of social solidarity through philosophical hermeneutics and Habermas's discourse ethics.

3.2 *The Decade of Internationalization*

Media ethics in the 1990s has shifted its emphasis from local and isolated concerns to the international arena. On occasion in the late 1970s, the world agenda was included; studies in press coverage of terrorism, for example, had no other choice. Anne Vander Meiden of Utrecht published a reader in 1980 for the International Association of Mass Communication Research, with contributors from Korea, Belgium, England, Germany, the United States, Finland, and the Netherlands. Also in 1980 Gudmund Gjelsten hosted an international conference on media ethics in Kristiansand, Norway, as did the Katholische Akademie in Stuttgart, Germany (Tompert, 1980). *Communication Research Trends* published an issue on international mass communication ethics in the Spring of 1980. The Gregorian University sponsored a series of conferences in the 1980s with scholars from several continents, the one in 1985 focusing on ethics and the conference in 1987 on moral development. Michael Traber of the World Association of Christian Communication in London edited a *WACC Journal* on media ethics in November 1979. Kaarle Nordenstreng's *The Mass Media Declaration of UNESCO* (1984) was a pathbreaker in international codes of ethics.

These efforts and others culminated in a methodical, aggressive cross-cultural approach to communication ethics at the turn of the present decade. The first comprehensive treatment by an international network of scholars, *Communication Ethics and Global Change*, appeared in 1989 edited by Thomas Cooper. Surveys of media ethics from 13 countries were included and integrative chapters emphasized three major areas of worldwide concern: truth, responsibility, and free expression. Throughout the 1990s, the Professional Education section of the International Association of Mass Communication Research has given mass media ethics a strong emphasis (Slovenia, 1990; Sao Paulo, 1992; Seoul, 1994; Sydney, 1996; Glasgow, 1998). The University of Paris convened a European/North American conference on ethics in 1993 (Bertrand, 1999), and the University of Tampere also hosted an international conference in 1993. Francis Kasoma edited a volume of ten theoretical and practical essays on *Journalism Ethics in Africa* which appeared in 1994. Pedro G. Gomes (1990) from the University of Sao Paulo grounds his ethical model in social communication and liberation theology. Hurst and White (1994) use local examples and examine Australian attempts to develop principles and monitor policies through press councils and codes of ethics. The textbook of Nicholas Russell (1994) and anthology of Valeria Alia *et al.* (1996) originate in Canada. Arnold De Beer *et al.* edited a special edition of *Ecquid Novi* in 1994 on media ethics. In addition, political realignments in Eastern Europe have made ethics central as a possible framework for writing new policies and generating national identity. Vaclav Havel's *Living in Truth* symbolises this effort as does the double issue on media ethics published in 1995 by the Polish journal of press studies, *Zeszyty Prasoznawcze*. Yassen N. Zassoursky's edited volume with Elena Vartanova (1998) includes the ethical dimension in analyzing the changed political and economic conditions in Central and Eastern Europe. The writings of Karol Jakubowicz (1998/99, 1999), Head of Strategic Planning for Polish Television, focus on ethics and policy, normative models of the media, and the media's role in social change. Antonio Pasquali (1997) of Caracas has developed an intersubjective model of communications ethics. Already in 1991, a special issue of *Communication Research Trends* had identified 70 academics in media ethics in 40 countries. The Silha Center bibliography (*Books in Media Ethics*) includes entries from 10 countries. Barrie MacDonald and Michel Petheram's *Key Guide to Information Sources in Media Ethics* (1998) is a reference handbook detailing extensive work in media ethics around the world.

Mass communication ethics in terms of issues, participation, and setting has passed the international watershed. Given the global character of mass media industries, it will be world-wide in character permanently. The challenge theoretically and methodologically is to replace the Eurocentric axis of communication ethics with a model of comparative ethics instead. This transformation has not occurred to date, with virtually all work across the globe depending on the deontological-teleological typology of the West. The first systematic attempt at developing a comparative model across 13 countries (India, Nigeria, Brazil, Japan, Taiwan, Poland, South Africa, Germany, Venezuela, Colombia, United Arab Emirates, for example) identified the sacredness of life as a universal protonorm which yields three ethical principles across cultures: human dignity, truthtelling, and non-violence (Christians and Traber, 1997; cf. Kim, 1998). In the same comparative spirit, Fred Casmir (1997) develops a 'third-culture model' of communication ethics. Tom Cooper (1998) looks for principles underlying cultural diversity by studying indigenous people groups.

Philosophical ethics has struggled with the cultural diversity issue since David Hume recognized that the multiplying discoveries of other cultures threatened philosophy's ordered world with diverse concepts of the good life that appeared to have nothing in common (*Treatise of Human Nature* [1739] and *Enquiries* [1748]). Kant's formal universalizability criterion (*Groundwork of the Metaphysics of Morals* [1785]) rejected Hume's empiricism of moral sentiments, but neither alternative satisfactorily dealt with cultural pluralism. Kant's view has been exclusionary and strategies of a Humean sort tend to reduce morality to social utility. As communication ethics internationalizes itself, the challenge is a thicker theory of comparative ethics that transcends the philosophical dilemmas of theory versus description and its progeny — rationalism versus relativism.

3.3 Critique

Applied ethics has sustained heavy criticism from academic philosophers since its beginnings in the 1980s. To some academics it has not seemed sophisticated enough theoretically and too accommodationist politically to serve as a framework for understanding professional morality. Except for medical ethics, the issues are not often considered intellectually interesting. In the last decade or two, ethics has been taken back from its isolation in one department and made accessible to the university as a whole. It is mediated through language appropriate to students and practitioners in the field. But the impact of applied ethics on the university's curriculum and educational policy is still marginal and its position insecure. Instead of being isolated *en bloc* in philosophy departments, it tends to be fragmented and marginalized piece by piece, feeding an ongoing academic dissatisfaction with all versions of applied and professional ethics.

Applied ethics is directed in principle to making actual choices in moral conflicts, without being separate from normative ethics in general. It intends to supplement the abstract structures of normative ethics by systematic attention to concrete moral decision making. It aims to draw on ethical theory in reaching or scrutinizing moral judgments. Professional ethics refers to ethical inquiry about professional conduct and, as part of applied ethics, is considered normative also. However, while the intention behind the busyness of the last two decades may have largely been the foundational work of normative ethics, the overall result has been non-philosophical descriptive ethics. While this social scientific enterprise is important in itself, it has not provided a normative framework for the media's professional ethos. The professional culture that took form in the 1890s remains true a century later:

> Communication ethics has emerged out of the ethos of professionalism that characterizes the... drive of upwardly mobile classes for professional status who identify with the historic myth of scientifically based progress. The internationalization of communication ethics has taken place in the context of worldwide modernization that is an extension of nations with an early lead in scientific technology and industrialization.... Alternative public philosophies of communication are developing in non-Western political and cultural contexts but these have so far not made a significant, coherent contribution to international discussions of communication ethics (White, 1989: 46, 65).

4. Conclusion

Three decades (1890s, 1920s, 1980s) and their overflow have been decisive in the formation of communication ethics as an academic enterprise. The fragility of the field is obvious, with virtually the same intellectual pattern repeating itself during these three outcroppings. In each case, a systematic framework emerges that is buried or besieged by larger intellectual currents. In the early 20th century,

moral philosophy isolated itself as metaethics in philosophy departments. Scientific naturalism as the university's prevailing worldview
in the middle of the century suffocated the vitality of the 1920s. The
explosion of the 1980s is hounded at present by a dramatic confrontation with modernist thought that most communication ethics
depends on and reflects.

Throughout this century, in and around the formative decades,
communication ethics in Europe and North America benefited little
from philosophical ethics generally. Where connections have
occurred, communication ethics suffered the same struggles and was
plagued by similar weaknesses. Therefore, a retrospective and new
direction must be embedded in ethical theory as a whole.

Ethical rationalism has served as the prevailing paradigm. Consistent with philosophical ethics generally since 1890, communication
ethics has presumed that rationality marks all legitimate claims
about moral obligations, so that the truth of those claims can be set-
tled by formal examination of their logical structure. The general
trend in serious-minded communication ethics entails an ethical
rationalism that requires autonomous moral agents to apply rules
consistently, formally, and self-consciously to every choice. Making
rational processes explicit has combined with the ancient Western
emphasis on the universality of reason to create basic rules of morality that everyone is obliged to follow and against which all counter-
claims about moral obligations can be measured.

Ethical rationalism is harassed from every side these days. A post-
Newtonian age no longer supports a metaphysical claim that good
and evil or right and wrong are formal properties that exist in
abstraction (cf. Bauman, 1993). Theories of truth that depend on a
simple correspondence between true statements and reality are
unusustainable on this side of Darwin, Freud, and Wittgenstein. The
utilitarian rationalism which all three periods represent has lost its
authority. And the dominant mode at present, professional and practical ethics, has been unable to address the complicated issues adequately. Dramatic technological innovation and the negative side of
market-driven global commerce have pulled the news profession
away from its traditional role in facilitating democratic life.

This historical study points to the need for an entirely new model
of communication ethics. Rather than searching for neutral principles to which all parties can appeal, or accepting moral relativism
uncritically, our ethical theory should rest on a complex view of

moral judgments as integrating facts, principles, and feelings in terms of human wholeness. Ethics is inscribed in our worldviews, which themselves are simultaneously embedded culturally and factually.

4.1 *Discourse Ethics*

Habermas's discourse ethics dominates the media ethics literature of the 1990s. The translation of his *Moralbewusstsein und kommunikatives Handeln* in 1990 and publication of *The Communicative Ethics Controversy* in the same year set the stage for the most important debates so far in communication ethics during this decade. In Section I, Benhabib and Dallmayr (1990) reprint a major section of Habermas's *Moralbewusstsein*, plus essays by Karl-Otto Apel and two of their students. The five chapters of Part II are composed of recent European reflections on the relevance of discourse ethics for theories of democratic institutions — ranging from Wittgensteinian language theory to Kantian idealism. Benhabib's 'Afterword' (pp. 330-69) clarifies the arguments in terms of Anglo-American philosophy as a whole.

Habermas (1990) replaces Kant's formal system — his universalizability criterion of non-contradiction — with a communication community representing their common interests. He develops a procedural model of moral argumentation; "justification is tied to reasoned agreement among those subject to the norms in question" (p. viii). Habermas understands language to be an agent of culture and social organization. Discourses are symbolic forms through which we think, argue, persuade, display convictions and establish our identities. Narratives contain in a nutshell the meaning of our theories and beliefs. Therefore, the overriding question is whether our myriad linguistic forms allow everyone's interests a representative hearing. Is the moral consciousness of the community's members reflected in our practical discourse? Competing normative claims can be fairly adjudicated in the public sphere under ideal speech conditions such as reciprocity and openness. Habermas makes a permanent contribution to the Frankfurt School by recognizing that the distributive fallacy can be overcome through universal pragmatics.

Habermas's critical theory contradicts the liberal democratic politics presumed by traditional approaches to communication ethics.

Nearly all the literature in communication ethics in the West during the twentieth century has taken for granted a liberal democratic political philosophy. For Habermas, moral consciousness must be nurtured instead under conditions of instrumental technocracy and institutional power that stifle autonomous action in the public arena.

But is media ethics thereby home free, repositioned through Habermas for intellectual leadership as the 21st century dawns? Indeed, cutting through our political assumptions is a major corrective, but still insufficient in terms of the current debates in philosophical ethics as a whole. Many of the major issues in contemporary life come to a head in ethical terms; they provide conditions which our theorizing in media ethics must meet in order to be intellectually viable — the Habermasian trajectory included. The challenges to Habermas revolve around three axes: gender, ethnicity and Enlightenment rationalism (see Benhabib, 1992):

1. In Nancy Fraser's view (1992, 1997), Habermas's public sphere is an abstraction which is not deeply holistic, gender inclusive or culturally constituted. It presumes a private-public dichotomy, with the nurturing of human intimacy constrained within the private domain.

2. Given Habermas's insistence that public discourse "conform to generalizable interests" (Cooper, 1991: 34), the potential ethnocentrism of his public sphere remains an ongoing concern. How can he ensure that the interests of marginalized subcultures "will become a part of generalizable interests"? (p. 34) Insisting in discourse ethics on full and open discussion does not itself guarantee that those without administrative power can interpret their own needs and position themselves in their own terms (Cooper, 1991: 40).

3. Foucault (1984) opposes both the liberal democratic presumption and Habermas's critical theory by questioning the very existence of autonomous citizens who may engage in rational discourse. Thoughtful self-reflexivity is impossible for Foucault without emancipation from the prevailing regime of oppressive practices. From his perspective, we ought to struggle against the economic and ideological state violence that constitute us as moral subjects. Meanwhile, the renewed interest in Marx's ethics suggests the possibility that more satisfactory critical ethics have yet to emerge, beyond both Habermas's modernity and Foucault's resistance (see Churchich, 1994; West, 1991).

4.2 *Feminist Communitarian Ethics*

Over the last decade, social and feminist ethics have made a radical break with the individual autonomy and rationalist presumption of utilitarian rationalism (cf. Koehn, 1998). The social ethics of Agnes Heller, Charles Taylor (1989, 1991, 1994), Carole Pateman (1985, 1988, 1989), Cornel West (1989, 1991) and Edith Wyschogrod, and the feminist ethics of Carol Gilligan, (1982, 1988), Virginia Held, (1993), and Seyla Benhabib (1992), are fundamentally reconstructing ethical theory (cf. Code et al., 1988). Agnes Heller (1988, 1990, 1996) and Edith Wyschogrod (1974, 1985, 1990, 1998) are two promising examples of ethical theory in terms of today's contingency and fragmentation. In Wyschogrod's *Saints and Postmodernism* anti-authority struggles are possible without assuming that our choices are voluntary. She represents a social ethics of self and Other in the tradition of Emmanuel Levinas. In Heller's trilogy, moral principles are conceivable in the context of good persons (rather than in abstractions). As a star student of Georg Lukács and professor at Budapest University until her dismissal in 1973, Heller contributes to social ethics an extraordinary understanding of resistance and emancipation (cf. Vajda, 1994; Despoix, 1994). Her dialogic ethics reconceptualizes the theory-practice relationship and brings communitarian social philosophy into maturity.

Feminist communitarian ethics is a normative theory that serves as an antidote to realist utilitarianism (cf. Denzin, 1997: 274-87). It presumes that the community is ontologically and axiologically prior to persons. Human identity is constituted through the social realm. In the communitarian perspective, our selfhood is not fashioned out of thin air. We are born into a sociocultural universe where values, moral commitments and existential meanings are negotiated dialogically. Social systems precede their occupants and endure after them. Therefore, morally appropriate action intends community. Fulfillment is never achieved in isolation, but only through human bonding at the epicenter of social formation. Contrary to the utilitarian dualism between individuals and society, we know ourselves primarily as whole beings in relation (cf. Sandel, 1998).

For communitarians, the liberalism of Locke and Mill confuses an aggregate of individual pursuits with the common good. Moral agents need a context of social commitments and community ties for assessing what is valuable. What is worth preserving as a good cannot be self-determined in isolation, but ascertained only within specific social situations where human identity is nurtured. The public sphere is conceived as a mosaic of particular communities, a pluralism of ethnic identities and worldviews intersecting to form a social bond but each seriously held and competitive as well.

In addition to resolving the anomalies in professional and practical ethics, feminist communitarianism helps establish a normative theory of the media to replace the objectivity model. Instead of the transmission of plentiful data, news is an agent of community formation. In this fundamental reorientation of the press's mission, the goal of reporting becomes civic transformation. A revitalized citizenship is seen as the press's aim — not merely readers and audiences provided with information, but morally literate persons. In the traditional view, the purpose of the news media has been to present evidence on which decisions can be based, to provide a bounteous fare — true, half-true, and false — which the public molds into a coherent body of knowledge. The received view characteristically supposes that the day's raw intelligence is democracy's lifeline, and for supplying that material we assign the press a strategic role. The press is said to advance society's interests by feeding our individual capacity to reason and make decisions.

However, from the perspective of a feminist communitarian ethics, the information function is too static and narrow, a half-truth at best. Getting one's head straight does not automatically generate intelligent social action. The question is what we need to improve society and how such transformation can be accomplished. The vocational axis for the news profession is activating the polis. Along these lines, communitarian ethics enriched by feminism establishes the way public communication ought to be organized to realize the social and political ideals of democratic life at present.

The vigor and resources of practical and applied ethics will keep them productive in the immediate future. However, the strategic direction for mass media ethics at present appears to be the social ethics of feminism and communitarianism. This normative model avoids the conundrums facing Habermas, and it provides a radical alternative to utilitarian rationalism.

References

ALIA, Valerie, B. BRENNAN, B. HOFFMASTER (eds.) (1996), *Deadlines and Diversity: Journalism Ethics in a Changing World*. Halifax (Nova Scotia), Fernwood.

ALMOND, B. (ed.) (1995), *Introducing Applied Ethics*. Oxford (UK), Blackwell.

AYER, Alfred Jules (1936), *Language, Truth, and Logic*. New York, Dover.

BALDASTY, Gerald (1992), *The Commercialization of News in the Nineteenth Century*. Madison, University of Wisconsin Press.

BAROSSO, Porfirio Asenjo (1984), *Códigos deontólogicos de los medios de communicación: Prensa, radio, televisión, cine, publicidad y relacíones publicas*. Madrid, Ediciones Paulinas.

BAUMAN, Zygmunt (1993), *Postmodern Ethics*. Oxford (UK), Blackwell.

BEAUD, Paul, Laurence KAUFMANN (1998), 'New Trends in French Communication Research' in *Javnost — The Public* 5(1998)1, pp. 5-31.

BENHABIB, Seyla, Fred DALLMAYR (eds.) (1990), *The Communicative Ethics Controversy*. Cambridge (MA) & London, MIT Press.

BENHABIB, Seyla (1992), *Situating the Self: Gender, Community, and Postmodernism in Contemporary Ethics*. New York, Routledge.

BELSEY, Andrew, Ruth CHADWICK (eds.) (1992), *Ethical Issues in Journalism and the Media*. London, Routledge.

BERTRAND, Claude-Jean (1999), *L'arsenal de la Démocratie: Médias, Déontologie, M.A.R.S.* Paris, Economica.

BOVENTER, Hermann (1984), *Ethik des Journalismus: Zur Philosophie der Medienkultur*. Konstanz, Universitatsverlag Konstanz Gmbh.

BOWIE, Norman (1982), 'Applied Philosophy — Its Meaning and Justification' in *Applied Philosophy* 1(1982)Spring, pp. 1-18.

CASMIR, Fred L. (ed.) (1997), *Ethics in Intercultural and International Communication*. Mahwah (NJ), Lawrence Erlbaum.

CHRISTIANS, Clifford (1977), 'Fifty Years of Scholarship in Media Ethics' in *Journal of Communication* 27(1977)4, pp. 19-29.

CHRISTIANS, Clifford, John P. FÉRRE, Mark FACKLER (1993), *Good News: Social Ethics and the Press*. New York, Oxford University Press.

CHRISTIANS, Clifford (1995), 'Review Essay: Current Trends in Media Ethics' in *European Journal of Communication* 10(1995)4, pp. 545-558.

CHRISTIANS, Clifford, Michael TRABER (eds.) (1997), *Communication Ethics and Universal Values*. Thousand Oaks (CA), Sage.

CHURCHICH, Nicholas (1994), *Marxism and Morality: A Critical Examination of Marxist Ethics*. Cambridge (UK), James Clarke.

CODE, Lorraine, Sheila MULLETT, Christine OVERALL (eds.) (1988), *Feminist Perspectives: Philosophical Essays on Methods and Morals*. Toronto, University of Toronto Press.

COOPER, Thomas W. (1989), *Communication Ethics and Global Change.* White Plains (NY), Longman.

COOPER, Thomas W. (1998), *A Time Before Deception: Truth in Communication, Culture and Ethics.* Sante Fe (NM), Clear Light Publishers.

CORCORAN, Farrel, Paschal PRESTON (eds.) (1995), *Democracy and Communication in the New Europe: Change and Continuity in East and West.* Cresskill, NJ, Hampton Press.

CRAWFORD, Nelson (1929), *The Ethics of Journalism.* New York, Knopf.

CURRAN, James, Jean SEATON. *Power Without Responsibility: The Press and Broadcasting in Britain,* 5th ed. London, Routledge.

DE BEER, Arnold, E. STEYN, G.N. CLAASEN (eds.) (1994), 'Special Edition: Focus on Media Ethics' in *Ecquid Novi: Tydskrif vir die Joernalistiek in Suider Africa,* 15(1994)1, pp. 1-172.

DENZIN, Norman K. (1997), *Interpretive Ethnography: Ethnographic Practices for the 21st Century.* Thousand Oaks (CA), Sage Publications.

DESPOIX, Phillippe (1994), 'On the Possibility of a Philosophy of Values: A Dialogue Within the Budapest School' in John BURNHEIM (ed.) *The Social Philosophy of Agnes Heller.* Amsterdam-Atlanta, Rodopi.

DICKEN GARCIA, Hazel (1989), *Journalistic Standards in Nineteenth-Century America.* Madison, University of Wisconsin.

DUCATEL, Ken *et al.* (eds.) (1999), *The Information Society in Europe: Work and Life in an Age of Globalization.* Lanham (MD), Rowman and Littlefield Publishers.

Editorial (1999), 'Key Issues in Global Communication' in *Media Development,* 46(1999)2, pp. 2-64.

ELLUL, Jacques (1969), *Propaganda.* Trans. K. KELLEN and J. LERNER. New York, Knopf.

ERMANN, M. David, M.B. WILLIAMS, M.S. SHAUF (eds.) (1997), *Computers, Ethics and Society,* 2nd ed. New York, Oxford University Press.

ESS, Charles (ed.) (1996), *Philosophical Perspectives on Computer-Mediated Communication.* Albany, State University of New York Press.

ETTEMA, James A., Theodore GLASSER (1998), *Custodians of Conscience: Investigative Journalism and Public Virtue.* New York, Columbia University Press.

FLINT, Leon (1925), *The Conscience of the Newspaper: A Casebook in the Principles and Problems of Journalism.* New York, D. Appleton.

FORTNER, Robert S. (1993), *International Communication: History, Conflict, and Control of the Global Metropolis.* Belmont (CA), Wadsworth.

FOUCAULT, Michel (1984), 'On the Genealogy of Ethics: An Overview of Work in Progress'; 'Politics and Ethics': 'An Interview' in Paul RABINOW (ed.), *The Foucault Reader,* Trans. C. PORTER. New York, Pantheon, pp. 340-380.

FRASER, Nancy (1992), 'Rethinking the Public Sphere: A Contribution to the Critique of Actually Existing Democracy' In Craig CALHOUN (ed.), *Habermas and the Public Sphere*. Cambridge (MA), MIT Press.
FRASER, Nancy (1997), *Justus Interruptus*. New York, Routledge.
GIBBONS, William (1926), *Newspaper Ethics*. Ann Arbor, University of Michigan.
GILLIGAN, Carol (1982), *In a Different Voice: Psychological Theory and Women's Development*. Cambridge (MA), Harvard University Press.
GILLIGAN, Carol et al. (eds.) (1988), *Mapping the Moral Domain*. Cambridge (MA), Harvard University Press.
GJELSTEN, Gudmund (1988), *Møte eller manipulasjon? Om etikk i massemedia*. Oslo, KKS Forlager.
GOMES, Pedro G. (1990), *Direito de ser: A ética da communicaó na América Latina*. Sáo Paulo, Ediciones Paulinas.
GORREN, Aline (1896), 'The Ethics of Modern Journalism' in *Scribner's Magazine* 19(1896)April, p. 507.
GUNARATNE, Shelton (1998), 'Old Wine in a New Bottle: Developmental Journalism and Social Responsibility' in Michael A. ROLOFF (ed.), *Communication Yearbook 21*. Thousand Oaks (CA), Sage Publications, pp. 277-321.
HABERMAS, Jurgen (1989), *The Structural Foundation of the Public Sphere: An Inquiry into a Category of Bourgeois Society*. Trans. T. BURGER. London, Polity Press.
HABERMAS, Jurgen (1990), *Moral Consciousness and Communicative Action*. Trans. C. LENHART and S.W. NICHOLSON. Cambridge (MA), MIT Press. (Originally published as *Moral Bewusstsein und kommunikatives Handeln*, 1983).
HABERMAS, Jurgen (1993), *Justification and Application: Remarks on Discourse Ethics*. Trans. C. CRONIN. Cambridge (MA), MIT Press.
HABERMAS, Jurgen (1998), *Between Facts and Norms: Contributions to a Discourse Theory of Law and Democracy*. Cambridge (MA), MIT Press.
HAMELINK, Cees J. (1983), *Cultural Autonomy in Global Communications*. New York, Longman.
HAMELINK, Cees J. (1994), *The Politics of World Communication: A Human Rights Perspective*. London, Sage Publications.
HAMELINK, Cees J. (1996), *World Communication: Disempowerment and Self-Empowerment*. New York (NY), St. Martin's Press.
HEINE, William C. (1975), *Journalism Ethics: A Case Book*. London (Ontario), University of Western Ontario Library.
HELD, Virginia (1993), *Feminist Morality: Transforming Culture, Society, and Politics*. Chicago, University of Chicago Press.
HELLER, Agnes (1988), *General Ethics*. Oxford (UK), Blackwell.
HELLER, Agnes, (1990), *A Philosophy of Morals*. Oxford (UK), Blackwell.

HELLER, Agnes (1996), *An Ethics of Personality*. Oxford (UK), Blackwell.
HENNING, Albert F. (1932), *Ethics and Practice in Journalism*. New York, R. Long and R.R. Smith.
HOCKING, William Ernest (1947), *Freedom of the Press: A Framework of Principle*. Chicago, University of Chicago Press.
HOLDEREGGER, A. (ed.) (1992), *Ethik der Medienkommunikation: Grundlagen*. Freiburg-Wien, Universitätsverlag Freiburg Schweiz.
HURST, John, Sally A. WHITE (1994), *Ethics and the Australian News Media*. South Melbourne, Macmillan Education Australia.
Hutchins Commission (1947), *A Free and Responsible Press*. Chicago, University of Chicago.
IGGERS, Jeremy (1998), *Good News, Bad News: Journalism Ethics and the Public Interest*. Boulder (CO), Westview Press.
JAKUBOWICZ, Karol (1998/99), 'Normative Models of Media and Journalism and Broadcasting Regulation in Central and Eastern Europe' in *International Journal of Communications Law and Policy* 2(1998/99) Winter, pp. 1-32.
JAKUBOWICZ, Karol (1999), 'Public Service Broadcasting in the Information Society' in *Media Development*, 46(1999)2, pp. 45-49.
JENSEN, J. Vernon (1997), *Ethical Issues in the Communication Process*. Mahwah (NJ), Lawrence Erlbaum.
JOHANNESEN, Richard L. (1997), 'Communication Ethics: Centrality, Trends, and Controversies' Unpublished paper. Share the Wealth Series, NCA Chicago.
JUUSELA, Pauli (1991), *Journalistic Codes of Ethics in the CSCE Countries: An Examination*. Tampere (Finland), University of Tampere Series B31.
KASOMA, Francis P. (ed.) (1994), *Journalism Ethics in Africa*. Nairobi, African Council for Communication Education (ACCE).
KIERAN, Matthew (1997), *Media Ethics: A Philosophical Approach*. Westport (CT), Praeger.
KIERAN, Matthew (ed.) (1998), *Media Ethics*. London, Routledge.
KIM, Yersu (1998), *Prospects for a Universal Ethics: Report on Ongoing Reflections; And A Common Framework for the Ethics of the Twenty-first Century* (30 March 1999). Paris, The UNESCO Universal Ethics Project: Division of Philosophy and Ethics.
KOEHN, Daryl (1998), *Rethinking Feminist Ethics*. New York, Routledge.
LAMBETH, Edmund B. (1991), *Committed Journalism: An Ethic for the Profession*, 2nd ed. Bloomington, Indiana University Press.
LICHTENBERG, Judith (1996), 'In Defence of Objectivity Revisited' in James CURRAN, Michael GUREVITCH (eds.), *Mass Media and Society*, 2nd ed. London, Edward Arnold.
LILLY, W.S. (1889), 'The Ethics of Journalism' in *The Forum* 4 (1889) July, pp. 503-512.

LIPPMANN, Walter (1922), *Public Opinion*. New York, Scribner's.

LUKES, Steven (1985), *Marxism and Morality*. New York, Oxford University Press.

Many Voices, One World: Communication and Society Today and Tomorrow (1980). London, Kogan Page.

MACDONALD, Barrie, MICHEL Petheram (1998), *Keyguide to Information Sources in Media Ethics*. London, Mansell Publishing.

MERRILL, John C. (1997), *Journalism Ethics: Philosophical Foundation for News Media*. New York, St. Martin's Press.

MILL, John Stuart (1865), *Examination of Sir William Hamilton's Philosophy and of the Principal Philosophical Questions Discussed in His Writings*. London, Longman, Green, Roberts & Green.

MILL, John Stuart (1893 [1843]), *A System of Logic, Ratiocinative and Inductive: Being a Connected View of the Principles of Evidence and the Methods of Scientific Investigation*, 8th ed. New York, Harper and Brothers.

MILL, John Stuart (1969), *Autobiography*. Boston, Houghton Mifflin.

MOORE, George Edward (1903), *Principia Ethica*. Cambridge (UK), Cambridge University Press.

MURPHY, Lawrence (1924), 'News Values and Analysis' *Journalism Bulletin* 2(1924)3, pp. 29-31.

NERONE, John (ed.) (1995), *Last Rights*. Urbana, University of Illinois Press.

NORDENSTRENG, Kaarle (1984), *The Mass Media Declaration of UNESCO*. Norwood (NJ), Ablex.

NORDENSTRENG, Kaarle, Hifzi TOPUZ (eds.) (1989), *Journalist: Status, Rights and Responsibilities*. Prague, International Organization of Journalists.

NORDENSTRENG, Kaarle (ed.) (1995a), *Reports on Media Ethics in Europe*. University of Tampere, Julkaisiya Sara B41.

NORDENSTRENG, Kaarle (ed.) (1995b), 'Special Issue on Media Ethics' in *European Journal of Communication* 10(1995)4, pp. 435-558.

NORDENSTRENG, Kaarle (1998a), 'Hutchins Goes Global' in *Communication Law and Policy*, 3(1998)3, pp. 419-438.

NORDENSTRENG, Kaarle (1998b), 'Professional Ethics: Between Fortress Journalism and Cosmopolitan Democracy' in Kees BRANTS, Joke HERMES, Liesbet VAN ZOONEN (eds.), *The Media in Question: Popular Cultures and Public Interests*. London, Sage Publications, pp. 124-134.

NORRIS, Charles (1994), *Truth and the Ethics of Criticism*. Manchester (UK), Manchester University Press.

PASQUALI, Antonio (1997), 'The Moral Dimension of Communicating' in C. CHRISTIANS, M. TRABER (eds.) *Communication Ethics and Universal Values*. Thousand Oaks (CA), Sage, pp. 46-67.

PATEMAN, Carol (1985), *The Problem of Political Obligation: A Critique of Liberal Theory*. Cambridge (UK), Polity Press.

PATEMAN, Carol (1988), *The Sexual Contract*. Stanford, CA: Stanford University Press.

PATEMAN, Carol (1989), *The Disorder of Women: Democracy, Feminism and Political Theory*. Stanford (CA), Stanford University Press.

PORTER, Vincent (1999), 'Introduction: The Economics and Politics of the New Media' (Special Issue) in *Javnost — The Public*, 6(1999)3, pp. 5-10.

PURCELL, Edward (1973), *The Crisis of Democratic Theory: Scientific Naturalism and the Problem of Value*. Lexington, University Press of Kentucky.

QUINE, W.V. (1953), *From a Logical Point of View: Nine Logico-Philosophical Essays*. Cambridge (MA), Harvard University Press.

ROSS, W. David (1930), *The Right and the Good*. Oxford (UK), Clarendon Press.

RUSSELL, Nick (1994), *Morals and the Media: Ethics in Canadian Journalism*. Vancouver, University of British Columbia Press.

SANDEL, Michael J. (1998), *Liberalism and the Limits of Justice*, 2nd ed. Cambridge (UK), Cambridge University Press.

SCHAUER, Frederick (1982), *Free Speech: A Philosophical Inquiry*. Cambridge (UK), Cambridge University Press.

SERVAES, Jan, Rico LIE (eds.) (1997), *Media and Politics in Transition: Cultural Identity in the Age of Globalization*. Leuven, Acco.

SIDGWICK, Henry (1997), *Practical Ethics*. New York, Oxford University Press.

SONNENBERG, Urte, Barbara THOMASS (eds.) (1997a), *Journalistic Decision-Taking in Europe: Case by Case*. Maastricht (Netherlands), European Journalism Centre.

SONNENBERG, Urte (ed.) (1997b), *Organizing Media Accountability: Experiences in Europe*. Maastricht (Netherlands), European Journalism Centre.

TAYLOR, Charles (1982), 'The Diversity of Goods' in Amartya SEN, Bernard WILLIAMS (eds.), *Utilitarianism and Beyond*. Cambridge (UK), Cambridge University Press, pp. 129-144.

TAYLOR, Charles (1989), *Sources of the Self: The Making of the Modern Identity*. Cambridge (MA), Harvard University Press.

TAYLOR, Paul W. (1963), *The Moral Judgment: Readings in Contemporary Metaethics*. Englewood Cliffs (NJ), Prentice-Hall.

THOMASSEN, Niels (1985), *Samvoer og solidaritet*, Copenhagen. Trans. J. IRONS, *Communicative Ethics in Theory and Practice*, London: Macmillan, 1992.

TOMPERT, Hella (ed.) (1980), *Ethik und Kommunikation: Vom Ethos des Journalisten*. Stuttgart, Katholische Akademie.

TONG, Rosemarie (1993), *Feminism and Feminist Ethics*. Belmont (CA), Wadsworth.

TOULMIN, Stephen (1988), 'The Recovery of Practical Philosophy' in *American Scholar* 57(1988)Summer, pp. 337-352.

TRABER, Michael (ed.) (1986), *The Myth of the Information Revolution: Social and Ethical Implications of Communication Technology*. London, Sage Publications.

TRACEY, Michael (1998), *The Decline and Fall of Public Service Broadcasting*. Oxford (UK), Oxford University Press.

VAN DER MEIDEN, Anne (ed.) (1980), *Ethics in Mass Communication*. Utrecht, State University of Utrecht.

VAN DER MEIDEN, Anne, *Reclame en Ethiek*. Leiden/Antwerp, H.E. Stenfert Kroese.

VENTURELLI, Shalini S. (1997), 'Informationsgesellschaft Europa' in *Europäische Öffentlichkeit: Entwicklung von Strukturen und Theorie*. Berlin, Vistas, pp. 123-145.

WEIBULL, Lennart, Britt BÖRJESSON (1991), 'The Swedish Media Accountability System: A Research Perspective'. University of Gothenburg: Unpublished paper MARS Forum, Paris.

WEST, Cornel (1991), *The Ethical Dimensions of Marxist Thought*. New York, Monthly Review Press.

WESTERMARCK, Edward A. (1932), *Ethical Relativity*. London, Routledge & Kegan Paul.

WHITE, Robert A. (1989), 'Social and Political Factors in the Development of Communication Ethics' in Thomas W. COOPER (ed.), *Communication Ethics and Global Change*. New York, Longman, pp. 40-65.

WHITE, Robert A. (1995), 'From Codes of Ethics to Public Cultural Truth' in *European Journal of Communication* 10(1995), pp. 441-60.

WHITE, Robert A. (1996), 'A Communitarian Ethic of Communications in a Postmodern Age' in *Ethical Perspectives* 3(1996)4, pp. 207-218.

WUNDEN, Wolfgang (ed.) (1989), *Medien Zwischen Markt und Moral: Beitrage zur Medienethik*. Stuttgart, J.F. Steinkopf Verlag.

WYSCHOGROD, Edith (1974), *Emmanuel Levinas: The Problem of Ethical Metaphysics*. The Hague, Netherlands, Martinus Nijhoff.

WYSCHOGROD, Edith (1990), *Saints and Postmodernism*. Chicago, University of Chicago Press.

WYSCHOGROD, Edith (1998), *An Ethics of Remembering: History, Heterology, and the Nameless Others*. Chicago, University of Chicago Press.

ZASSOURSKY, Yassen N., Elena VARTANOVA (eds.) (1998), *Changing Media and Communications: Concepts, Technologies and Ethics in Global and National Perspectives*. Moscow, Faculty of Journalism/Publisher ICAR.

NEW APPROACHES TO MEDIA ETHICS: MORAL DIALOGUE, CREATING NORMATIVE PARADIGMS, AND PUBLIC CULTURAL TRUTH

Robert A. White

In many countries of the world today, there is widespread dissatisfaction with the quality of public communication systems. This is often summed up as a crisis of communication ethics. The dissatisfaction is felt, of course, by the general public, but also by professionals, regulatory agencies and by the media industries themselves. Some suggest that we need new legislation and regulatory control. Others argue that a more stringent application of codes of ethics is necessary. The libertarians, on the other hand, suggest a removal of all controls. Some degree of dissatisfaction is perhaps a normal part of the ongoing debate, but many would suggest that we are at moment of profound cultural and political change.

It is the thesis of this chapter that the source of the crisis of communication ethics today and the root of general dissatisfaction with the state of public media is the widespread feeling that the 'moral claims', that is, the rights of people in the area of public communication, are being violated. Conspiracy theorists would be quick to lay the blame on one or another actor, but in some way all the actors are to blame and none are to blame. The problem lies more in the lack of a formula of moral consensus which enables all claims to be respected in an equitable way. Throughout history, virtually every major epoch of sociocultural and political economic change has witnessed a similar reorganization of the formula of consensus for adjudicating moral claims in the public sphere. The ability of a society to reach a new moral consensus with relative ease and thoroughness depends very much on finding an adequate procedure for dialogue among major social actors.

To understand the nature of the current debate, it is helpful to examine the sense of 'violation' of moral claims of major actors. First of all, the public itself. Virtually every survey of citizen attitudes toward the public media indicates a growing distrust of the media and the feeling that the media are a self-serving, manipulative institution. In a survey by a major newspaper in the United States, only 25% held the opinion that "The news media help society solve its problems" while 71% thought that "The news media gets in the way of society solving its problems" (Merritt, 1995: xv). A very concrete evidence of this declining credibility is the declining readership of newspapers and the declining audiences of virtually all major broadcasters.

Journalists themselves are increasingly disillusioned. In a survey of journalist satisfaction in 1982 and 1983 only one in ten journalists was dissatisfied, but in 1993 one in five journalists said that they were planning to leave the profession in the next few years (Merritt, 1995: 4). Most cited as the reason the increasing violation of their professional ideals by the news organizations that are ceasing to serve public needs and are simply an income-generating enterprise.

Still another voice of moral outrage are the media critics who see themselves as the defenders of a public that often suffers in silence. Critics see the growing invasion of privacy as a prime example of the increasing transgressiveness of the media industry. Very wealthy and powerful people, especially those close to decisions of the media industry, can protect their privacy. Franklin and Pilling ask, "Who is entitled to privacy? The drive of market forces and the thrust of the law could well mean that very few — apart from media moguls — have this right... The most serious casualties of this journalistic trend will be ordinary people... Lacking the financial and legal resources to halt press intrusion, their everyday lives and experiences can be transformed into a commodity which can sell newspapers" (1998: 120).

The media industry, on the other hand, point to the enormous economic pressures and the large number of media enterprises that have failed in recent years. They feel that the moral demands that media critics are making are utterly utopian. The public is interested in light entertainment and sensationalism. For the industry the first moral obligation is to give to the public what it wants and not to judge the motives of this public. If a large percentage of all video cassettes sold in the United States are pornographic, it is the public which has to decide what its moral rules are.

This brief survey reveals that virtually all of the actors in the arena of public communication feel that other actors are imposing, through power relationships, demands that make it impossible for them to fulfill their moral obligations. For example, certain key sectors of the public such as parents feel that the media are forcing on them material which is totally unacceptable for a family and there is virtually nothing they can do about it. Journalists feel news organizations force them to violate their conscience in news selection and presentation and, again, there is nothing that can be done except to leave the profession. The media, on the other hand, argue that they would like to provide better quality programming, but the ratings are all powerful and must be followed (Ang, 1991)

From this perspective, it is easy to see why the traditional approach to 'ethics' in public communication in terms of 'professional ethics' and deontological codes have such limited significance. This media ethics tradition "has more to do with standards of personal or professional conduct than with public concerns" (McQuail, 1992: 14-15). The moral education of media professionals in terms of codes of ethics has tended to reinforce what Weaver and Wilhoit (1986: 104-145) refer to as the routine, disseminator and adversary roles rather than the interpretative role of journalists. This encourages conformity to media organization routines and discourages the broader social and cultural questions. There is very little evidence that the self-regulatory action of media professionals is based on criteria of adherence to codes of media ethics (Boeyink, 1994). Codes become more of an alibi to keep media critics and the consumer demands of the public away from direct influence on media standards (Pasquali, 1997).

What is occurring, then, is that each major actor is putting forth moral claims, but few actors are listening to or respecting the moral claims of others. The ethical decisions of a journalist, television producer or other communicator in the public sphere are based not simply on a solitary dialogue with her or his conscience but imply a relation of interpretative listening and negotiation among all major actors in the public sphere. An effective morality of public communication is a dialogical process in which each major actor recognizes the moral claims of other actors and is willing to work toward common symbols of morality in which all actors can recognize something of their moral claims.

Historically, when a more effective moral consensus has emerged, this has usually been the result of broad support for a particular formula which defines both obligations and rights of all the actors. The public consensus which finally recognized the freedom of the press took almost three centuries to work out, but eventually it was a formula that accepted the claims of the printers and harmonized this with the claims of the new commercial entrepreneurs, the new sciences, the new political movements, the more conservative religious traditions, and even the constitutional monarchies themselves (Siebert, 1965). Marzolf (1991), in her description of how the particular US version of the social responsibility formula or paradigm emerged, indicates that there was support from many social actors: the families of the general public, the business community, newspaper publishers such as Pulitzer and Ochs, academics promoting the professional degree courses, the founders of professional media associations proposing codes of ethics, and, finally, media operatives who were looking for higher, professional status.

In the 1920s and 1930s, when radio introduced a new set of actors and claims in the sphere of public communication, virtually every major country of the world worked out a different formula to respect the moral claims of major actors. In the US, with its strong free-enterprise tradition, a formula was devised which respected the importance of media entrepreneurs, the desire for local community and regional control, and, to protect services to the public, a certain measure of public regulation (a very new concept at the time) (Head and Sterling, 1989). In the Netherlands there emerged a very different formula based on the rights and obligations of religio-political-cultural communities of Protestants, Catholics, more secularized socialists and eventually other communities that could establish a moral claim to public communication.

Movements for media reform do fail if there is not real dialogue and negotiation. The movements in Latin America from 1960 to 1985 to consolidate the communication rights of the general public and to establish obligations of broadcasters failed in large part because the political-economic interests refused to dialogue, but also because the promoters of reform left out some of the major actors, especially the sectors of the general public such as the middle class (Fox, 1988: 6-35; Martín-Barbero, 1993). Horwitz, in his careful study of the history of deregulation in the United States, concludes that the social responsibility-public service model of regulation was built on a process of dialogue among the major parties involved (1989: 85-89). The process broke down when some of the new actors began to make demands of public service that seemed to entrepreneurs too utopian. The pressures for change made the old formula for adjudicating claims through regulatory agencies unrealistic. In the circumstances of rapid technological change, the paradigm of public regulation seemed unable to guarantee the moral claims of nearly all the major actors.

1. The Concept of 'Actor' in the Sphere of Public Communication

An 'actor' in public communication refers to groups of individuals who see their political-economic or cultural interests to be affected by a particular organization of services of public communication. These individuals have discovered sufficient 'community of interest' to organize a network of intercommunication constituting a social movement of leaders and followers seeking change in the decision process regarding public communication. For example, in many nations parents and others concerned about the negative influence of broadcasting in the socialization of the young have formed associations of concerned media consumers to force broadcasters to respect the moral implications of socialization.

Secondly, each actor also recognizes that it represents a community of values, experience and expertise that is somehow of crucial importance in helping public communication institutions fulfill their mission in society. Media consumer associations, for example, feel that they are an important source of normative reference regarding cultural values, order and solidarity. Journalists feel that they are of crucial importance in maintaining the freedom and open debate of the system. Media owners feel that they are of importance in opening up new media services and greater media diversity.

Thirdly, an actor tends to define its relation to other actors in terms of its own particular role and sphere of interest. The creative producers tend to define their claims in relation to others who have some role in the production. We could chart professionals in production in a kind of hierarchy of generality of responsibility in production quality (Cf. Figure 1). The fact that Figure 1 represents only one plane of rights and obligations suggests the complexity of interaction of actors in the sphere of public communication.

Figure 1: *Major social actors establishing the normative culture of public*

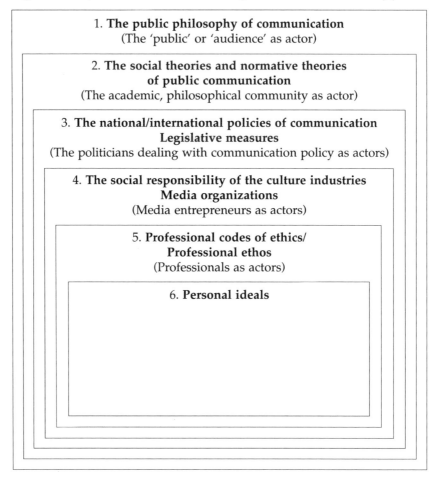

1. **The public philosophy of communication**
(The 'public' or 'audience' as actor)

2. **The social theories and normative theories
of public communication**
(The academic, philosophical community as actor)

3. **The national/international policies of communication
Legislative measures**
(The politicians dealing with communication policy as actors)

4. **The social responsibility of the culture industries
Media organizations**
(Media entrepreneurs as actors)

5. **Professional codes of ethics/
Professional ethos**
(Professionals as actors)

6. **Personal ideals**

Finally, an actor tends to be delimited in terms of moral claims, that is, in terms of rights and obligations that are defined not arbitrarily by the community of individuals that represent an actor but by the demands of the common good of the whole society.

2. The quality of the dialogue for establishing
a formula of common moral rights and obligations

In the examples of how a relatively satisfactory moral consensus has been constructed in a given historical context, the quality of the dialogue among major actors has been a crucial factor of success or failure (Habermas, 1991; Pasquali, 1997). If a dialogue is able to evoke a sense of respect for the moral claims of all actors and a search for a formula that does justice to all claims, then it is fulfilling its role. The following criteria are at least suggestive of the dimensions that should be present.

1. The process should encourage all potential actors to have an internal process of decision-making regarding its community of interests and its moral claims. Often, giving a constituency a 'seat on a board' or an 'office in a building' provides a stimulus to defining its role.

2. All affected parties should be encouraged and invited to be present in the negotiation process. If some parties are not present, then a proposed formula will lack support from this group in the eventual political process and the group may even block the proposed formula as 'illegitimate'. This suggests that there be an official 'organizing body' which is recognized as impartial and which represents the moral foundations of the society. Whether this be a public legislative body or a group of citizen trustees depends on how the society has typically adjudicated moral authority.

3. The claims of all parties need to be taken not simply as a pragmatic interest, but as a 'moral claim'. All participants should be encouraged to define their claims in moral terms, that is, in relation to the constitutive common good of the society and for the defense of fundamental human rights and human dignity. At times what actors initially put forward as a very pragmatic claim gradually becomes defined as a moral claim because the discourse has been framed in moral terms. An example of this is the moral discourse introduced by Lord Reith in the definition of the constitution of the BBC in Britain. Initially, advertising was rejected as a source of funding for the BBC in very pragmatic terms, namely a concession to the newspapers who feared that broadcasting would draw away their advertising revenues. Later the elimination of advertising was widely accepted as a moral issue, namely, that some areas of public media need to be free from the influences of advertising for the common good of the national culture (Paulu, 1981: 13-14, 54-60).

4. The negotiation procedures will have greater success in reaching agreement in so far as the discussion is located in a discourse of overarching values which are 'above' the interests of any one group but which, at the same time, guarantee the interests of all groups.

Usually, these statements of values including some or all of the following:
— Service to the people and the recognition of the people's 'right' to good service;
— Appeal to the impersonal, universalistic sense of 'professional responsibility', the assumed categorical duty to serve all clients and colleagues regardless of the situation;
— Appeal to common values such as the progress of the whole community;
— Appeal to whatever aspects of the 'mythic' national and international values and symbols which have been accepted in the past as the ultimate justifications of common action.
— Appeal to whatever 'new' and emerging common values seem to be of interest to all of the parties involved.
The creation of this kind of 'moral discourse' rooted in some version of a categorical obligation beyond the arbitrary construction of culture is the foundation of all appeals to respect the moral claims of others (Christians, 1997). The ability to call into play a moral discourse depends on the integrity of the leadership of the process. If the leadership is perceived as not representing universal moral values but, rather, its own pragmatic interests, then the appeal will have less power for bringing the parties to negotiation.

5. The formula for negotiation does not require any party to 'give up' part of its fundamental moral claims, but rather creates a 'higher' level of more generalized cultural symbols in which all can recognize something of their moral claims.

Underlying the desire for negotiating is the realization that the breakdown in procedures to elaborate a new formula will be detrimental to all involved. Especially important is a commonly accepted *moral* foundation, that is, willingness to carry out an action simply because it is the 'good' thing to do, even if it has no immediate pragmatic benefit for me personally or for my party (Kohlberg, 1980). The alternative is a regime in which brute power, the law of vendetta or the law of personalistic agreements among friends and family hold sway. Once the values of sectarian leadership dominate, then leaders compete to show that they can reward their sectarian constituencies better than other patrons. Likewise sectarian leaders try to outdo each other in attempts to destroy any kind of consensus because consensus would undermine their form of leadership.

3. The Role of Normative Paradigms in Public Communication

If the quality of the dialogue among major actors is important for arriving at a satisfactory normative consensus in public communication, no less important are the rules for elaborating a formula of consensus which respects all moral claims. Indeed, the history of philosophical and scientific reflection on communication from the earliest treatises of Plato and Aristotle regarding rhetoric have been attempts to define what constitutes a formula for good public communication (Poulakas, 1995). We may refer to these proposals as theories because they generally try to 'explain' how such an ideal state of public communication comes into existence and then how it contributes to efficient, democratic collective decision-making. Different theories have highlighted the importance of different aspects of public communication. For example, Plato tended to emphasize the importance of the objective, philosophical truth of public discourse. The movements for freedom of the press in the early modern era of Europe tended, naturally, to emphasize the dimension of expression of authentic personal conscience. Other theories have emphasized the social responsibility of all actors or the radical democratization of the system. Whatever the emphasis of the particular normative theory, it must be able to explain to the major actors why they have a moral obligation to act in a way that respects the moral claims of other major actors.

A new normative formulation becomes important when normative consensus among the major actors has broken down and public communication has become a chaotic situation in which 'might makes right'. Major public actors do not seem to be bound by any moral order and do not feel that older formulations apply in this new situation. As we have noted, arriving at a satisfactory normative theory is not easy and often does falter or fail in some major way. One condition is the quality of the dialogue. Another condition is the quality of the normative theory which is sought through the dialogue. By quality in this case is meant the degree to which all major actors agree to abide by established moral norms of good public communication such as freedom, diversity of content, objectivity and credibility, and order (McQuail, 1992). A normative theory of public communication emerges in the context of a particular socio-political movement which seeks a reorganization of society and a public communication system that will be part of that society (White, 1989).

The concept of normative theory of public communication began
to take shape as central to contemporary communication science
with the landmark book, *Four Theories of the Press*, composed by
Siebert, Peterson and Schramm (1956), to explain why there are such
profound differences in public communication systems in different
parts of the world. They located the difference at the level of moral
philosophies underlying different political systems and political cultures, and they identified four major press theories: authoritarian,
libertarian, social responsibility and communist. Later, major textbooks in communication theory have taken up the concept originally
proposed by *Four Theories of the Press* and integrated this into a general framework of communication as 'normative theory' in contrast
to and complementary to 'empirical theory' (McQuail, 1987; Grossberg, Wartella, Whitney, 1998). That is, while empirical theory
explains the existing processes of public communication, normative
theory provides a systematic explanation of how the communication
institutions *should* function in some ideal context.

Some discussions of normative theory suggest that there are not
several normative theories such as *Four Theories of the Press* proposed, but rather that there is one body of normative theory which
has gradually developed in different historical periods various paradigms and schools of thought (Nerone, 1995). It is useful to briefly
review the history of normative theory of public communication as a
background for understanding the conditions and functions of normative theory in the formation of normative consensus in public
communication.

4. The Historical Search for a More Adequate Normative Theory

4.1 *The Origins of the Corporatist Paradigm in the Mediterranean City-State*

It is significant that the earliest writings in Western society proposing an ideal of good public communication can be traced back to the
introduction of direct democracy in Athens about 600-500 BC
(Poulakos, 1995). Once the government dominated by the traditional
families of Athens was opened up to new commercial classes, as
many as 5,000 citizens came together in the public forum to debate
the collective decisions. Ability to influence outcomes depended on
the ability to present persuasive proposals to the public, and, in the

commercial atmosphere of the port city, a class of professional teachers of persuasive political eloquence, the sophists, promised a training certain to win an outcome in public debate.

Although the sophists wrote their own textbooks in ancient Athens, the most influential thought about good public communication was not that of the sophists but rather that of Plato who attacked the teaching of sophists as a major cause of the decline of good government in Greece. The writings of Aristotle, who felt that the sophists did not offer a systematic understanding of good public communication, carried Plato's position to a more objective treatise. It was largely Platonic thought, however, that provided the foundations for what later became the 'corporatist' conception of public communication, dominant through the Greco-Roman and Medieval Christian era.

For Plato the error of the sophists was to see good communication as simply winning public arguments and defending personal interests regardless of whether this was in the long-term interests of good government and truth. For Plato truth lies, not in the surface pragmatic solutions, but in the eternal unchanging verities, the underlying metaphysical natures of things that are known through philosophical reflection. To make good proposals for government it is necessary, for example, to understand the essential nature of justice which can be applied as the criterion of justice in any particular public decision. In the pluralistic melting pot of tribal cultures in the Mediterranean, this view of an underlying law of natures provided a useful basis for a more universal law of the Roman empire. The Christian kingdoms of northern Europe in turn built their legal and moral systems on that of the Roman Empire.

In the context of the Roman empire and the medieval society, this view of the moral foundations of society provided a convincing model of how to adjudicate the moral claims of all major actors in society. In this perspective, the centuries of social experience and the accumulated reflection of wise people provide a conception of the good society which is far superior to momentary currents of public opinion and the influence of powerful demagogues. In the chaotic state of early medieval Europe with its continual barbaric war, people dreamed of a good society as organic in which every social role — from monarch to peasant — and every institution has its defined role of service to the integrated well-being. One is intrinsically oriented toward fulfilling one's own personal contribution to the whole by one's rational nature, talents, social position and vocation. Happiness lies in harmony with one's human nature, social position and in harmony with the whole ensemble of society and creation. The best definition of communication in this organic, harmonic conception of reality is *wisdom*, the ordering of all things toward their ultimate goal. The church and theologians were the depositories of wisdom. Any view contrary to the established wisdom was treated as nonsense.

For people in this era the organic, corporatist conceptions of communication seemed quite convincing. During the Middle Ages it was taken for granted that craft guilds and the market towns controlled sellers and craftsmen tightly (Preston, 1975: 35). The aim was to serve the good of the community. In the period of the Tudor kings of Britain, the view that printing should be licensed was seen as a means of protecting the people. The printers were pleased that their business was guaranteed and that good standards were upheld.

4.2 *The Libertarian Tradition*

In the late Middle Ages of Europe, with the growth of an increasingly complex multiplication of social roles — commerce, industry, science and government — the simple corporatist view of society ceased to offer a good moral foundation for public communication. The monarchies held on to the idea of a tightly controlled society as the best path to the modern nation, while the new commercial classes felt free enterprise offered the most efficient model of national growth. For the new entrepreneurial classes the view that truth could be summed up in the perennial philosophy, in the church or in the symbols of the ceremonial monarchy were viewed as simply an ideology to protect entrenched power and privileges. The abuses and hypocrisy in these traditional institutions were only too apparent. This led to a new norm of truth: the integrity of individual conscience. Development of society is achieved by allowing free individual initiative and free circulation of ideas.

Libertarians like to trace their intellectual tradition back to the *Areopagitica* of Puritan dissenter, John Milton, a booklet attacking prior censorship and licensed printing. Milton argued that if the merits of any proposal are allowed to be debated freely, even if there are erroneous ideas, at least a pragmatic truth will triumph through what would today be called the self-righting principle of the marketplace of ideas.

Eventually, the libertarian tradition worked out a formula which protected the moral claims of all major actors in the sphere of public communication. All printers were allowed to seek profits and express ideas freely. All philosophies, religions and personal views were free to express themselves as they wished. The new democratic political movements had the freedom to propagate their ideas. Intellectual life, literacy and education were stimulated. The freedom to criticize led to better government and better services in general. Even constitutional monarchies eventually found the means in the free press to build a new myth of the royal families.

4.3 *The Social Responsibility Tradition*

In the nineteenth century the socio-political-cultural conditions of the libertarian formula changed. The industrial revolution created the conditions which brought together masses of immigrants from the rural villages into the great cities. The new liberal democracies gradually gave the vote to all people living within national boundaries. The press evolved from many small voices of political opinions into the mass daily newspaper of millions of copies. For the ordinary citizen, the mass newspaper was the only way to be informed about public decisions, yet, in the view of many, the new sensationalist popular journalism was totally irresponsible. The proprietors now hired 'reporters' to gather news, often semi-literate people themselves. The public began to call for government regulation of such an important institution for democracy as the press.

In the context of mass society, pluralism, anonymity and upward social mobility of the popular classes, the liberal ideal of enlightened self-interest rapidly degenerated into rampant charlatanism and opportunism. No one could trust medical doctors, medicines, manufactured foods, bankers, lawyers — or newspapers — any longer. The heart of the drive to rebuild social bonds of trust in a mass society where few people knew each other very profoundly was to develop in the service trades an internal sense of moral mandate modelled after the classical professions of medicine, law and the clergy. People working in the media joined this movement to form professional associations with the adoption of codes of ethics, requirement of a university degree, and the development of communication as a university-based science. The media professions developed an ethos of objectivity, accuracy, fairness to sources and freedom of any collusion with government or other powerful institutions (Marzolf, 1991).

With the introduction of broadcasting, the media began to accept a certain measure of government regulation in the public interest and the competition of public service broadcasting directed by government or para-governmental agencies.

By mid-twentieth century the 'social responsibility' formula had negotiated a new respect for the moral claims of major actors. Media proprietors admitted that freedom of the press had become an ideology to defend itself from public regulation and adopted a new policy of public service. Media workers, formed into professions, gained a new prestige. With its public service ideals, the press could present itself as the central institution defending democracy. In times of national crisis the public gained confidence in the media as social critics and as accurate objective reporters of events such as wars and catastrophes.

5. How normative paradigms provide
a moral foundation for media activities

A normative theory or paradigm fulfills multiple functions which resolve the dissatisfaction and moral conflict which exist at any one moment.

1. Relates pragmatic activities to an overarching moral purpose so that pragmatic activities are transformed into moral activities. Media activities are now given a basis of moral obligation.

2. Provides a formula of moral purpose which shows how a given media activity can respond to the moral claims of all major actors and at the same time satisfy and enhance both the pragmatic and moral claims of the party in question. The formula thus harmonizes conflicting moral claims.

3. Attacks former abuses of the media as something not really inherent in media activity but as an aberrant ideology that can be discarded and purified.

4. Transforms media use into a form of public philosophy with transcendent values. Using media is now a moral, quasi-religious activity.

5. Provides a basis for codes of ethics that have a moral meaning, not just a positivistic convenience meaning. All of the major values associated with good media — freedom, objectivity, diversity, and contributing to social solidarity — are infused with a moral sense.

6. Provides criteria for quickly identifying abuses of norms and helps to establish consensus in the proffession on how to avoid these abuses.

7. Provides sets of ideals for the individual media worker and a basis for the socialization of media personnel into these values.

8. Provides guidelines for media policy and media legislation. The work of the politician is transformed into a service to society, not just gaining favors for one's own party and constituency.

Each aspect of the function of these normative paradigms can be illustrated in each case by the example of the 'social responsibility-public service' paradigm which is sufficiently a matter of history to confirm the validity of the argument. The moral formula of social responsibility theory is that the media are the foundations of modern liberal democracy and the foundation for the rights of the citizen by providing information and other services.

Through this formula the media pragmatically increase usage because one cannot be a good citizen without using media. As contexts for advertising the media pass their prestige to the advertiser.

Just as the classical professions gained their prestige by proclaiming that their scientific expertise was now dedicated to the good of society and the good of their clients, the formula which links media to democracy, the economic progress of the nation and the dignity of the individual, now differentiates all of the major media roles — journalists, editors, proprietors, photographers, correspondents, film directors and gives them a quasi-sacred meaning as a 'artistic creator'. These roles are no longer simply part of an economic enterprise, like factory workers, but each responds to her or his independent artistic genius to create the sacred community of the nation.

This enhances the moral significance of media work so that, ideally, all are satisfied. Newspaper proprietors and editors must now respect the independence of reporters as professionals, just as all medical doctors must respect other medical doctors.

The normative paradigm transforms the entertaining use of media into a sacred duty as a citizen. Being vigilant that all of the values of democracy are found in this newspaper and becoming a 'critical' user of media is now part of one's sacred duty.

The moral claims of the politician are now satisfied because the politician now becomes the formulator of policy and legislation to insure that the media do serve democracy. The moral claims of the media scholar are satisfied because there is now moral purpose in evaluating media's role toward democracy.

6. Normative Theories and Public Cultural Truth

One of the essential concerns of public communication is the truthfulness of what is presented in the public sphere. If the statements of individual actors are not true, then the final outcome of public debate may be fundamentally vitiated. The debating community loses contact with the reality in which it lives. The problem lies in determining what is truth in public communication.

One set of criteria argues that objectivity, accuracy and fairness to sources is the basis of truth. Is this enough? As we have noted above, what news says may be perfectly accurate and fair, but may not be reflecting the real issues of the society at all.

A more adequate norm for truthfulness of the media is what may be referred to as 'public cultural truth'. The criterion of truthfulness is not just correspondence to reality in an epistemological sense, but justice, that is, respect for the sense of human dignity and the dignity of all other forms of existence. Public communication is debate about the best decisions of the community, and the best decisions are those based on justice and compassion. The movements to question the truthfulness of a statement arise out of the sense of alienation, the sense that one's existence is in some way denied and destroyed. Thus, the public cultural truth is the systematic representation of the 'problems', the proposed lack of justice, that the members of the society must be collectively aware of and must resolve if that society is to exist as a unity. Since the definition of what is a 'problem' depends on the particular cultural movements and cultural values in play at a given moment, the public cultural truth is a continually shifting construction of meaning.

One of the crucial tasks of the search for a more normative paradigm is to continually redirect the media toward an assessment of its capacity to question the current construction of the public cultural truth in terms of justice and human dignity. There is an constant tendency for public communication to be absorbed into its pragmatic, self-serving activities and to forget its moral purpose. The media are then held hostage by an ideology and are no longer capable of being truthful. It is at this time that new socio-political movements begin to carve out a new space for alternative communication which has a new foundation of moral value. A new paradigm of normative theory then comes into existence and provides new dimensions of normative theory.

For many media scholars the movement toward a communitarian foundation of public communication represents this kind of search for a more adequate normative paradigm (Christians, Ferré and Fackler, 1993). A very specific aspect of a move away from the libertarian paradigm toward a communitarian paradigm is the public journalism movement.

7. The current search for a more adequate normative paradigm
   of public cultural truth: The public journalism movement

There are many evidences of a move toward a communitarian normative paradigm: the worldwide movement of community and public access media; the use of more participatory approaches to communication at all levels, from group communication to national communication; the application of new research paradigms focusing on audience construction of meaning. The public journalism movement, however, is closer to the center of the media industry (Lambeth, 1998).

The falling circulation of newspapers and falling use of other media, especially news media and notably among younger people, has been a widespread concern among more reflective leaders in the culture industry. One ploy is to lower the analytic level of newspapers to 'newsbytes' or forms of superficial sensationalism. The declining use of news media is paralleled by falling participation in the political and cultural affairs of communities.

Newspaper editors themselves have been quite aware that, because of financial constraints, they have relied more on prefabricated news from politicians, public relation offices and news agencies. Often these agencies have their own self-serving interests in making up issues that distract the public from more serious issues. This has meant less responsiveness to the real issues that the public are concerned about. In part this is due to the fact that the media industry has become a kind of professional 'priesthood', dialoguing among themselves, but cut off from the people. Journalists see themselves as constructing the news agenda and the news narratives in terms of their own interests, not in terms of the interests of the public. Truth has been defined in terms of photographic objectivity and accuracy, but there is often no connection between bits of information. The public do not feel involved and feel that it is useless to be more informed because they can do nothing about the events.

A major practice of public journalism is to make a conscious effort to find out what are the cultural, political and economic issues of the public and to follow the development of debates about these issues in a 'connected' way. In some cases, newspapers have carried out surveys of how the public sees issues or the newspapers have linked with civic leaders to hold a series of public meetings in the communities. These issues are then put before political candidates or other public officials to force them to respond to this.

Another practice is to consciously abandon the 'horse race' reporting of election campaigns — that is to simply recount who is ahead at a given time — and to focus on the issues of the candidates. The media try to avoid collaborating with the pseudo events of political candidates, which are often manipulative of both the media and the public.

Still another practice is to reorganize newsrooms so that departments are not just following routine beats collecting public relation handouts with little intercommunication between departments. Rather all the departments follow together a series of issues in a way that enables each department — economic affairs, political affairs, religious affairs, etc. — to present a different specialized in-depth aspect of the same issue.

The most controversial practice is to select news not in terms of the size of the event from the official perspective, but the size of the event in terms of justice and compassion of the people. Thus, the criterion for news selection is not simply the number of people who have died in a public tragedy, but the size of the neglect by public officials or the size of the injustice being perpetrated against the people.

Conclusions

The present chapter has attempted to sketch out a 'theory' of communication ethics. The very prolific outpouring of texts on communication ethics and the history of ethics over the last fifteen years have provided a rich source of materials for building such a theory. Typically, our texts present an outline of the moral duties of journalists or other media professionals. But where do such deontological lists come from and what is the criterion for including one list of duties rather than another. What is the relation of codes of ethics to the broader normative issues such as media policy, normative theory, and moral theory. The present chapter attempts to provide a kind of theoretical map to guide us toward the deeper foundational questions of communication ethics.

This theoretical effort took as its point of departure some of the major current issues of media ethics that some consider evidence of a major crisis. The conclusions are that a crisis consists of the following:
— The lack of respect for the moral claims of major actors and the lack of dialogue among major actors for achieving moral consensus;
— The lack of a widely accepted normative theory that will provide a formula for consensus;
— The lack of criteria of an adequate normative theory, namely, the move toward public cultural truth;
— The lack of clear criteria of public cultural truth in terms of justice and human dignity
We hope that the map provides a vision of a way forward to create dialogue among major actors in the public sphere and a more satisfying formula of normative theory for moral consensus. For many, communitarian normative theory of public communication is the way forward. Only greater dialogue among the major actors will prove that to be true.

References

ANG, Ien (1991), *Desperately Seeking the Audience*. London, Routledge.
BOEYINK, Burton J. (1994), 'How Effective Are Codes of Ethics? A look at Three Newsrooms' in *Journalism Quarterly*, 71(1994)4, pp. 893-904.
CHRISTIANS, Clifford, John FERRÉ, Mark FACKLER (1993), *Good News: Social Ethics & the Press*. New York, Oxford University Press.
CHRISTIANS, Clifford (1997), 'The Ethics of Being in a Communications Context' in, Clifford CHRISTIANS, Michael TRABER (eds.), *Communication Ethics and Universal Values*. London, Sage Publications.

Fox, Elizabeth (1988), 'Media Policies in Latin America: An Overview' in Elizabeth Fox (ed.) *Media and Politics in Latin America: The Struggle for Democracy*. London: Sage Publications, pp 6-35.

Franklin, Bob, Rod Pilling, 'Taming the Tabloids: Market, Moguls and Media Regulation' in Matthew Kieran (ed.) *Media Ethics*. London, Routledge, pp 111-122.

Grossberg, Lawrence, Ellen Wartella, D. Charles Whitney (1998), *Media Making: Mass Media in a Popular Culture*. London, Sage Publications.

Habermas, Jürgen (1991), *Moral Consciousness and Communicative Action*. Translated by Christian Lenhardt, Shierry Weber Nicholsen. Cambridge (MA), The MIT Press.

Head, Sidney, Christopher Sterling (1989), *Broadcasting in America*. 6th Edition. Dallas, Houghton-Mifflin.

Horwitz, Robert Britt (1989), *The Irony of Regulatory Reform: The Deregulation of American Telecommunication*. New York, Oxford University Press.

Kohlberg, Lawrence (1980), 'Stages of Moral Development as a Basis of Moral Education' in Brenda Munsey, (ed.) *Moral Development, Moral Education and Kohlberg*, Birmingham (Al), Religious Education Press, pp. 15-100.

Lambeth, Edmund (1998), 'Public Journalism as a Democratic Practice' in Edmund L. Lambeth, Philip Meyer, Esther Thorson (eds.) *Assessing Public Journalism*. Columbia, University of Missouri Press, pp 15-35.

Martín-Barbero, J. (1993), *Communication, Culture and Hegemony*. London, Sage Publications.

Marzolf, Marion T. (1991), *Civilizing Voices: American Press Criticism 1880-1950*. New York, Longman.

McQuail, Denis (1987), *Mass Communication Theory: An Introduction*. London, Sage Publications.

McQuail, Denis (1992), *Media Performance*. London, Sage Publications.

Merritt, Davis (1995), *Public Journalism and Public Life: Why telling the News is Not Enough*. Hillsdale (NJ), Lawrence Erlbaum Associates, Publishers.

Nerone, John C (ed.) (1995), *Last Rights: Revisiting Four Theories of the Press*. Urbana, University of Illinois Press.

Pasquali, Antonio (1997), 'The Moral Dimension of Communicating', 24-45, in Clifford Christians, Michael Traber, (eds.), *Communication Ethics and Universal Values*. London, Sage Publications.

Paulu, Burton (1981), *Television and Radio in the United Kingdom*. London, Macmillan Press.

Poulakas, John (1995), *Sophistical Rhetoric in Classical Greece*. Columbia, University of South Carolina Press.

PRESTON, I.L. (1975), *The Great American Blow-Up: Puffery in Advertising and Selling*. Madison, The University of Wisconsin Press.

SIEBERT, Frederick Seaton (1965), *Freedom of the Press in England, 1476-1776*. Urbana, University of Illinois Press.

SIEBERT, Frederick Seaton, T. PETERSON, W. SCHRAMM (1956), *Four Theories of the Press*. Urbana, University of Illinois Press.

WEAVER, David H., G. Cleveland WILHOIT (1986), *The American Journalist: A Portrait of US News People and Their Work*. Bloomington, Indiana University Press.

WHITE, Robert A. (1989), 'Social and Political Factors in the Development of Communication Ethics' in Thomas COOPER, Clifford CHRISTIANS, Frances FORDE PLUDE and Robert A. WHITE (eds.), *Communication Ethics and Global Change*. New York, Longman, pp. 40-66.

THE STRUCTURAL CONTEXT OF MEDIA ETHICS

How Media Are Regulated in Democratic Society

Kaarle Nordenstreng

Media ethics — seen from different angles and at different levels as articulated in the other chapters of this textbook (especially Robert White above) — depends on and grows out of a certain media system and its relation to the rest of society. By media system we refer to the political, economic and legal structures which constitute what are typically called 'media institutions', namely the concrete units of production and distribution (newspapers, radio and television stations, etc.), which make available all the message flow and content, which for its part is (or is not) received or consumed by the audience. The media systems and structures in this sense do not deal with the substance of ethics at all; instead, our attention is drawn to the socio-economic-political preconditions, which determine (more or less directly) the media output and its reception among the public. Accordingly, we have the 'hard' media structure, on the one hand, and the 'soft' media culture, on the other.

The media structures and systems can be classified and analyzed in a number of ways, including a historical evolution of normative paradigms, as shown in Robert White's chapter. The focus of the present chapter is on the 'regulatory' aspect of media systems, leading to two basic questions: *What is the place and role of the media in society under democratic conditions?* and *What are the overall mechanisms by which the media institutions are linked to the rest of society?*

These media-society links operate basically in two directions: (1) the media are *contracted by* society to carry out certain tasks, and (2) the media are *accountable to* society for their performance. The term 'media regulation' refers strictly speaking to the latter accountability relationship and the laws by which it is handled, but the term is often used in a broader sense to cover also the political, economic and even philosophical elements of the media-society relationship. This chapter takes a broad approach by addressing the above two questions, each as a separate passage. In addition, a third passage at the end focuses on a particular form of self-regulation: the media councils.

Media and Society[1]

A basic approach to the topic is to place the media in relation to power holders on the one hand and to the citizenry on the other hand. This is done below by means of two figures.

Figure 1.

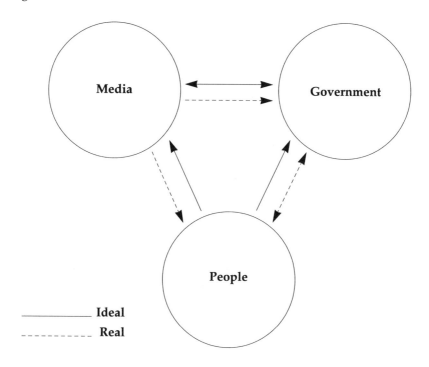

[1] This passage is based on the concluding chapter in *Sananvapaus* ('Freedom of Speech', in Finnish), a collection of articles relating to my project for the Academy of Finland and published in 1996 (Helsinki: WSOY). An English version was published in *Nordicom Review*: Nordenstreng, 1997.

Figure 1 presents the media in a classic representative democracy.[2] The media are positioned in relation to the public (People) and to political power (Government). In the theory of democracy — in an ideal world — the media provide the people with a channel for both the dissemination of information and for discussion. In a way the media serve the people in the same way as an elected government, which, in theory at least, acts to take care of the affairs of the country in the best interests of the people. Thus the essential relation of influence is from the people to the media and from the people to the government, as prescribed by the doctrine of the sovereignty of the people. According to the same theory of democracy the ideal relationship of influence between the government and the media works in two directions: on the one side the government elected by the people has the mandate (under the Constitution) to be responsible among other things for the overall activity of the mass media, while on the other side the media are mandated to control the government on behalf of the people by exposing politics to constant surveillance (like a watchdog) and by putting across to the government the thoughts and sentiments of the people.

This setup represents the theory of democracy, with ideal relationships between media, government and people.[3] Parallel to it there are other relationships of the actual situation in a modern representative democracy. These real relationships elevate the media into a key position: their main line of influence goes towards both the people and the government. Meanwhile, the relationship of real influence between the people and the government is more or less two-way. It is true that the media derive content to a great extent from the people and the government, but in shaping that content and setting the agenda for political debate the media wield considerable power. The ideal and real relationships of influence are thus virtually opposites, when in point of fact the people have become the *target* of influence where according to the theory they should have been the *source* of influence.

Admittedly the figure generalizes and simplifies the situation, ignoring for example the complex nature of the media, including the alternative press. Nevertheless the message of the figure cannot be

[2] Taken from my article, which examines the paradoxical nature of the journalist's profession: Nordenstreng, 1995a: 119.

[3] On theory of democracy in general see e.g. Held, 1996. On the relation between the media and democracy see Keane, 1991; Nordenstreng, 2000a.

denied. Democracy does not function as it ought to according to the theory, and the media and its practitioners are at the heart of the problem of democracy. In order to improve the situation — to achieve democratization — the media must come closer to the people and the actual relationship of influence between these two must work in two directions.

Figure 2

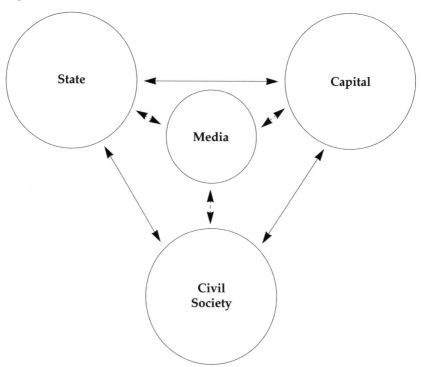

Figure 2 has been taken from Johan Galtung, in whose three-sided model the pillars of society are the State, Capital (market forces), and Civil Society.[4] In this setup the media are not found at the apex of the triangle but rather float somewhere between the pillars. In the history of many countries the media have found their place first close to the state, then drifting towards civil society, and more recently more and more towards the markets.

[4] Galtung presented his model as a paper read at the MacBride Round Table in Honolulu, January, 1994, and later at a postgraduate seminar at the University of Tampere in June 1994. The paper is published in Vincent *et al.*, 1999.

Galtung does not predict that market forces will completely absorb globalizing society; he also sees a burgeoning strength in the civil society with its new movements. Thus the media take a challenging place in a field of conflicts. The media are a vital channel not only for Civil Society in relation to the State and the Capital, but also in communication between the State and Capital in order to ensure a common public sphere and dialogue in society. If the media succeed in attaining a strong and independent position in this triangle, they could, according to Galtung, assume the status of a fourth pillar in the power structure of society.

It is typical to exaggerate the power of the media to exert influence by ignoring the fact that communication is not generally an independent power, but rather a continuation of more fundamental social forces.[5] However, there have been in recent years — in conditions of the so-called information society — good reasons to speak of the 'mediatization' of social relations and of the significant power position of the media in society. The media have become kingmakers in the field of politics at the same time as the party institution has lost ground. In the old days newspapers were typically an extension of politics, and newspapermen (indeed mostly men!) were politicians. Today politics and the media have split up into two institutions, and the media frequently appear to be the stronger.

Traditionally the influence of the media has been emphasized by talk of the 'fourth estate' or 'fourth branch of government' alongside the legislative (Parliament), executive and judiciary branches. This view has gained new impetus from the perspective of the 'media society'. For example, the Finnish discussion among constitutional lawyers has generated a proposal that the classic doctrine of the three branches is no longer valid and should be complemented by such contemporary branches as trade unions, market forces — and mass media.

The basic setup, however, is clear and the core question remains, what is the relation of the *media power* to the *people's power*. Going from the basis for freedom of speech the task of the media and of journalism in particular is to serve the people and not those who wield power, be that power political or economic. Thus in Galtung's figure the media should take up a position closer to civil society. It is not healthy for the cause of democracy that the media should

---

[5] For a discussion of the question of media power, see Nordenstreng, 2000b.

move from the political camp to the economic camp and remain the tool of the elite of society while the people continue on their own path as consumers and spectators.

From this position in the United States a start has been made to seek for new forms of journalism, not only through investigative reporting, but also *civic journalism* or *public journalism* seeking out the grassroots.[6] The premiss here is that the people are not only lacking information but also democracy, and that journalism should pose the questions in the manner of the man or woman in the street, not as the political and economic elite would do it. The fault thus lies not with people but with elitist information alien to everyday life. This populist trend has achieved the support of some publishers, who are concerned about the decrease in the amount of papers read, especially among the young.

Civic journalism seeks to support local democracy not so much by inundating citizens with information filtered by the elite but by bringing citizens to discuss and act on issues which concern them. In such a case the media and the journalists are transformed from apparently objective reporters to moderators supporting citizen participation. The objective is to activate citizens who have become cynical and to revive the community adrift from its ties — to return from individualism to communitarianism (Christians *et al.*, 1993).

It is, however, doubtful to what extent journalism and the media can be of assistance in the structural repair of the foundations of society. Projects of a popular journalistic nature more likely reflect the rhetoric of the civil society than reality, and this particularly in the United States. One may furthermore ask whether or not the national and supranational media scene is with 'deregulation' becoming more anti or pro freedom of speech. On the other hand the encounter of the global and the local opens up a new positive perspective — *glocal* — for both the civil society and the media (Tehranian, 1999).

My thesis is that behind all those contradictory developments, the long-term thinking about the media, or media paradigm, is changing, and despite the well-known trends towards concentration, tabloidization, etc., the change is for the better, for more democratic

---

[6] For more on 'public journalism' or 'civic journalism' as presented by those who developed the concept, see Merritt 1995 and Rosen 1994. A contemporary collection of assessments is offered in Glasser 1999. A brief review is presented in White's chapter above.

and ethical direction. In the ideal world of normative media theories, if not in the real world of media practices, the image of self-sufficient media and a public passively receiving information is being replaced by a new image of media working as extensions of democracy and serving its citizens. Accordingly, the citizen is on the way from the sidelines into the arena.

I have examined elsewhere (Nordenstreng, 1997) the concept of freedom of speech in the light of long-term trends of media ideologies in Western Europe, particularly Finland, and that study suggested indeed a *paradigm shift* with five aspects:

1. The dominant frame of reference in freedom of speech is no longer the question of *censorship* — the advance surveillance of heroic media by a villainous state — but of human rights. Each individual has an inalienable right to information and its dissemination, and also to an opinion and its expression, namely the *right to communicate*.

2. The masters of freedom of speech are not the mass media and the journalists, i.e. *media* — an avant garde party fighting valiantly for their freedom — but the *citizens* for whom freedom of speech ensures both democracy and quality of life.

3. Because it is the media that organize the use of citizens' freedom of speech, it is they who are *responsible* to the citizens for their performance, both individually and collectively. In order that this relation of responsibility be fulfilled there must be both general social norms and particular *self-regulation* by the media.

4. Democracy requires both *openness* in the wielding of power and citizens' effective *participation* in the social debate and in decision-making which concerns them. Freedom of speech serves these ends by maintaining *pluralism* in communication in relation to the views and interest groups in society.

5. Freedom of speech in a democracy requires a *public arena* at local, regional and national as well as international (EU) level. This state of affairs is not guaranteed merely by a judicial system which ensures freedom of discussion among the citizenry; there must also be *material facilities* for the realization of public information and debate.

In brief, the suggested new thinking emphasizes on the one hand the *right of citizens to communicate* (points 1 and 2), and on the other *pluralism in public affairs* (points 4 and 5) as well as the *responsibility of the media* which serves these ends (point 3).

There is no doubt about this kind of a paradigm shift among a good number of media scholars and activists of various media reform movements such as the MacBride Round Table (Vincent *et al.*, 1999), the Cultural Environment Movement *CEM* (Duncan, 1999), or the Peoples' Communication Charter *PCC* (Hamelink, 1994). Symptomatic of the same paradigmatic development is a *media ethics boom* as documented by a phenomenal growth of literature on this topic (Christians, 1995). Nevertheless, it remains a question, how widely held — or how marginal — this paradigm shift is in the real media world today. At least in the USA the situation is well characterized by a recent book title 'Rich Media, Poor Democracy' (McChesney, 1999), suggesting a gloomy picture of the role of media in society. But even that book is inspired by a wish for reform, with a set of recommendations about how to turn the media system more democratic and how to improve its ethical performance. Thus there remains a margin of hope.

Media Regulation

After reflections around media and democracy we shall now focus on the mechanisms of media responsibility and accountability (the third aspect of the above list of paradigm shift). A good frame of reference is provided by Denis McQuail (1997: 518).

Figure 3

FREE MEDIA
have
RESPONSIBILITIES
in form of
OBLIGATIONS
which are either:
ASSIGNED CONTRACTED SELF-IMPOSED or DENIED
for which they are held
ACCOUNTABLE
(legally, socially or morally)
either in the sense of:
LIABILITY   or   ANSWERABILITY
for harm caused   for quality of performance

Accordingly, even the freest media have responsibilities and they are accountable either in the sense of liability or answerability. While McQuail discusses in detail the lines of accountability, Christians *et al.* (1998) ask what are the parties to which media professionals are responsible and accountable: To whom is moral duty owed? They single out five parties: (1) Duty to ourselves; (2) Duty to clients/subscribers/supporters; (3) Duty to our organization or firm; (4) Duty to professional colleagues; (5) Duty to society.

In the European tradition, the mass media are part and parcel of the legacy of Enlightenment and human rights, whereby they should be free — free from coercion by the power holders and free for the pursuit of truth and exercise of creativity. However, no social institution can be absolutely free, and even the freest media are always tied to some social forces, serving some political objectives — often indirectly and even unintentionally, but still sociologically speaking far from absolutely free. The question, then, is not whether media are free or controlled, but what are the mechanisms of social 'control' and accountability.

Three main mechanisms of media control can be distinguished (Bertrand, 1998): (1) *Law* promulgated by the Parliament and other state bodies and executed by the courts; (2) *Market* based on private property, commercial advertising, etc.; (3) *Media* themselves through various means of maintaining 'ethics'.

These are not mutually exclusive categories, and in most countries today (all countries in Europe) they coexist. Thus the last-mentioned category of self-regulation is always accompanied by some degree of legal regulation — not to censor but to guarantee that minimum standards of democratic order and human rights are respected (Hamelink, 1999). On the other hand, heavy-handed legislation and effective self-regulation are typically seen as alternatives, and there is a clear trend today to favour unafficial self-regulation over official legislation. Similarly, at the time of media concentration and tabloidization, it is natural to favour self-regulation over commercial markets.

Accordingly, while self-regulation is always accompanied by legal and market regulation, we should take it as a most valuable form of regulating the media in society. It is one aspect of a mega-trend in contemporary Western thinking, whereby established political institutions, including nation states, lose their importance — at least in terms of their intellectual potential — and are gradually replaced by more flexible structures, grassroots approaches, networking, etc. Part and parcel of this trend is a new emphasis on (ordinary) people as the main subject in communication — as consumers, citizens and 'owners' of the right to freedom of information — instead of journalists and media proprietors.

In fact, one could add to the above list of regulatory mechanisms a fourth one: *citizens* and their civil society. Yet, in reality regulation on the part of civil society is possible only in small vehicles of communication owned by members of associations and in information networks formed by restricted interest groups. Citizens can bring influence to bear on the main media only marginally, by their own consumer behavior and by participating in the activities of pressure groups. On the other hand, we must remember that citizens constitute the electorate which ultimately determines, in theory at least, what Parliament and the government — the whole state apparatus — is doing with the media.

The idea that the media are responsible for the general public made up of citizens is widely accepted, not least among journalists.[7] Journalists see themselves as using freedom of speech as the representatives of the citizens, and the professional ideal of the journalist typically embodies the roles of both a watchdog and an educator. On the other hand journalists, not to mention media owners, are anxious to remain independent, at least regarding the state, and therefore they are reluctant to accept laws to concretize the abstract responsibility. Accordingly, while media professionals speak warmly about responsibility, they remain lukewarm about accountability.

Upon closer examination the media present a constitutional dilemma. On the one hand we have freedom of speech and a ban on advance censorship written into the Constitution (the US First Amendment and corresponding provisions in many countries including Finland). On the other hand the media, like any institution in society, including free enterprise, are to a certain extent accountable to a democratic society. The responsibility of communication

---

[7] Laitila (1995) shows that the European codes of journalistic ethics clearly attach more importance to responsibility to the public and to sources than to responsibility which journalists give the state, the employer and their own profession. Heinonen (1998) documents how positively Finnish journalists approach the issue of social responsibility, particularly through the code of ethics and the media council. Weaver (1998) shows that the same overall attitude has practically a universal appeal.

has been specified in international agreements on human rights which both guarantee freedom of opinion and expression and set limitations on the dissemination of racist and warmongering propaganda, for example. In general, human rights instruments set clear boundary conditions for the media, just as there are boundary conditions on other aspects of life. It is thus impossible for the media to use freedom of speech to justify their setting themselves above social norms and institutions. They have, on the contrary, a special responsibility, for in a democratic society both constitutional protection for freedom of speech and human rights agreements place the media in the position of a tool in the service of citizens.

As noted above, self-regulation of the media is a widely accepted mechanism of regulating the responsibility of the media in relation to the citizens. In practice this boils down to professional *codes of ethics* and independent *media councils*. A newcomer to the modes of self-regulation is *media criticism* — a scientifically and professionally based analysis which facilitates the debate between media producers and consumers and the influence-hungry political and economic interest groups on various aspects of media coverage (Nordenstreng, 1999a).

Self-regulation, however, is quite a weak form of regulation compared to official laws and perpetual market forces. Moreover, self-regulation tends to remain cosmetic window-dressing of the media industry and its professionals — a repertoire of good intentions with little or no impact on practical media operation and performance. Even if media people were honest and not just tactical in their willingness to be accountable to the public, their professional values and work practices, supported by a culture of autonomy, easily leads to 'fortress journalism' where professionalism rather inhibits than promotes the fulfilling of the citizens' communication needs (Nordenstreng, 1995a; 1998). It thus becomes necessary both to intensify the effects of self-regulation on professional practice and to monitor critically the state of self-regulation.

For self-regulation this means that the main function shifts from protecting media professionals to protecting ordinary citizens. This does not suggest to dilute the idea of media self-regulation. On the contrary, taking a little distance from the media themselves and taking the role of the audience and citizen more seriously brings self-regulation closer to what it is supposed to be in the theories of democracy.

Actually self-regulation can and should be justified not just on the basis of defensive strategies on the part of the media but first and foremost seen through the public interest — ultimately as an innovative approach to democracy. I have suggested elsewhere (Nordenstreng, 1999a) the rationale as a four-step logical progression:

1. Media are influential (operating and perceived as a powerful socio-political institution)

2. Media are free (autonomy guaranteed by national and international law)

3. Media are accountable (responsibility determined by social relations and legal provisions)

4. Media accountability is best achieved by proactive self-regulation.

This logic was articulated with a view to new forms of self-regulation: media criticism based on systematic monitoring of media performance. But it fits equally well with the old ways of media self-regulation: councils and codes. Given the ever more vital role played by the media — including the so-called new media — in the emerging information society, it is a great challenge for both media professionals, media academics as well as media politicians to promote self-regulation.

Self-regulation is the most obvious answer to the question, how to ensure the freedom and responsibility of the mass media in society. Claude-Jean Bertrand (1998) refers to it as *media accountability systems MAS* and lists over thirty different ways to uphold the quality and responsibility of the free media. These include media criticism and monitoring, public access to the media and even training — the education of both professionals and consumers. However, the most important and internationally recognised mechanisms of self-regulation are independent media councils and professional codes of ethics.

The codes of ethics are covered in a separate chapter by Huub Evers below. Here we shall continue with a factual review of media councils in Europe.

Media Councils[8]

Table 1 lists the European countries where media self-regulation operates through councils and codes. The table shows graphically

---

[8] This passage is based on Nordenstreng, 1999b, which for its part reports data from Nordenstreng, 1995b (by Laitila and Sonninen).

Table 1. European countries which have a press council and/or a professional code of ethics (Sources: Nordenstreng, 1995b; www.uta.fi/ethicnet; www.u-paris-2.fr/ifp_Deontologie/ethic)

Country	Council	Code
Armenia	-	+
Austria	+	+
Belarus	-	+
Belgium	+	+
Bulgaria	-	+
Croatia	-	+
Czech Republic	-	+
Cyprus	+	+
Denmark	+	+
Estonia	+	+
Finland	+	+
France	-	+
Germany	+	+
Greece	*	+
Hungary	-	+
Iceland	+	+
Italy	(+)	+
Latvia	-	+
Lithuania	+	+
Luxembourg	(+)	+
Malta	(+)	+
Netherlands	+	+
Norway	+	+
Poland	(+)	+
Portugal	*	+
Romania	(+)	+
Russia	(+)	+
Serbia	-	+
Slovakia	-	+
Slovenia	(+)	+
Spain	+	+
Sweden	+	+
Switzerland	+	+
Turkey	+	+
United Kingdom	+	+

that codes are more widespread than councils. Every one of the 35 countries listed has a document of principles and practices typically called 'code of ethics', adopted by an independent media organization (UK has two codes). Meanwhile, less than 25 countries have a body to function as a court of honour mostly called 'press council'. Considering the nature of these means of self-regulation this is understandable: a code is relatively easy to adopt by a single professional association, whereas a council requires agreement between several parties (journalists and publishers often in conflict with each other) and an institutional commitment far beyond a single resolution. Some of the councils are no longer or not yet operational, or their status as an independent body is under dispute, which is marked by brackets in Table 1 (altogether 7 cases). In addition, the councils which are instruments of governmental regulation rather than professional self-regulation are marked by asterisk in Table 1 (2 cases).

For a council to be an agency of self-regulation, it must be independent of the political and judicial system. Thus an official body incorporated in the state apparatus does not qualify as a self-regulatory media council. Yet there are two countries, Denmark and Lithuania, where a media council has been established by laws passed by Parliament, and thus formally speaking it has an official character, but in reality it operates like any independent self-regulatory body. Most broadcasting councils are official state bodies in this respect, and therefore they are omitted here, although such radio and/or television councils may in some cases have quite a professional and pluralist orientation. Since the media councils are first and foremost established for and by the print media — although most of them today also cover the electronic media — they are usually called 'press councils'.

Table 2 shows how the first press councils emerged in the beginning of the century, at around the same time as did the first ethical codes of journalists. The real boom of the councils started, however, only after the Second World War and peaked in the 1960s, when several already existing councils also began to be remodeled or revised. The most important example for the later councils was the now defunct British 'General Council of the Press', founded in 1953. For instance the German *Presserat* is a copy of the former British body. Even if it served as a model for other councils especially in Europe, the British Press Council was not the first of its kind. The Scandinavian journalists were years ahead of their British colleagues, the Swedish Court of Honor being founded as early as in 1916, the Finnish and the Norwegian bodies in the late 1920s.

Table 2. Founding and revision of the councils

Decade	Original	Revision
1910s	Sweden 1916	
1920s	Finland 1927	
	Norway 1928	
1930s		
1940s	Slovenia 1944	
	Netherlands 1948	
1950s	United Kingdom 1953	
	Germany 1956	
1960s	Austria 1961	Netherlands 1960
	Denmark 1964	Austria 1963
	Iceland 1965	Finland 1968
1970s	Switzerland 1972	Norway 1972
	Portugal 1975	Switzerland 1976
1980s	Luxembourg 1980	Germany 1986
	Poland 1984	
	Belgium 1985	
	Turkey 1988	
	Malta 1989	
1990s	Cyprus 1990	Portugal 1990
	Romania 1990	United Kingdom 1991
	Estonia 1991	Denmark 1992
	Spain 1992	Slovenia 1992
	Italy 1995	Finland 1997
	Lithuania 1996	
	Russia 1998	

After the opening move by the Scandinavian journalists, the councils spread around the world. At the end of the 1970s there were around 50 media councils or similar organizations throughout the world. And as shown in Table 2, further councils were established in Europe in the 1980s and 1990s — among these the councils in Greece and Portugal sponsored by the state (the latter not recognized by the Syndicate of Journalists). The British body went through a crisis and was reborn in 1991 as the Press Complaints Commission (without participation of the National Union of Journalists). Russia is in its own class, with the 'Chamber for the Adjudication of Information Disputes' under the President of the Russian Federation established in the mid-1990s and an independent 'Grand Jury of the Media' set up by the Union of Journalists in 1998.

Although there are considerable differences between the various media councils, they also have much in common. Their main task everywhere is twofold. First, the councils protect the rights of the public (audience, sources and referents of the content) in relation to the mass media. By giving the public the opportunity to complain about bad or unethical journalism, the councils give the public at least some empathy if not a direct voice in media performance. The council investigates complaints by the public on certain cases and makes a statement that the medium in question, if found to have violated good journalistic practice (as defined in the code of ethics), is asked to publish a retraction within a given period and with due prominence.

Secondly, the councils protect the mass media themselves. Here the quarter to be protected against is mainly the state and other powers in the public as well as private sector, but also various interest groups among the general public. Thus self-regulation is also a way for the journalists and publishers to demonstrate that the media are responsible, with no further official regulation needed. Many councils, including the first in Sweden, were in fact founded under public interest pressure.

Most independent media councils have been established by journalists and/or publishers, and are typically composed of representatives of these professionals and proprietors, appointed by the respective national associations of journalists and publishers. Ethics committees of journalists' associations only may not be taken as councils proper, but nevertheless some such cases are included in this presentation (among those bracketed in Table 1). In addition, more often than not a media council also has 'lay members' — people representing the general public. The selection of these lay members remains a problem, because in this case one obviously does not want to resort to Parliament as a representative sample of the population. However, the members of the general public have proved to be an important asset to the councils, adding to their credibility.

References

BERTRAND, Claude-Jean (1998), Key-note speech. Proceedings of the Information Seminar on Self-regulation by the Media held at the Council of Europe, Strasbourg, 7-8 October 1998 (s:\mmsep\98\seminar\ documents\asem7.98), 7-12. (A French version: Les M*A*R*S: Moyens (non-governementaux) d'assurer la responsabilité sociale des medias. *MediaPouvoirs*, numero d'automne 1998.)

CHRISTIANS, Clifford (1995), 'Review Essay: Current Trends in Media Ethics' in *European Journal of Communication* 10(1995)4, pp. 545-558.

CHRISTIANS, Clifford, Mark FACKLER, Kim B. ROTZOLL, Kathy Brittain McKEE (1998), *Media Ethics: Cases and Moral Reasoning*. 5th edition. New York, Longman.

CHRISTIANS, Clifford G., John P. FERRE, P. Mark FACKLER (1993), *Good News: Social Ethics and the Press*. New York, Oxford University Press.

DUNCAN, Kate (ed.) (1999), *Liberating Alternatives: The Founding Convention of the Cultural Environment Movement*. Cresskill (NJ), Hampton Press.

GALTUNG, Johan (1999), 'State, Capital, and the Civil Society: The Problem of Communication' in VINCENT *et al.* (1999), pp. 3-21.

GLASSER, Theodore (ed.) (1999), *The Idea of Public Journalism*. New York, The Guilford Press.

HAMELINK, Cees (1994), *Trends in World Communication: On Disempowerment and Self-empowerment*. Penang, Southbound and Third World Network.

HAMELINK, Cees (1995), *The Politics of World Communication: A Human Rights Perspective*. London, Thousand Oaks — New Delhi, Sage Publications.

HAMELINK, Cees (ed.) (1999), *Preserving Media Independence: Regulatory Frameworks*. Paris, UNESCO Publishing.

HEINONEN, Ari (1998), 'The Finnish Journalist: Watchdog with a Conscience?' in WEAVER (1998), pp. 161-190.

HELD, David (1996), *Models of Democracy*. 2nd edition. Stanford (CA), Stanford University Press.

KEANE, John (1991), *The Media and Democracy*. Cambridge, Polity Press.

LAITILA, Tiina (1995), 'Codes of Ethics in Europe' in NORDENSTRENG (1995b), pp. 23-56. (Abridged version in *European Journal of Communication* 10(1995) 4, pp. 527-544.)

McCHESNEY, Robert (1999), *Rich Media, Poor Democracy*. Urbana (IL), University of Illinois Press.

McQUAIL, Denis (1997), 'Accountability of Media to Society' in *European Journal of Communication* 12(1997)4, pp. 511-529.

MERRITT, Davis (1995), *Public Journalism and Public Life*. Hilldale, Lawrence Erlbaum.

NORDENSTRENG, Kaarle (1995a), 'The Journalist: A Walking Paradox' in P. LEE (ed.), *The Democratization of Communication*. Cardiff, University of Wales Press, pp. 114-129.

NORDENSTRENG, Kaarle (1995b), *Reports on Media Ethics in Europe*. University of Tampere, Publications of the Department of Journalism and Mass Communication, Reports B 41.

NORDENSTRENG, Kaarle (1997), 'The Citizen Moves from the Audience to the Arena' in *Nordicom Review* 18(1997)2, pp. 13-20.

NORDENSTRENG, Kaarle (1998), 'Professional Ethics: Between Fortress Journalism and Cosmopolitan Democracy' in K. BRANTS, Joke HERMES, Lisbet VAN ZOONEN (eds.), *The Media in Question: Popular Cultures and Public Interests*. London, Sage, pp. 124-134.

NORDENSTRENG, Kaarle (1999a), 'Toward Global Content Analysis and Media Criticism' in Kaarle NORDENSTRENG, Michael GRIFFIN, (eds.), *International Media Monitoring*. Cresskill (NJ), Hampton Press, pp. 3-13.

NORDENSTRENG, Kaarle (1999b), 'European Landscape of Media Self-regulation' in *Freedom and Responsibility: Yearbook 1998/99*. Vienna, OSCE Representative on Freedom of the Media, pp. 169-185.

NORDENSTRENG, Kaarle (2000a), 'Media and Democracy: What Is Really required?' in Jan VAN CUILENBURG, Richard WURFF (eds.), *Media and Open Societies*. Amsterdam, Het Spinhuis.

NORDENSTRENG, Kaarle (2000b), 'Mass Communication' in Gary BROWNING, Gary, Abigail HALCLI, Frank WEBSTER (eds.), *Understanding Contemporary Society: Theories of the Present*. London, Sage, pp. 328-342.

ROSEN, Jay (1994), 'Making Things More Public: On the Political Responsibility of the Media Intellectual' in *Critical Studies in Mass Communication* 11(1994)4, pp. 362-388.

TEHRANIAN, Majid (1999), 'Where is the New World Order? At the End of History or a Clash of Civilizations?' in VINCENT *et al.* (1999), pp. 23-63.

VINCENT, Richard, Kaarle NORDENSTRENG, Michael TRABER (eds.) (1999), *Towards Equity in Global Communication: MacBride Update*. Cresskill (NJ), Hampton Press.

WEAVER, David (ed.) (1998), *The Global Journalist: News People Around the World*. Cresskill (NJ), Hampton Press.

MEDIA AND DEMOCRACY

Michele Nicoletti

1. Media and Democracy: A Constitutive Relationship

The relationship between rights, the media and democracy, which appears to be both relevant and decisive for civic life today, is indeed rather old. It concerns the nature of democracy itself and its twofold meaning.

1.1 Democracy as a Form of Government

In the strictest sense, the term 'democracy' refers to a 'form of government.' According to classical definitions from Plato to Montesquieu, 'democracy' indicates a form of government in which power is not exercised by a monarch or aristocracy, but by people who are in a position to make decisions concerning their own political community, either in a direct or indirect way through their representatives. Democracy is based on the fundamental assumption that a political community has the right to choose freely its government and its political leaders. This entails, on one hand, the recognition of the principle of *self-determination*, and on the other, the recognition of the principle of *consent*. Such a twofold recognition excludes the right 'to choose for others,' that is to say, to decide on relevant questions without consulting all members of a community and without having the consent of the majority.

According to this definition, democracy is a form of social organisation and procedural decision-making. In this context, a constitutive relationship between communication and democracy exists insofar as the large number of people involved in the decision-making process involves at least: (a) Communication 'to' subjects about issues upon which they must deliberate: setting an order of importance, information, documentation, and procedures for the discussion and the deliberation. Of course, the use of adequate media is required here. (b) Communication 'of' subjects among themselves in order to discuss the questions and come to a decision: exchange of information and opinion, argumentation and persuasion strategies, etc.

1.2 *Democracy as an Ideal, as an Ethos and as a Form of Life*

Nevertheless, democracy cannot be reduced to a mere form of social organisation. As a type of government, with its procedures of collective decision-making and selection of political leaders, democracy is not neutral and value-free, but also calls into question practical principles, rules, institutions, customs, etc. In this light, democracy is understood as a specific way of civil life that is rooted in the ethical dimension of every human being.

In this context as well, democracy has a constitutive relationship with the media. Authentic communication and adequate media are thus required: (a) To research and discuss the (epistemological, anthropological and ethical) elements of democracy; (b) As a procedure of argumentation and discussion on rules and institutions; (c) As a dimension of life containing premises that are ethically relevant, including the equality of all human beings as rational beings, who are able to dialogue and understand one another despite conflicts. Such a 'dialogical attitude,' intrinsic to democratic procedures, as Karl-Otto Apel has shown, is not only a presupposition, but is also an aim of democracy, a 'virtue' that must be practised. As Montesquieu has pointed out (1748: III, 3) 'virtue' is a constitutive element of democracy, since equality is neither naturally nor automatically accepted. On the contrary, in most cases, equality is instinctively intolerable.

2. Democracy and Public Opinion: An Ambivalent Relationship

The constitutive relationship between media and democracy is nonetheless ambivalent. This has become particularly clear today because of the nature and development of media, and because of their political and economic misuse. We cannot help but wonder whether the media are pillars of democracy or rather its gravedigger. Despite this, it would be erroneous to ascribe the ambivalence in question to the media themselves. Indeed, ambivalence is rooted in the relationship between politics and truth or, to be more precise, in the relationship between political power and the communication of truth. It is pertinent to recall Socrates' words in Plato's *Apology*:

> "For I am certain, O men of Athens, that if I had engaged in politics, I should have perished long ago, and done no good either to you or to myself. And do not be offended at my telling you the truth: For the truth is, that no man who goes to war with you or any other multitude, honestly striving against the many lawless and unrighteous deeds which are done in a state, will save his life; he who will fight for the right, if he would live even for a brief space, must have a private station and not a public one." (*Apology of Socrates*, 31d-32a.)

It is not so much that the search for truth is in collision with the political order — something that can be carried on, perhaps, in the inwardness of one's own conscience — but rather, the communication for truth. Of course, one needs to ponder whether the search of truth without its communication is possible at all. Definitely not for Plato, for whom truth is a distributive good, a good to be spread, to be handed out to others in order to be enjoyed.

This is the dynamic of the search for truth that Plato's myth of the cave illustrates. (*Republic*, VII, 514-517) The prisoner who becomes free and is able to see things for what they really are and contemplate the idea of the Good, feels compassion for his former companions that are still in the cave. He goes back and tries to communicate the truth to them, but they do not show any enthusiasm for such a revelation and actually laugh at him. Truth questions the social and political structures of power that are founded on error and false opinion. This is why the prisoner who has become free is then put to death. Here, the conflict between the communication of truth and political power is anticipated. Although it is not a necessary, inevitable conflict it remains possible. Communication of truth questions power's legitimacy by revealing the falsehood on which it is based. This potential conflict between the communication of truth and political power is a recurrent theme in Plato's thought. It is found again in the *Gorgias*, a dialogue that deals with rhetoric. Rhetoric does not look for truth, it is an adulatory practice, which seduces and dominates the interlocutor by communicating pleasant things. Philosophy, on the contrary, is the search for truth and seeks to communicate it, but in so doing, it does not convey immediate pleasure, rather it often causes suffering, yet it sets one free.

Even in the dialogue between Jesus Christ and Pilate (*Jo. 18-19*), as it has been interpreted by Hans Kelsen, as the symbol of the conflict between absolute truth and relative democracy (the democratic crowd chooses Barabbas, not Jesus, i.e., the truth), a similar conflict recurs. (Kelsen, 1948: 101ff; 1955-56). Such a conflict may not be exaggerated, but its possibility should not be removed either. It emerges not only between absolute truth and political power, but also between factual truth and political power. Factual truth shows that reality cannot be entirely manipulated, it is not entirely at man's disposal. (Arendt, 1972)

The irruption of truth into reality, the communication of truth, is the radical affirmation of man's finitude and of the relativity of human power: It is the end of man's absolute power. For this reason, the political power, which tends to preserve and extend itself, can hardly tolerate it. Truth sets one free. Not only those in power, but also those who are governed, do not want to be set free, to be liberated.

Hence, the ambivalence in the relationship between political power and the communication of truth, which itself is at the heart of the relationship between democracy and media, is radical.

The political power has its own communicative logic: It can hardly tolerate any reference to truth because such a reference questions its pretension of permanence and absoluteness. For this reason, political power attempts to pervert the original relationship between truth and words. It empties and deprives words of their meaning, it uses them as objects, purely as polemical instruments. This is why the communication of truth must begin with a criticism of words, sometimes even with silence. This is also why a political power tends to evade the universe of words, which can be criticised, and takes refuge in the universe of images. (Sartori, 1997) Goethe had captured, in one of his poems, the difference between images and words, long before the advent of television:

Dummes Zeug kann man viel reden,
Kann es auch schreiben;
Wird weder Leib noch Seele töten,
Es wird alles beim Alten bleiben.
Dummes aber vors Auge gestellt

Hat ein magisches Recht:
Weil es die Sinne gefesselt hält,
Bleibt der Geist ein Knecht.

The ambivalence between communication and power becomes all the more evident once so-called 'public opinion' is born. (Habermas, 1962). At the beginning of 19th century, the enthusiasm for public opinion is great and absolute trust is put in it. Jeremy Bentham, in a writing of 1816, speaks of public opinion in very optimistic terms, employing a language that sounds almost 'theological'. Public opinion seems to have become a new god, it is compared to a supreme court of justice that is 'incorruptible,' and that comprehends the whole of wisdom and the sense of equity of a nation. (Bentham, 1843: II, 229ff) It is clear that Bentham is here opposing the politics of *arcana imperii* and defending the principle of transparence in public affairs.

In these early years, the relationship between public opinion and truth is very strong. Guizot, for instance, is convinced that the representative system leads citizens to search for truth: Thanks to the discussion, public power is obliged to search for truth; thanks to the freedom of the press, citizens themselves are stimulated to look for truth and communicate it to the power. While this may sound very naive today, it does reflect the spirit of the time. (Guizot, 1851, II, 10ff)

The general confidence and trust in public opinion declines shortly thereafter. John Stuart Mill, for example, writes in his essay *On Liberty*: "The general tendency of things throughout the world is to render mediocrity the ascendant power among mankind... At present individuals are lost in the crowd. In politics it is almost a triviality to say that public opinion now rules the world... Those whose opinions go by the name of public opinion ... are always a mass, that is to say, collective mediocrity... In this age, the mere example of nonconformity, the mere refusal to bend the knee to custom, is itself a service. Precisely because the tyranny of opinion is such as to make eccentricity a reproach, it is desirable in order to break through that tyranny, that people should be eccentric." (Mill, 1848). In the same way, Tocqueville (1835-40) and Kierkegaard see in public opinion the danger of the levelling down of society, the mass society in which everybody conforms to the majority's opinion because one wants to avoid the labour of thinking for oneself and the suffering involved in distinguishing oneself as an individual. This society is dominated by the Public, an omnivorous monster that lives in "a state of indolent laxity." (Kierkegaard, 1978) The public is always bored, and in suffering from boredom, it looks for some variety, a piece of news. Thus, every day it creates new events and then devours and consumes them.

This ambivalence has been even more present in the totalitarian regimes of our century. It was the triumph of the media used for propaganda to replace truth. It was the triumph of stupidity, as Dietrich Bonhoeffer wrote in 1943. Yet, in a situation like that of totalitarianism, of the tyranny of propaganda, it is still the recourse to the media that liberates. Traditional media such as books, journals, but also handmade leaflets, such as those of the Resistance Movement. A good representation of the ambivalence between propaganda media and resistance media is found in the conflict between the huge machinery of Nazi propaganda and the leaflets against Hitler written by the students of the *Weisse Rose* and distributed clandestinely at the University of Munich in 1943. (Dumbach, Newborn, 1986; Scholl, 1982) These leaflets are also media and as the previous President of Germany von Weizsaecker said, they have restored dignity to the German people. Other examples of alternative media are the letters of Bonhoeffer written while in prison and the many books of philosophy and theology written in prison. In a certain sense, even in *1984*, this ambivalence is present: the Big Brother informative apparatus on one hand, and the book that Winston reads in secrecy in his room, on the other hand. This book represents his freedom.

3. The Political and Institutional Role of the Media in Modern Societies

The ambivalence at the heart of public opinion is also reflected in the media, which are seen either as an essential instrument or as a danger for democracy. The media are undoubtedly part of the institution of democracy, so much so that they have been interpreted as the 'fourth power' next to the three traditional powers of the state: legislative, executive and judicial. In particular, in the American experience, the press has been conceived as the 'watchdog' of citizens against abuses of the government, a function that was certainly exercised in the Watergate scandal.

Nevertheless, it is difficult, and perhaps even dangerous, to assign the media a fixed political and institutional position once and for all.

It is rather more opportune to think of a dynamic role that places the media in a dialectical (and non-opposing) relation with the other powers.

From this point of view, it is interesting to recall the evolution of juridical sensibility. As far as the right of information is concerned, we cannot help but notice different nuances. In the French *Déclaration des droits de l'homme et du citoyen* of 1789, article 11 states: "La libre communication des pensées et des opinions est un des droits les plus précieux de l'homme: tout citoyen peut donc parler, écrire, imprimer librement, sauf à répondre de l'abus de cette liberté dans les cas déterminés par la loi." Here, the accent is posed on the free expression of thought. Therefore, this article has represented the juridical basis for the right of the press against censorship. 150 years later, in the *Universal Declaration of Human Rights* of 1948, article 19 underlies the right of "searching, obtaining, propagating information" as distinguished from the right of free speech. Here, the accent is more on the right of the citizen and not so much on the right of the journalist or editor. Nowadays, the jurist would most likely put the accent on the right of privacy, to protect citizens against the invasion of the media.

Originally, because of the idea of freedom, the media, in the age of the press, were essentially pluralists; in the age of radio and television, the media were first under the control of state monopolies, both in liberal as well as totalitarian states; later, with the advent of commercial television, they enjoyed pluralism again. Finally, the advent of Internet was initially characterized by anarchy, which only now, and not without difficulties, has begun to be regulated.

The dynamic and dialectical roles of the media point to the nature of the media. They are not institutions, but technological instruments.

4. Technopolitics: A Challenge for Democracy

The influence the media have on the citizens is one of the most controversial aspects of the relationship between the media and democracy. (McQuail, 1994) Despite the many preoccupations expressed by researchers towards a possible, radical and total manipulation of the minds by the media (as evoked in the famous novel by George Orwell, *1984*), empirical studies offer a very diversified, sometimes even contradictory, picture which does not allow for definite or uni-lateral conclusions.

Nobody would deny that the media have played a crucial role in the political ascent of leaders such as Ross Perot or the Italian Berlus-coni. It remains nonetheless difficult to say whether the media have artificially created a political opinion out of nothing, or if they have rather amplified and affirmed an already existing opinion.

In the case of Berlusconi, the first reactions of political scientists both in Italy and in Europe were terrifying and went as far as defin-ing Berlusconi's success as a *"coup d'état mediatique"*. (Virilio, 1994) Ricolfi, a political sociologist, wrote an essay presenting the results of his empirical research on the phenomenon. (Ricolfi, 1994) He analysed a panel of 2500 citizens inquiring how many of them had changed their political orientation during the electoral campaign. His results were that television, both state and commercial televi-sion, i.e., Berlusconi's television, had displaced 4 million votes (38%). In his analysis, half of them had been displaced from the right to the left and from the left to the right. The other half represented a change of party within the left or the right.

Such a study was negatively criticised (Mazzoleni, 1998) both on theoretical and methodological grounds: (1) It put electoral intention and electoral choice on the same level; (2) It adopted a deterministic framework (stimulus-response); (3) It ignored the fact that media abuse during electoral campaigns could also produce reaction and rejection of the political message.

In conclusion, in the Italian debate, there is recognition that the media influence political opinions, but not in the sense that they pro-duce a determining conditioning of the electoral results. Berlusconi was defeated in the 1996 elections by the center-left party (*Ulivo*), even though he has control over a significant part of state television along with his own commercial television empire. It is nevertheless the case that 'media' politicians such as Berlusconi have contributed to transforming politics into a virtual spectacle. (Rodotà, 1997) Let us consider the impact of the media on democracy with regard to four dimensions of a citizen's life.

4.1. *Information*

The necessary prerequisite for an authentic democracy is that citi-zens possess the necessary information and knowledge in order to make independent decisions.

The question is obviously very delicate, and it is precisely on this point that the elitist theorists focus their criticism. They believe that a popular democracy is not possible, since the number of people who actually possess the necessary specific information in order to make adequate decisions corresponds to no more than 10% of the total population, whereas about 30% possess generic information. (Sartori, 1987) It is therefore necessary to measure the level of democratic distribution of information among citizens in relation to the unprecedented growth of the media, an issue that is extremely relevant for democracy itself.

It is clear that the recent development of the media has provided citizens with an amount of information which is, greater than in the past. It remains however controversial whether such a huge amount of information has actually increased the number of well-informed citizens. The results of empirical studies in this regard are rather discouraging. According to Entman, in a study conducted 10 years ago, the American citizens know as much about politics as they did 20 years earlier, despite the increase of sources of information. (Entman, 1989: 4) According to Davis, at the end of the day, half of the televiewers have only a very superficial idea of about half of the news broadcasted. The 30% that are better informed can actually recall only the main issues of a third of the news. A great deal of what is apprehended is rapidly forgotten. (Davis, 1990: 173)

Why does this happen? Why is there such a disproportion between information supply and knowledge? Why the paradox of disinformation in a society of hyperinformation? The responsibility lies with both the media and citizens. As far as the media are concerned, political information is conveyed in a superficial manner; it tends to be sensationalist, it privileges scandal, it makes excessive use of images, often very poor ones, and tends to be very boring. (Graber, 1994: 331-346) A classical example is the recent Clinton Sexgate and the defeat of the media by the media. As far as citizens are concerned, they show very little interest for politics, they view or listen to the media for entertainment purposes and not for information, they privilege sport and local news, and above all, they have no awareness of their degree of disinformation. If it is true that many people who are not informed do not participate in political decisions, it is also true that many others, while disinformed, believe themselves to be in possession of the necessary information to make a decision. (Delli, Keeter, 1996) In the latter case, there is a disin-

formed participation in the decision-making process, which is primarily based not on rational evaluation, but on ideological convictions, particular interests, sociological factors, symbolic identification,
and so on. This does not seem to be a development of the more
recent years since the classical work of Walter Lippmann, *Public
Opinion*, already examines the influence exercised by the symbolic
dimension on political opinion. (Lippmann, 1922)

It is worthwhile to focus our attention on this aspect. The media
seem to exercise a great deal of influence on the symbolic horizon
and on the semantic context, rather than on the information as such.
Although the content is easily forgotten and is seemingly less important, much more relevant are the way and the order of importance in
which information is communicated. The media's influential power
is exercised more at the level of *agenda setting* than at the level of
news processing, that is to say, in the process of establishing the
agenda of what to say, the order and the space ascribed to each news
item. (McQuail, 1994: 64-69) A correspondence has emerged between
the order of importance given by the media and what citizens consider important. This power of influence of the media is due to the
fact that the agenda setting follows models of communication of
advertising which do not require authentic apprehension, but only a
minimal awareness of the issues.

Because of the significance of the agenda setting, there arise the
most relevant ethical questions, both for the information operators,
who elaborate and provide news, and the citizens, who select and
order it.

Some final observations: (1) the paradox of disinformation in a
society of hyperinformation must not lead to less political information; a different type of information is needed as well as more education of citizens; (2) the way in which media have been providing
political information has not increased the number of informed citizens: this must change, and citizens must demand a different, more
serious and less spectacular way of media coverage; (3) media information can produce more positive effects when it is accompanied
and supported by other forms of communication in politics, especially interpersonal communication. (Lenart, 1994)

4.2 *Equality*

In every case, the elitist theoreticians of popular democracy see
equality among citizens as a real problem. If a full, active political

citizenship can be achieved only where knowledge and critical appreciation exist or where information, discussion and knowledgeable deliberation are present, the problem of the well-informed citizen is not only a problem of the quantity and quality of political information, but also one of public accessibility. An unfair distribution of information, where a discrepancy exists between a well-informed minority and an uninformed mass, would create certain problems regarding the substantial nature of a democracy.

In this regard, it would not prove futile to examine the influence of the media, objectively understood, in relation to the fulfilment of minor and major conditions of equality. It is evident that the media employ language that requires certain skills in order to be understood, and they have certain economic means in order to carry out their desired goals. They also use technology, which requires the assistance of highly trained technicians. If one examines the history of technology over the last two centuries, one notices that as new media emerged, the complexity of the technology varied. The press, for example, was geared toward a literate audience, and hence, in the 1700s and 1800s, was fairly complex. Radio and television were characterised by a remarkable immediacy and enjoyment level that were both achieved at a reasonable cost. New information technologies (data banks, web rings and electronic voting) are highly selective in so far as they require different skills and are of varying costs. It is not only a question of the medium being user-friendly, but also a question of economic accessibility.

Naturally, a greater or lesser accessibility is linked with the greater or lesser amount of information a certain medium makes available. For example, Internet access is more complex and costly than listening to television information. It is also more informative. Moreover, a greater or lesser accessibility is also linked with issues of control, discussion and decision-making. In the radio and television eras, the problem of equality among citizens never arose, at least in the beginning, as ethically and politically relevant. Such considerations, in their radicality, only came to the fore with the advent of new technologies.

In this regard, one can speak of "the risk of a new hierarchy of information haves and have nots" (Rodotà, 1997:90) and the danger of veritable "information apartheid." (Bikson and Rodotà, 1997:91) At this point it would be useful to examine data compiled by the Rand Corporation. According to research carried out between 1984 and 1993, the appearance of new technologies has not helped to reduce traditional inequalities, but in fact, has contributed to the creation of new ones.

> The percentage of computer users belonging to the group of highest income earners rose from 11% to 56%, whereas the group of lowest income earners witnessed an increase from 2% to 7.5%. Examining various cultural groups, higher educated individuals saw an increase of 17% to 50%, whereas those of a lower educational level only saw an increase from 4.5% to 13%. An analysis was also carried out in terms of race. Whites saw an increase from 11% to 42%, whereas blacks saw an increase from 3.5% to 12.5%. Age saw different, more complex results. For those under 19 years of age, there was an increase from 13.5% to 31%. For those between 20 and 39, an increase from 10.5% to 29% was present, and for those between 40 and 59 years of age, and increase from 2% to 11%. (Rodotà, 1997: 91)

Clearly, the traditional variables of income, level of education and ethnicity were used. Age, as a new variable, was introduced into these traditional categories. The aforementioned study not only reveals information concerning access to consumer goods, but also, more profoundly, access to tools that are becoming more and more indispensable in order to participate in a democracy.

The question becomes more sensitive when such telecommunication systems are used not only by commercial agencies or private information agencies, but also by central or local governments. In such cases, the problem arises of providing a truly universal service as desired by OCSE (Rodotà, 1997: 93), which is based on universal fee schedules, the presence of local affiliates throughout the country and the literacy of the users of the service. By only mentioning these problems, one begins to see how difficult it is to achieve an effective, open, accessible telecommunication system for all citizens, including seniors and those who live in remote areas far away from 'electronic highways.'

Even the most optimistic analysts believe that it would be difficult to reach more than 2/3 of the population with such a service. It would appear that Peter Goltz's prophecy regarding teledemocracy has been fulfilled. On this point, the following observations can be made:

(1) First, it should be noted that the inequality between information haves and have nots is caused, in the beginning anyway, by the

distribution of new information and communication technologies. This widespread inequality is typical with the introduction of new technologies. Strong social and cultural groups have the advantage in the use of new technologies. This is not to say that such a discrepancy will remain constant. There will be an attempt to curb the inequality. In this sense, one can situate the proposals of governments to give every student a personal computer (Tony Blair). Some say that the project sounds more demagogic than real, especially given that the problem is not only instrumental but also political (placing conditions on citizens accessing information) and educational.

(2) Even if one was to promote openness and attempt to curb discrimination, new technologies, unless they are accessible to all citizens, cannot act as substitutes for the traditional media of both the state and its citizens.

(3) If we posit that these new technologies cannot substitute for traditional media, one must also think about a larger role for single individuals, groups and institutions as facilitators of the new communication technologies.

4.3 Participation

A third element, according to which one can measure the relationship between democracy and the media, is the participation of citizens. Participation is defined as the exercising of active citizenship on the part of the individual who experiences himself or herself in a pluralistic context: from basic voter participation to participation in individual political initiatives (referenda, campaign financing, demonstrations, protest letters or letters of solicitation) to the participation in movements or the registration in a political party as an individual member or organiser. Even in this case, the reality presented is complex. To simplify matters, we can distinguish certain historical periods.

4.3.1 Birth of Democracy

The first period refers to the birth of modern democracy and the establishment of democracies in the 1800s and 1900s. This is the period belonging to the press. The press first appeared as private initiatives. Later, gazettes were used by governments, and over time, became soapboxes for political parties as in the case of the Jacobins in the French revolution. The *Political Register (1816)* was the first newspaper to print over 50 000 copies, and was the political voice of the chartist movement. In this period, participation, especially in European countries, and the media grew (from flyers to newspapers of political parties.) The media helped facilitate greater participation while at the same time benefiting from this greater participation. Here, the media worked from 'below.'

4.3.2 *Participation via Radio*

In the second period, i.e., the period of the radio, new communication media were used from 'above.' They were in the control of monopolies. Here, participation, which continued in the same manner as in the previous period, included mass gatherings, processions and crowds gathered round to hear the voice of their leaders. Participation began to change, political activity gave way to violent activism or protests. But the history of radio also includes significant non-totalitarian moments like the broadcasts of Radio London to the resistance in World War II.

4.3.3 *Television Time*

The third period, when television became the instrument of information and political campaigns, participation began to dwindle. Already in 1948, two American researchers, Lazarsfeld and Merton, spoke of 'narcotic dysfunction' of the mass media, which encourages citizens to be passive, thereby transforming them from participants to spectators. Here, information does not induce participation, but the contrary. "Political activity leads citizens to follow the news, but the news does not normally lead people to political action." (Schudson, 1995:27) Like football, politics has also become an arm chair 'sport.' How was the relationship between the development of the media and participation viewed in this period? Scholars have developed two interpretative models. (Fabbrini, 1999) First, the fetishistic approach. This approach views public opinion as the public of that particular show which is politics. Second, there is the structuralist approach. It sees public opinion as an institution that regulates a particular type of relation to the market, namely, the 'market of ideas.'

(1) According to the first approach, politics is essentially a show, or better still, an artificial reality constructed by actors and, in larger

part, by the audience. It is a fetish. The definition of politics as a show, however, is not new, especially if one thinks of King James I of England, who said, "A king is always on stage." The newness of the first approach consists in the radicality of how the artificiality of politics or the affirmation that all "politics is a show" is thought. In this approach, the apathy of citizens is constitutive of the political scene. The more politics becomes a show, with its use of images, symbols and rites, the more passive the audience becomes. In this particular show, the media play a crucial role in so far as they represent the actual stage upon which the whole political show will take place. Politics must respect the time frames of the media. The political event is a political declaration (not a fact, but a declaration, or even better, a witty remark) delivered just before the evening news, made in such a way as journalists are able to be present in order to broadcast the declaration on the evening news. The logic that governs political actors is the very same logic that governs a show. Hence, politics, like the television show, seeks to increase its number of spectators and earn critical acclaim. For this reason, the political event is considered a dramatisation, a simplification, a personalisation. Biographical facts are introduced into the show, and the logic of the encounter of the political protagonists is that of friend-foe. Moreover, the news coverage must necessarily be ambiguous in order not to antagonise the audience, thereby capturing the largest share of viewers as possible. It is not easy to ascertain how much and how far this political show succeeds in manipulating public opinion. What is certain, though, is that such political shows succeed in capturing the attention of viewers in their moments of boredom and/or discontent over the current state of affairs (Berlusconi, Perot), even periodically shifting votes from one camp to another. The show can never become absolutely unilateral, for that would alienate a large audience. The media must appear neutral and objective. But even in doing so, the media cannot help imposing their own agenda, as they decide which events deserve the attention of the public.

Political shows encourage passivity, thereby generating little political interest, especially given that both the time the media devote to political coverage and the size of the viewing audience have decreased. "The three major American TV networks (ABC, CBS, NBC) devoted only 15 hours of coverage to the Democratic Party convention of 1992 held in New York, whereas in 1988, they devoted 34 hours of coverage. In 1972, 90 hours of coverage were granted.

The last convention of the Republican Party was followed by 25 million spectators (10% of the US population), whereas Hubert Humphrey's radio address at the Democratic Party Convention had 60 million listeners." (Rodotà, 1997:28) Another fact: "The time of direct media communication by candidates has progressively decreased, falling from an average of 42.3 seconds in 1968 to 9.8 seconds in 1988 and 7,3 seconds in 1992." (Rodotà, 1997:29)

Italy has witnessed a progressive increase of voter no-shows with the advent of the television period, and this has occurred despite the massive use of private television stations in the electoral campaign of 1994. With regard to the actors, the political show has resulted in a 'politics of inauthenticity,' in which the politician is viewed as perennially committed to saying what the public wishes to hear. Such an approval, which is a popularity quotient, does not, in fact, demonstrate a real consensus or the following of party lines. Popularity and consensus have become disassociated from one another, which can lead one not to know and interpret correctly the will of the people. And this is the risk of vainglory that Max Weber condemned as the sin of the politician (Weber, 1989) because such vanity renders the politician blind and dependent upon the volatile moods of the public. How this confusion between popularity and consensus can become lethal is seen in totalitarian states, where popular leaders have confusingly interpreted the applause of a crowd as the real willingness of the people to sacrifice themselves for a given cause.

(2) The second interpretative approach views the 'space' of public opinion as a 'market of ideas,' and emphasises the transformation of collective, political subjects as provoked by the development of the media. This approach views the television era as representing the decline of traditional political parties, and with them, the weakening of the competitive edge that weaker social groups acquired by organising themselves within the internal structures of popular parties. This can be verified by examining the new media: Television permits a communication between elites and the masses, and even to those elites who do not root themselves in a popular base. Public opinion polls: They are tools used to discover the trends of behaviour of citizens. They are not only used in planning election strategies, but also used by governments to test beforehand certain proposed policies and measures. These sometimes run the risk of flattening public sentiment toward certain proposed measures or policies of reform. For

those who have the financial means, public opinion polls permit one to know popular sentiments without even having one's own proper base of survey respondents: telephone banks or direct mailings facilitate contact between electors and candidates that is no longer mediated by the work of activists and volunteers.

The development of the media in the television era tends to substitute an electoral politics based on a large quantity of work with huge capital. The media, therefore, end up favouring politicians who have financial resources and who are not necessarily politicians of organised, popular movements.

4.3.4 *Computer Era*

Finally, the last period is that of the computer. The new medium appears to facilitate a closer relationship between media and participation. It is, however, to early to say, quantitatively, whether any significant results have ensued from the aforementioned relationship. Qualitatively, one can say, however, the new computer media are more interactive and require more than a passive comportment. They require certain activities, including research, selection of news items, even the expression of one's opinion, in some cases, etc.

New means of technology are creating new modes of participation, including:

(1) *civic nets*: These nets are characterised by the efforts of the public administrators to make available, by means of the net, information relevant for the political lives of a local municipality or national government. These nets, however, do not only make available certain relevant information, but also try to elicit participation in relevant discussions. (Cf. Amsterdam 1994, Santa Monica 1989)

(2) *electronic town meetings*: These are the modern day equivalent of the early New England town meetings that happened in public squares. In such town meetings, people gathered to discuss and make decisions about their communities. (This is described in Tocqueville's *Democracy in America* I, I, V.) Today, public gatherings occur in both real and virtual spaces. A moderator is selected, and there is free access to panelists either through telephone, fax or e-mail, thereby fostering an open discussion with a wide array of people. Panelists are chosen ahead of time, and they discuss issues based on information that already exists in the public sphere and which is already well known.

(3) *consensus conferences*: These conferences are organised to discuss specific problems relative to a certain place or group of citizens. They are open, and try to achieve some sort of common understanding regarding a specific problem by proposing laws, political solutions or strategic initiatives of one sort or another. Participants make use of pre-existing laws, or they formulate certain bills or resolutions that can be introduced into parliaments and various types of political fora.

(4) *deliberative polls*: Usually organised by the aforementioned interests, deliberative polls are electronic referenda. They are often used in remote areas where transportation is difficult e.g., Hawaii and Alaska. Deliberative polls help facilitate normal, regulated voting procedures, but they are not absolute substitutes for them.

What are the new elements connected with the use of these procedures? As has been shown (Rodotà, 1997), these new technologies help promote a 'continuous democracy' in which everyone, ideally and progressively, can be involved in the various processes of decision making and power. In fact, in the traditional forms of democracy, voting occurred at particular times under certain conditions and limits, and for this reason, one can speak of an 'intermittent democracy' — a democracy that runs the risk of representatives no longer representing the popular will, once they have been elected. To be sure, this was one of the grave reservations of Rousseau and the theorists of direct democracy. Moreover, there is also the risk of having too many vehicles for direct democracy. For example, referenda, facilitated by new computer technology, can reinforce the tendencies of plebiscites, thereby diminishing the role of the democratically elected representative. With respect to the aforementioned risks, the new computer media, even in areas where the population is small, seem to allow an integration of representative democracy and direct democracy, especially where participation is not based on the decision of citizens, but on the power of control and consultation that accompanies political decisions. Such new technologies are used "less in the dimension of decision-making, and are more dispersed throughout the whole process of democratic deliberation." (Rodotà, 1997:116)

There is a positive element: The use of these new technologies tend to associate the formation of public opinion and political will with being well-informed (often a very high level of information is assured, given the vast amount of information available on the net) critical discussion, and therefore, rational reflection.

Problematic, however, is the question of intersubjectivity. In so far as intersubjective relations remain mediated by electronic means, and are, therefore, highly artificial, the authenticity of collective subjectivities is undermined.

4.4 *Information and Privacy*

We shall now investigate how the relation between the media and democracy can be measured by another relevant aspect, namely, the privacy of the citizen. We shall do so because respect for privacy is not only ethically relevant, but also politically relevant.

Our preliminary question is: Can a democracy which does not respects privacy beconsidered as a real democracy? The question is relevant, especially if we consider that, in the past some models of democracy made no provision for what we consider an irrevocable right to the protection of one's own personal sphere of privacy from invasive elements of certain public powers and the market. In the name of equality for all citizens, or in the name of the primacy of the common good with respect to the individual good, or because of the exigencies of the transparency of communal life, certain models of society used to exert control over one's personal life without respecting one's privacy and personal autonomy. In this regard, one automatically thinks of Ancient Greece, where one cannot speak of the rights of the individual. Even in certain modern or contemporary models of democracy, from certain puritan experiments with democracy to the Jacobin models in their various forms, one cannot speak of the rights of the individual subject.

Here, we find the conflict between the demands of democracy and the demands of liberalism, which we know are not always compatible with one another. With respect to our present-day situation, the example of totalitarianism has been most illuminating in this regard.

There have been determined dictatorial governments that pretended to realize democracy without respecting privacy. They tried to control the personal sphere, regulating private life, and more, the sphere of interiority. They wished to colonise the soul, control thought. Many great thinkers and writers, including George Orwell, denounced this. But the issue of a colonisation of human soul was not only a literary invention: it has been a real political attempt. This very issue came up in certain trials like von Moltke and Delp in Nazi Germany. The judge, who was in charge of those trials, declared explicitly that the Nazi regime demanded more than the external loyalty of its citizens: it demanded their soul (Cf. von Moltke, 1985).

The aforementioned examples have shown us that various trials bent on the expropriation of the personal sphere, the colonisation of the soul, do not have as their outcome the desire to construct a society of equals. Rather, they seek to create a termitary of individuals reduced to machines or animals, governed by a select group of power. Far from fulfilling the condition of equality, the totalitarian model of government bases itself on the systematic discrimination against individuals who are not considered homogeneous and on the dehumanisation of society.

The tragic outcome of this totalitarian line of thinking is the persecution of the Jews and their internment in extermination camps. In the diaries of many of the protagonists of the Nazi persecution, one finds tales of the systematic stripping of camp interns, placing them in lines. This was done as a form of symbolically and psychologically annihilating the independence of their persons, on the one hand, and affirming total power, on the other hand. The same is also true of the slave trade. Reading certain accounts of the slave trade in the 1800s, which was denounced by certain enlightened Europeans, the theme of nudity appears. Slaves were nude, stripped them of all that would have protected them. The relationship between nudity and slavery still has a symbolic force that is not easily forgotten. It was Paul Valadier (1998) who underlined the political, anthropological, and ethical value of 'modesty' as the guarding of a personal good that could not be handled as merchandise for a given political power. Totalitarianism is antithetical to the construction of democracy, where democracy refers to self-government. The colonisation of the soul eliminates the principle that makes possible the self-government of the human subject.

It is justified, therefore, that every invasion of privacy be viewed with some suspicion, not only by liberals, but also by democrats. Democracy cannot truly exist without personal liberty. This is not only valid for totalitarian governments, but also for constitutional governments, given those ethico-social conditions of democracy, as previously demonstrated (Habermas, 1998), cannot be reproduced by the system itself. They need an autonomous sphere of personal, family and social life, in which individuals can find meaning not reproducible by administrative means, and without which political systems cannot function.

There is another fact about totalitarianism that causes us to reflect. Regimes that have proceeded to force human beings to strip do not solely arise out of a violent hold on power by a select group or movements that have oppressed people. Totalitarianism has also risen from 'below' as a consequence of being exhausted by freedom, being tired of thinking for oneself. In exchange for tranquillity, well being, order and protection, entire peoples have turned over rights of decision-making to a select few. As Etienne de la Boetie recognised, there even exists a 'voluntary servitude,' which remains at the base of tyranny. This dynamic is also present in the process of the colonisation of the soul, which we denounced earlier. In today's version of this dynamic, we see that the media do not stop at anything in order to sell information. The media constantly scrutinise the private lives of individuals with the intention of sensationalising people's lives, their personal stories. The colonisation of the soul also happens here, and not so much for political ends, but more for economic ends.

The transforming of the soul into a public spectacle, however, is not only the fault of unscrupulous media, but also stems from the desires of human beings who do not jealously guard their privacy. They want to sensationalise and make public their private stories. Often, this is done to earn money, but sometimes people share their stories publicly because it is the only way for them 'to be,' to be present to us.

Here, we see how complex the issue of privacy can be. Privacy is constrained on three fronts. First, by the political powers that tend to reinforce the powers of the citizen. Second, there are economic powers that transform the private sphere into merchandise that can be commercially exchanged. Finally, there are information powers that tend to collect personal data in order to generate or solicit news.

Privacy is a serious issue in democratic societies. It can be understood as the democratically sanctioned "right to the free development of one's personality" (Art 2, Bundesverfassung Deutschland), which cannot be guaranteed by a system of laws, professional codes and customs.

It is not possible to underline all the important aspects of the issue of privacy. Nevertheless, it is worthwhile to outline some important considerations. We shall follow the work of Rodotà (1997) in this regard.

First, how is the question of privacy raised in our society?

(1) Whereas in traditional societies, where individuals controlled personal information (apart from statistical and information and

police records) today our personal information seems to be shared by a plurality of subjects. (2) In the past, the main concern was to avoid a transmission of personal information to outside sources. Today, it is almost the opposite in so far as the prime concern has become how to slow down the flow of information (e.g., commercials) into the personal sphere. (3) In the past, privacy was seen as a privilege reserved for particular individuals. Today, it is seen as a right of all individuals. (4) A significant problem is the question of how to guarantee privacy while simultaneously guaranteeing access to information in the public sphere. Often, the invasion of privacy of the media results in the opposite situation: Maximum clarity and openness in private life and an obfuscated public sphere. M.L. Goldschmidt (1954: 401), nearly half a century ago, recorded the same observations: "There are two worrisome tendencies: First, there is a lack of consideration of the individual's right to privacy. Second, not enough publicity, thereby resulting in more secrecy with regard to matters that ought to be public."

What are the strategies employed to protect privacy? (1) The right of citizens to oppose certain determined forms of the collection and treatment of personal information by private and public individuals. A specification of this right is the right "not to know," which can be valuable in certain cases relevant to one's personal life (e.g., the releasing of information related to one's health,) or even to matters concerning commercial information (e.g., the sending of junk mail across fax lines without the permission of the owner of the fax line.) (2) Statute of limitations: Personal data must be restricted to a specific use by a specific individual. Hence, personal data cannot be used by unauthorised individuals for purposes other than those specified (e.g., magazine subscriptions or similar things) (3) The right to the closure of records when certain specific limitations and terms of use have been fulfilled.

With respect to these problems, it is evident that the issues are related. Auto-regulation by individuals is not enough, even more so when regulated by the market. Hence, a regulation based on contracts between providers and consumers of goods is insufficient given there exist inalienable goods! Legislation (with certain flexibility) and professional codes outlining the comportment to be followed by workers and users is needed. A shared ethical perspective is also necessary. A substantial respect for privacy can only be achieved only where there is an ethics of respect for oneself and the inviolability of the other.

It is interesting to note how the problem of privacy is raised in different ways that follow the development of the media. In the press and television media, which find their audience to be more passive, violation of privacy happens when the citizen is treated like an object of information, and, hence, news and images of the person in question are circulated in the public sphere. In the case of the new media, violation of privacy can happen through the very interaction with new technology, or when the citizen becomes an 'active subject', and enters the world of the net. This obviously presents a problem because, in the case of the former, a defensive strategy concerning the privacy of the individual could have been introduced, which did not necessarily imply the renunciation of the active participation of the citizen. In the case of the latter, the active exercise of citizenship poses the risk of 'being watched.'

5. Conclusions

The analysis of the impact of the new media on the dynamics of democracy has brought to light once again the question of ambivalence. The task of a media ethics is that of reinforcing those dynamics that can render fruitful the introduction of new media for democracy.

For this reason, a constant commitment to production and critique in order to attempt a reconnection of the means of communications with its scope, or the communication of truth and the relation with the other, must be undertaken. One must take care to distinguish and not confuse the diverse levels of communication, which are also diverse levels of relation. In which direction?

First and foremost, in the direction of a reinforcing the sense of the personal sphere, of the safeguarding of one's own proper interiority and primary, personal relations. The political relevance of interiority and the subjection of the personal sphere to the invasive gaze of the other, to jealousy and morbid curiosity were, I think, brought to light. By means of laws, professional codes, traditions, it is necessary to safeguard the soul, the personal space of one's own intimate thought and the difference between public and private. The same holds true for the spheres of family and friends, but in a more profound manner. Everyone who understands the silences and words articulated to one's own God, between men and women, between parents and children, between friends in the night, understands that they belong to the realm of secrecy and not to the public domain. Every time that the media reveal these private words, often violating secrecy, not only do they offend moral sensibilities, but they also disregard the essential link which enables one to trust another without having to place himself or herself in the trust of the public. A democracy needs to guard the intimate sphere of communication.

Second, communication also exists in the societal sphere, which is dominated by the market. It includes the worlds of work, production with its languages of competition and marketing, but also solidarity, conviviality, movements, groups and churches. There are both competitive and co-operative socialities. Between and among themselves, they must allow expression and communication. Their messages must be measured in light of this two-fold reality, and not exclusively by means of the thought of exchange. Certainly, communication is subject to the logic of the market, but we have also seen how interpersonal communication in groups and associations is important.

A democracy must fix rules of communication, which facilitate the free exchange of information and knowledge among subjects, but it must also favour the life of groups and associations which wish to avoid a certain levelling.

Finally, we must consider the public sphere understood, in its most authentic sense, as universality. This space is not only the space of reason, but it is also the space in which a reference to the truth cannot be negated. Politics always sinks its roots in existence, which is always historical, particular, tending to the infinite and facing loss in the face of its own finitude and imminent death. Here, reasoning not only comes into play, but also passions expressed in symbols, myths and ideals. Politics, however, does not exhaust itself in the expression of a need for protection and defence. It is also an attempt to inscribe the protection of the community and its need for identity in an horizon that is broader, which is the horizon of all human beings, namely, the horizon of the true and the just.

A democratic order cannot lose its reference point in the search for truth and justice. This is a painful reference point because one discovers that every power finds the very dissolution of its absoluteness. But without this reference point, democracy ends up being arid, and transforms itself into something other than it is. From this perspective, communication between human beings, with its means and various levels of communication, is, in its foundation, the very possibility of its own renewal.

References

APEL K.O, M. KETTNER (eds.) (1992), *Zur Anwendung der Diskursethik in Politik, Recht und Wissenschaf.* Frankfurt a.M., Suhrkamp.

ARENDT H., (1972), *Wahrheit und Luge in der Politik: zwei essays.* München, Piper, 1972.

BAUDRILLARD J., *Simulacres et simulation.* Paris, Galilee, 1983.

BENTHAM J., (1843), 'An Essay on Political Tactics' in *The Works of Jeremy Bentham,* ed. Bowring. Edinburgh, Vol II.

BIKSON T.K., (1996) *New Inequalities,* Paper presented at the First Information Imperative International Inquiry, Washington, 4-5 June 1996, 1.

BONHOEFFER D. (1970), *Widerstand und Ergebung. Briefe und Aufzeichnungen aus der Haft* , tr. it. *Resistenza e resa.* Milano 1988.

DAVIS D.K. (1990), *News and Politics* in D.L. Swanson, D.D. Nimmo (eds.), *New Directions in Political Communication.* Newbury Park, 1990.

DELLI CARPINI M.X., S. KEETER (1996), *What Americans Know about Politics and why It Matters.* New Haven, Conn.

DUMBACH, A.E., J. NEWBORN (1986), *Shattering the German Night. The Story of the White Rose.* Boston/Toronto.

EDELMANN M. (1988), *Constructing the Political Spectacle.* Chicago.

ENTMAN R.M. (1989), *Democracy without Citizens. Media and the Decay of American Politics.* New York.

FABBRINI S. (1999), *Il Principe democratico. La leadership nelle democrazie contamporanee.* Roma-Bari.

FERGUSON T. (1995), *Golden Rule: The Investment Theory of Party Competition and the Logic of Money-Driven Political Systems.* Chicago.

FRANKLIN B. (1994), *Packaging Politics. Political Communications in Britain's Media Democracy.* London.

GINSBERG B.E. (1986), *The Captive Public. How Mass Opinion Promotes State Power.* New York.

GRABER D. (1994), 'Why Voters Fail Information Tests: Can the Hurdles Be Overcome?' in *Political Communication* 11(1994), pp. 331-346.

GUIZOT F. (1851), *Histoire des origines du gouvernement représentatif en Europe.* Bruxelles, Vol. II.

GOLDSCHMIDT M.L., 'Publicity, Privacy and Secrecy' in *The Western Political Quarterly,* 7(1954).

HABERMAS J. (1962), *Strukturwandel der Öffentlichkeit,* tr.it. *Storia e critica dell'opinione pubblica.* Roma-Bari, 1995.

HABERMAS J. (1973), *Legitimationsprobleme im Spätkapitalismus*, tr.it. *La crisi della razionalità nel capitalismo maturo*. Roma-Bari, 1978.

KELSEN, H., (1955-56), 'Foundations of Democracy' in *Ethics* 66(1955-56)1.

KELSEN, H. (1948) 'Absolutism and Relativism in Philosophy and Politics' in *The American Political Science Review* 42(1948).

KIERKEGAARD, S.A. (1847), *En literair Anmeldelse*, tr. it. *Una recensione letteraria*. Milano, 1995.

KIERKEGAARD, S.A. (1978) *Two ages. The Age of Revolution and the Present Age. A Literary Review*, E.H. HING (ed.), Princeton (NJ).

LA BOETIE, E. (1576), *Discours sur la servitude volontaire ou le Contr'un*. tr. it. *Discorso sulla servitù volontaria*. Milano, 1996.

LAZARSFELD P.H., MERTON R. (1948), *Communication, Taste and Social Action*, in L. BRYSON (ed.), *The Communication of Ideas*. New York.

LENART, S. (1994), *Shaping Political Attitudes. The Impact of Interpersonal Communication and Mass Media*. Thousand Oaks, California.

LIPPMANN W., *Public Opinion* (1922), tr. it. *L'opinione pubblica*. Roma 1995

MAZZOLENI G., *La comunicazione politica*. Bologna 1998.

MCCOMBS M.E., SHAW D.L. (1972), 'The Agenda-setting Function of the Mass Media' in *Public Opinion Quarterly* 36(1972), pp. 176-187.

MCQUAIL D. (1992), *Media Performance. Mass Communication and the Public Interest*, tr.it. *I media in democrazia. Comunicazioni di massa e interesse pubblico*. Bologna, 1995.

MCQUAIL D. (1994), *Mass Communication Theory. An Introduction.* tr.it. *Sociologia dei media*. Bologna, 1996.

MILL J.S. (1848), *On liberty*, tr.it. *Sulla libertà*. Roma 1996.

MOLTKE, Helmuth James von (1985), *Futuro e resistenza: dalle lettere degli anni 1926-1945*. Brescia.

MONTESQUIEU (1748), *Esprit des lois*, tr. it. *Lo spirito delle leggi*, in Id., *Opere*. Torino, 1982.

OCSE (1991), *Le service universel et la restructuration des tarifs dans les télécommunications*. Paris, 1991.

RICOLFI L., 'Elezioni e mass media. Quanti voti ha spostato la TV' in *Il Mulino* 43(1994), pp. 1031-1046

RODOTÀ S., *Tecnopolitica. La democrazia e le nuove tecnologie della comunicazione*. Roma-Bari, 1997.

SARTORI G. (1987), *Democrazia e definizioni*. Bologna.

SARTORI G. (1997), *Homo videns. Televisione e post-pensiero*. Roma-Bari.

SCHOLL, I. (1982), *Die Weisse Rose*. Frankfurt a. M. 1982.

SHUDSON M. (1983), *The News Media and the Democratic Process*. New York.

TOCQUEVILLE A. DE (1835-40), *La democratie en Amerique*, tr.it. *La democrazia in America*. Milano, 1992.

VALADIER P. (1990), *Inevitable Moral*, tr. it. *Inevitabile morale*. Brescia, 1998.

VIRILIO P. (1994), 'Le coup d'Ètat médiatique' in *Le Monde des débats*, 19-5-1994, p. 2.

WEBER M. (1919), *Politik als Wissenschaft* , tr.it. *La politica come professione* in Id., *Il lavoro intellettuale come professione*. Torino, 1989.

CAN HUMAN RIGHTS BE A FOUNDATION FOR MEDIA ETHICS?

Cees J. Hamelink

1. Foundations for Ethics: Why Be Moral?

The debate on foundations for ethics has a long and complex history. It reflects the perennial and puzzling question, 'why be moral?' We find the philosophical search for foundations of human morality already in Plato's *Republic*. In the discussion Socrates has with Glaucon and Adeimantas, Glaucon wants to learn from Socrates why people should be righteous. He wants to hear an argument that explains why justice is superior to injustice. His brother Adeimantus points out that the unjust person often lives much more comfortably than the just person, and he adds that people will only act justly, if they get something out of this behaviour or if they will be punished for unjust conduct. The brothers search for the foundation of moral obligations. (pp. 43-55) This is no simple matter because throughout history most philosophical and theological efforts to find a legitimate foundation for norms and values are flawed. As a result, the validity of any argument that justifies moral principles can be contested.

The search for moral foundations becomes particularly complex in democratic, pluralist and multi-cultural societies. In such societies, moral standards cannot simply be imposed; they can evolve legitimately only through dialogue among all those concerned. As the German social philosopher Jürgen Habermas proposes, moral standards are valid only when all those concerned give their consent to such standards in the course of their common deliberations. (Habermas, 1993: 66) This insight constitutes the basis of what has been termed a communicative or discursive ethics. (Apel, 1988) Societal dialogue explores the *'minima moralia'* upon which societies can find a basic and common agreement.

It is a difficult challenge to identify foundations for moral judgments that can be accepted by all those concerned, given their divergent cultural, political and social histories. Post-modernist thinkers
are inclined to reject the possibility of such common foundations.
They suggest that norms and values are historically determined and
therefore are not universally valid. The German moral philosopher
Karl-Otto Apel disagrees: if our morality is relative only to time and
place and no universal standards can exist, we cannot condemn
Nazi practices. (Griffioen, 1990: 13) Following the relativist position,
the Holocaust could be justified with the argument that opinions
about genocide in Nazi Germany were determined by the specific
historical conditions of the time. If we accept global responsibility
for the worldwide effects of our technological and economic activities, we absolutely need, according to Apel, interculturally and universally binding norms. (p. 13)

The metaphysical arguments through which theologians attempt
to justify norms and values will usually convince only believers. If
the moral foundation is revealed through the 'Word of God,' this
has authority only for those who accept the validity of this revelation.

If moral principles are founded upon the nature of the human
being, this foundation will fail because it moves in unexplainable
ways from a descriptive statement about human nature to a normative statement about human conduct. Moreover, upon which dimensions of human nature should moral principles be based? Human
dignity? But this is a very vague notion with many different and
conflicting interpretations. Upon qualities such as human skills?
Those are however very unequally distributed among human beings
and this would imply that rights and duties are assigned to different
people in different ways. Can human needs provide a foundation?
But someone's need for alcohol does not provide a right to liquor or
the moral duty for others to get those in alcoholic need their drinks.
It is difficult to argue that people should always be entitled to the
satisfaction of their needs.

In recent thinking about the development of morality — for example, the Canadian philosopher of science Michael Ruse — some
emphasis has been placed upon an evolutionary model that per-
ceives of moral acting as a genetically programmed altruism. It
remains, however, unclear why some species (human beings in this
case) are able to make, on the basis of biological facts, specific moral

claims. Those who defend the rights of animals argue that acknowledging or rejecting moral claims based on biological definitions inevitably leads to serious discrimination.

We could also relate the foundations for the distinction between good and evil to our personal intuition. This, however, renders arguments for or against certain moral choices subjective and arbitrary to the extent that a serious dialogue with others becomes impossible. And, in the end, it is only through dialogue that we can discover the moral foundation of social ethics. The essential contestability of all normative foundations forces us to engage in this dialogue. In this way, searching for the justification of norms and values changes "from a logical into a social and historical" issue. (Reinders, 1995: 20) It would seem that this search could be successfully based upon the political consensus which the international community has achieved through the adoption of those basic moral principles that are codified in the international human rights conventions.

2. International Human Rights as an Instrument of Moral Guidance in Media Ethics

2.1 *Human Rights*

The human species does not distinguish itself by an historical record that radiates benignity. For most of its history, the male human being has carried out (and the female to a more limited extent) an impressive variety of humiliating acts against his fellow human beings. Against this gross indecency of human history, the more enlightened individuals have, throughout the ages, committed themselves to the articulation and codification of basic moral standards that were intended to restrain human aggression, arbitrariness and negligence. Most of such moral prescriptions had a limited scope in terms of the agents they addressed and/or the geographies they covered. This changed dramatically in 1945. In response to the assaults against human dignity during the Second World War, the United Nations began to develop a universal framework of moral standards. This was to become the international convention on human rights.

Before 1945, human rights declarations existed, including the Magna Carta of 1215, the British Bill of Rights, the American Declaration of Independence and the French *Déclaration des droits de l'homme et du citoyen.* In 1945, this long history of the protection of human dignity acquired a fundamental new significance.

The novelty of the international human rights convention, as it was established after 1945, was the articulation of the age old struggle for the recognition of human dignity and the desire to protect human dignity by formalising a catalogue of legal rights. Moreover, the political discourse shifted from the 'rights of man' to the more comprehensive 'human rights.' The protection of human dignity, which earlier was mainly a national affair, was put on the agenda of the world community. Herewith, the defence of fundamental rights was no longer the exclusive preoccupation of national politics. It became an essential part of world politics. The judgement of whether or not human rights had been violated was no longer the exclusive monopoly of national governments.

More importantly, the enjoyment of human rights was no longer restricted to privileged individuals and social elites. The revolutionary core of the process which began at San Francisco with the adoption of the UN Charter in 1945 consisted in the fact that that 'all people matter.' Basic rights were to apply to everyone and to exclude no one. The new conventions that transcended all earlier moral codes claimed universal validity. This claim has time and again been challenged. Yet, the celebration in 1998 of the 50th anniversary of the Universal Declaration of Human Rights clearly articulated the fact that international human rights conventions embody the only global moral framework we have at present. This was, after much discussion, also confirmed by the 1993 United Nations World Conference on Human Rights in Vienna.

> The World Conference on Human Rights reaffirms the solemn commitment of all States to fulfil their obligations to promote universal respect for, and observance and protection of, all human rights and fundamental freedoms for all in accordance with the Charter of the United Nations, other instruments relating to human rights, and international law. The universal nature of these rights and freedoms is beyond question. (United Nations, 1993: 3-4)

Although this was an important step, the recognition of universal validity did not resolve the question of the admissible variety of cultural interpretations. Universal validity does not mean that all local forms of implementation will be similar. A variety of cultural interpretations remains possible. This has provoked the question of the degree to which local cultural interpretations can be accepted.

There is increasing support for the view that culturally determined interpretations reach a limit when they violate the core principles of human rights law. Moreover, this view holds that the admissibility of the interpretation should be judged by the international community and not by the implementing party. An important characteristic of these rights is that they are formulated in very similar ways in a variety of international, regional and national constitutional conventions. Therefore, it seems sensible to accept the political reality and adopt the moral standards of the human rights convention as guidance for human conduct in all domains of social activity. This obviously includes the field of media and communication. Actually, particularly for this domain human rights have enormous importance.

The new conventions evolved around a set of basic texts (some codified as legally binding conventions and others adopted as customary law) and mechanisms for their enforcement. The foundation for the conventions was laid down in the United Nations Universal Declaration of Human Rights (adopted on December 10, 1948 by the UN General Assembly) and the two key human rights treaties, the International Treaty on Economic, Social and Cultural Rights (in force since January 3, 1976) and the International Treaty on Civil and Political Rights. (in force since March 23, 1976)

In these three documents, commonly referred to as the International Bill of Rights, one finds seventy-six different human rights. If one were to take the totality of some fifty major international and regional human rights conventions, the number of rights would obviously increase even further. Presently, there is also a tendency among human rights lobbies to cast more and more social problems within a framework of human rights, thus adding to the number of human rights.

Since the aforementioned proliferation of rights does not necessarily strengthen the cause of the actual implementation of human rights, various attempts have been made to establish a set of core human rights that are representative of the totality. One effort concludes by articulating the existence of twelve core rights. (Jongman & Schmid, 1994: 8) These are:

1. The right to life.
2. The right not to be tortured.
3. The right not to be arbitrarily arrested.
4. The right to food.
5. The right to health care.
6. The right not to be discriminated against.
7. The right to due process of law.
8. The right to education.
9. The right to political participation.
10. The right to fair working conditions.
11. The right to freedom of association.
12. The right to freedom of expression.

These rights are the legal articulation of fundamental moral principles and their implied standards of human conduct. These principles and standards are:

> Equality and the implied standard that discrimination is inadmissible.
>
> Inviolability and the implied standard that intentional harm against human integrity is inadmissible.
>
> Liberty and the implied standard that interference with human self-determination is inadmissible.

2.2 *Media Ethics and Human Rights*

Media ethics inspired by human rights principles would start from a general obligation to promote respect for human rights. The recognition of the importance of human rights and even the mere knowledge about them cannot be taken for granted. This needs a major effort in education and information. As the media are capable of reaching out to large audiences and play an important role in people's informal education, the promotion of a 'human rights culture' should be among their prime tasks. 'Human rights culture' refers to a social situation within which knowledge about human rights, awareness of their importance, concern about human rights violations, and sensitivity to their protection is widely spread. The role of human rights is constituted as an essential yardstick against which the quality of media products should be measured.[1]

---

[1] In the negotiations leading to the formulation of the International Treaty on Economic, Social and Cultural Rights, the Australian and Swedish delegations proposed the following paragraph for the preamble: "Realizing also that the individual, having duties to other individuals and to the community to which he belongs, is under a

On a more specific level, this implies that media practices should be guided by the three core human principles of equality, inviolability and liberty.

2.2.1 *Media Ethics and the Principle of Equality*

The principle of equality implies that there is equal entitlement to the conditions of self-empowerment. Among the essential conditions of people's self-empowerment are access to and use of the resources that enable people to express themselves, the communication of these expressions to others, exchanging ideas with others, informing oneself about events in the world, creating and controlling the production of knowledge and sharing the world's resources of knowledge.

These resources include technical infrastructures, knowledge and skills, finances, and natural systems, such as outer space. The unequal distribution of their usage among the world's people obstructs the equal entitlement to the conditions of self-empowerment and, therefore, should be considered a violation of human rights.

Equality also implies the right not to be discriminated against on the basis of such factors as race, ethnic origin, religion or nationality.

Article 4 of the International Convention on the Elimination of All Forms of Racial Discrimination and Article 20.1 of the International Covenant on Civil and Political Rights prohibits the dissemination of ideas based on racial superiority, the incitement of racial hatred and national or religious hatred in domestic law.

2.2.2 *Media Ethics and the Principle of Inviolability*

Human rights conventions propose standards of conduct against attacks upon people's physical, mental and moral integrity. The right to the protection of privacy, as provided in Article 12 of the Universal Declaration of Human Rights and in Article 17 of the International Treaty on Civil and Political Rights, protects people against arbitrary interference with their private sphere and against unlawful attacks on their honour and reputation.

responsibility to strive for the promotion and observance of the rights recognized in this Covenant." This became the fifth preambular paragraph of the two human rights conventions. The formulation was motivated by the insight that individuals must contribute to the implementation of the provisions of the conventions. (Daes, 1983: 21)

The right to the presumption of innocence as provided in Article 11 of the Universal Declaration of Human Rights and in Article 14 of the International Treaty on Civil and Political Rights guarantees that people accused of a criminal offence are presumed innocent until proven guilty by public trial.

Article 5 of the Convention on the Elimination of All Forms of Discrimination against Women demands the elimination of stereotyped representations of roles for men and women and prejudices based upon the idea of the inferiority or the superiority of either of the sexes.

Concerning the protection of people's integrity, both incitement of genocide (in the Convention on the Prevention and Punishment of the Crime of Genocide) and apartheid (in the International Convention on the Suppression and Punishment of the Crime of Apartheid) have been declared criminal acts.

2.2.3 Media Ethics and the Principle of Liberty

There are various international and regional conventions which provide for the protection of freedom of expression and information. These conventions provide for the right to freedom of expression, the limitations on this right, the legitimacy of these limitations, and legal recourse against violations of these provisions.

Human rights conventions have developed a threefold test to establish the legitimacy of limitations to the liberty of expression. Limitations must be provided by law, they must serve purposes expressly stated in the treaties, and they must be shown to be necessary in a democratic society.

In this context the jurisprudence of the European Court of Human Rights in relation to freedom of expression cases deserves to be mentioned. The Court has stated in several judgments that not only do the mass media have a right to impart information, they also have the responsibility "to impart information and ideas on matters of public interest," and the public has a right to receive such information and ideas. The Court has ruled that the media are both purveyor of information and public watchdog. (Barthold case, 1985; Sunday Times case 1991; Observer/Guardian case, 1991; Open Door case, 1992) The preceding decision is similar to the classic 1969 opinion of the US Supreme Court in 'Red Lion Broadcasting versus the FCC' in 1969, where the Court stated that "the right of the viewers and listeners, not the right of broadcasters, is paramount."

3. Concluding Observation

There is a worldwide political consensus that 'all people' (and some would add 'all sentient beings') are entitled to treatment in accordance with the moral principles that undergird international human rights conventions. This consensus provides an important foundation for media ethics. This does not mean that human rights principles should be used to construct a human rights-inspired Code of Conduct for journalistic practices. As will be argued in Part III, this would constitute a conventional deductive approach to moral reasoning which is highly ineffective and inadequate. Rather, the essential function of human rights in media ethics is to provide (a universally acceptable moral source of) inspiration for the professional-ethical dialogue.

References

APEL, K.-O. (1988), *Diskurs und Verantwortung*. Frankfurt, Suhrkamp.
DAES, E.-I. (1983), *The Individual's Duties to the Community and the Limitations on Human Rights and Freedoms under Article 29 of the Universal Declaration of Human Rights*. New York, United Nations.
GRIFFIOEN, S. (ed.) (1990), *What Right does Ethics have? Public Philosophy in a Pluralistic Culture*. Amsterdam, VU uitgeverij.
HABERMAS, J. (1993), *Moral Consciousness and Communicative Action*. Cambridge (Mass.), The MIT Press.
JONGMAN, J.J., SCHMIDT, A.P. (1994), *Monitoring Human Rights*. Leiden, PIOOM.
PLATO, *The Republic*. Penguin edition of 1955. Translation by Desmond Lee.
REINDERS, J.S. (1995), 'Human Rights from the Perspective of a Narrow Conception of Religious Morality' in: A.A. AN-NA'IM, J.D. GORT, H.
United Nations (1993), *Vienna Declaration and Programme of Action*, UN General Assembly, A/CONF. 157/23.

PART II

THE CULTURAL AND
ECONOMIC CONTEXT

MEDIA CULTURE AND IDENTITY CONSTRUCTION THE SHIFT FROM MODERNITY TO POSTMODERNITY

Luc Van Poecke

Philip Schlesinger's argument that the theme of collective identity "is certain to become increasingly central in the human sciences" (Schlesinger, 1991: 137) actually implies that something which previously seems to have been experienced as unproblematical, namely (collective) identity, will be considered less and less self-evident in the future. Indeed, it now appears that fewer people find their identity in traditional pregiven categories, structures and in ascribed characteristics. "So, class, gender and ethnicity," according to Crook *et al.* (1992: 35), "decline in social significance and so also do some of their characteristic forms of expression." Instead, people are more and more constituting their identity on the basis of their active consumption of products offered to them by the leisure, media, and consumer goods industries (Crook *et al.*, 1992; Featherstone, 1991a; Friedman, 1992; Pakulski and Waters, 1996; Willis, 1990). As is known, these industries are increasingly transnational, offering their products to a global public.

These two movements (the reduction in relevance of the old forms of bonding and solidarity, on the one hand, and, on the other, the finding of one's identity in the consumption of what is offered to a global market) are, of course, linked to each other and have given rise to two opposing points of view.

The supporters of the 'cultural-imperialism' thesis point out that this globalisation leads to a cultural homogenisation or cultural synchronisation at the cost of cultural diversity and existing ethnocultural identities. (Hamelink, 1983) But there is also a more optimistic viewpoint that can be found, among others, revolving around the project of an ethnography of media audiences formulated by Morley within the British cultural studies tradition (Fiske, 1992a; Moores, 1933; Morley, 1992a; Turner, 1996). Here, it is posited that the media consumer may not be seen as a passive mass public, "stupid and naive" (Seiter *et al.*, 1989), but that, on the contrary, people actively and creatively make use of what the global media system offers them to construct their own local culture and identity:

> As we have seen, ethnographies of media audiences emphasise, and tend to celebrate, the capability of audience groups to construct their own meanings and thus their own local cultures and identities, even in the face of their virtually complete dependence on the image flows distributed by the transnational culture industries. (Ang, 1990: 250-1)

The questions that can be posed here are the following. Supposing that this last position is adopted, could not the messages that are presently offered by the cultural industries offer the public, more than previously, the opportunity to construct their own meaning? The question, in other words, is about a historical perspective (which, in my opinion, often is lacking in these and similar approaches.) Second question: Would this evolution from a more closed text to a more open one not have to be situated in a more global social evolution — an evolution in which the changes in the media have undoubtedly played an important role but whereby one would have to beware of any form of determinism?[1]

The position that I want to defend here is that these shifts can be explained in terms of the shift from modernity to postmodernity.[2] I will now try to sketch this shift on three interactive levels: the socio-economic, the socialisation system (thus related to identity construction) and the production of symbolic goods. With regard to the last of these, I will try to illustrate this in the second part of this chapter on the basis of changes in the television text because of the central place this medium occupies in our societies. Before beginning this sketch, however, I would like to say a word about identity.

---

[1] I have in mind, for example, the work of Meyrowitz (1985) in which often interesting observations are constantly distorted by the most rabid technological determinism in the manner of Innis and McLuhan (i.e., changes in media technology cause social changes.)

[2] For my part, those who are allergic to the concept of 'postmodernism' can use another concept like 'late modernism.'

1. Identity

First, identity, both individual and collective, is not an "essence that expresses itself," but is produced in a socialisation process. Second, identity is a matter of boundaries and of a "category system." As Morley and Robins (1989: 12) rightly point out, structuralism has taught us that people and things have no meaning or identity of themselves, but obtain it in relation to other people and things, that is, in a category system. There is no *I/we*, therefore, without an *other/they*. "Difference", according to Morley and Robins, "is consti-tutive of identity". Or, in the words of the sociolinguist Fishman (1972: 52-3): Identity is the result of a "contrastive self identifica-tion." In order then for people and things to find their position *vis-à-vis* each other in a category system, they must (and this structural-ism has also taught us) have a characteristic that simultaneously brings them together and distinguishes them. That which brings people and things in contact with each other and distinguishes them is a boundary.

Without a boundary, without contact and communication with the other/they, there is no I/we. But each contact, each communication with the other implies a threat for one's own I/we, namely, the dan-ger that one will be contaminated or even absorbed by the other (*cf.* for example, the anxiety noted above for cultural imperialism, homogenisation, Americanisation, etc.). Communication and iden-tity are thus always, as is demonstrated in the work of Lévi-Strauss (Clément, 1987), a matter of the drawing of boundaries and the preservation of the proper distance; a matter, too, as Mary Douglas (1966) has shown, of dirt and pollution. With Leach (1976: 61), who relies on Douglas here, it can be said that:

> The more sharply we define our boundaries, the more conscious we become of the dirt that has ambiguously got into the wrong side of the frontier. Boundaries become dirty by definition and we devote a great deal of effort to keeping them clean, just so that we can pre-serve confidence in our category system.

Finally, a distinction must be made with regard to identity between, on the one hand, the identity that the individual adopts in the inti-macy and informality of what Goffman (1959) has called the "back region" or "backstage" and, on the other hand, the impression that he/she gives to others in the "front region," where an attempt is expected of him/her "to give the appearance that his activity in the region maintains and embodies certain standards" (Goffman, 1959: 107). Here, too, it is again a question of how sharply the boundary between the two regions is drawn.

1.1 *From Modernity to Postmodernity*

In my sketch of the shift from modernism to postmodernism, I want to proceed from the often stated position that the shifts on the economic level are linked to a shift in the class system due to the rise of a (postmodern) post-industrial service class or 'new middle class' (cf., among others, Bell, 1973; Betz, 1992; Crook *et al.*, 1992; Featherstone, 1991a; Lash, 1990; Lash and Urry, 1987; Pakulski & Waters, 1996; Sulkunen, 1992; Vidich, 1995). In this regard, reference is often made to Bourdieu (1984: 354-71), who sarcastically describes new intellectuals or the "new *petite bourgeoisie* of new cultural intermediaries who provide symbolic goods and services" (Featherstone, 1991a: 60), the members of which refuse to find their identity in the old (modern) category system. According to Bourdieu, they see themselves as 'unclassifiable' and thus refuse "to be pinned down to a particular site in social space" (Bourdieu, 1984: 370). It is thus clear that the old (modern) categorization or classification system has lost a great deal of its relevance or, in other words, that the manner of socialisation and thus of identity constitution of the new middle class is different from that of the old one.

For the shift in education and socialisation, I will now make use of the insights of the British language and education sociologist Basil Bernstein. Bernstein has pointed out that identity and socialisation can be defined on the basis of, on the one hand, the prevailing *principles of classification*, that is — and Mary Douglas's influence is apparent here — the degree of insulation or degree of boundary maintenance applied within a culture or subculture and, on the other hand, the *principles of control*. These latter principles determine with whom the control of the socialisation process resides (and thus of the acquisition of identity), namely, with the transmitter, the one who socialises, or with the acquirer, the one who is socialized. Bernstein uses the concept of *framing* for these control principles.

For Bernstein, as regards both the principles of classification and of framing, a shift is demonstrable within what he calls the 'transmitting agencies,' such as family, work, education, the peer group, and leisure. Bernstein's ideas and concepts will now serve as my primary guidelines for the rest of this text (cf. Bernstein, 1971, 1975, 1981, 1987, 1990, 1996).[3]

1.2 From a Citizen of a Modern Nation State to a Postmodern Consumer in a Global Media and Culture of Consumption

On the socio-economic level, modernity can be related to the growing emphasis placed on capitalism, rational control and standardisation of production/consumption. Harvey (1989) and Crook *et al.* (1992), among others, speak in this context of 'Fordist modernism,' which is characterized by "relative fixity and permanence (fixed capital in mass production, stable, standardized, and homogeneous markets, a fixed configuration of political-economic influence and power, easily identifiable authority and meta-theories, secure grounding in materiality and technical-scientific rationality, and the like" (Harvey, 1989: 338-9).) This also implies the generation and development of modern industrialized and bureaucratic nation states (Crook *et al.*, 1992: 18-20; Gellner, 1983) in which the personalised and arbitrary power of the *Ancien Régime*, according to Harvey (1989: 213), is replaced by the "faceless, rational and technocratic (and hence more systematic)" power of the modern state. The modern individual must find his/her collective identity in his/her being a citizen of this state.

Although modern states were often formed by calling upon the nation, the *People*, by creating and taking advantage of ethnic longings and ethnic solidarity by an elite (Brass, 1991), there prevailed on the cultural level, as Gellner (1983) and others have noted, the policy that local linguistic and cultural diversity must disappear to be replaced by the standard language and the literate 'high' culture of this elite. For the dissemination and passing on of this language and culture, a centrally organized educational system was critical. Modernity, as we will see, was thus marked by an explicit, cultural-educational project whereby the result, or better, the objective was:

> ... the establishment of an anonymous, impersonal society, with mutually substitutable atomized individuals, held together above

---

[3] In this context, reference can be made to the work of Dimaggio in which Bernstein's concepts of 'classification' and 'framing' are operationalised in the same way as I will do. (Dimaggio, 1982a, 1982b, 1987)

all by a shared culture of this kind, in place of a previous complex
structure of local groups, sustained by folk cultures reproduced
locally and idiosyncratically by the micro-groups themselves. (Gellner, 1983: 57)

In other words, this is the well-known shift from a *gemeinschaftliche*
to a *gesellschaftliche* organisation of society, the latter being characterised by strong structural or functional differentiation (Crook *et al.*,
1992: 3-6). Here, the individual must find his/her identity in pregiven structures and ascribed roles, as will be demonstrated.

Crook *et al.* (1992: Ch. 3) argue that these modern states have
developed to become what they call "bureaucratic corporate states,"
characterised by "economic planning, central management and the
overall co-ordination of social activities. This includes, above all,
control over interest articulation." (Crook *et al.*, 1992: 84) They sketch
how Western European corporatist states, which are characterised by
a licensed pluralism, can be placed between the U.S.A., where this
corporatism is the weakest and where "despite the concentration of
power, the overall structure looks more plural, diverse and fragmented" (Crook *et al.*, 1992: 90), and the Fascist and Communist versions of the corporatist state, where, of course, there was no pluralism at all. This modern Western European pluralism does not at all
mean a postmodern "multiplicity of voices," but rather a distribution of power, money and ideological influence by "functionally
organized interest pillars" and major political parties among themselves. (Crook *et al.*, 1992: 88) Only those who are willing and have
the ability to play by the rules of the game, a game that is based on
compromising and reaching consensus, are allowed to play. We find
this licensed pluralism in all cultural institutions of the liberal corporatist states. The public broadcasting institutions of Western European states — which, I will argue below, have best realized the principles of modern television — are a good example of this.
Centralistic and bureaucratic, they are above all politically patron-
ised: Either they were forced into political and ideological neutrality
or they scrupulously had to reflect political and ideological pluralism. (McQuail *et al.*, 1992: 9)

According to Harvey (1989: 141), an economic crisis has been
developing in the West since the middle of the 1960s to which the
rigid Fordism could provide no solution. Hence, a shift can be seen
to occur to what he calls postmodern flexible accumulation: Flexibility regarding the labour process, labour market and consumption.

There is an accelerating shift from a goods economy to a service economy and to what the popular culture industry offers. From production/producer, the centre of gravity is moving to consumption/consumer. In the consumer culture thus formed, one no longer tries to homogenise and standardise consumption but, on the contrary, to react flexibly to the divergent personal desires of the consumer. This happens by means of such things as the generalised introduction of rapidly changing styles and fashions; by a segmentation of the market into "'segments', 'niches', 'lifestyles' and 'life-stages'" (Willis, 1990: 131), whereby the previously applied category system loses part of its relevance; and primarily by the selling of products not so much on the basis of their use value but on the basis of their sign value, in other words, on the basis of the meaning that these products have for the identity of the consumer. (Featherstone, 1991a, 1992a, 1995; Lash, 1990: 37-52; Leiss *et al.*, 1990) To use the words of Fiske (1987: 311): What our consumer culture offers is "meaning, pleasure, and social identity for the consumer." The subject, in other words, is invited to find his/her identity no longer in pregiven structures and ascribed roles but, by means of his/her consumption, to make, to create, to style, to design himself/herself. Featherstone speaks in this regard of the "aestheticization of everyday life" on the basis of a "rapid flow of signs and images which saturate the fabric of everyday life in contemporary society." (Featherstone, 1991a: 67) Moreover, the products and messages that are offered are produced increasingly for a global market by corporations that are becoming more and more transnational.

All of this means that an identity is much less ascribed to a subject as a citizen of a nation state, but rather, that he or she has to achieve an identity as an active member of a global consumer and media culture. The modern state itself, threatened by a move towards the local and regional and by this globalization, loses meaning and authority as a result. (Crook *et al.*, 1992: Ch. 3; Hall, 1991; Hjarvard, 1993; Morley and Robins, 1989; Ohmae, 1995) In this process, special attention has to be given to the role played by information and communication technologies. Citing Rath (1988: 203), Morley and Robins (1989: 22) state:

> ... it is undoubtedly the case that the new information and communication technologies are playing a powerful role in the emergence of new spatial structures, relations and orientations. Corporate communications networks have produced a global space of elec-

tronic information flows. The new media conglomerates are creating a global image space, a "space of transmission [that] cuts across — as a new geographic entity, which has its own sovereignty, its own guarantors — the geographies of power, of social life, and of knowledge, which define the space of nationality and of culture."

The shift I have tried to sketch above, therefore, can be summarised with Elliot (1982: 244) as a "shift from involving people in society as a political citizen of nation states towards involving them as consumption units in a corporate world." Let us now look at how this shift is accompanied by a shift in the socialisation proces.

1.3 *From Visible to Invisible Socialisation*

As already noted, the shifts sketched above are often related to what Bernstein (1975: 16) has called "the shift of emphasis in the division of labour from the production of goods to the production of services." Durkheim, according to Bernstein (1975: 121-2), described only one form of organic solidarity, namely, the form that produced *abstract individuals*. This form is characteristic of what at present can be called the old, modern class system, whereby the middle class based its power "upon ownership/control over specialised physical resources, although it would include entrepreneurial professional occupations such as lawyers, medical consultants, solicitors, accountants." (Bernstein, 1975: 18) What Durkheim could not foresee was that this form of organic solidarity would be succeeded by a new form in which the stress is placed on the *concrete person*. In other words, there is a shift from an "individualized organic solidarity" to a "personalized organic solidarity." This last form of solidarity is characteristic of and propagated by the new, post-industrial middle class or service class, which bases its power "upon ownership/control over dominant and specialized forms of communication" (Bernstein, 1975: 18).

1.3.1 *The Visible Socialisation of the Individualised Organic Solidarity*

The old, modern, working and middle class is, according to Bernstein (1971, 1975), marked by a positional role system and by what he calls visible socialisation and control. 'Positional' means that the subject, beginning with the primary socialisation in the family, is ascribed an identity through occupying positions in pregiven and highly differentiated and hierarchised structures. A positional family is thus characterized by a strong role segregation and a formal division of responsibility and power in function of age, gender, and status. The rules and norms are explicitly formulated and imposed from above on the basis of 'positional appeals': The one who is regulated, Bernstein (1971: 157) holds, is "explicitly linked to others who hold a similar universal or particular status" ('boys don't cry.') In this way, ignoring the personal unicity of the subject, one creates an *abstract individual* who knows his/her place in a functionally differentiated whole, or, as I quoted Gellner (1983: 57) above, "mutually substitutable atomized individuals." "Individuality of this kind," Fiske (1992b: 161) contends, "is a top-down product: individuals are differentiated according to the demand of the system, and individuation becomes a disciplinary mechanism." In short, in this way one creates individuals who fit into the rigid Fordist organisation of the economy and into the modern *gesellschaftliche* organisation of society. Strongly influenced by the work of Mary Douglas (*cf.* above), Bernstein states that this form of socialisation is marked by strong boundary maintenance. This implies, among other things, that this socialisation leads to "unambiguous role identities and relatively inflexible role performances." (Bernstein, 1975: 122) The subject is, in other words, highly aware of his/her specific identity, which he/she shares with others. Hence, the great sensitivity to 'dirt,' the impure, everything that affects the self from within or from without.

This, which Bernstein calls visible education or socialisation, is now marked by strong classification and framing. As noted, Bernstein uses the notion of framing to indicate where the control over the socialisation process resides. In modern socialisation, it resides with the one who socializes and thus the process takes place top down. Strong classification is marked by strong boundary maintenance between people and things. I have already pointed out that this strong and continuous structural or functional differentiation is generally considered one of the most salient characteristics of modernity.

Three comments can now be made with regard to these matters. First, as stated, the modern state, although based on a strong functional differentiation or classification, is marked by a constant striving to impose a unifying, supracommunal language and culture. (Bauman, 1992: 7) Each culture, of course, classifies and each classification contains a hierarchy and value judgements. Typical for modernity, according to Gellner (1983: 10-11) and Bauman (1992: 7), however, is that the higher must supplant the lower, that is, in the words of Bauman, "mere superiority turned into hegemony." The high, literate culture must supplant the low popular culture, the standard language the dialects, the universal standards of truth the local conceptions and misconceptions. The explicit educational project that is implied by this is based on the idea that human beings can be improved, humanised, civilised. (Bauman, 1992: 3)

Second, the task that the modern intellectual sees for himself/herself in all of this is two-fold. First, "as prospective and potential legislator" (Featherstone, 1991a: 140), to create order, to set and supervise boundaries and standards, to combat deviation. Second, as "confident educator, who possesses confidence in his judgement of taste and the need to mould society in terms of it" (Featherstone, ibidem), to integrate the subject into this ordering. Hence, the missionary drive, the proselytism, the idea of a cultural crusade of the modern intellectual. (Bauman, 1992)

Third, the discourse that ultimately constitutes the hallmark of the modern intellectual can be described as rational and decontextualised and as having universal pretensions. Authors like Gouldner (1976), Stallybrass and White (1986), Bauman (1992), and Gellner (1992) describe how since the Reformation and the Enlightment a rational public discourse has been developed with which the modern individual attempts to acquire autonomy for himself/herself. The right was demanded to investigate reality, to produce universal truth and to create order exclusively on the basis of the facts on the one hand, and, on the other, on the basis of the "eternal and unchangeable laws of reason." Gouldner (1976) speaks in this regard of an ideal of a self-grounded rationality: Between the facts and the rational judgement nothing may any longer intervene, and, therefore, one can no longer legitimate one's claim to the truth by referring, for example, to the magisterium of the Church, the tradition, local morals and customs, or the *doxa* of the community, that is, the "opinions and beliefs of common understanding." (Bauman, 1992: 116) This discourse must also be separated from the concrete communication context. It may, in other words, no longer draw its power of persuasion from contingent factors such as the personal characteristics of the sender (his/her *ethos*) or by taking advantage of the emotions of the public (*pathos*). What remains is *logos*, a discourse out of which the sender and the receiver, as creatures of flesh and blood with their desires and emotions, have to evacuate themselves. (Featherstone, 1992b: 161) Gouldner (1976) speaks here of decontextualisation. Stallybrass and White (1986: 97) note that "the emergence of the public sphere required that its spaces of discourse be *delibidinized* in the interests of serious, productive and *rational* intercourse."

It is in this way that this discourse produces an 'I' that can distinguish and knows to distinguish itself from the others. (Maffesoli, 1988: 188) This 'I' cannot be considered a concrete person, but is an abstract individual, an author constructed on the basis of his/her discourse, situatable, quotable, and thus of significance in a particular discursive field, which, in its turn, has been separated from daily life. It is in this way also that the modern individual becomes master of himself, becomes an autonomous individual with an autonomous discourse. On the one hand, he/she liberates himself/herself from external authorities, "from the court and the church on the one hand and the market square, alehouse, street and fairground on the other." (Stallybrass and White, 1986: 93-4) On the other hand, the internal forces that threaten to overwhelm the rational ego are also suppressed/sublimated (the irrational, the 'lower', the bodily, the emotional, the libidinal.) One can equally state that this is the price that the modern individual must pay for his/her autonomy. It is only by yielding the communal ties with the others and by the suppressing of his/her desires that he/she acquires this mastery. (Bauman, 1992; Friedman, 1988; Lash, 1990)

1.3.2 *The Invisible Socialisation of the Personalized Organic Solidarity*

As stated above, there now stands opposed to the modern visible socialisation the invisible socialisation of postmodernity, with its weak classification and weak framing. Bourdieu (1984: 219) speaks in this regard of a 'gentle, invisible education.' This invisible socialisation, according to Bernstein, no longer produces abstract individuals but *concrete persons*. A similar notion is also met in Maffesoli (1988: 93), who is of the opinion that one can show a shift from *modern individuals*, typified by contractual, rational associations, to *postmodern persons*, who seek out each other in affective 'tribes.' He uses here the concept of person in its etymological meaning (persona = player's mask) in order to indicate the flexible, the underdetermined, the 'tragically superficial' of the postmodern subject. (Maffesoli, 1988: 98-99; see also Shields, 1992)

Long before the concept of postmodernism was launched and such ideas became popular, all this was already formulated by Bernstein:

> Whereas the concept of the *individual* leads to specific, unambiguous role identities and relatively inflexible role performances, the concept of the *person* leads to ambiguous personal identity and flexible role performances. (Bernstein, 1975: 122)

And in 1996 Bernstein worked this idea out in this way:

> Much has been written about postmodernism, late modernism, and the localising of identities (...) and I have no wish to rehearse this literature here. However, it does seem clear that, in the old speak, those identities which were given a biological focus (age, gender, age relation), 'ascribed identities', have been considerably weakened, are ambiguous and to some extent can be achieved. These cultural punctuations and specialisations (age, gender, age relation) are now weak resources for the construction of identities with a stable and collective base. Further, again in the old speak, locational 'achieved' identities of class and occupation have become weak resources for stable unambiguous identities. This weakening of stable, unambiguous, collective resources for the construction of identities, consequent upon this new period of transitional capitalism, has brought about disturbance and disembedding of identities and so created the possibility of new identity constructions. (Bernstein, 1996: 76)

For Bernstein (1971: 153), the socialisation that is person-oriented is marked by a "reduced segregation and less formal definition of roles." Hence, abstract, standardised individuals are no longer produced, but the subject is communicated with on the basis of his/her "unique social, affective and cognitive characteristics." (Bernstein, 1971: 157) In this way, the subject must achieve a particular identity, an identity that is ascribed from above in the visible socialisation. The socialisation is, in other words, such that the subject is invited (or thinks he/she is entitled) to construct his/her own role and identity by means of interaction with others. In this way, according to Bernstein (1971: 185) "the boundary between self and other is blurred." Elsewhere, he states: "Strong, well-marked social types are less likely to be produced, for here selves are inextricably interrelated." (Bernstein, 1975: 10) In the words of Maffesoli (1988: 87): While the modern individual, who is free *de jure*, enters into relations with others on a rational-contractual basis, the postmodern person is tributary to others. In this way, a flexible subject (weak classification) is created who must socialise himself/herself in interaction with others (weak framing) and is capable of coping "with ambiguity and ambivalence." (Bernstein, 1971: 154) To this can be added that rules and norms are no longer imposed from above. The subject, on the contrary, must acquire them himself/herself within specific communication contexts. This means also that, to cite Bauman (1992: 202), these "negotiated rules remain by and large precarious and under-determined." In short, the new middle class "stand[s] for variety against inflexibility, expression against repression, the inter-personal against the interpositional." (Bernstein, 1975: 123) It is in this way that subjects are produced which fit perfectly into the post-Fordist flexible accumulation and into the growing service economy in which one must deal more with people and less with objects.

In a (rare) moment of playfulness (and clarity,) Bernstein (1975: 142-145) illustrates his theory by means of the gradual distinction between two lavatories. On the one end of the continuum, he situates a lavatory that looks totally like a lavatory (neat, everything in its place, nothing that does not belong there) and is used exclusively as a lavatory. There is a door that can be locked. This is the modern lavatory, with its strong classification and framing: there is a concept of a lavatory, and everything that does not fit into it does not belong in it; there is a sharp partition between the lavatory and the other spaces; every improper use, every blurring is absolutely forbidden. All of this is based on explicit, easy to understand rules and visible authorities (strong framing): "all that is needed is the following of the command 'Leave the space as you found it.'" (Bernstein, 1975: 144) Therefore, modernity is based

> ... on the rule 'things must be kept apart,' be they persons, acts, objects, communication; and the stronger the classification and frames, the greater the insulation, the stronger the boundaries between classes of persons, acts, communications. (Bernstein, 1975: 143)

The result of this is, as stated, that 'pollution is highly visible' (Bernstein, 1975: 142) in modernity and that the modern individual is very sensitive to contamination, the lower, the other, the alien. (Stallybrass and White, 1986) This system, however, also has its advantages: those who use the modern lavatory lock the door behind them. In other words, there is a sharp separation between the public and the private self, between front region and back region behaviour. Time and space are given to the modern subject in which he/she can withdraw from the control of the others. (Bernstein, 1975: 143)

The postmodern lavatory looks entirely different. Here, the apparent 'anything goes' of postmodernism applies, with its chaos, eclecticism, and deformalisation. The walls are covered with posters; reading material is scattered around; the towel does not hang in its place; if there is a door, it cannot be locked. Moreover, the users often leave it open so that there is communication between the lavatory and the other spaces (weak classification.) Explicit rules and visible authorities are lacking: the user must discover the prevailing principles for himself/herself (weak framing.) Postmodernism is, therefore, based on the rule "things must be put together" (Bernstein, 1975: 144) and has been oriented to something that is abhorrent to the modern subject, namely, the creation of ambiguity. (Bernstein, 1971: 166) By the blurring of the boundaries between the public and the private, the front and the back region, however, all of this also means that it is much more difficult for the subject to evade the implicit control of the others. Postmodernism, one could say, creates social situations that come across as relaxed and informal, that encourage personal expression, creativity, and choice, and where no explicit hierarchy or authority is present. At the same time, however, the possibility of total control that embraces all aspects of life is built in. The subject, in other words, is invited (has the duty) to open himself/herself in the affective and emotional proximity of Maffesoli's (1988) postmodern tribes:

> At the level of classification the pollution is 'keeping things apart'; at the level of framing the violation is 'withholding'; that is, not offering, not making visible the self. (Bernstein, 1975: 140)

All of this does not mean that what previously remained hidden in the private sphere, the back region, or what belonged to the most intimate thoughts, desires, and emotions of the subject is now brought out in public. Rather, one must state with Meyrowitz (1985) (in his discussion of the effects of television) that this blurring of the boundaries between front and back regions has created a "middle region," that is, a behavioral pattern that "contains elements of both the former onstage and offstage behaviours but lacks their extremes." (Meyrowitz, 1985: 47) This observation of a reduction of contrasts, of sharp opposition, and an increase of variation, is described in the sociology of civilisation of Norbert Elias as a process of increasing informalisation whereby, as Wouters (1990: 144-5) notes, it is expected that the subject will open himself/herself more to the other but also that he/she will regulate this self-disclosure in a more subtle and more flexible manner. What Wouters calls "controlled decontrolling" (cf. also Featherstone, 1991a: 59) is, in other words, nothing other than what Meyrowitz describes as middle-region behaviour. I will elaborate on this in the second part of this chapter.

All of this can be found in the pre-school and infant pedagogy of the new middle class. (Bernstein, 1975: Chapters 5 and 6) I will examine this briefly in order to introduce certain aspects of the invisible socialisation that I will need to explain certain shifts within the television discourse to be discussed in the second part. More specifically, this addresses the shift from the Protestant work ethic to what has been called the hedonistic and therapeutic ethic of the postmodern subject. (cf. Bell, 1976) By this I mean, first of all, the obsession of the postmodern subject that everything that he/she does must be pleasurable:

> Thus, whereas the old morality of duty, based on the opposition between pleasure and good, induces a generalised suspicion of the 'charming and attractive,' a fear of pleasure and a relation to the body made up of 'reserve', 'modesty' and 'restraint,' and associates every satisfaction of the forbidden impulses with guilt, the new ethical avant-garde urges a morality of pleasure as a duty. (Bourdieu, 1984: 367)

Second, and linked to this, there is the constant duty 'to work on oneself.' In other words, the concept "of the self as an enterprise", as Bonner and du Gay (1992: 88) express it, dominates. (cf, also Lasch, 1979; Lipovetsky, 1983; Lears, 1983; Leiss et al., 1990)

Typical for this pedagogy, therefore, is, first of all, the blurring between learning and playing, between labour and entertainment: "play is work and work is play." (Bernstein, 1975: 118) Second, the child is invited (obliged) in this play with others to explore and express himself or herself, while the educator remains in the background observing and evaluating: "play is the means by which the

child exteriorizes himself" (Bernstein, 1975: 118.) This invisible pedagogy develops in the child the sensitivity for his/her unique self
("implicit nurture reveals unique nature" (Bernstein, 1975: 120)) and
creates in this way what has come to be called contemporary narcissism (Lasch, 1979), whereby the subject receives the life-long task
(right) to work on this unique self. Hence, as Bourdieu (1984: 367)
notes, the drive of the postmodern subject not to place experiences
and problems in a more general and abstract framework ('politicisa-
tion'), but to personalize them much more via 'moralisation' and
'psychologisation'.

All of this, Bourdieu (1984: 368) goes on to say, can only happen
"when 'relating' to others ('sharing experiences') through the inter-
mediary of the body treated as a sign and not as an instrument." (cf.
also Featherstone, 1991b) In this seeking out of others, therefore, a
return to a certain form of a *Gemeinschaft* becomes visible, but then
"more (...) on the basis of *Wahlverwandtschaft* than on the basis of
inherited or ascribed characteristics." (Dobbelaere, 1991: 221 — my
translation) In this way, society is segmented and fragmented in
often ephemeral, coalescing and dissolving, 'emotional-affective
communities,' 'communicative networks,' 'tribes,' 'proto-communi-
ties,' etc. without strong organisation, project, or cause. Membership
involves no long-term obligations and can easily be revoked. (Meyrowitz, 1985: 315-7; Balandier, 1985: 160; Maffesoli, 1988; Willis, 1990;
Sulkunen, 1992)

Typical for such communities is, first of all, that they often take
form within what can be called the 'media- and consumer culture,'
whereby consumption, as stated above, "must not be understood as
the consumption of use-values, a material utility, but primarily as
the consumption of signs." (Featherstone, 1991a: 85) It is in this way
that different groups develop their own style and identity and so
distinguish themselves from the others (Featherstone, 1991a: Chap.
6; Bauman, 1992: 223).

Second, it must be noted with Willis (1990: 141) that such groups
both can come into existence on the basis of "direct communication
around a 'consuming interest'" and can be "serial", that is, "not connected through direct communication but through shared styles,
fashions, interests, empathies, positions and passions — sometimes
shared simultaneously 'off-air' through the communication media."

Third, since the subject must fill in his/her identity himself/her-
self, the messages within this consumer culture must be produced in

such a way that they deliver the subject material for this filling in. The principle of the self-socialisation of the subject by means of consumption, in other words, implies open texts that acquire a specific meaning only in consumption. Willis calls this "made messages" and speaks of the "grounded aesthetics" of a "common culture," whereby — and one recognizes in this all the principles of invisible socialisation — identity is now constructed "from below" and in "leisure and play": "Making (not receiving) messages in your own context and from materials you have appropriated is, in essence, a form of education in the broadest sense." (Willis, 1990: 136)

With regard to the postmodern subject, therefore, one speaks of a 'self-constitutor' (Poster, 1990: 68; Bauman, 1992: 193, ff.), a *bricoleur* (Hebdige, 1979: 102-4), a nomadic subject (Meyrowitz, 1985; Balandier, 1985: 204; Grossberg, 1987; Melucci, 1989). In any event, this shift "from what Jameson (1984) calls a depth (stage) model of autonomous selves with inner essence and outward expression to a surface (screen) model of an interconnected self constituted in a network of relationships" (Tseëlon, 1992: 121) is now accompanied by a shift on the level of the production of meaning. Since these postmodern communities, as Willis suggests, are often not based on direct communication, but on what Balandier (1988: 168) has called "mediated proximity," and so can be described as electronic communities or networks (Ang and Morley, 1989; Morley, 1992b), I will treat this shift in the remainder of this chapter on the basis of the shifts within the textual universe of television.

2. From Paleo- to Neo-Television

An interesting sketch of these changes is given by Casetti and Odin (1990), who speak of a shift from *paleo-television* to *neo-television*.[4] Paleo-television is modern television, best realized in the Western European public broadcasting institutions before their monopolies were broken in the 1980s and the mediascape was shaken up by "commercialisation, internationalisation, decentralisation and indus-

---

[4] It is noteworthy that both Hayward and Kerr (1987: 7) and Connel and Curti (1985: 102-3) refer to Umberto Eco (who is not actually named by Casetti and Odin) with regard to this distinction. Further, one can point out that, for Casetti and Odin, neither of the two types occur in a pure form but that a clear evolution to neo-television is demonstrable.

trialisation" (Siune *et al.*, 1992: 2), which marked the beginning of era of the neo- or postmodern television.

2.1 *Paleo-Television*

Typical for this kind of television, according to McQuail *et al.* (1992: 9), is its national character. It was designed

> ... to serve audiences and social institutions within the national territory, centre-peripheral in form of organisation, expected to protect national language and culture and (however implicitly) to represent the national interest. As an aspect of their national character, broadcasting institutions were also usually monopolistic or quasi-monopolistic in their form of control.

The task of paleo-television was, therefore, to contribute to the creation of what one can, with Anderson (1983), call an 'imagined community' for the modern nation state. (Ang, 1991; Brants and Siune, 1992; Martin-Barbero, 1993; Morley and Robinson, 1991; Scannel, 1990) In other words, the public broadcasting institutions were expected to create a particular public sphere, an audio-visual space for the state. Following the principles of modern strong classification, an imaginary boundary was drawn between a *we* and a *they*, the latter being those the broadcasters were not addressing (regardless of wether or not they could receive the broadcasts.) (Van den Bulck and Van Poecke, 1996a, 1996b) In this regard, television had the following classic and explicitly formulated responsibility: *popular education*, as an extension of the national educational system; *information*, to which every citizen of a modern state has the right (and the obligation); and *entertainment*, "to encourage the expression of a national culture ... to create a new cultural community around televised works, domestic or foreign." (Desaulniers, 1986: 114) In other words, together with the rest of the cultural apparatus, television, by means of education, information, and entertainment (which had to be strictly segregated from each other) had to promote social integration, supracommunal homogeneity, and assimilation into the dominant, high culture:

> There was the idea of television as a centripetal, societally integrative force. In Katz's (1985) words, it offered 'the opportunity of shared experience . . . contributing to authenticity by connecting the society to its cultural centre and acquainting the segments of society with each other. (Blumler, 1992a: 11)

This does not mean that modern television offered no diversity or was not pluralistic. On the contrary, diversity and pluralism were values that modern television thrust strongly to the fore and that are now being threatened after "the commercial deluge." (Blumler, 1992a, 1992b) But this diversity and this pluralism meant (and can mean nothing else than) the licensed pluralism described above. In practice, this meant that power and influence were neatly divided among the most important interest pillars and political parties. They were the ones who, from the point of view of their ideology, interests, concerns, values, and taste, determined what the interests, concerns, values, and taste would be of the audience groups they thought they represented. Modern or paleo-television followed in this respect the double movement that marks modern society: On the one hand, a strong differentiation between groups and categories of people; on the other hand, the need to bind these groups with each other, to bring them in contact with each other, and thus to integrate them into a structured whole.

> Individual audience members, differing in taste and concerns, should also have a wide range of selection and choice, while the chance of coming into contact with the interests and ways of life of others should encourage the understanding and tolerance on which democracy depends. (Blumler, 1992b: 32)

This was expressed the best in the unique Dutch system in which each recognized pillar on the social level was assigned a broadcasting pillar. (McQuail, 1992a)

Diversity in programming also meant that sufficient popular entertainment had to be present. But, here too, the principles of the modern, visible pedagogy with its sharp demarcation between seriousness and pleasure, between work and play applied. On the basis of the philosophy "after playtime, back to the classroom," entertainment was used to lure the audience to the better programmes (Burns, 1977: 42) — a strategy that could hardly fail because of the monopoly position held. "In the past, our public, after entertainment, also watched the better programmes. Now they stay with the banalities," complains Karel Hemmerechts, who for years helped determine the policy of Flemish public broadcasting. (Hemmerechts, 1990. My translation.)

In short, modern television was marked by the "cultural-educational or cultural-pedagogic logic" (Brants and Siune, 1992: 110) described above. The result was that, both for those who set broadcasting policy and for those who implemented it, the idea was strongly and explicitly present that television was one of the most powerful weapons in what Bauman (1992: 97) has called the cultural crusade of the modern intellectual: the people must be educated, emancipated, liberated from their backwardness, their prejudices, their vulgar pleasures, and their dialects. The medium must convey the best of what was created artistically and intellectually, and the public must be given the opportunity to become acquainted with it (Blumler, 1992a). Thus, it need not be surprising that modern television was "colonized by the intellectuals of the professional middle class." (Elliot, 1982: 250) As "legislator and educator" (*cf. supra*), the modern intellectual felt perfectly at home in this visible pedagogy. He/she considered himself/herself to be "the viewer's guide to whatever was culturally worthwhile" (Blumler, 1992a: 11) and saw his/her audience as vulnerable and helpless (an argument that was used to repel every attack on the monopoly.) "From this notion of the audience", Richard Collins argues, "follows the need for a protector, a Platonic Guardian required to regulate broadcasting in the audience's interest because the audience is unable to identify its own interests unaided." (Collins, 1989: 14)

As is known, the benevolent paternalism that typifies paleo-television was realized in its sharpest form in the *Reithian Ethos* that marked the BBC, the mother of all public broadcasting institutions, in its initial period. (Ang, 1991; Scannel, 1990) Reith's philosophy was "to give the public a little more than it wants" (cited in Leitner, 1983: 58), whereby it was ultimately the educator, according to the principles of the visible pedagogy with its strong framing, who knew what the subject who was to be educated really wanted. "It is occasionally indicated to us," Reith stated, "that we are apparently setting out to give the public what we think they need — and not what they want, but few know what they want, and very few what they need." (Cited in Briggs, 1988: 55) And although this paternalism gradually lost its sharp Reithian edges, it remained the case that "despite the greater pluralism of public broadcasting in the 1960s and 1970s 'ordinary people' were still spoken about far more often than they spoke for themselves." (Murdock, 1992: 31) In Schrøder (1992: 199-203), one can read how calls for quality in television even in the 1980s needed to yield nothing to Reith.

Now all of this had its repercussions on the programming and the textual strategies of modern television. Founded on an explicit, cultural-educational project, according to Casetti and Odin (1990: 10-1), paleo-television functions on the basis of what they call a "vectorised pedagogical contract" whereby the audience, as it were, constituted one large class with the broadcaster as their schoolmaster. (McQuail's *transmission model* of mass communication; *cf.* McQuail, 1994: 49-50; Ang, 1991: 29)

This pedagogical contract may be described as follows. The object is to transfer various forms of knowledge. The communication process has the form of one-way traffic, whereby total control was in the hands of the broadcaster and in which there is a strong differentiation and hierarchisation of the roles: there are those who possess knowledge and those to whom one wishes to communicate this knowledge. The programme flow is so conceived that each programme component is clearly distinct from the others and that the broadcaster and receiver are bound by a specific sub-contract for each component. The latter intends a sharp separation between the three classic genres — information, education, entertainment — and should also be interpreted as such by the receiver (this is information and must be received as information, etc.) There is also a clear differentiation between the audience groups. Although this kind of television is based on the idea of a "regular mass television audience viewing the main national channel" (McQuail *et al.*, 1992: 15-6), the various programmes are aimed at audience groups that could be distinguished on the basis of the modern interpositional category system (for adults, children, women, the man in the street, intellectuals, etc.) In short, paleo-television manifests all the characteristics of the sharp boundaries and the strong framing of visible socialisation that marks the modern positional family. It is thus these families to which paleo-television directed itself: "breadwinner father, homemaker mother and growing up children." (Haralovich, 1988: 38) The best characterisation of these concepts of television, I still think, is the way in which the Glasgow Media Group (1980: 251) described the newsreader in the classic news programme: a schoolmaster at his lectern with a blackboard behind him, in the form of devices such as back projection or chromokey.

2.2 Neo-Television

2.2.1 The New Television Marketplace

In the beginning of the 1980s, there arose what Blumler (1991) calls "the new television marketplace." The breakdown of the oligopolistic (United States) or monopolistic (Europe) system created a "new and hectic competitive environment... engendered by multichannel television." (Blumler, 1991: 195) The increasing competition that this deregulation engendered, together with the introduction or increasing spread of new communication technologies and the fact that more and more families owned several television sets caused the same shift occurring in broadcasting that we saw when we spoke of the evolution from a Fordist to a post-Fordist economy. Broadcasters are no longer assured of a stable and faithful audience that they can subdivide according to the standard category system, but they are now confronted with an audience that segments itself in function of personal taste and preference, that has an enormous range of choice available to it, and that reacts unpredictably to what is offered. (cf. also McQuail, 1992b: 312; Eco, 1994: 110). There is, in other words, as regards the control over the communication process (framing,) a shift from the producer to the consumer. Moreover, while the Western European public broadcasting institutions maintained a sturdy linkage between culture and politics but remained free from commercial influences, they, too, are now confronted with what Ang (1991:29), using a concept of McQuail (1987:44-6; 1994:51-2), calls the attention (or publicity) model of American commercial television. In this model the audience is not seen as "a public to be served with enlightened responsibility" (Ang, 1991: 29), as citizens to whom, following the principles of the *transmission model*, information has to be dispersed and who have to be united around a specific national culture and specific national values and opinions, but rather as a market which has to be conquered. In this model, the communication process is seen as succesful as soon as the receiver pays attention to the message, whatever the quality or the impact of the message may be. In this sense, audio-visual products are not seen as cultural products, but as another service, aiming at the largest possible audience (which in turn can be sold to the advertisers.)

> Television is a business, more or less like any other, and a broadcasting market, shaped by consumers' viewing decisions, is analogous to a popular democracy, governed by citizens' voting decisions. As channels increase, broadcasters should be transformed from public trustees to marketplace competitors, and 'the public interest should be defined by the public's interest.' (Fowler and Brenner, 1981) Presumed societal and cultural goods are subordinate or irrelevant in this model — at any rate they simply have to

take their chances in the rough and tumble of marketplace outcomes. (Blumler, 1991: 195-6)

Additionally, the pressure to gain the largest possible number of
viewers, the uncertainty about the audience's reactions to a particular product and the ever increasing production costs, force the large
media companies to produce more and more products which are
acceptable to "multiple markets, both domestic... and global."
(Blumler, 1991: 202)

Ang (1991), amongst others, has shown how the Western-Euro-
pean public broadcasting organisations have tried to counter the crisis in which they found themselves as a result of deregulations, privatisation, and increasing competition, by relinquishing their
patronising philosophy and by moving strongly towards this attention model, "thinking in terms of 'what the audience wants' rather
than 'what it needs.'" (Ang, 1991: 166) All this threatens the characteristics of modern television — its national character, the functions
that it saw itself serve, the values for which it stood. "The term
'national culture' fits the reality of television less and less though it
has been an important goal in the past and in a programmatic and
'scaled up version' promises to do so in the future", states Richard
Collins (1990: 200), who, with this last clause, alludes to the idea —
a modern idea *par excellence* — of creating a European 'national'
identity via a European media culture. The transnationalisation of
the culture, Collins goes on to say, means that "in time *cuius regio
eius culturo* will be as quaint an archaism as *cuius regio eius religio.*"

It is within this changing constellation that Bourdieu's 'new intellectuals' or new *petite bourgeoisie* will take over the place of the old
modern intellectuals. As the 'avant garde' in the postmodernisation
process, they are armed as no other to play a crucial role in the
process "of producing and reproducing skilful and eager consumers,
rather than obedient and willing subjects of the state." (Bauman,
1992: 17)

As indicated, these shifts have repercussions on the textual strategies of television. The function of modern television was to create an
'imagined community' that was situated *outside* the medium,
namely, the creation of national identity and solidarity. The medium
is, therefore, used in this pedagogical project as an instrument to
achieve an external objective. This is no longer the case in neo-television. In view of the internal dynamic of the medium itself and of

the more general developments at the economic and social level, neo-television now has a different function. Neo-television does not create an 'imagined community' outside the medium. Instead the medium constitutes together with its audience its own postmodern 'electronic community,' with the constitution of such communities as a goal in itself. Postmodern communities, according to Maffesoli (1988: 30), possess no project, for all the energy is expended in their own creation. They are *in actu*. The contract for Casetti and Odin (1990), who are clearly influenced by Maffesoli, is therefore replaced by the *contact*. The same point of view is found in Eco.

> The principal characteristic of neo-television is that it speaks less and less (...) of the outside world. It talks about itself and of the contact made with its own audience. It doesn't matter what it might say and of what it might speak (...) [N]eo-television tries to hold the viewer, saying to him: 'I'm here, I'm me, and I'm you.' (Cited in Connel and Curti, 1985: 103)

If one wishes to use Jakobson's now classic typology of the language functions, one can say that the phatic function dominates in neo-television. (*cf.* also Martin-Barbero, 1993: 216-8) This function is fulfilled when that which is said is less important than that something is said and that, in this way, a contact, a bond of solidarity is created or reconfirmed. Small talk fills this function perfectly. (Jakobson, 1960) If the metaphor of the classroom can be used for modern television (in its ideal form,) then the metaphor of the neighbourhood, the living room, or the local pub, *Café du Commerce*, is indicated for postmodern television (in its ideal form.) (Casetti and Odin, 1990: 13; cf. also Maffesoli, 1988: 26)

In the remainder of this chapter, I will try to discuss this shift on the basis of a number of specific characteristics of neo-television. These characteristics I will try to place in three groups.

First, in neo-television there is a blurring of the previous boundaries between genres, programme components, and audiences.

Second, and this seems to me to be the most central characteristic in the light of my thesis that postmodern television constitutes a community in itself, there is a blurring of the boundary between the public and the private sphere. (*cf.* Silverstone, 1994)

Third, this blurring between the institutional and the everyday is strongly enhanced by the shift of the centre of gravity from the sender to the receiver in the communication process of postmodern television. Concretely, this means that texts are produced which are 'open', to which a certain meaning is given only in the reception. In other words, postmodern television produces an active viewing audience.

2.2.2 *Things Must Be Put Together*

Postmodern dedifferentiation, i.e., the blurring of boundaries, makes *hybridisation* one of the most salient characteristics of our time. In regard to neo-television, of course, one must first of all mention the often criticised blurring of the differences (and thus also the breakdown of the hierarchy) between the programme categories of 'information,' 'education,' and 'entertainment,' In addition, the blurring of the boundaries between work and play, between seriousness and entertainment, in short the 'fun ethic' of postmodernism (Bourdieu, 1984: 368-9) causes the 'new television marketplace' to be affected by what Blumler (1991: 206-7) calls 'a hedonistic bias.' As a result, the blurring between the previous, sharply divided categories not only gives rise to the development of hybrid genres but also to the contamination of the higher (information, education) by the lower (entertainment): *infotainment* — news as a show, dramatic entertainment, story telling, happy talk, as part of popular culture (Brants, 1998; Altheide and Snow, 1991: 46-47; Blumler and Gurevitch, 1995, 1996; Connell and Curti, 1985: 106; Dahlgren and Sparks, 1992; Hartley, 1982: 46-7; 142-6; Larsen, 1992; Snow, 1983: 141); *edutainment*;[5] *infomercials*; *reality shows* (Wegener, 1994), etc. In neo-television, according to Casetti and Odin (1990: 17), contamination and syncretism have become the principles of organisation. The prototype in this regard is what they call the *omnibus* programme, a mix of variety show, information, game shows, and advertising. With regard to such 'hold-all programs,' Connell and Curti react as follows to the complaints about the increasing contamination of 'the factual' and 'the serious' by the 'fictional' and the 'frivolous':

[5] In the 'scientific show series' (a ghastly combination to modern ears) on the body (*Over mijn lijf*) of the Flemish Public Broadcasting Company (BRTN), use was made on 2 October 1991 of such elements as a ballerina, bodybuilders (male/female), tightrope walkers, an elephant, two people from the public (male/female) who had to get drunk during the broadcast. Another good example of the evolution to the creation of hybrid genres are the highly controversial advertising campaigns of *Benetton* in which the advertising message is also used to make a moralising statement to the world.

What is fundamentally at stake here is not only the categorisation of different cultural areas, but also their ranking. Broadly, 'fictional' and 'entertainment' forms are ranked as inferior, and it is this which inspires all the concerns about increasing spectacularization and fictionalization of popular broadcasting. (1985: 106-7)

Many critics, according to Connell and Curti, who follow the principles of the invisible pedagogy ('My playing is my learning,') "often find it difficult to accept that entertainment can not only be informative but also explanatory and educative."

This increasing trend to de-differentiation can also be derived from the fact that, where in modern television the programme components had been neatly divided from each other, postmodern television is marked by a continuous flow. (Casetti and Odin, 1990: 110) Raymond Williams (1989: 24-29) was one of the first to point this out after what was for him a disconcerting encounter with American television. In the meantime, this phenomenon has become generalised, and television is marked more and more by "a continuous succession of images which follows no laws of logic or cause and effect, but which constitutes the cultural experience of 'watching television.'" (Fiske, 1987: 98) MTV is a good example of this, but this trend is present elsewhere too. Thus, Larsen compared the way in which the Norwegian public broadcasting station (NRK) broadcasts the news (still in the 'modern' way in discrete units that find their place in a hierarchical structure) with the way in which CNN works:

> The CNN programme, on the other hand, is an example of the never-ending 'flow' characteristic of most modern international commercial television systems. Most of the time, short segments, usually no more than two minutes long, follow after each other — 'headlines,' 'updates,' 'reports' and 'interviews' are mixed with commercials, promos and trailers for coming attractions. (Larsen, 1992: 129)

Third, there is a shift in the way in which the public is perceived. The situation of modern television is paradoxical in this respect. On the one hand, one knew that one had a mass audience (the viewer had no other choice); on the other hand, as we have noted, this audience was subdivided on the basis of standard socio-economic criteria so that programmes and audience groups contrasted sharply with one another. The situation of postmodern television is totally different. As I have cited Blumler above and as is also noted by Casetti and Odin (1990: 16), neo-television attempts to address everyone, so that the more specific programmes (sports, films, news, music, culture, etc.) are now more reserved for specialty channels, which often must be paid for. The disappearance of the sharpest contrasts reminds Meyrowitz (1976: 176) of a cocktail party where the guest-list is expanded "to include people of all ages, classes, races, religions, occupations, and ethnic backgrounds." Hence, according to Meyrowitz (*ibid.*), less and less distinction is made between "'men's programming' and 'women's programming' or between 'adult programs' and 'children's programs.'" In other words, television is here following what I have noted above as the reduction of contrasts and the increase of variations. The contrasts between programmes and between population categories, which are so typical for the modern strong classification, blur and, on both levels (categories of programmes and of the population) one can speak of variations. It is on the basis of this blurred but not eliminated group identity that the public now chooses from the large supply of programmes, offered by multi-channel television, and in this way segments itself. The result is that "[t]here will be many more different audiences and 'sets' of viewers or readers, constantly recomposing along lines of taste and consumption patterns." (McQuail, 1992b: 310) While the strategy of modern television used to consist of bringing the different categories of the population together in one nationwide audience and, by means of strong diversification in the programming, have them become acquainted with each other, we now have a situation that is described by Morley (1992: 289) as "the era of narrow casting and audience segmentation", in which "it may well be (...) that many of us will have less broadcast 'experience' in common with anyone else."

2.2.3 *Television as the Extension of Everyday Life*

The second group of characteristics concerns the blurring between the public and the private sphere. I have indicated above how modernity produces a public discourse that can be called 'decontextualised,' which implies, among other things, that it must be separated from everyday life and must struggle out of the *doxa*. In neo-television, a recontextualization is now demonstrable. Neo-television, which replaces the pedagogical contract by contact, the hierarchical relationship by a relationship of proximity, is, according to Casetti and Odin (1990: 12), no longer a space where people are formed from the outside and from above, but a space that is marked by conviviality. The television personnel and studio audience, on the one hand, and the home audience, on the other, constitute one single community.

Thus, typical for postmodern television discourse is that it takes the form, to use the words of Bernstein (1975: 117), of "an ongoing inter-actional present in which the past is invisible and so implicit." Expressed less academically: neo-television can be seen as the extension (sometimes the replacement) of the babble of everyday life (Casetti and Odin, 1990: 13), with characteristics such as: "an emphasis upon the present" and "an emphasis upon heterogeneous knowledge, the disorderly babble of many tongues." (Featherstone, 1992b: 161) In this respect, neo-television exploits fully 'the now-ness' or 'presentness' of the medium (*cf.* Fiske, 1987: 22; Flitterman-Lewis, 1992: 218), i.e., the characteristic that, whatever is broadcast, it always has a life-character in one way or another such that "events are somehow co-present with the viewer, shared rather than witnessed from outside." (Ellis, 1992: 137) At the same time, neo-television understands more clearly than paleo-television that, unlike movies, it is not the picture but the sound that is the most important. (*cf.* Altman, 1986; Ellis, 1992; Martin-Barbero, 1993: 217; Morse, 1985)

This clearly conversational, interactive character of neo-television is expressed not only in the massive presence and popularity of genres in which little happens but in which there is all the more talk, such as *talk shows*, *sitcoms*, and *soaps*, but also from the fact that, more than previously, the capabilities of the medium for direct address are used. (Allen, 1992: 113-27) In neo-television, the television personnel not only constantly converse with each other but also constantly address themselves directly and as naturally as possible to the viewer, who, moreover, is invited to participate and react as actively as possible. The viewer not only can participate as a member of the studio audience but also is invited to react at home immediately by telephone (e.g., *televoting*) or by mail after the broadcast or, even better, by videopost and so on (Rath, 1988: 36). Typical for this, as Casetti and Odin (1990: 14-5) observe, is the evolution in television news. Postmodern television news wants to be as interactive as possible, which is expressed both in the choice of what is broadcasted and in the interactive presentation of the news staff and the continual addressing of the audience. The anchor person, who must bring all of this together, functions no longer as a school teacher but as a kind of *gentil organisateur*, who "operates from a position much closer to the audience." (Larsen, 1992: 134) The ethnomethodologists Heritage, Clayman, and Zimmerman come to the same conclusion:

> The use of news material that incorporates a social interactional dimension has become common in recent years. News producers (and, in some cases, news makers) increasingly prefer to use material displaying the qualities of informality and spontaneity that are characteristic features of other areas of TV output. Interpersonal interaction is perhaps the prime medium through which these qualities can be exhibited. Thus the apparently preferred way of conveying the current state of health of the president of the United States is via a shouted conversation from the window of a hospital room rather than a press statement or interview. The sentiments of released hostages' relatives are depicted through the interactions of family members rather than through statements to the camera regardless of how intrusive the former procedure might be held to be ... The steady growth in the program makers' preference for the interactive presentation of news is also manifested in the development of studio practices. Increasingly, the older film report to cameras employed by foreign correspondents has, facilitated by improvements in world-wide communications technology, given way to immediate on-air interactions in which correspondents are interviewed by anchor personnel. Moreover, inside the studio itself, news presentation, which was once regarded largely as a matter of 'reading the printed word aloud' (Whale, 1977), is now developed through quasi-conversational interaction that is facilitated by the ubiquitous 'two-anchor' presentational format. (Heritage *et al.*, 1988: 79)

Second, this merging of the everyday and the institutional in neo-television is expressed in the fact that, as Casetti and Odin (1990: 13-14) observe, the everyday is becoming more and more the referent of the broadcasts. Temporally, according to Casetti and Odin, neo-television adapts the organisation of its time to the way in which time is organized in daily life, beginning with breakfast television and ending with the light-erotic programme before the audience goes to sleep. (Scannell, 1988: 23-7). In the organisation of space, we obtain the same logic: the studio is furnished like a living room or a local pub, people descend into the street to ask the opinion of the common person, one goes to people at home, and so on.

In the content, too, the attention shifts to the everyday life-world of the audience, and this with regard to both fact and fiction. For the informational programmes, this is expressed in a shift from the hard to the soft genres, that is, increasing attention is being given to human interest and the immediately recognizable. "[P]ublic affairs, and political coverage comes under increasing pressure," according to Blumler (1991: 207), "[b]roadcast local news is booming in both late afternoon and late-night slots ... Feature material tends to drive out 'hard' stories (...) [A]nalysis and discussion tend to flag." It hardly needs to be pointed out that this movement fits in with the aversion of the postmodern subject to anything that smacks of abstract and generalised knowledge and only wants to take up information (or can be morally mobilised) when this knowledge is depoliticised and recontextualised, that is, psychologised and emotionalised, in short, personalised.

The same occurs in fiction, where both the narrative form and the content are focused on the everyday and where, therefore, more and more is drawn from what Liebes and Katz (1990: 140) have called the universal (and thus universally comprehensible and everywhere marketable) "primordial themes of human relations." With this is intended the concrete but at the same time fundamental aspects of everyday life that we share with our fellow men and about which are so curious: the body, both in its functioning and in its dysfunctioning and as the seat of desire and pleasure; family ties; love and hate; life and death; anxiety and doubts; joy and sorrow; faithfulness and betrayal, and so on; "in short, the stuff of daily life and experience." (Scannell, 1988: 21; cf. also Meyrowitz, 1986: 48, 107; Rath, 1988: 34)

The massive presence and great success of *soap operas* in neo-television can thus be accounted for by the strong presence in this genre of two qualities that are characteristic of everyday life, namely, seriality and these primordial themes. In this respect, the soap opera is a genre that is extremely well suited for the creating of electronic communities. Ultimately, we know the *neighbours* of the Australian soap of the same name better than our own neighbours. The former come to visit us, with the latter we have no longer any communal ties. Therefore, Liebes and Katz (1990: 143), on the basis of their reception analysis of Dallas, state the following:

> Involvement in these characters and their stories does not only reflect their enactment of human texts which are familiar to us but also reflects our week-to-week familiarity with them. We are connoisseurs not just of the situation but also of these very people who visit us so regularly.

With regard to these primordial themes, I must note one of the (to modern eyes) most astonishing and fascinating phenomena that, as a consequence of the above mentioned postmodern therapeutic ethos and narcissism, has arisen in recent years not only on television but also in the other media (radio, magazines, the 'light prose' of the semi-autobiography), namely, what I would like to call the *media confession*. (cf. White, 1992) In this genre, people (both ordinary people and celebrities) are invited to make public their most intimate affairs: drug addiction; couples with relational problems; victims of incest; how one discovered one's homosexuality (transsexuality, travestitism, paedophilia, exhibitionism/voyeurism, sadomasochism, etc.) and learned to cope with it, and so on. I have already noted above how in the invisible socialisation, withholding, "that is, not offering, not making visible the self" is forbidden (Bernstein, 1975) and how this is expressed in the blurring of the boundary between back and front regions, as reported by Meyrowitz (1985). Postmodern narcissism, Lipovetsky (1983: 91-92) states, referring here to Sennett (1977), includes not only the passion to know oneself but also the drive to reveal this self in all its intimacy to the others. Whether now, with regard to this phenomenon, one adopts the pronounced pessimistic conservativism of authors like Lipovetsky ("the obscenity of intimacy") or the view of Wouters (1989) who argues that this decontrol is done in a controlled manner, the fact remains that these forms of self-disclosure do not happen in face-to-face interaction but before an audience of millions. Everyday reality becomes in this way television (melo)drama and, as Holthof (1993: 5) aptly remarks, morality is no longer in the hands of the church, the state, or even the individual, but it is shifting to the electronic community. The *media confession* thus seems to me to be a good example of how the media, led by television, have succeeded in blurring the boundaries between the public and the private, whereby this blurring corresponds with the blurring in the postmodern subject between the public self (appearance) and the real self (being).[6] I will return to this in my discussion of postmodern celebrities.

That neo-television is marked by what is called above the "emphasis upon heterogeneous knowledge, the disorderly babble of many tongues" of everyday life (Featherstone, 1992: 101), however, is best expressed in the proliferation of the *talk show*. The talk show, according to Casetti and Odin (1990: 12-13), clearly shows that it is no longer a matter in neo-television of transmitting specific knowledge from top down. The talk show demonstrates, on the contrary, that, first, everything is open to discussion in neo-television or, as Meyrowitz (1985: 176) expresses it, "no issue from infant care to incest is left untouched, yet technical jargon and highly focused ideas and discussions are banished to more specialised areas." Second, it demonstrates that, in neo-television, not only does everyone have access to all this, as has been noted, but also that everyone can have and wants to have his/her say about all this.

In the talk show, therefore, no longer are the various arguments weighed against each other for their intrinsic value or does a master's discourse establish the final interpretation as is customary in the modern debate and panel discussion. On the contrary, we have here the return of *doxa*, which Connell and Curti (1985: 109) welcome as a possibility to "introduce orders of discourse other than the official sanctioned ones." In his analysis of popular journalism, Fiske points out that, while the "official" news and its extensions, like debates and current-affairs programs, are marked by a top-down communication process and a strongly decontextualized discourse "distanced from the materiality of everyday life" (Fiske, 1992c: 49), genres like the popular chat shows, on the contrary, recontextualise the information and knowledge and anchor them in the everyday lives of the viewers who, in this way, are invited to "construct

---

[6] With regard to this mediated intimacy, see Poster's commentary on the way in which the *Minitel-messagerie*, with which one can communicate via the computer, is used in France. By means of a game with masks — the adoption of differing identities, "in a position beyond responsibility" — very intimate conversations are achieved. In this way, according to Poster (1990: 119-21), "the *messageries* provide a new form of sociability, a 'community' in the era of the mode of information, "whereby" computer conversations are often considered more important than conventional ones as when some users admit they reveal more intimacies on the Minitel than they do with long-time spouses. Invented subjectivities may be more 'authentic' than the 'real' self."

aspects of the public sphere as relevant to their own." (*Ibid.*: 57) Not only, Fiske goes on to say, is it customary in such programmes for members of the studio audience to intervene in the discussion and introduce their own experiences, opinions, and solutions, but such talk shows are also so constructed as to encourage the home audience to discuss the matter during and after the broadcast and to form their own opinions. Fiske points out that such programmes never end on a final, concluding truth, but have a radically open structure. In this way, the centre of gravity shifts in the communication/socialisation process to the receiver/the subject to be socialised, to whom an active role is now assigned. In their analysis of what they call "access programmes, talk shows and audience discussion programmes" Livingstone and Lunt (1994) arrive at the same conclusions. Their analysis shows that such programmes have all the marks of what has been referred to as weak classification and framing of postmodernity: blurring of the boundaries and of the hierarchical relationship between information and entertainment, between the knowledge of invited 'experts' and ordinary or common-sense knowledge, between "ideas and emotions, argument and narrative" (*ibid.*: 37), between the public and the private.

Before I consider this active viewer in the last section of this chapter, I want to note the following as a conclusion to this section. The blurring of the boundaries between the public and the private has resulted in what Langer (1981) has called the "television's personality system", a system that departs substantially from the classic (modern) Hollywood star system. (Ellis, 1992: 106-8; King, 1992; Martin-Barbero, 1993: 217)

The classic star was characterised by a sharp separation between, first, the private, authentic self, second, the public image of the person, and, third, the imaginary characters that he/she impersonated at irregular intervals on the screen. In other words, the star played someone else, and his/her task was "to imbue the assigned role in the film with one's personal 'aura' or 'character.'" (Rath, 1991: 91) Moreover, the star attempted anxiously to keep separate what Tseëlon (1992: 186) calls 'private realities' and 'public appearances' (the case of Rock Hudson is a good example of this.) The result was that the modern star was constructed as a public figure who was "remote, extraordinary, and exceptional." (Langer, 1981: 356)

The postmodern media personalities or celebrities, whether they are known from fiction or non-fiction programmes, are cast from

another mould. First, they must be taken up in what Langer (1981:
356) calls the "ritual regularity" of television, that is, they must, by
means of repeated appearances in this "reign of intimacy", build up
"a knowable and known 'television self.'" In contrast to the stars,
they must not seem to be inaccessible but familiar, immediate, commonplace:

> Television, both in its conception of programming and in its social
> setting suggests that there is a reduction of distance between itself
> and the viewer, that both television personalities and viewers exist
> within a common universe of experience, a kind of community of
> like minds where television is merely an extension of everyday life.
> (Langer, 1981: 361)

This also means that the audience of such celebrities may expect that
they will reveal themselves in multiple interviews and talk shows,
that they make it clear that they, too, are only creatures of flesh and
blood. King (1992: 38) calls such media celebrities 'hypertypes', that
is, "individuals whose point of interest is not what they are, let alone
what they do, since they have the emotions and foibles we have, but
where they do it: in public and at the centre of the social imaginary,
television." Now this does not mean that the subject is expected to *be*
himself/herself (for this would assume a distinction between
appearance and being, between front and back region,) but it does
mean that the subject should *play* himself/herself. (Langer, 1981:
355) "[T]he boundary between the socially symbolic field of the narrative and the private biography of the actor ... is eroded," according
to King (1992: 39), who speaks in this regard of a managed sincerity.
(*cf. supra*: the media confession.) However, this also means that,
where the public image of the classic star was his/her commodity
(and the subject, for the rest, could be himself/herself in the private
sphere, back stage), we now, as King rightly observes, obtain a self
that has been commodified in its totality by this blurring of the
boundaries between the real I and the persona that is constructed
according to the demands of the situation.

The fact that the postmodern subject plays himself or herself, that
"appearances do not mask reality but are reality" (Tseëlon, 1992: 125)
also causes neo-television to be marked by ambiguity and instability,
playful self-reflexivity and self-irony, and pastiche-like personalities,
which are so typical of postmodernism. (Tseëlon, 1992: 125) In this
regard, see, for example, Kellner's (1992) analysis of the shifts that

are demonstrable in the characters of television fiction or analyses that both Tolson (1991) as well as Brand and Scannell (1991) have made of different forms of broadcast talk. These last analyses, for example, show how, on the basis of the "awareness of the performed nature of the displayed self" (Brand and Scannell, 1991: 215), "the popular public sphere now appears increasingly ironic about itself, reflexive about the forms in which it presents itself, and at times totally ambiguous in its ability to differentiate between sincere and insincere talk." (Tolson, 1991: 198) Self-reflexivity is, therefore, one of the most striking characteristics of neo-television (cf. also J. Collins, 1989), and this is also expressed in the fact that, where paleo-television, like the movies, still wanted to be a transparent window on the world and therefore anxiously hid away all recording equipment, neo-television shamelessly shows this equipment and, in this way, makes it clear to the public that it is dealing with a construction of reality. (Eco, 1985: 189-92)

2.2.4 *Open text-active viewer*

With respect to talk shows, we have already seen how the centre of gravity in the communication process in neo-television has shifted to the receiver. One could now formulate the hypothesis that neo-television, and this completely according to the principles of weak framing of the invisible socialisation, stresses more than paleo-television open texts that assume active audience groups. In the reception of these texts, these groups establish a particular interpretation and use it "as a part of their own cultures, that is, use it to make meanings that are useful to them in making sense of their own social experiences and therefore of themselves." (Fiske, 1992a: 300) With regard to this shift to more open texts in television discourse a good deal of historical research is certainly still to be done. What, for example, concerns advertising, Leiss *et al.* (1990) have, in my opinion, convincingly demonstrated that a historical evolution is demonstrable from closed ('hard sell') to more open texts ('soft sell.') And Kellner (1992: 173-4) concludes on the basis of concrete analyses that "in a postmodern image culture, the images, scenes, stories, and cultural texts of so-called popular culture offer a wealth of subject positions which in turn help structure individual identity."

In any event, the idea that television offers open texts to an active audience has become an important (but also contested) approach in audience research ("reception studies" — cf. Jensen and Rosengren, 1990). The reasoning that is followed here can be reproduced as follows. (Fiske, 1987: 319-26; 1989; 1992a; 1992b; 1996)

I have pointed out that postmodern, multichannel television is aimed at everyone, irrespective of age, gender, class, ethnicity, nationality, or culture. In addition, (and the one follows logically from the other) the supply is quite homogeneous in spite of the great range of choice. The programmes that multichannel television offers must thus be seen more as variations of each other in which the sharpest contrasts disappear and "a new 'middle region' content for programs" arises. (Meyrowitz, 1985: 176)

These at first sight identical series, serials, talk shows, etc., made according to tried and tested formats in which always the same 'primordial themes' occur, however, are now characterised by openness and polysemy, by Bakhtinian *heteroglossia*. Postmodern television is, in other words, marked by a multiplicity of contradictory voices and thus by a struggle for the interpretation of reality.

This absence of an authorial centre that establishes a meaning and concludes the text is convincingly demonstrated by Newcomb. (1988; *cf.* also Newcomb and Hirsch, 1984) Newcomb's analysis shows that constantly conflicting opinions, which implicitly dialogue with each other, on all kinds of ever-recurring basic problems are given not only in one episode of, for example, a soap serial but also within the entire television discourse as it is offered to the audience day in and day out via a multiplicity of channels. Of course, this polysemy and diversity is constrained and structured, but this does not alter the fact that "this conflicted mixture of meaning and socio-cultural problems and ideas is the essence of television." (Newcomb, 1989: 101) Newcomb points out, for example, that one of the basic procedures of soap operas consists of having the same event commented upon and interpreted by different sets of characters in different ways. "Report of an infidelity, an unwanted pregnancy, an illness", according to Newcomb (*ibid.*), "moves through the community of characters. Each report means something different to each pair or triangle or family... Events occur, but it is concern *about* events that interests the audience."

It is by this "liberation of local rationalities" (Vattimo, 1992: 9) that the viewer is invited to take a position, to establish an interpretation, to take sides, and all of this accompanied or not by a discussion with others who are watching or have watched the programme. Such 'made messages' (Willis, 1990) or 'producerly texts' (Fiske, 1987: 95-9), which are only completed in the reception, place the viewer in the position of "a *bricoleur* who matches the creator in the making of meanings. Bringing values and attitudes, a universe of personal experiences and concerns to the texts, the viewer selects, examines, acknowledges, and makes texts of his or her own." (Newcomb and Hirsch, 1984: 69)

All of this also makes it clear that such texts not only supply material to the subject for his/her identity constitution but also, and this is typical for this form of socialisation (Bernstein, 1971: 153-4), offer alternatives. This textual instability and openness corresponds, in other words, to the instability and openness of the postmodern subject.

> Rather than identity disappearing in a postmodern society, it is merely subject to new determinations and new forces while offering as well new possibilities, styles, models, and forms. Yet the overwhelming variety of subject positions, of possibilities for identity, in an affluent image culture no doubt create highly unstable identities while constantly providing new openings to restructure one's identity. (Kellner, 1992: 174)

3. Conclusion: Toward a Generalized Creolisation?

I have pointed out that I consider the central characteristic of postmodern television to be the blurring of the boundaries between the public-institutional and the private-everyday through which postmodern television no longer creates an 'imagined community' that lies outside itself but now forms imagined communities itself together with its audience. Neo-television, according to Eco (1994: 110), "adresses an audience that is part of the programme."

Postmodern television is thus both an extension of everyday life and a "domestication of public space." (Silverstone, 1994: 65) In these electronic communities, the viewer is addressed less as an abstract individual, a citizen of a nation state who is being given the task of being informed, educated, and entertained, but rather is addressed as a concrete person who, by watching, becomes a participant in and gives meaning to the personal problems, emotions, joys, and sorrows within this community. Such communities are formed, as I have said, on the basis of what the transnational culture indus-

tries offer and are, in contrast to what used to be the case, no longer
bound to a spatial locality. "Experience," according to Morley
(1992a: 280), "is both unified beyond localities and fragmented
within them."

While before, as one can argue with Hamelink (1993: 371),
national products were exchanged internationally, transnational
media companies now produce global products, of which they hope
they will appeal to consumers anywhere in the world. As Hamelink
notes, a global culture is being formed which misses the characteristics which the notion of culture has always had, that is, spatial and
temporal limitation. The Swedish anthropologist Ulf Hannerz, therefore, predicts the end of a world which could be seen "as a cultural
mosaic, of seperate pieces with hard, well-defined edges." (Hannerz,
1991: 107; see also Hannerz, 1992, 1996) As a result of a process of
globalisation on the cultural as well as the economic and political
level, Hannerz claims, a *global ecumene* is taking shape. This global
ecumene does not resemble an egalitarian 'global village,' but is typified by a fundamental assymmetry: there is a constant stream from
the centre, the West, to the periphery, the Third World. The result of
this is that "[t]ransnational cultures are thus, usually, in different
ways extensions or transformations of the cultures of Western
Europe and North America." (Hannerz, 1992: 150) As far as media
and popular culture are concerned, it is obvious that these are American. At the same time, however, it is important to realise that concepts such as 'American media culture' or 'American popular culture' do not necessarily refer to products specifically produced in the
US or with American capital. Rather, it refers to products which
reproduce a particular life style (with its emphasis on consumption
and pleasure, on the pleasure of consumption) and use a grammar of
production which not only universalises this life style, but increasingly forces itself on the world as a universal 'language.' (Martin-
Barbero, 1993: 142ff.)

All of this has consequences for the way in which identities are
formed and one cannot but agree with Ang (1990:253) when she
writes that "in the increasingly integrated world system there is no
such thing as an independent cultural identity; every identity must
define and position itself in relation to the cultural frames affirmed
by the world system." (see also Ang, 1996: part 3)

In the Introduction, I pointed to two possible attitudes. The first,
pessimistic, attitude, known as the 'media imperialism' or 'cultural

imperialism' thesis, was dominant mainly in the seventies and eighties. It points at the unbalanced flow of media products between the centre and the rest of the 'ecumene,' the spreading of the Western/American ideology through the whole world, etc. (e.g., Sreberny-Mohammadi, 1996: 178-181). Hannerz calls this thesis, which at least has the advantage of being simple and sounding dramatic, the *saturation-scenario*: the centre colonises the rest of the world culturally to such an extent that in the end the colonised will totally depend on and be totally saturated by the dominant culture. Cultural globalisation in this way leads to cultural homogenisation or synchronisation (Hamelink, 1983) — called Cocacolonisation, McDonaldisation, or Dallasification (De Bens *et al.*, 1992) — which threatens to destroy local identities and cultures.

This scenario is increasingly opposed in recent years. It has been remarked, for instance, that this approach only looks at the market (the 'unbalanced flow') and ignores other factors in the process, such as the way in which the products and the production grammar are used locally. (Hannerz, 1991, 1992, 1996) Another element of criticism is that when concepts such as 'local identity' and 'local culture' are supposedly under threat, one is actually usually referring to national identity and culture, which, as was argued above, has suppressed what is really local for the sake of national unity. (Sreberny-Mohammadi, 1996:199)

I have already pointed out that other, more relativizing approaches are possible. Without succumbing to an exaggerated optimism, Hannerz (1991, 1992, 1996) proposes what he calls the *maturation-scenario* instead of the saturation-scenario. He remarks not only that, as has been suggested here, local receivers use the global products actively, but also that local producers appropriate the production-grammar of the global culture and adapt it to the local culture. In this way, mixed cultures and genres develop a process coined *creolisation* by Hannerz, refering to a concept from sociolinguistics.[7] Others call this process *hybridisation*, of which Nederveen Pieterse (1995: 53) gives the following witty examples:

---

[7] Unlike the pidgin from which it has evolved, a creole language is a fullfledged and autonomous language that has native speakers. Creolisation (and pidginisation) can be illustrated by the following simple formula: X — *Creole language* — Y. Whereby X symbolises the local language (languages) and Y the dominant (e.g., colonial) language. (Bauer, 1987)

How de we come to terms with phenomena such as Thai boxing by Morrocan girls in Amsterdam, Asian rap in London, Irish Bagels, Chinese tacos and Mardi Gras Indians in the United States, or "Mexican schoolgirls dressed in Greek togas dancing in the style of Isidora Duncan?" (Rowe and Schelling, 1991: 161) How do we interpret Peter Brook directing the Mahabharata, or Ariane Mânouchkine staging a Shakespeare play in Japanese Kabuki style for a Paris audience in the Théâtre Soleil?

This process of creolisation/hybridisation has a number of consequences. This global culture, as I have tried to illustrate by referring to the television discourse, is a *bricoleur*-culture: the global product only acquires meaning in local consumption; the universal grammar of production is transformed locally. Because this global culture can only be encountered where it is locally interpreted, adapted and inserted, one can agree with Stuart Hall who says that this culture always appears as decentred and segmented. Hall offers a good illustration of what is meant by 'creolisation' in this context when he claims that, while this global culture is undoubtedly Western and its language is English, this culture no longer speaks the Queen's English:

> It speaks English as an international language which is quite a different thing. It speaks a variety of broken forms of English: English as it has been invaded, and as it has hegemonised a variety of other languages without being able to exclude them from it. It speaks Anglo-Japanese, Anglo-French, Anglo-German or Anglo-English indeed. (Hall, 1991: 28)

This 'global-local nexus' (Morley and Robins, 1989:13) or 'glocalisation' (Robertson, 1985) is understood very well by industry, as is illustrated by Coca-Cola's contention, "We are not a multi-national, we are a multi-local" (Morley, 1992:289) or by the 'global localisation' philosophy of Sony, summarised in the by now classic slogan *Think Globally, Act Locally*:

> It is Sony's philosophy that global corporations have a responsibility to participate actively in the countries in which they operate, a philosophy of 'a global localization.' This means think globally, while acting locally — being sensitive to local requirements, cultures, traditions and attitudes. (Sony USA, cit. Sreberny-Mohammadi, 1996: 124)

It is also clear that this process of creolisation/hybridisation, or glocalisation will blur the strong and sharp distinctions between identities and cultures, typical of modernity, because creole cultures, being variations of the dominant culture, have to be seen as variations of each other. This blurring of boundaries between *we* and *they*, implies of course a certain loss of authenticity, but it implies also a reduction of the sensitivity to dirt, pollution, contamination by the other. This postmodern less stable feeling of identity can probably also lead to a "society in which reality presents itself as softer and more fluid, and in which experience can again acquire the characteristics of oscillation, disorientation and play." (Vattimo, 1992: 59) Wouters, following Norbert Elias, refers to a decrease of contrasts and an increase in variation, a process which makes people more tolerant towards each other. (Wouters, 1990)

In all this, one should not, however, forget that although ethnographic audience research may contend "that meaning is not exported *in* Western television programming but created *by* different cultural sectors of the audience in relation to their already-formed cultural attitudes and political perceptions" (Sreberny-Mohammadi, 1996: 190), this does not detract from the fact that the idea is exported in such a way that every individual has the right (read, the duty) to fill in his/her identity by means of consumption and to become a member of a global consumer culture.

References

ALLEN, Robert C. (1992), 'Audience Oriented Criticism and Television' in Robert C. ALLEN (ed.), *Channels of Discourse, Reassembled: Television and Contemporary Criticism*. 2nd ed. Chapel Hill & London, The University of North Carolina Press, pp. 101-137.

ALTHEIDE, David L., Robert P. SNOW (1991), *Media Worlds in the Postjournalism Era*. New York, Aldine de Gruyter.

ALTMAN, Rick (1986), 'Television/Sound' in Tania MODLESKI (ed.), *Studies in Entertainment. Critical Approaches to Mass Culture*. Bloomington & Indianapolis, Indiana University Press, pp. 39-54.

ANDERSON, Benedict (1983), *Imagined Communities*. London, Verso.

ANG, Ien (1990), 'Culture and Communication, Towards an Ethnographic Critique of Media Consumption in the Transnational Media System' in *European Journal of Communication*, 5(1990)2/3, pp. 239-260.

ANG, Ien (1991), *Desperately Seeking the Audience*. London & New York, Routledge.

ANG, Ien (1996), *Living Room Wars: Rethinking Media Audiences for a Postmodern World*. London, Routledge.

ANG, Ien, David MORLEY (1989), 'Mayonnaise Culture and Other European Follies' in *Cultural Studies*, 3 (1998) 2, pp. 133-143.

BALANDIER, Georges (1985), *Le Détour: Pouvoir et Modernité*. Paris, Fayard.

BALANDIER, Georges (1988), *Le Désordre: Eloge du Mouvement*. Paris, Fayard.

BAUER, Anton (1987), 'Pidgin und Kreolsprachen' in Ulrich AMMON, Norbert DITTMAR, Klaus J. MATTHEIER (eds.), *Sociolinguistics/Soziolinguistik*, Vol. I. Berlin & New York, Walter de Gruyter, pp. 344-352.

BAUMAN, Zygmunt (1992), *Intimations of Postmodernity*. London, Routledge.

BELL, Daniel (1973), *The Coming of Post-industrial Society*. New York, Basic Books.

BELL, Daniel (1976), *The Cultural Contradictions of Capitalism*. London, Heineman.

BERNSTEIN, Basil (1971), *Class, Codes and Control*. Vol. 1: *Theoretical Studies towards a Sociology of Language*. London, Routledge & Kegan Paul.

BERNSTEIN, Basil (1975), *Class, Codes and Control*. Vol. 3: *Towards a Theory of Educational Transmissions*. London, Routledge & Kegan Paul.

BERNSTEIN, Basil (1981), 'Codes, Modalities, and the Proces of Cultural Reproduction: A Model' in *Language in Society*, 10(1981)3, pp. 327-63.

BERNSTEIN, Basil (1987), 'Social Class, Codes and Communication' in Ulrich AMMON, Norbert DITTMAR, Klaus J. MATTHEIER (eds.), *Sociolinguistics/Soziolinguistik*. Vol. I. Berlin & New York, Walter de Gruyter, pp. 563-579.

BERNSTEIN, Basil (1990), *Class, Codes and Control*. Vol. 4: *The Structuring of Pedagogic Discourse*. London, Routledge.

BERNSTEIN, Basil (1996), *Pedagogy, Symbolic Control and Identity: Theory, Research, Critique*. London. Taylor & Francis.

BETZ, Hans-Georg (1992), 'Postmodernism and the New Middle Class' in *Theory, Culture & Society*, 9(1992)2, pp. 93-114.

BLUMLER, Jay G. (1991), 'The New Television Marketplace: Imperatives, Implications, Issues' in James CURRAN, Michael GUREVITCH (eds.), *Mass Media and Society*. London, Edward Arnold, pp. 194-215.

BLUMLER, Jay G. (1992a), 'Public Service Broadcasting before the Commercial Deluge' in Jay G. BLUMLER (ed.), *Television and the Public Interest: Vulnerable Values in West European Broadcasting*. London, Sage, pp. 7-21.

BLUMLER, Jay G. (1992b), 'Vulnerable Values at Stake' in Jay G. BLUMLER (ed.), *Television and the Public Interest: Vulnerable Values in West European Broadcasting*. London, Sage, pp. 22-42.

BLUMLER, Jay G., Gurevitch, MICHAEL (1995), *The Crisis of Public Communication*. London, Routledge.

BLUMLER, Jay G., Gurevitch, MICHAEL (1996), 'Media Change and Social Change: Linkages and Junctures' in James CURRAN, Michael GUREVITCH (eds.) *Mass Media and society*. 2nd ed. London, Arnold, pp. 120-137.

BONNER, Frances, Paul DU GAY (1992), 'Representing the Enterprising Self: Thirtysomething and Contemporary Consumer Culture' in *Theory, Culture & Society*, 9(1992)2, pp. 67-92.

BOURDIEU, Pierre (1984), *Distinction: A Social Critique of the Judgement of Taste*, transl. R. Nice. London, Routledge & Keagan Paul.

BRAND, Graham, Paddy SCANNELL, (1991), 'Talk, Identity and Performance: The Tony Blackburn Show' in Paddy Scannell (ed.), *Broadcast Talk*. London, Sage, pp. 201-226.

BRANTS, Kees (1998), 'Who's Afraid of Infotainment' in *European Journal of Communication*, 13(1998)3, pp. 315-335.

BRANTS, Kees, Karen SIUNE (1992), 'Public Broadcasting in a State of Flux' in Karen SIUNE and Wolfgang TRUETZSCHLER (eds.), *Dynamics of Media Politics: Broadcast and Electronic Media in Western Europe*. London, Sage, pp. 101-115.

BRASS, Paul R. (1991), *Ethnicity and Nationalism: Theory and Comparison*. London, Sage.

BRIGGS, Asa (1985), *The BBC: The First Fifty Years*. Oxford, Oxford University press.

BURNS, Tom (1977), *The BBC: Public Institution and Private World*. London & Basingstoke, Macmillan.

CASETTI, Francesco, Roger ODIN (1990), 'De la Paléo — à la Néo-télévision: Approche Sémio-pragmatique' in *Communications*, 51(1990), pp. 9-26.

CLÉMENT, Catherine (1987), *Le Goût du Miel*. Paris, Grasset.

COLLINS, Jim (1989), 'Watching Ourselves Watch Television, or Who's Your Agent' in *Cultural Studies*, 3(1998)3, pp. 261-281.

COLLINS, Richard (1989), 'The White Paper on Broadcasting Policy' in *Screen*, 30(1989)1/2, pp. 6-23.

COLLINS, Richard (1990), *Television: Policy and Culture*. London, Unwin Hyman.

CONNELL, Ian, Lidia CURTI (1985), 'Popular Broadcasting in Italy and Britain: Some Issues and Problems' in Phillip DRUMMOND, Richard PATERSON (eds.), *Television in Transition*. London, BFI, pp. 87-111.

CROOK, Stephen, Jan PAKULSKI, Malcolm WATERS (1992), *Postmoderniza-tion: Change in Advanced Society*. London, Sage.

DAHLGREN, Peter, Colin SPARKS (eds.) (1992), *Journalism and Popular Cul-ture*. London, Sage.

DE BENS, Els, Mary KELLY, Marit BACKE (1992), 'Television Content: Dal-lasification of Culture?' in Karen SIUNE, Wolfgang TRUETZSCHLER (eds.), *Dynamics of Media Politics: Broadcast and Electronic Media in Western Europe*. London, Sage, pp. 75-100.

DESAULNIER, Jean Pierre (1985), 'Television and Nationalism: From Cul-ture to Communication' in Phillip DRUMMOND, Richard PATERSON (eds.), *Television in Transition*. London, BFI, pp. 112-122.

DIMAGGIO, Paul (1982a), 'Cultural Entrepreneurship in Nineteenth Cen-tury Boston: The Creation of an Organisational Base for High Cul-ture in America' in *Media, Culture and Society*, 4(1982)1, pp. 33-50.

DIMAGGIO, Paul (1982b), 'Cultural Entrepreneurship in Nineteenth Cen-tury Boston, part II: The Classification and Framing of American Art' in *Media, Culture and Society*, 4(1982)4, pp. 303-322.

DIMAGGIO, Paul (1987), 'Classification of Art' in *American Sociological Review*, 52(1987)4, pp. 440-455.

DOBBELAERE, Karel (1991), 'Over Godsdienst en de Kerk in Vlaanderen in 2000' in *Onze Alma Mater*, 45(1991)3, pp. 205-229.

DOUGLAS, Mary (1966), *Purity and Danger*. London, Routledge & Kegan Paul.

ECO, Umberto (1985), *De Alledaagse Onwerkelijkheid*. Transl. F. DENISSEN *et al*. Amsterdam, Bert Bakker.

ECO, Umberto (1994), *Apocalypse Postponed*. Bloomington, Indiana, Indi-ana University Press/ London, BFI Publishing.

ELLIS, John (1992), *Visible Fictions*. London, Routledge.

ELLIOT, Philip (1982), 'Intellectuals, the "Information Society" and the Disappearance of the Public Sphere' in *Media, Culture and Society*, 4(1982)3, pp. 243-253.

FEATHERSTONE, Mike (1991a), *Consumer Culture and Postmodernism*. Lon-don, Sage.

FEATHERSTONE, Mike (1991b), 'The Body in Consumer Culture' in Mike FEATHERSTONE, Mike HEPWORTH, Bryan S. TURNER (eds.), *The Body: Social Process and Cultural Theory*. London, Sage, pp. 170-196.

FEATHERSTONE, Mike (1992a), 'Postmodernism and the Aestheticization of Everyday Life' in Scott LASH, Jonathan FRIEDMAN (eds.), *Moder-nity and Identity*. Oxford, Blackwell, pp. 265-290.

FEATHERSTONE, Mike (1992b), 'The Heroic Life and Everyday Life' in *The-ory, Culture & Society*, 9(1992)1, pp. 159-182.

FEATHERSTONE, Mike (1995), *Undoing Culture: Globalization, Postmodernism and Identity*. London: Sage.

FISHMAN, Joshua (1972), *Language and Nationalism*. Rowley (MA), Newbury House.

FISKE, John (1987), *Television Culture*. London, Methuen.

FISKE, John (1989), 'Moments of Television: Neither the Text nor the Audience' in Ellen SEITER, Hans BORCHERS, Gabrielle KREUTZNER, Eva-Maria WARTH (eds.), *Remote Control: Television, Audiences and Cultural Power*. London & New York, Routledge, pp. 56-78.

FISKE, John (1992a), 'British Cultural Studies and Television' in Robert C. ALLEN (ed.), *Channels of Discourse, Reassembled*. 2nd ed. Chapel Hill & London, The University of North Carolina Press, pp. 284-326.

FISKE, John (1992b), 'Cultural Studies and the Culture of Everyday Life' in Lawrence GROSSBERG, Cary NELSON, Paula TREICHLER (eds.), *Cultural Studies*. New York & London: Routledge, pp. 154-173.

FISKE, John (1992c), 'Popularity and the Politics of Information' in Peter DAHLGREN, Colin SPARKS (eds.), *Journalism and Popular Culture*. London, Sage, pp. 45-63.

FISKE, John (1996), 'Postmodernism and Television' in James Curran and Michael Gurevitch (eds.), *Mass Media and Society*. 2nd ed. London, Edward Arnold, pp. 53-65.

FLITTERMAN-LEWIS, Sandy (1992), 'Psychoanalysis, Film, and Television' in Robert C. Allen (ed.), *Channels of Discourse, Reassembled: Television and Contemporary Criticism*. 2nd Edition. Chapel Hill & London, The University of North Carolina Press, pp. 203-245.

FRIEDMAN, Jonathan (1988), 'Cultural Logics of the Global System: A Sketch' in *Theory, Culture & Society*, 5 (1988) 2/3, pp. 447-460.

FRIEDMAN, Jonathan (1992), 'Narcissism, Roots and Postmodernity: The Constitution of Selfhood in the Global Crisis' in Scott LASH, Jonathan FRIEDMAN (eds.), *Modernity and Identity*. Oxford, Blackwell, pp. 331-366.

GELLNER, Ernest (1983), *Nations and Nationalism*. Oxford, Basil Blackwell.

GELLNER, Ernest (1992), *Reason and Culture. The Historical Role of Rationality and Rationalism*. Oxford, Blackwell.

Glasgow Media Group (1980), *More Bad News*. London, Routledge & Kegan Paul.

GOFFMAN, Erving (1959), *The Presentation of Self in Everyday Life*. Garden City (NY), Doubleday Anchor Books.

GOULDNER, Alvin (1976), *The Dialectic of Ideology and Technology: The Origins, Grammar and Future of Ideology*. London, Macmillan.

GROSSBERG, Lawrence (1987), 'The Indifference of Television' in *Screen*, 28(1987)2, pp. 28-45.

HALL, Stuart (1991), 'The Local and the Global: Globalization and Ethnicity' in Anthony D. KING (ed.), *Culture Globalization and the World System*. London, Macmillan, pp. 19-39.

HAMELINK, Cees J. (1983), *Cultural Autonomy in Global Communication*. New York, Longman.

HAMELINK, Cees J. (1991), 'Internationale Communicatie, Wereldpolitiek en de Rechten van de Mens' in *Onze Alma Mater*, 47(1991)4, pp. 366-390.

HANNERZ, Ulf (1991), 'Scenarios for Peripheral Cultures' in Anthony D. King (ed.), *Culture Globalization and the World-System*. London, Macmillan, pp. 107-128.

HANNERZ, Ulf (1992), *Cultural Complexity: Studies in the Social Organisation of Meaning*. New York, Columbia University Press.

HANNERZ, Ulf (1996), *Transnational Connections: Culture, People, Places*. London, Routledge.

HARALOVICH, Mary Beth (1988), 'Suburban Family Sitcoms and Consumer Product Design: Addressing the Social Subjectivity of Homemakers in the 1950's, in Phillip DRUMMOND and Richard PATERSON (eds.), *Television and its Audience*. London, BFI, pp. 38-60.

HARTLEY, John (1982), *Understanding News*. London & New York, Methuen.

HARVEY, David (1989), *The Condition of Postmodernity*. Oxford, Basil Blackwell.

HAYWARD, Philip, Paul KERR (1987), 'Introduction' in *Screen*, 28 (1987)2, pp. 2-8.

HEBDIGE, Dick (1979), *Subculture: The Meaning of Style*. London, Methuen.

HEMMERECHTS, Karel (1990), 'Interview met Karel Hemmerechts' in *De Standaard der Letteren*, 20.10.1990.

HERITAGE, John C., Steven CLAYMAN, Don H. ZIMMERMAN (1988), 'Discourse and Message Analysis: The Micro-Structure of Mass Media Messages' in Robert P. HAWKINS, John M. WIEMANN, Suzanne PINGREE (eds.), *Advancing Communication Science: Merging Mass and Interpersonal Processes*. London, Sage, pp. 77-109.

HJARVARD, Stig (1993), 'Pan European Television News: Towards an European Political Public Sphere' in Phillip DRUMMOND, Richard PATERSON, Janet WILLIS (eds.), *National Identity and Europe: The Television Revolution*. London, BFI Publishing, pp. 71-94.

HOLTHOF, Marc (1993), 'Love Letters: De Privatisering van de Moraal' in *Andere Sinema*, 114(1993), pp. 5-11.

JAKOBSON, Roman (1960), 'Closing Statement: Linguistics and Poetics', pp. 350-377 in Thomas A. SEBEOK (ed.), *Style in Language*. Cambridge, M.A., The MIT Press.

JENSEN, Klaus Bruhn, Karl Erik ROSENGREN (1990), 'Five Traditions in Search of the Audience' in *European Journal of Communication*, 5(1990)2/3, pp. 207-238.

KELLNER, Douglas (1992), 'Popular Culture and the Construction of Post-modern Identities', in Scott LASH, Jonathan FRIEDMAN (eds.), *Modernity and Identity*. Oxford, Blackwell.

KING, Barry (1992), 'Stardom and Symbolic Degeneracy: Television and the Transformation of the Stars as Public Symbols' in *Semiotica*, 92(1992)1/2, pp. 1-47.

LANGER, John (1981), 'Television's Personality System' in *Media, Culture and Society*, 3(1981)4, pp. 351-365.

LARSEN, Peter (1992), 'More than Just Images, the Whole Picture: News in the Multi-Channel Universe' in Michael SKOVMAND, Kim Christian SCHRODER (eds.), *Media Cultures: Reappraising Transnational Media*. London & New York, Routledge, pp. 124-141.

LASCH, Christopher (1979), *The Culture of Narcissism: American Life in an Age of Diminishing Expectations*. New York, Norton.

LASH, Scott (1990), *Sociology of Postmodernism*. London & New York, Routledge.

LASH, Scott, John URRY (1987), *The End of Organized Capitalism*. Oxford, Polity Press.

LEACH, Edmund (1976), *Culture and Communication: The Logic by which Symbols are Connected*. Cambridge, Cambridge University Press.

LEARS, Jackson T. (1983), 'From Salvation to Self-Realization: Advertising and the Therapeutic Roots of Consumer Culture' in Richard W. FOX and Jackson T. LEARS (eds.), *The Culture of Consumption*. New York, Pantheon.

LEISS, William, Stephen KLINE, Sut JHALLY (1990), *Social Communication in Advertising: Persons, Products and Images of Well Being*. 2nd edition. London, Routledge.

LEITNER, Gerhard (1983), 'The Social Background of the Language of Radio', in Howard DAVIS, Paul WALTON (eds.), *Language, Image, Media*. Oxford, Basil Blackwell.

LIEBES, Tamar, Elihu KATZ (1990), *The Export of Meaning: Cross-Cultural Readings of Dallas*. New York & Oxford, Oxford University Press.

LIPOVETSKY, Gilles (1983), *L'Ere du Vide: Essais sur l'Individualisme Contemporain*. Paris, Gallimard.

LIVINGSTONE, Sonia, Peter LUNT (1994), *Talk on Television: Audience Participation and Public Debate*. London, Routledge.

McQUAIL, Denis (1987), *Mass Communication Theory: An Introduction*. 2nd. ed. London, Sage.

McQUAIL, D. (1992a), 'The Netherlands: Freedom and Diversity under Multichannel Conditions', in Jay G. BLUMLER (ed.), *Television and Public Interest: Vulnerable Values in West European Broadcasting*. London, Sage.

MCQUAIL, Denis (1992b), *Media Performance: Mass Communication and the Public Interest*. London, Sage.

MCQUAIL, Denis (1994), *Mass Communication Theory: An Introduction*. 3rd. ed. London, Sage.

MCQUAIL, Denis, Rosario DE MATEO, Helena TAPPER (1992), 'A Framework for Analysis of Media Changes in Europe in the 1990's' in Karen SIUNE, Wolfgang TRUETZSCHLER (eds.), *Dynamics of Media Politics*. London, Sage, pp. 8-25.

MAFFESOLI, Michel (1988), *Le Temps des Tribus: Le Déclin de l'Individualisme dans les Sociétés de Masse*. Paris, Méridiens Klincksieck.

MARTIN-BARBERO, Jesus (1993), *Communication, Culture and Hegemony*. London, Sage.

MELUCCI, Alberto (1989), *Nomads of the Present: Social Movements and Individual Needs in Contemporary Society*. Philadelphia, Temple University Press.

MEYROWITZ, Joshua (1985), *No Sense of Place: The Impact of Electronic Media on Social Behavior*. Oxford & New York, Oxford University Press.

MOORES, Shaun (1993), *Interpreting Audiences: The Ethnography of Media Consumption*. London, Sage.

MORLEY, David (1992a), *Television, Audiences and Cultural Studies*. London & New York, Routledge.

MORLEY, David (1992b), 'Electronic Communities and Domestic Rituals: Cultural Consumption and the Production of European Cultural Identities' in Michael SKOVMAND, Kim Christian SCHRODER (eds.), *Media Cultures: Reappraising Transnational Media*. London & New York, Routledge, pp. 65-85.

MORLEY, David, Kevin ROBINS (1989), 'Spaces of Identity: Communications Technologies and the Reconfiguration of Europe' in *Screen*, 30(1989)4, pp. 10-34.

MORSE, Margaret (1985), 'Talk, Talk, Talk — The Space of Discourse in Television' in *Screen*, 26(1985)2, pp. 2-15.

MURDOCK, Graham (1992), 'Citizens, Consumers, and Public Culture' in Michael SKOVMAND and Kim Christian SCHRODER (eds.), *Media Cultures: Reappraising Transnational Media*. London & New York, Routledge.

NEDERVEEN PIETERSE, Jan (1995), 'Globalization as Hybridization' in Mike FEATHERSTONE and Scott LASH (eds.) *Global Modernities*. London, Sage, pp. 45-68.

NEWCOMB, Horace C. (1988), 'One Night of Prime Time: An Analysis of Television's Multiple Voices' in James W. CASEY (ed.), *Media, Myths and Narratives: Television and the Press*. London, Sage, pp. 88-112.

NEWCOMB, Horace C., Paul M. HIRSCH (1984), 'Television as a Cultural Forum' in Willard D. Roweland and Bruce Watkins (eds.), *Interpreting Television: Current Research Perspectives*. London, Sage, pp. 58-73.

OHMAE, Kenichi (1995), *The End of the Nation State: The Rise of Regional Economics*. New York, The Free Press.

PAKULSKI, Jan, Malcom WATERS, Malcolm (1996), *The Death of Class*. London, Sage.

POSTER, Mark (1990), *The Mode of Information: Poststructuralism and Social Context*. Oxford, Polity Press.

RATH, C.-D. (1988), 'Live/Life: Television as a Generator of Events in Everyday Life' in P. DRUMMOND, R. PATERSON (eds.), *Television and its Audience*. London, BFI, pp. 109-204.

RATH, Claus-Dieter (1991), 'Life television and its Audiences. Challenges of Media Reality' in Ellen SEITER, Hans BORCHERS, Gabriele KREUTZNER, Eva-Maria WARTH (eds.), *Remote Control: Television, Audiences and Cultural Power*. London & New York, Routledge, pp. 23-37.

ROBERTSON, Roland (1995), 'Glocalization: Time-Space and Homogeneity-Heterogeneity' in Mike FEATHERSTONE, Roland ROBERTSON (eds.) *Global Modernities*. London, Sage, pp. 25-44.

SCANNELL, Paddy (1988), 'Radio Times: The Temporal Arrangements of Broadcasting in the Modern World' in Phillip DRUMMOND, Richard PATERSON (eds.), *Television and its Audience*. London, BFI, pp. 15-31.

SCANNELL, Paddy (1989), 'Public Service Broadcasting and Modern Public Life' in *Media, Culture and Society*, 11(1989)2, pp. 135-66.

SCANNEL, Paddy (1990), 'Public Service Broadcasting: The History of a Concept' in Andrew GOODWIN, Garry WHANNEL (eds.), *Understanding Television*. London, Routledge, pp. 11-29.

SCANNELL, Paddy (1991), 'Introduction: The Relevance of Talk' in Paddy SCANNELL (ed.), *Broadcast Talk*. London, Sage, pp. 1-13.

SHIELDS, Rob (1992), 'The Individual, Consumption Cultures and the Fate of Community' in Rob SHIELDS (ed.) *Lifestyle Shopping: The Subject of Consumption*. London, Routledge, pp. 99-113.

SCHLESINGER, Philip (1991), *Media, State and Nation: Political Violence and Collective Identities*. London, Sage.

SCHRØDER, K.C. (1992), 'Cultural Quality: Search for a Phantom', in Michael SKOVMAND, Kim CHRISTIAN Schroder (eds.), *Media Cultures: Reappraising Transnational Media*. London & New York, Routledge.

SEITER, Ellen, Hans BORCHERS, Gabriele KREUTZNER, Eva-Maria WARTH, (1991), '"Don't treat us like we're so stupid and naïve": Towards an Ethnography of Soap Opera Viewers', in Ellen SEITER, Hans

BORCHERS, Gabriele KREUTZNER, Eva-Maria WARTH (eds.), *Remote Control: Television, Audiences, and Cultural Power*. London & New York, Routledge.

SENNETT, Richard (1977), *The Fall of Public Man*. New York, Knopf.

SILVERSTONE, Robert (1994), *Television and Everyday Life*. London, Routledge.

SIUNE, Karen, Denis MCQUAIL, Wolfgang TRUETZSCHLER (1992), 'From Structure to Dynamics' in Karen SIUNE, Wolfgang TRUETZSCHLER (eds.), *Dynamics of Media Politics: Broadcast and Electronic Media in Western Europe*. London, Sage, pp. 1-7.

SNOW, Robert P. (1983), *Creating Media Culture*. London Sage.

SREBERNY-MOHAMMADI, Annabelle (1996), 'The Global and the Local in International Communications' in James CURRAN, Michael GUREVITCH (eds.), *Mass Media and Society*. 2nd ed. London, Arnold, pp. 177-203.

STALLYBRASS, Peter, Allon WHITE, Allon (1986), *The Politics and Poetics of Transgression*. London, Methuen.

SULKUNEN, Pekka (1992), *The European New Middle Class: Individuality and Tribalism in Mass Society*. Aldershot, Avebury.

TOLSON, Andrew (1991), 'Televised Chat and the Synthetic Personality' in Paddy SCANNELL (ed.), *Broadcast Talk*. London, Sage, pp. 178-200.

TSEËLON, Efrat (1992), 'Is the Presented Self Sincere? Goffman, Impression Management and the Postmodern Self' in *Theory, Culture & Society*, 9(1992)2, pp. 115-128.

TURNER, Graeme (1996), *British Cultural Studies: An Introduction*. 2nd ed. Boston, Unwin Hyman.

VAN DEN BULCK, Hilde, Luc VAN POECKE (1996a), 'National Language, Identity Formation and Broadcasting in the Modern-Postmodern Debate: The Case of the Flemish and German-Swiss Communities' in Sandra BRAMAN, Annabelle SREBERNY-MOHAMMADI (eds.), *Globalization, Civil Society and the Public Sphere*. London, Hampton Press, pp. 157-177.

VAN DEN BULCK, Hilde, Luc VAN POECKE (1996b), 'National language, Identity Formation and Broadcasting: Flanders, the Netherlands and German-speaking Switzerland' in *European Journal of Communication*, 11(1996)2, pp. 277-233.

VATTIMO, Gianni (1992), *The Transparent Society*. Transl. D. Webb. Oxford, Polity Press.

VIDICH, Arthur J. (ed.) (1995) *The New Middle Classes*. London, Macmillan.

WEGENER, Claudia (1994) *Reality-TV: Fernsehen zwischen Emotion und Information?* Opladen, Leske und Budrich.

WHITE, Mimi (1992), *Tele-Advising: Therapeutic Discourse in American Television*. Chapel Hill & London, The University of North Carolina Press.

WILLIAMS, Raymond (1989), *Raymond Williams on Television: Selected Writings*. London & New York, Routledge.

WILLIS, Paul (1990), *Common Culture: Symbolic Work at Play in the Everyday Cultures of the Young*. Milton Keynes, Open University Press.

WOUTERS, Cas (1990), *Van Minnen en Sterven: Informalisering van Omgangsvormen rond Seks en Dood*. Amsterdam, Bert Bakker.

MEDIA ETHICS AS A CULTURAL DIAGNOSIS OF THE TIMES

Walter Lesch

In this article[1] I will first reconstruct some of the characteristics of the now over twenty year-old discussion of the so-called 'post-modernity', so as to set forth the semiotic core of this characterisation. Thereafter, I will explain what such a view signifies for the understanding of the times in general and for the working out of a cultural diagnosis of the times. From this, consequences arise for the relationship between cultural contemporaneity and normative ethics, and for the basic concepts of a media ethics, the outlines of which we will sketch.

1. The discussion about postmodernity:
   the paths and detours of a debate that is not simply theoretical

If one wants an approximate characterisation of the new postmodern thinking,[2] the recourse to the *visible* changes in architecture and the accompanying discussions in architectural theory in the 1970s commend themselves[3]; since it is these which have most enduringly

---

[1] Translated from the German by Paul Crowe.

[2] An informative accounting, to which I am indebted for many inspirations, is offered by a rich double-issue of *Merkur. Zeitschrift für europäisches Denken* 52(1998)9-10. An explanatory overview of the most important topoi, in the form of informative essays and lexicon articles, is to be found in Stuart SIM (ed.), *The Icon Critical Dictionary of Postmodern Thought*. Cambridge, Icon Books, 1998. Cf. also Wolfgang WELSCH, 'Topoi der Postmoderne' in Hans Rudi FISCHER, Arnold RETZER, Jochen SCHWEITZER (eds.), *Das Ende der großen Entwürfe*. Frankfurt a.M., Suhrkamp. 1992, pp. 35-55. The locating of oneself 'after' the post of postmodernity was adopted relatively early, as in Andreas STEFFENS (ed.), *Nach der Postmoderne*. Düsseldorf/Bensheim, Bollmann, 1992.

[3] Cf. Diane GHIRARDO, *Architecture after Modernism*. London, Thames and Hudson, 1996.

impressed themselves upon the public consciousness beyond the small circle of experts.[4] From 1975 on, especially the American author Charles Jencks, has spoken out on behalf of the program of new building he himself terms postmodern.[5] He defines himself polemically in opposition to the modern 'international style': a style which has worn itself out with its straight lines, sober glass and steel structures (Le Corbusier, Mies van der Rohe), and a rigid refusal of ornamentation. For him the enlightened program of the architectonic modern has turned into a functionalist uniformity and unimaginativeness, which has contributed greatly to the desolation of our cities that has since become a byword.[6] In opposition to this, postmodern constructions evidence, on the one hand, a new spirit of stylistic multiplicity and a use of new materials, while they are not afraid to imitate older styles, this mostly being done in an ironic fragmentary way. In this way the elitist abstractness of the modern is broken up and interspersed with popular, playful forms that facilitate an emotional access to the building. For a building is something more than pure form and function: it 'communicates' with its surroundings and produces connections in space and time.

The debates in architectural theory contain *in nuce* all those aspects which would become typical for the further course of the modern/postmodern controversy; the dissolution of a rationality that understands itself as universal, the historicising reanimation of traditional elements of form, the pluralisation of styles, the unabashed intercourse with tradition and the ironic play with cita-

---

[4] The notion 'postmodern' had already surfaced in American literary criticism. Cf. Wolfgang WELSCH, *Unsere postmoderne Moderne*. Weinheim, VCH Acta Humaniora, 1987, pp. 14-17. In this context the postmodernisation of literature was above all a struggle against the elitist distinction between high and popular culture. Good books are distinguished by being written in both an intelligent and entertaining way. At the same time, many authors have seen the path to success in the double-encoding of their texts, such that they can be read as exciting stories that are pleasant to read, even when not all allusions and stylistic devices are deciphered. In this way the opposition between a cheap literary commodity for the uneducated, and a serious culture only accessible to a dedicated public collapses. Similar developments also characterise film production under the sign of postmodernity, e.g., the work of David Lynch.

[5] Cf. Charles JENCKS, *The Language of Postmodern Architecture* [1975]. London, Academy Editions, 4th revised edition, 1984.

[6] Alexander MITSCHERLICH, *Die Unwirtlichkeit unserer Städte. Anstiftung zum Unfrieden*. Frankfurt a.M., Suhrkamp, 1965; *Thesen zur Stadt der Zukunft*, Frankfurt a.M., Suhrkamp, 1971.

tions.[7] All of this is, of course, also open to negative comment. Then the pluralisation of a supposed unity of reason is seen as a fundamental attack upon rationality. Multiplicity becomes arbitrariness, historical citation becomes a lack of historical standpoint and a strategy of forgetting and repression, ironic distance becomes a cynical and nihilistic game. Obviously the protagonists of the postmodern have struck a very sensitive nerve in defenders of the holy grail of modernism and have thereby provoked a correspondingly fierce counter-reaction. For only this could explain the humourlessness of so many discussions over the past couple of decades.[8] It is precisely these ironic forms of expression that have frequently been misunderstood and intolerantly attacked. But for all that, the point of the postmodern critique is not so new. Similar doubts about the Enlightenment's optimistic philosophy of history, about the unidimensionality of the rigid conception of rationality, and about the neutrality of rational viewpoints, are as old as the history of modernity itself, which can be understood as the grand project of emancipation from traditional authorities and the legitimation of standards of every kind before the forum of reason.[9] The twentieth century, however, is full of events that have called forth justified criticism of this foundationalist pride, such that postmodernism has no cultural-historical monopoly over the critique of reason, which rather, in several variants of 'Dialectic of Enlightenment' (Horkheimer/Adorno), belongs inseparably to the process of modernisation.

The renunciation of authority could not in the end leave science undisturbed, the legitimacy of which, at least for the limited field of research, was relatively uncontested, even though it has since become evident that scientific discoveries and technical applications can be employed for both beneficial and destructive purposes. At the same time, the prestige of the ritualised academic system was shattered by the protest movement that by May 1968 could no longer be

---

[7] Consequently architecture and urban studies are excellent fields for detailed case-studies and critical diagnoses of the times. Cf. on this point Josef FRÜCHTL, 'Gesteigerte Ambivalenz: Die Stadt als Denkbild der Post/Moderne' in *Merkur* 52(1998)9/10, pp.766-780.

[8] Cf. on the relation between private irony and public discourse: Richard RORTY, *Contingency, Irony, and Solidarity*. Cambridge, Cambridge University Press, 1989.

[9] Cf. On the most important structural characteristics of the Modern: Hans VAN DER LOO, Willem VAN REIJEN, *Modernisierung: Projekt und Paradox*. München, Deutscher Taschenbuch Verlag, 1992.

ignored. The theoretical discussions of the 60s and 70s articulated a discontent that did not remain confined to intellectual circles, but was made concrete in the conduct of life, where a strong tendency to pluralisation of lifestyles and a loss of the plausibility of all-encompassing models of interpretation could be noticed. This *Zeitgeist* found a dense summary in Jean-François Lyotard's small text *La condition postmoderne* (1979), which came about as a commissioned report on knowledge in modern technological and media societies and is now viewed as a prelude to the philosophical controversy over the status of the modern.[10] Lyotard suggests that the 'great stories' of Christianity and Marxism, which until now could claim a certain validity as models of interpretation in the philosophy of history, have lost their credibility. He also proposes a connection between the changed cultural situation and the new information and communications technologies, which have contributed in an unusual degree to the acceleration of the dynamic of civilisation and to the swifter ageing of received certainties.

Similar theses and questions, which today scarcely disturb us, do not really explain the tempest of indignation and the sharpness of the polemics that after 1979 have set the tone for a good decade. This temporal delimitation does not seem to me to be accidental. For 1989 saw the fall of the Berlin wall, and along with it the collapse of totalitarian socialism and one of the last of the 'great stories' of modernity: the Marxist ideal of a emancipation of man from the shackles of capitalism. With this the staging of the opposition between modern and postmodern positions lost a backdrop that had been essential to it: the sharp confrontation between the Left's engagement in the service of enlightenment and freedom on the one hand, and conservative sympathy for historicist arbitrariness and bourgeois aestheticism on the other.[11] In the German-speaking discussion after 1989 this front-line has not entirely disappeared, but it has become ever more porous. By contrast, before reunification (*die 'Wende'*), one had to reckon with ideological positions the role of

---

[10] Jean-François LYOTARD, *La condition postmoderne. Rapport sur la savoir.* Paris, Minuit, 1979.

[11] The most prominent English-speaking critics of postmodernism in the USA and Great Britain are engaged Marxist culture-theorists, Cf. Frederic JAMESON, *Postmodernism, or, The Cultural Logic of Late Capitalism.* Durham (North Carolina), Duke University Press, 1991; Terry EAGLETON, *The Illusions of Postmodernism.* Oxford, Blackwell, 1996.

which in anchoring the conflict over the postmodern should not be underestimated.[12]

In retrospect, the clear differences in style of discussion in the individual linguistic and cultural regions are very informative. In the USA the debate over the modern was intense, but was conducted with comparatively greater calm, as socio-cultural differentiation and the process of pluralisation were clearly much further advanced and popular culture had a far greater prestige. In Europe there was a remarkable polarisation between French and German intellectuals, this having to do with the fact that a larger part of the writings critical of reason and modernity arose from French authors. Seen from the outside, this led to a widespread identification of postmodernism with current French philosophy. This simplification is no less grotesque than the reduction of the German-speaking contribution to the defence of the 'unfinished project of the modernity' espoused by Habermas.[13] To be sure, the spokesmen in the debate were themselves not entirely innocent of exaggeration, obstinacy, and distortions which inhibited a fair dialogue. In his programmatic book of 1979 Lyotard put Habermas firmly in his sights and thereby triggered sharp reactions aimed at defending the ethical and aesthetic substance of modernity.[14]

In 1983 and 1985 two books, important then as now, made clear the irreconcilable positions: in 1983 Lyotard's *Le différend*,[15] and in

---

[12] Of value for the history of this period is the document of a conference on the theme 'Postmodernism', which was held by the (East-) Berlin Central Institute for Literary History at the end of 1988 during the (at the time unforeseen) final phase of the DDR: Robert WEIMANN, Hans Ulrich GUMBRECHT (eds.), *Postmoderne — globale Differenz*. Frankfurt a.M., Suhrkamp, 1991. Reading between the lines of what was said there concerning the legitimation of authority, one can in retrospect recognise a few changes in the political and cultural landscape.

[13] The speech 'Die Moderne — ein unvollendetes Projekt', which Habermas gave on the occasion of the award of the Adorno Prize, counts as a milestone in international discussion. It is printed inter alia in Jürgen HABERMAS, *Kleine Politische Schriften I-IV*. Frankfurt a.M., Suhrkamp, 1981, pp. 444-464.

[14] It is in fact quite misleading to link a theory of moral discourse with the 'terror of the universal'. Habermas's ethics of discourse and his theory of civil society and the democratic constitutional state are in the end not to be read as exhaustively developed answers to such objections. In addition there are also a series of excurses in the field of aesthetics. Cf. on architecture and the defence of modernity against 'neo-conservatism': Jürgen HABERMAS, 'Moderne und postmoderne Architektur' in his book, *Die Neue Unübersichtlichkeit: Kleine Politische Schriften V*. Frankfurt a.M., Suhrkamp, 1985, pp. 11-29.

[15] Jean-François LYOTARD, *Le Différend*. Paris, Minuit, 1983

1985 Habermas' *Der philosophische Diskurs der Moderne*[16]. Habermas' book, that in the following years would take on the function of a influential guide to the labelling of philosophical approaches, is a heartfelt plea for the unexploited potential of the enlightenment and for the combating of an irrationality which the author identifies in a few chiefly French works and their reception of Heidegger and Nietzsche. Lyotard, on the contrary, resists the idea of a unity of reason and the ideal of arriving at a consensus in practical discourse, working out the incompatibility of language games the conflict of which cannot be resolved by a central judicial instance.[17]

In hindsight, it is not surprising that many of the contributions to the postmodern debate have attached themselves to the positions of Lyotard and Habermas, and sometimes even became fixated on them.

At the end of the eighties and the beginning of the nineties the debate that in other human and social sciences had long ago lost the attraction of its novelty, started up after the usual delay in theological circles. The enthusiasm for postmodern theory in theology and in the Church was felt as enormously unsettling — at least in the first round of discussions.[18] Those who expressed such sympathies were suspected of arbitrariness and of betraying the truth. On this point conservatives and the avant-garde left of the new political theology[19] were in full agreement, such that quite some persuasion and convincing was required before the academic discussion with the suspect authors could find a platform.[20] And indeed this discussion was

---

[16] Jürgen HABERMAS, *Der philosophische Diskurs der Moderne: Zwölf Vorlesungen.* Frankfurt a.M., Suhrkamp, 1985. The fact that the first four chapters of the book were originally given as lectures at the Parisian Collège de France has great symbolic value.

[17] Cf. Manfred FRANK, *Die Grenzen der Verständigung: Ein Geistergespräch zwischen Lyotard und Habermas.* Frankfurt a.M., Suhrkamp, 1988.

[18] In any case, the constructive reception of these themes in Catholic as in Protestant theology remained the exception. Cf. Hermann TIMM, *Das ästhetische Jahrzehnt. Zur Postmodernisiering der Religion.* Gütersloh, Gütersloher Verlagshaus Gerd Mohn, 1990.

[19] Kuno FÜSSEL, Dorothee SÖLLE, Fulbert STEFFENSKY, *Die Sowohl-als-auch-Falle: Eine theologische Kritik des Postmodernismus.* Luzern, Edition Exodus, 1993.

[20] Cf. e.g. Walter LESCH, Georg SCHWIND (ed.), *Das Ende der alten Gewißheiten: Theologische Auseinandersetzung mit der Postmoderne.* Mainz, Grünewald, 1993. A very good overview of the international discussion is conveyed by the contributions in Pierre GISEL, Patrick EVRARD (ed.), *La théologie en postmodernité.* Genève, Labor et Fides, 1996 (with an exhaustively annotated bibliography).

no more free of conflict than shortly before the intercourse with the Frankfurt School, with the theory of communicative action, and finally with discourse-ethics had been. Now, however, it seemed finally the salvation of the West was at stake, so that when in doubt theology supported modernity in Habermas' sense. As always, exceptions prove the rule. In any case, however, the situation from which it arose, which we have just described, makes the much-debated postmodern syndrome an exceptional topic of interest for both theology and communications theory.[21]

Obviously, some of the growths that have sprouted from the soil of intellectual fashion are to be enjoyed only with the greatest caution. There are approaches to the critique of rationality that overshoot the mark and in the end produce nothing but arrant nonsense, yet which profit from a media environment in which fashionable constructs with the pathos of the new and the fundamental are highly marketable. To that extent, the relationship between postmodernists and the media is a multi-layered phenomenon, since the media have played a considerable part in staging and marketing the theoretical discussions, something that cannot be achieved without the aid of simplifications and stereotypes. The features and cultural programs on radio and television are not usually the object of consideration in media-ethics. It would be naive to think, however, that there are no power and profit motives at play in this area. It is precisely here that 'agenda-setting' aimed at securing market-share is extremely influential. The complexity of postmodernist themes arises not only from their sometimes quite demanding philosophical background and their interdisciplinary multiplicity of perspectives, but also from the simultaneity and non-simultaneity of developments, which for the purposes of simpler presentation are linked with or set off against each other. Thus, for example, there has been much discussion in the past years over the aesthetic stamp of our times. Certainly, the *aesthetic tendencies* of certain postmodern concepts cannot be denied, something that can then be worked up with a strategic polemical intent into an accusation of arbitrariness. Simultaneously, however, we are experiencing

---

[21] The function of a mediator was (involuntarily) taken on by the work of Emmanuel Levinas, to whom those interested in theology and philosophy of religion felt strong affinities and thereby discovered the role Levinas had played in the thought of Lyotard and Derrida. Cf. Joachim VALENTIN, *Atheismus in der Spur Gottes: Theologie nach Jacques Derrida*. Mainz, Grünewald, 1997, pp. 87-110.

a *moralising* of public discourse to a degree rarely known: a development that can only be judged as anything but arbitrary. In the search for something binding, the old consensus-paradox of modernity expresses itself: we long for ever greater agreement, while at the same time the things we have in common are being dissolved. In other words, there is good reason for a new survey of old controversies with the more relaxed attitude that comes with a greater distance from the inception of the polemics. In this way a modest contribution can be made to the improvement of the level of argumentation, that even meets the justified claims of fashionable philosophy.

2. The semiotic core of the discussion about 'postmodernity'

Among the different varieties of postmodern phenomena in present-day culture, there is one basic structure they have in common. It is the departure from firmly fixed horizons of meaning and their dissolution in an unpredictable play of signs, which in their materiality no longer stand for a univocal content, but are perceived in their pure signitivity. Following the distinction introduced by the Genevan linguist Ferdinand de Saussure at the beginning of the century, one can say that the signifier (signification-bearer) is linked with a signified (signification-content) through convention. While within the framework of the traditional concept of truth this signification appears to be secured by a reality beyond the sign, the postmodern denial[22] of such a guarantee confers upon the functioning of the signifiers a new value. They are not merely a means of transport for contents independent of them, but become the substrate that can be described with the limited means of human reason.[23] They are not only the packaging but prove to be constitutive for the transferred message. McLuhan's famed slogan, "The medium is the message", coined already in the sixties, underwent a further intensification in structuralist, semiotic, and postmodern

[22] To some extent this denial coincides with so-called post-structuralism, though the ways of identifying one's own position and that of other within semiotics and structuralism is extremely confusing.

[23] Cf. Jochen KÖHLER, 'Sprachkritik statt Ideologiekritik. Die Konjunktur der Zeichen in Strukturalismus und Poststrukturalismus' in Peter KEMPER (ed.), '*Postmoderne' oder Der Kampf um die Zukunft*. Frankfurt a.M., Fischer, 1988, pp. 37-58.

contexts.[24] Measured by the traditional philosophical and theological theory of truth this could only be seen as a relativist attack on previously accepted standards.[25]

Yet the disenchantment of structures of meaning is not an exclusive mark of the postmodern. The 'linguistic turn' had long since infected other theories, for example, the theory of communicative action in the form advocated by Habermas. Thus the postmodern dramatisation of the alleged loss of meaning is perhaps perceived as exaggerated because the foundation of action theory by speech theory takes it for granted that there exists no permanently fixed meaning content, but only ever fallible meaning claims that have to be proved in fair discourse or otherwise be revised. If this evaluation is correct, then the postmodern gesture of farewell to a metaphysics that is no longer viable ultimately expresses a much greater emotional bond with traditional models than many of the variants of modern pragmatism, which, without any trace of melancholy, set out from a sober diagnosis of the present and relinquish ultimate certainties with relative ease.[26]

In the cultural constellation just described there is an interesting crossover of modern and postmodern styles of thinking, insofar as the advocates of modernity, despite their programmatic commitment to enlightenment values, sometimes appear more modest than so-called postmodern theorists. For the latter, while refusing the

---

[24] From the perspective of the history of philosophy, one can observe that the problem of nominalism is hidden in the background here. According to nominalism only the sensuously perceptible individual can be known, and not any reality lying behind it. Only the names of things are available to us, not the reality of the things themselves. It is thus no accident that Umberto Eco's novel *Il nome della Rosa* (Milano, Bompiani, 1980), with its allusions relating to this philosophical and theological problem, should come to be a showpiece of postmodern literature.

[25] One need only think of the ontologically founded sign theory of the sacraments in Catholicism in order to gauge the theoretical distance. Cf. on the ontosemiology of being and meaning and the dissolution of its plausability from the perspective of media-analysis: Jochen HÖRISCH, *Brot und Wein: Die Poesie des Abendmahls*. Frankfurt a.M., Suhrkamp, 1992. Also the much discussed afterword by Botho STRAUß, 'Der Aufstand gegen die sekundäre Welt: Bemerkungen zu einer Ästhetik der Anwesenheit', to the book by George STEINER, *Von realer Gegenwart: Hat unser Sprechen Inhalt?* München/Wien, Hanser, 1990, pp. 303-320 (the original version which resonated internationally: *Real Presences*. London, Faber and Faber, 1990).

[26] Cf. for this kind of critique of reason: Jürgen HABERMAS, *Nachmetaphysisches Denken: Philosophische Aufsätze*. Frankfurt a.M., Suhrkamp, 1988.

emphasis on earlier concepts of truth, justice, and solidarity, are at the same time quite willing to consider often spectacular scenarios of old and new themes. Thus the critique of modernity has in fact not led to its complete disenchantment, but, on the contrary, released new semantic potential and mythological creations, that have even been sceptically acknowledged by the defenders of reason. It is a commandment of fairness, not simply to reduce postmodern thought to the derogatory slogan 'Style rather than content' ('*Design statt Bewusstsein*') but instead analyse without prejudice these new institutions of meaning beyond the trusted expressions of rationality.

The constantly heard misgiving that most contemporaries are purely and simply overwhelmed by the unbridled multiplication of signs, should be taken in all seriousness, all the more so since it is a dangerous ideology to assert the pure self-referentiality of signifying systems and thereby refuse responsibility for the consequences of one's use of signs. Indeed, mixed into the postmodern debate there is talk of 'the death of man', of 'the end of the subject', and of anti-humanism, that profits from the gesture of farewell to modernity. What is at issue here it is not just a rhetorical delirium, but a sophisticated excuse-mechanism for a generation that seems to believe that it cannot in any way influence the course of things and finds a welcome explanation for this in post-structuralist jingles like 'language speaks' ('*die Sprache spricht*'). In the face of so many apocalyptic murmurings, a hermeneutic of suspicion is advisable. If we were really caught in the web of signs, then any project of reforming the current state of things would have no chance. Although many people are plagued by feelings of powerlessness, they fortunately do not share in the idea that an automatism of meaning-shifts in the chain of signifiers determines our reality. Much rather they display an intuitive confidence in language when, for example, they demand *justice*, and thus assume that despite various different formulations for this demand there is an interculturally intelligible core which cannot be driven from the world by any intellectual relativism.

The considerations sketched out to this point should have made sufficiently clear that between the cultural trends we have described and the emergence of a media society a close symbiosis is obvious, inasmuch as the media have taken on a new value of their own over and above a service function, a value that has arisen out of the semiotic deep-structure of our age.[27] As speaking and symbolically inter-acting beings we are dependent on material structures of communi-cation, something which can on the one hand be experienced as a limitation, but on the other sets free a wholly new creativity. This need not necessarily amount to the megalomaniacal aim of creating the world anew. It can also mean using, with a twinkle in the eye, the historical stock of signs in a bric-a-brac (*bricolage*) of old elements so as to bring about interesting new structures. One can see this quite easily in the already mentioned example of architecture. While the constructions of classic modernism are marked out by pure, severe forms and for this pay the price of monotony and faceless-ness, postmodern construction has brought colourful touches to public spaces that are greeted with enthusiasm rather than disap-proval by those who use and visit the building.

The cultural postmodern of the past decade has to a great degree coincided with a aestheticisation of the lifeworld and its correspond-ing repercussions on philosophical discourse, which is now far more polyphonic.[28] Similar consequences would also be apparent in the religions as well, but for the disapproving attitude at the official level of church and theology, which has meant that they have only found a place in the religious niches of subcultures. Aesthetic think-ing, according to the cultural assumptions of our tradition, is a bedazzling phenomenon that must be met with mistrust and hostil-ity. Obviously, this is all a question of perspective and of avoiding absurd exaggerations. No serious person would claim that aesthetics is a solution for the burning problems of today. This would be not only be being blind to reality, but under the circumstances, would be cynical as well. The postmodern is less about a romantic religion of art than about a re-evaluation of sensuous perception, which is the starting-point for aesthetic experience but which also has value beyond the narrower field of art appreciation. If we live in an 'age of

---

[27] Closely bound up with this is the remarkable career of the communications and media sciences that have developed from marginal subjects to leading disciplines within the social sciences and at the same time have participated in a transformation of philology. Cf. Daniel BOUGNOUX. *Introduction aux sciences de la communication*. Paris, La Découverte, 1998; Peter LUDES, *Einführung in die Medienwissenschaft: Entwicklungen und Theorien*. Berlin, Erich Schmidt, 1998.

[28] Cf. Wolfgang WELSCH (ed.), *Die Aktualität des Ästhetischen*. München, Fink, 1993. Theological perspectives are to be found in Walter LESCH (ed.), *Theologie und ästhetis-che Erfahrung: Beiträge zur Begegnung von Religion und Kunst*. Darmstadt, Wis-senschaftliche Buchgesellschaft, 1994.

signs',[29] then in a culture dominated by visual impulses it is a worthwhile skill to be able to manage this excess of signals and work to civilise anonymous signifying systems. The postmodern omnipresence of the aesthetic is frequently understood to mean that we are being misled by alluring appearances, which in the interests of enlightenment have to be unmasked through an ideology critique so as to fend off the threat to freedom posed by the manipulation of art. Certainly, such warnings often attest to the lack of humour of authors who use a sledgehammer to crack a nut. Yet it is true that communications media have acquired a new position of importance and that through these channels influence can be exerted. The signifying systems of language, image, and sound are not just neutral tools, but can at any time be misused. Aesthetic concepts can, for example, be employed for political or commercial ends. In the first case, after the terrible events of our century the aestheticisation of the political is chiefly associated with fascism, such that one encounters the (often malicious) imputation of fascist motives as a frequently effective cudgel for the discrediting of postmodernism.

The second tendency, the aestheticisation of the commodity world, finds its visible expression in the ever more sophisticated (and thereby ever more self-reflexive) aesthetics of advertising. The serious problems that result from the inclusion of the media in globalised economic processes can only be mentioned here and not dealt with in depth. This background, however, is important for understanding noteworthy aspects of the leftist fundamental critique of postmodernism. In addition, it also relates to the basic political question of the possibility of controlling complex systems in a fragmented world.[30]

Fortunately, cultural transformations are linked with learning processes that should somewhat alleviate our cultural pessimism in the face of the above mentioned tendencies. Less and less do I have the impression that we are moving exclusively in a virtual world of

---

[29] Hans-Joachim HÖHN, 'Zeit der Zeichen — oder: Sehnsüchte in der Gegenwartskultur' in Forum medienethik 1(1998), pp. 6-15.

[30] Cf. Klaus VON BEYME, Theorie der Politik im 20. Jahrhundert. Von der Moderne zur Postmoderne. Frankfurt a.M., Suhrkamp, 1991. On the relation between globalisation, postmodernism and mass media: Peter V. BRINKEMPER, Bernhard VON DADELSEN, Thomas SENG (eds.), World Media Park. Globale Kulturvermarktung heute. Berlin, Aufbau Taschenbuch Verlag, 1994; Niels WERBER, 'Jenseits der Zeitmauer: Globalisierung als Erbe der Postmoderne?' in Merkur 52(1998)9-10, pp. 981-987.

simulations produced by media technologies. Rather, we consistently distinguish between fiction and reality and see through the ridiculousness of so many of the inhabitants of cyberspace. Even if the aesthetic fashion now and again produces some unusual blooms, on the whole it has brought a refreshing disrespect into our dealings with the world of images, which have now finally lost that aura which raised them above doubt. Art products of all kinds are viewed in their materiality and as a product of their times, and must prove themselves in a process of critical reception. If this assessment is correct, then postmodern aestheticisation is less dangerous than is often claimed. On the contrary, it sharpens our sense of relativity and so helps to make exaggerated claims and clichés explode like soap bubbles. This in turn results in a less apocalyptic way of dealing with shifts in the media landscape, which is withdrawing more and more from central control by a public-legal morality and is seeking out a new public on the free market; a public we should not too quickly judge as being stupid. Of course, the constant themes of discussion in media ethics, pornography and the representation of violence, remain unsolved problems that clearly cannot be eliminated by prohibition. Self-regulation by producers and media-pedagogic offerings for consumers can only be first steps in the right direction.

The semiotic revolution that has taken place as the backdrop to the pluralisation of our society, does not lead automatically to an atmosphere of indifference. Much rather it sets free the forces that see in the accentuation of difference a victory for democratic freedom and therefore concern themselves with tying the colourful aesthetic of the variety of ways of life, with an ethic of responsibility for the respectful interaction with this plurality. On just this basis, I hold many condemnations of postmodernism in the name of an enlightened modernism to be an expression of anxiety and insecurity in the face of the unsolved problems of modern society. Obviously, the recognition of difference is conceivable within the framework of the 'incomplete project of modernity'. However, it should not be overlooked that the deserved claims of feminism and multiculturalism first gained their long-deserved cultural recognition only in association with postmodern theorems. If one succeeds in unmasking the signifying system of our age as a masculine and eurocentric dominated apparatus of power, then in postmodern difference thinking there lies hidden more ethical potential than many of the beneficia-

ries of classic modernism would have it. In this sense, I would plead
for a less heated way of dealing with a cultural development, from
which in the last decade ethics has in the end only derived advantages. Instead of living parasitically upon the contemporary crisis of
direction that it is often discussed along with the postmodern and
instead of constantly giving old answers to new questions, it would
be more constructive to enter into the logic of our civilisation
dynamic and to train our diagnostic gaze on new challenges.

3. Media-ethical discourse as bound to its times

It is under the conditions analysed to this point, that media-ethical
discourse, as a critical commentary on developments that race
ahead ever more quickly, has become conscious of its being bound
to it times. It does not wish to draw up any revolutionary new professional ethics for the field of journalistic labour, especially since
there are already good foundational works in this regard.[31] Here it
is less a matter of a professional ethics analysis of individual cases
as of a conceptual agreement over a theoretical framework, the
knowledge of which could then be made fruitful in concrete applications. Of course, anyone who is occupied with such basic questions runs a double risk. On the one hand the generality of the
expression makes its practical utility appear in an unfavourable
light; this is the (hopefully healthy) delayed effect that is part of all
theoretical endeavours. On the other hand, it can easily happen that
one is refuted through confrontation with a swiftly changing reality.
The danger of being shown up if one over- or under-estimates technological developments has accompanied media ethics since its
beginnings, and seems to belong to the professional risks of the ethicist generally.

Insofar as it is a task of philosophy to comprehend the current age
in thought, we will not be able to dispense with this sometimes
uncomfortable form of contemporaneity and are left with the task of
provisionally clarifying the questions that present themselves. Let us
turn first of all to two essential functions of media communications
and their transformation in the postmodern; the creation of a public

---

[31] Cf. Daniel CORNU, *Journalisme et vérité: Pour une éthique de l'information*. Genéve,
Labor et Fides, 1994.

space relevant to the functioning of democracy, and public entertainment. According to the categories of modernity, the definition of the relations between these two functions was relatively clear. Priority fell to a normatively loaded concept of public space, while entertainment had a less positive image and was controlled through morally influenced conceptions of good taste. Today the situation has just about been turned on its head. The traditional distinction between private and public is being bypassed by the progressive privatisation and commercialisation of the media system. Moreover, private life as a repertoire of sensational topics (*Boulevard*) is gaining an ever greater importance, shifting the heart of journalistic work towards a summarising analysis of the day's events, which, where possible, should be reported under the guise of entertainment (infotainment). Measured by the standards of quality journalism this may sound like a story of decline. Yet it is entirely possible to derive something positive from this development. Through the differentiation of programs there also arises new opportunities for broadcasting more discriminating projects in formats that do not have to worry about the pressure to be entertaining. Besides, it is not only a drawback when there is no longer just one forum for political exchange between citizens, but rather many smaller public spaces offering occasions for understanding and networking. The internet is just such an integrative medium that opens up a wealth of new perspectives that until now did not exist in this immediacy.

The ever faster communication of data gives a few critics cause for great concern, in that while it creates a sense of immediacy, it can also lead to a feeling of menace. The new information and communications media make us in a certain way independent of pregiven spatial structures and create virtual meeting points that are freely accessible to all users of the medium. Associated with this is the promise of the creation of an unlimited communications community that could never have existed without digital means.[32] The downside of this new control over space and time is a loss of the sense of having to overcome any resistance and of the sense for the concrete needs of one's actual communication partner.

---

[32] I nevertheless take the talk of a 'technological pentecost', which was coined on the basis of a formula of McLuhan's, to be a gross exaggeration. Cf. in this regard Welsch, *Unsere postmoderne Moderne*, p. 216. The most important objection arises from the fact that free access to a complete media network is still limited to a small part of the world's population.

The critique of the negative effects of the process of modernisation, which has been fed from quite varying sources, has therefore always taken up a cautionary attitude to the 'racing standstill' that has been brought about by limitless acceleration.[33] Today we have just about accustomed ourselves to accepting with a certain fatalism the ever more hectic movement of the *Zeitgeist* and the tempo of technological innovation, as if the achieved level of living conditions in a media and service society can no longer be in any way altered. In extreme cultural theories this diagnosis is sharpened into the idea of 'posthistory': a state beyond the laborious history of emancipation that has come to an end with the achievement of the liberal economy and the constitutional state. Within this framework, that has been won once and for all, history only simmers away on a low flame such that we will not have to contend with any really new developments.[34]

In actual fact, however, it is precisely journalistic activity that is the best antidote to the illusion of a frozen age and an end of history, for it consists in summarising and evaluating with seismographic accuracy the shifts in power relations from day to day.[35] Through such activity it should become clear to any half alert contemporary, that the historical process has in no way reached a desirable endpoint and that for better or worse the future is still open.[36]

4. Between description and evaluation

The project we have favoured here, of a contemporaneity of media ethics combined with a diagnostic sharpness and a capacity for con-

---

[33] Paul VIRILIO, *L'inertie polaire*. Paris, Christian Bourgois, 1990. Cf. in this regard the critical observations of Jochen HÖRISCH, 'Non plus ultra: Paul Virilios rasende Thesen vom rasenden Stillstand' in *Merkur* 47(1993)9-10, pp. 784-794.

[34] Cf. Francis FUKUYAMA, *The End of History and the Last Man*. New York, The Free Press, 1992; Rainer ROTHERMUNDT, *Jedes Ende ist ein Anfang: Auffassungen vom Ende der Geschichte*. Darmstadt, Wissenschaftliche Buchgesellschaft, 1994.

[35] Cf. on the 'daily labour' of journalism: Jacques DERRIDA, *L'autre cap suivi de La démocratie ajournée*. Paris, Minuit, 1991.

[36] On the historical-philosophical consideration of this dimension of our times: Walter LESCH, 'Verlorenes Paradies und befristete Zeit. Variationen über Geschichtsphilosophie und Apokalyptik' in Daria PEZZOLI-OLGIATI (ed.), *Zukunft unter Zeitdruck: Auf den Spuren der 'Apokalypse'*. Zurich, Theologischer Verlag Zürich, 1998, pp. 33-65. On the media-theory and communications-technology aspects of the consciousness of the times: Georg Christoph THOLEN, Michael O. SCHOLL (ed.), *Zeit-Zeichen: Aufschübe und Interferenzen zwischen Endzeit und Echtzeit*. Weinheim, VCH Acta Humaniora, 1990.

structive criticism, has to be a two-tracked one. It has both descriptive as well as evaluative moments, and the transition from the one to the other is not easy to formulate. On the descriptive level, it is to my mind a question of finding a reliable way of taking a snapshot of the current situation. Such a project has obviously to take into consideration the methods of empirical social research.[37] But to this one can also add the range of instruments provided by a critical philosophy of culture which can argue in a broader framework and at times even test working hypotheses which with time may show themselves to be problematic.[38] The entire postmodern debate of the last decade seems to stand on such an unstable foundation, but its continuing heuristic function cannot be denied. On the contrary, these theoretical discussions sharpen the focus of those dealing with empirical details. and in this way have made a valuable contribution to the clarifying the self-conception of an epoch. Naturally, in the course of this, evaluations have also slipped in which have still to be proved. It is often better, however, to have such premises than to search for cultural trends completely without orientation or imagination.

The consideration of the possible foundations for ethics in a philosophy of a culture can make an essential contribution to detecting the blind spots in the specialised field of so-called 'applied ethics'. For an interest in background cultural assumptions need not necessarily lead to an aestheticisation of the ethical, but can above all help to integrate larger theoretical lines of thought into arguments specific to certain fields. To that extent draft projects for a postmodernist ethics[39] have made a quite substantial contribution to the expansion of the ethicist's spectrum of perception. What is now at stake is making the results of the thinking of plurality and difference fruitful for the evaluation of media systems and for the activity of media producers and users.

An example of this is the media ethics analysis of the communication structures in the public spaces of cities, in which modern and

---

[37] Cf. the thoughts of Hans-Joachim Höhn on the relation of structural reflection to the diagnosis of the times in social ethics, 'Im Zeitalter der Beschleunigung: Konturen einer theologischen Sozialdiagnose als Zeitanalyse' in *Jahrbuch für Christliche Sozialwissenschaften* 32(1991), pp. 245-264.

[38] Cf. Carl-Friedrich GEYER, *Einführung in die Philosophie der Kultur*. Darmstadt, Wissenschaftliche Buchgesellschaft, 1994.

[39] Cf. e.g., Zygmunt BAUMAN, *Postmodern Ethics*, Oxford/Cambridge (Mass.), Blackwell, 1993.

postmodern theoretical constructs make themselves concrete. Cities
are not only the place where modern media systems arise; they are
also the stage for political manifestations and democratic decision
processes, for changing forms of life, and for cultural experiments.
The language of media theories is stamped with the spatial
metaphors of urban life-worlds. We speak of forums and market-
places, streets and boulevards, as the symbolic places of a multiply
differentiated public realm. In particular, the metropolises of the
twentieth century have become the essence of technological modernisation, the ambivalence of which we have since become conscious of
— not least in regard to the mega-cities of the southern hemisphere.
Increased freedom and isolation, economic success and poverty, tolerance and violence, cultural riches and banality, memory and forget-
fulness; these are only a few of the facets of something which began
with great hopes and has lead us to great insecurity, and which, with
the disappearance of concrete places into virtual space, has gained a
new dimension. In the media we communicate not only *about* these
conditions, but as well *in* structures the legitimacy of which often has
only a dubious basis. We can only *act* responsibly then, if we do not
separate moral *judgements* from the unprejudiced *seeing* of reality.
Exactly for this reason, ethics is also dependent on the work of interpreting the confusing and contradictory signs of the times, which to a
considerable degree are only accessible via the media. Through this,
ethics and journalism necessarily become involved in a very close
working relationship. It is a relationship that in the interests of mutual
learning processes should be cultivated and, for example, can begin
on the level of cooperation with media in the home and work-place,
though it is not necessarily limited to any one area. To that extent, the
vision of the global village has now become a reality, at least for a few
privileged media users. It has allowed an alternative to modern met-
ropolitan culture to spring up, because the new networks are poly-
centric and provide a counter-weight to the old centres of power.

   Having been for ten or twenty years a virgin territory in the field
of ethics, the confrontation with the ambivalence of modernity has
since become quite familiar terrain. It is thus of secondary importance whether we stick with the concept of postmodernism or prefer
with Ulrich Beck to speak of a second modernity.[40] The important

---

[40] The theoretical presuppositions for the development of the concepts of a risk
society, reflexive modernisation and a second modernity have been expounded by

thing is the expansion of horizons that allows us not to cling desperately to one normative concept of the public realm, while around us the world has changed so much that the old categories are only partially applicable. An up-to-date *ethics of the public realm*, besides its necessary engagement as a professional ethics in journalistic education and practice, operates as well at the interface of ethics and aesthetics, economics and politics, technology and philosophy. Only in these inter-disciplinary constellations and on the basis of a hermeneutic flexibility can it succeed in understanding and critically following current developments — even at the price of revisions that may prove to be appropriate in the course of the ever faster development of media technologies.[41]

The more concrete it becomes the more ethics shares this destiny with a critically-minded journalism, which likewise cannot occupy any completely independent observer's standpoint, but which in all its efforts to be objective is caught up in the controversies of its societal environment. An ethics that has the ambition to be socially critical and to be a diagnosis of the times, will get its most effective hearing when it is familiar with how society sees itself from within, including its media systems, and gathers together in dense descriptions the arguments and convictions espoused therein.[42]

Beck in a programmatic outline: Ulrich BECK, 'Vom Veralten sozialwissenschaftlicher Begriffe: Grundzüge einer Theorie reflexiver Modernisierung' in Christoph GÖRG (ed.), *Gesellschaft im Übergang: Perspektiven kritischer Soziologie*. Darmstadt, Wissenschaftliche Buchgesellschaft, 1994, pp. 21-43.

[41] Cf. Dennis MÜLLER, 'L'éthique, prise de vitesse par le cours du monde?' in *Le Supplément. Revue d'éthique et de théologie morale*. 190(1994), pp. 51-69.

[42] This hermeneutic-ethical understanding of critical contemporaneity takes its orientation from Michael WALZER, *Interpretation and Social Criticism*. Cambridge (Mass.) — London, Harvard University Press, 1987, where the "the path of illumination" (through religious inspiration) and the "path of discovery" (of completely context-dependent norms) are contrasted with a more feasible "path of interpretation", upon which the social critic moves with the competence and vulnerability of a contemporary.

THE NEED FOR UNDERSTANDING
MASS PSYCHOLOGY IN MEDIA ETHICS

Bart Pattyn

The total amount of time spent working in a day in Europe divided by the number of Europeans above 15 years of age amounts to an average of around 3.33 hours a day. The same calculation based on the number of hours of television viewed in a day gives a result of 3.05 hours. This, at least, is what we learn from data published in 1991, but, since then, we have little reason to believe that people work much more than they watch television. On the contrary. In Belgium, for example, the amount of time devoted to work in a normal working day in 1998 divided by the number of Belgians above 15 was 3.1 hours, whereas television viewing, with 3.02 hours, differed by only 8 minutes. The least one could say on the basis of this calculation is that a great deal of time is invested in viewing audio-visual media.

The reason that is normally cited in order to explain this success is rather simple: a lot of television is being viewed because television offers something people need. People choose to spend their evenings watching television because news editors and production studios deliver products that meet the need for information and recreation. Information is a very broad concept. It involves things like weather reports, scientific studies but also various bits of trivia concerning all sorts of national and international occurrences, conflicts and scandals, or reports of disasters, technical breakthroughs or sporting events. Likewise, the need for recreation can assume many diverse forms. For instance, people enjoy going to see a romantic film or a thriller, they follow one of the soaps or they challenge their intelligence with one game show or another etc. Modern technology has made it possible nowadays to meet all these kinds of preferences in a differentiated way, and this is precisely why television has become such an influential medium.

In the sort of explanation just cited, questions are seldom raised about the moral and cultural differences of quality among needs, and about the heterogeneity of the circumstances under which they have come about. It appears to be of little importance where these needs come from and what their value is. Important is the fact that needs exist. Also important is the question of how these needs are going to be fulfilled. Producers will make little effort to discover whether a need for information, for example, is based on a political interest, a scientific curiosity, a social expectation pattern or an instinctual upsurge. For them, it is sufficient to know that such a need exists and in what way it can be successfully satisfied. The same applies to academically trained economists. In their scientific research, they intentionally abstract from theories about the genesis or the moral and cultural quality of preferences. In their opinion, qualitative considerations regarding preferences and needs have, by and large, a subjective and unscientific character, and have nothing to do with what economic research should ultimately be about, namely, the most efficient strategy for optimally matching the supply with the demand.

The morally neutral tone of the economic approach makes it very attractive outside the sphere of economic thought. Now that people feel mature enough to distance themselves from the stuffy and pedantic tone in which needs and desires used to be spoken about in schools and churches, a thought framed in terms of consumers and producers offers an attractive alternative. Liberal theories about the subjective meaning of evaluations and preferences help to wash away the bitter taste of guilt and contrition that had been induced by meticulous moralists. The liberating idea that no authority can determine what someone else should consider good or important has contributed to economic language, thereby becoming the standard language, not only when one speaks about the media, but also about culture, academic education, social security, health care and so on.

There are undoubtedly many additional reasons for the current success of the language of producers and consumers, and any attempt to provide a comprehensive survey would lead us too far afield, but I would like to examine one of these additional reasons because I will return to it later in the discussion. Economic language makes it possible to believe that everything is all right as long as a person's 'natural' and personal needs and preferences are taken care of in a reasonable and timely fashion. Some of his or her desires might be slightly aberrant or somewhat unrefined, but they are not murderous desires, certainly not where the majority is concerned. In the producer-consumer context, human discord, aggression and xenophobia are often interpreted as the consequence of frustrations encountered when one is unable to satisfy certain of these desires. Hooliganism and racism, for example, are regularly explained as the consequence of declining material circumstances. It is in this sense that the prevailing economic language helps us, without our being aware of it, to forget that a human being can indeed be a frightening creature. It helps us to cover up the fact that *Dasein* — to speak like Heidegger — is a poignantly open question, a project in an incomprehensible world, in anticipation of an equally incomprehensible death. Speaking in terms of producers and consumers keeps this kind of dark speculation at a safe distance and maintains the illusion that, as a result of developments in science and technology, every consumer possesses a world of unforeseen possibilities and opportunities that no other human being could previously have been offered.

The language of consumers and producers is quite common. It forms an element of our individualistic culture. In this paper, I will discuss some pessimistic presuppositions from Émile Durkheim, Gustave Le Bon and Sigmund Freud. These authors confront us with anti-individualistic and unconventional views on human nature and offer a mass psychological understanding of the way in which the audio-visual media became so time consuming.

1. Collective Spheres of Emotions

Modern people have a tendency to assume that decisions are by definition the result of independent reflection and consideration and that choices are made on the basis of personal preference. Even when what motivates our behaviour is attributed to 'unconscious' processes, the 'blame' is ascribed more often than not to our personal life history. When we reflect on the multiplicity of things that can happen to a person, it is the individual we tend to place before our mind's eye. When it comes to community formation, there are those who would defend the notion that society is only possible because agreements and understandings are achieved between autonomous individuals. The accepted conceptual sequence implies that, in the first instance, there are individuals, who form communities only in the second instance. The individual is considered to be the *arché* of society.

At the beginning of this century, a number of researchers in France became convinced that this conceptual sequence needed to be turned on its head, believing that community had priority over the individual, and that persons with an individual character developed only later and certainly not always and everywhere. Such a point of departure implies that in our culture, individualism is a fairly recent development[1] and that in the past, and to a certain extent still today, human life was and is regulated by a communal, 'trans-individual' reality.

Indeed, there exist phenomena in every culture which are not simply the mean of what individual people desire, think or do. Such phenomena are 'trans-individual,' referring, for example, to concepts such as 'group-sentiment,' 'mentality,' 'public opinion,' 'ambience,' 'current,' 'tendency,' 'trend,' etc. In ancient communities, according to Émile Durkheim, this 'trans-individual instance' made individual thinking unusual and unnecessary because in any given circumstance, an individual thought and did what would be considered proper for a community member to think and do.[2] It rarely occurred to the individual to take a 'personal' stand with respect to common understanding. Durkheim referred to this 'trans-individual' reality with the term 'collective consciousness.' What he intended by this term can best be understood against the background of the idea that what people respect, what they consider to be 'worth the effort' depends on something beyond the capacities of the individual. In contrast to what is often assumed, the respect we nurture for ourselves or for others or for this or that custom or institution is not only dictated by individual motives, but falls back on a sort of participation in an instance which transcends the individual. The individual does not have this instance at his or her 'disposal.'

---

[1] The best known contribution to this debate is undoubtedly that of Marcel MAUSS, 'Une catégorie de l'esprit humain: la notion de personne, celle de «moi»', reprinted in M. MAUSS, *Sociologie et antropologie*. Paris, Quadrige-PUF, 1991.

[2] The idea that the community is completely dominated at the start by the transindividual 'collective consciousness' was developed by Durkheim in *De la division du travail social*. Paris, Alcan, 1893 – Paris, Quadrige-PUF, 1991, although it continued to play a fundamental role in his later work.

When the collective consciousness is dominant in a society, this does not necessarily have something to do with a kind of un-democratic balance of power. The individual as an autonomous entity is in many situations not really aware of his obedience to what is expected of him. We can say that even in our culture, the dominance of common presuppositions or commitments is real, but we do not mention this dominance because it does not occur to us to question these common presuppositions and commitments.

Because it is impossible to study ancient group sentiment directly, since sentiments and emotions can only be noticed by feeling them, Durkheim analysed moral codes and civil law as expressions of the collective consciousness. In studying their evolution, he came to the conclusion that the legal systems of ancient societies were geared towards the sanctioning of any violation of group sentiment with a punishment which raised just as much emotion as that unleashed by the violation itself. The choice of terrible punishments such as quartering, beheading, torture and such things was not the result of tyrannical whim, but was a response to necessity. Without some counterweight, without a response that is just as impressive as the original transgression, respect for order and authority, religion and government would vanish, and society would disintegrate.

In modern societies, where internal cohesion is more a matter of economic dependence, this emotional connotation seem no longer to be a part of the legal system. The purpose of a modern legal system is no longer atonement but reparation. Now, there is less talk of shame and disgrace. The degree of punishment is no longer necessarily equivalent to the degree of collective indignation; it is measured in time and cost by objective facts and formal legal rules.

Can one conclude from this, however, that collective emotions have come to play a much more restricted role in modern societies, as Durkheim initially seems to have believed? It is possible that what was previously expressed in repressive jurisprudence now manifests itself in other ways, through the mass media for instance. No one can deny that modern society is also awash with collective feelings of emotion: collective mourning for the violent death of a prominent princess, collective indignation and gloating over the sexual delinquencies of a president, collective enthusiasm or despair during the course of football's world cup. All these sorts of reports have one thing in common: they affect the mood of the crowd.

2. Sensation, Honour, Courage and Trust

Sensation has to do with collective emotions. No one would contest this, but when it comes to describing what collective emotions are and what their impact is on a person's motivation, then this unanimity is put to the test. A collective emotion is usually conceived as a sum of individual emotions. The emotion experienced by a person X, for example, in learning of the misadventures of president C would be strengthened by a similar emotion in person Y, Z, etc., and in this way a collective emotional feeling would arise that results in immense public interest. Durkheim's point becomes more original from the moment that he begins to build on this type of reasoning. The personal emotion of person X is not merely strengthened by the personal emotion of person Y and Z, etc., but is also strengthened by the collective emotion as such. In other words, a self-strengthening movement arises that contributes to giving the collective emotion a life of its own. This implies, for instance, that when an emotionally charged trend acquires a collective character, no one is still able to say, 'I shaped this trend,' whereas sometimes the opposite can be said: 'someone is shaped by this trend.' Even if someone refuses to be taken in by a certain atmosphere or tendency, the atmosphere still presents itself as an objective given, a reality *sui generis*. Durkheim stresses this by continually emphasising that the whole cannot be reduced to the sum of the parts. Whoever attends musical concerts or visits the theatre has undoubtedly had many opportunities to notice that musicians or actors, at certain privileged moments, are able to derive inspiration from a certain mood that takes over the concert-hall or theatre in order to give their music and words a renewed intensity. Looking back over their careers, many musicians and actors consider these experiences as the most gratifying, even though they do not have the slightest rational explanation for what happened to the audience and performers at such moments. As is well known, Durkheim considered this sort of sacred, objective group emotion to be the source of religious feelings, practices and ideas which initially were thought to leaven every segment of social life. He also believed that, in modern societies, social institutions such as justice, politics and education derived their authority from this kind of collective emotion.

Durkheim also went a step further. He believed that collective emotions also generate courage and self-confidence. Someone who

is part of an energetic professional team, surrounded by an enthusi-
astic family, or a member of a winning football team, for instance,
discovers that his personal self-confidence grows. And the opposite
is true as well: a member of a family in which there is a painful dis-
unity, of a governmental department where things are dealt with
slowly and bureaucratically, or of a company where bankruptcy
appears inevitable, will undoubtedly experience difficulties in carrying out his tasks in a careful manner. The feeling of being someone,
of doing valuable work, of counting for something, or being
involved in something meaningful — all of this is related to the
atmosphere in which people live and work together with others. The
groups in which a person participates, whether they be the family,
the workplace, a neighbourhood, a religious community, a cultural
association or hobby club, each in their own way inspire ideals that
transcend the individual's self-interest and ensure that when a person takes these ideals to heart, his or her self-respect, courage and
self-confidence increase. By participating in groups, an individual is
capable of surpassing himself and taking initiatives that would be
foolish from a purely rational point of view. As long as there is an
audience who can give an individual the feeling that what he or she
does is essential, there will be people who are capable of heroic acts.
This can be seen in family life, in work situations, in health care, in
the theatre, in sport, etc.

If one bears in mind this inspirational power, one can understand
why human beings are indeed social animals. It is not so much a
result of some natural need to be together, but rather because their
soul, their *virtus*, self-respect, honour, courage and self-confidence
are all the result of their participation in the group. Conversely, people who fall back on themselves and do not maintain the slightest
relation with the outside world, friends or family, will wither away
unless they direct themselves to a virtuous alterity, or an alterity that
is not of this world. People are not very well aware of this kind of
dependence because the prevailing individualistic ideology over-
shadows the importance of group feelings and attachments. A person's observable behaviour, however, clearly shows the interest in
those groups that affect their identity. The supporters of a football
team are extremely interested in the latest achievements of their
club, citizens in the recent election results, workers in the results of
their company. Government leaders, for instance, must take great
care, when ordering troops to be deployed for humanitarian reasons,

that no compatriots are killed in the intervention, and to ensure this there are often a large number of 'enemy' casualties. If government leaders did not do this, they would run the risk of public opinion unanimously turning against them, obstructing any further form of participation in international peacekeeping missions. What else is at stake here than group solidarity?

3. Television Viewing and Group Participation

Now that I have recalled Durkheim's observations in this regard, I would like to return to the matter of the needs that exist in connection with the television medium. It is often said that we live in an individualistic time. Individualism is presented, following Tocqueville's definition, as a withdrawal from social life and a turning inwards with family members and friends: 'cocooning,' we would say nowadays. Bearing in mind the fact that family life is often fragmented, one concludes that individualism has never been so radical as it is today.

It is true that people withdraw, but they do not do it by completely separating themselves from the outside world. They keep an eye on what takes place in politics, in their neighbourhood, and even with their rivals and idols. They have an informant, quite a good informant, one who knows the kind of information people are sensitive to. One who tells them about all those places where things happen: where decisions are taken, trends are set, films conceived, important matches played, the future created and riddles solved. What these places mean to our culture can be compared with what Versailles was for the French nobility under Louis XIV. The nobles who were not at court had the feeling that they had been exiled. The closer the contact with the monarch, the more important they felt. Nothing important happened if it happened outside the king's court. Now, nothing happens unless it is reported on CNN. Television broadcasts with large viewing audiences have a similar power. People watch them in the belief that they will see what they have to see in order to be 'in touch,' in order to belong to the world. Successful television is able to give citizens the feeling that they will see what is going on at the very heart of the group which affects their identity. This means that news reports are devoted to mass meetings, a political event, a shocking revelation by a well known personality. In the entertainment industry, it is a matter of a spectacular show, a performance by a popstar, a soap opera, a sporting event, etc.

There has been a significant shift in recent years in the medium of television. Previously, the public broadcasters had the lion's share of the viewing public; now however, many new broadcasters have entered the arena (in Europe, from 21 in 1980 to 119 in 1997), each of which serves a fraction of the viewers. One can, for this reason, no longer claim that television keeps people uniformly informed about what is going on in their society. Instead of this, it seems at first sight that they are being offered a wide variety of television programmes. This view must be qualified somewhat on the basis of market share statistics. In each national state, half of the market, per language, is shared by at most two broadcasters. In light of the enormous interest in the medium of television, these broadcasters enjoy a very large reach. In addition, more broadcasters do not necessarily imply a completely different sort of information being offered. The difference of emphasis between reports from different networks is usually minor. One network's editors keep an eye on the bulletins from the other networks. If the competition has some interesting news, they will attempt to report on the same news as soon as possible. This is also true of entertainment. There is usually little difference in the concept or the form with which various successful entertainment programmes and talk shows are constructed. It is true that each broadcaster has its own atmosphere, and that people respond to what various broadcasters are offering, but in spite of this diversity people will remain fascinated by programmes that involve a strong 'we feeling,' i.e., a feeling of 'us against them.' Because this feeling is strengthened by the idea that a large number of viewers are watching the same programme at the same time, television will always be a business with a few large broadcasters and many small, specialised ones.

The ideas that have taken shape up to now boil down to the following: People spend a significant portion of their valuable time with television because television provides them with information about groups that affect their identity. Choosing to be on top of things, being alert to what is going on in society, is not voluntary, but has to do with affective relations that people have with groups that they consider as their own. More must be said about the affective relation between the individual and his group. One of the theoretical

concepts that can be useful here is undoubtedly the concept of identification.

4. Identification and the Power of Groups

Persons, groups and institutions with the ability to attract someone
into identifying with them have power over the identifier, which can
be a good thing if these persons, groups and institutions have good
intentions similar to responsible parents and educators. This power,
however, can also be terrifying. In our time, these ambivalent consequences of the process of identification often remain hidden because
we tend to use the term 'identification' in an active sense, creating
the impression that during this process the subject is in control. In
other words, he or she makes up his or her own mind about who he
or she will or will not identify with, and he or she is able to give up
previous engagements. This habit makes us forget how easily identification can turn people into accomplices to mass murder or similar
horrors. For historical reasons, it would be better to define identification as 'the semi-unconscious process of being seduced into identifying with someone or something, a process which, once it has
taken place, is impossible to undo without leaving scars.' One
should keep in mind that identification is like 'falling in love.'
Indeed, even without recognizing it, people are aware that their self-
respect is dependent on what their identification models value. They
are usually prepared to do foolish things to gain their approval.
Even in the modern world, people are extremely sensitive to what
significant others think of them.
   In his treatment of the identification process, Freud often speaks
of 'self-respect.' In his view self-respect relies on a reinvestment of
energy into the self, a process which triggers the narcissistic associations of omnipotence. It is interesting that in this context, he makes
use of a metaphor which makes us attentive to those interpersonal
processes that we tend to overlook in our individualistically oriented
understanding. The way Freud conceives it, it is as if energy, desire
or love, the terms are frequently interchangeable, can flow from one
person to another like some measurable quantity. A person loses the
amount that has been invested in someone else, making that person
feel disconsolate, unsure and dependent — like someone in love.
What the other person has 'received' increases one's personal energy,

resulting in a feeling of pride, self-respect and omnipotence. Such a physicalistic paradigm seems absurd because none of us would accept that personal feelings can be quantitatively transferred from oneself to another, and yet this metaphor can point out certain observations that are dissimulated by the current conceptual framework. This metaphor will indeed seem less absurd when one realizes that courage, resilience and vitality are closely allied with self-respect, self-assurance and even with a certain feeling of omnipotence, and that all these phenomena are linked with the support, love, encouragement and appreciation which has been shown or is currently shown to us by those in our immediate environment. On the other hand, if our initiatives are unappreciated or if our requests for love go unanswered, then we feel shame. At such moments our self-respect and self-assurance have disappeared and we have the feeling that we no longer have any meaning.

The conclusion here is the same: An individual's attitude regarding people to which he is attracted to identify with is always ambivalent, since others can both encourage and destroy the motive and the meaning of what is personified.

What is crucial to our argumentation is the fact that people tend to misinterpret the existence of this ambivalence. Either they think that 'to identify with something' is just a cognitive process with the same connotation as 'to recognize something,' or they are convinced that the people with whom they identify are just like friends and mean well. Most often they do both. They have the impression that they can choose their own group of friends and fellow citizens in the same way as they are convinced that they can rationally decide which values they want to follow, and secondly they believe that they can participate in the groups with which they identify without provoking dissension. This would seem to be correct. It is possible that a group without any internal dissension comes into existence, but fortunately that happens rarely because that kind of collusion usually has dangerous features. Freud was dealing with this kind of group in *Massenpsychologie und Ich-Analyse*. But before turning to a discussion of that book, we should say something about Gustave le Bon and his famous *Psychologie des foules*, a work that inspired *Massenpsychologie* as a comment.

The first publication by Durkheim on group sentiment was mentioned at the beginning of this discussion. It did not come into existence in a vacuum. A number of prominent researchers, with whom he would later engage in a dialogue, published material on the same topic around the same time. Three years prior to Durkheim's study, Gabriël Tarde's *Les lois de l'imitation*[3] appeared (1890) and five years later Gustave le Bon's striking *Psychologie des foules*[4] (1895). This latter publication was considered the most authoritative work on the psychology of the masses for fifty years after its publication.

Concerning the individuals who make up the masses, le Bon wrote that they tended to experience a feeling of invincible power, losing their sense of responsibility in the anonymous crowd. Such individuals are quickly influenced or 'infected' by the behaviour of the other individuals who constitute the masses, undergoing a sort of persuasion akin to hypnotic suggestion. The masses as such are impulsive, unstable, irritable, easily manipulated and gullible. Someone wanting to take advantage of the masses would do best not to employ reasonable arguments, but rather should offer fascinating visual images which they should repeat again and again. The masses as such shelter no doubts. For this reason, they are able to offer blind faith in a particular authority and maintain a position of unlimited intolerance. The only positive thing le Bon has to say is that the masses can raise the moral standards of the individual. "While the personal advantage of an isolated individual is more or less his or her only motivation, this is seldom the case where the masses are concerned."[5] The masses, however, do not increase the moral standards of an individual by appealing to his or her capacity to reason, but rather on the basis of emotional influence.

Le Bon's denigrating choice of words goes back to his initial aversion towards the socialist movements which he viewed, from his middle-class conservative standpoint, as a phenomenon of a counterfeit culture. The pessimistic tone of his work also stems from the delimitation of his topic. Indeed, le Bon did not have in mind an organized society, but rather the ephemeral masses.

Le Bon's *Psychologie des foules* was the point of departure for Sigmund Freud's (1856-1939) *Massenpsychologie und Ich-Analyse*[6] published in 1921. Fascinated by le Bon's observations, Freud asked him-

---

[3] G. TARDE, *Les lois de l'imitation. Étude sociologique*. Paris, Alcan, 1895.

[4] G. LE BON, *Psychologie des foules*. Paris, Alcan, 1895, 1926[34]; (Quadrige, 14), Paris, PUF, 1983.

[5] ID., *op. cit.*, 1926[34], p. 42.

[6] S. FREUD, *Gesammelte Werke*, vol. 13, p. 71-161; Eng. Transl.: *Standard Edition*, Vol. 18, p. 67-143.

self how it is possible that people can be so strongly tied to one another despite the ambivalent nature of interpersonal relations and how it was possible that the intellectual capacity of the individual was so powerfully inhibited in a group situation. In an effort to offer an answer to these questions, he proposed the following hypothesis: The masses emerge when individuals equate their ideals with the will of a single leader or with a single abstract system of ideas, and thereby, come to identify with one another. When the 'ego ideal,' which Freud at that moment considered to be a rational instance, became completely equated with the common ideal, then personal rationality would tend to vanish. The feeling of omnipotence experienced by the individual in a group context harks back to the narcissistic origin of his or her emotional capacity which has crossed over to the ideal of the group. In such a group, every imperfection is projected onto people and institutions that are commonly believed to be 'bad,' situated outside the circle of 'fellow feeling.' When conformity comes under threat, the individual is affected at a level which constitutes his or her personal identity, namely, his or her 'ego ideal.' Given the fact that the 'ego ideal' is charged with narcissistic wilfulness, the emotions released by the threat to the 'ego ideal' are akin to the impulse of self-preservation. In this regard, Freud wrote: "In the undisguised antipathies and aversions which people feel towards strangers with whom they have to do, we may recognize the expression of self-love — of narcissism. This self-love works for the preservation of the individual, and behaves as though the occurrence of any divergence from his own particular lines of development involved a criticism of them and a demand for their alteration... it is unmistakable that in this whole connection men give evidence of a readiness for hatred, an aggressiveness, the source of which is unknown, and to which one is tempted to ascribe an elementary character."[7]

As we saw with le Bon, Freud also had the ephemeral masses in mind. He was well aware that masses which completely absorbed the individual were rather rare phenomena. "Each individual is a component part of numerous groups, he is bound by ties of identification in many directions, and he has built up his ego ideal upon the most various models."[8] With this theoretical background in mind,

---

[7] *Standard Edition*, Vol. 18, p. 102.
[8] *Ibid.*, p. 129.

we will now return to our earlier conclusions in order to see if our observations open some other perspectives on why television is so time-consuming.

5. Freedom and the Attraction of the Audio-Visual Media

Freedom is normally defined as the ability to do what one wants. But it seems unlikely that people feel free just to the extent that they have the means to do what they wish. Someone in financial need has the feeling of being fixated on material concerns, of course, but how is it that some people in the same dire circumstances feel more free and less worried than others? The feeling of being trapped is even more common in people who have little or no commitments. What is it then that leads to the feeling of not being free? The feeling that one is trapped has undoubtedly to do with the awareness that one is not able take part fully in social life, and in this way we come to a discovery that is closely related to the conclusions of the previous paragraphs: People can feel quite free even when they are suffering under all sorts of unbearable demands, on the condition that they feel they are participating in something that is at the core of the group life of which they are a part. Apparently what works in a liberating manner is the 'we feeling.' This kind of involvement explains why people are so keenly interested in what happens to the groups that affirm their identity.

It is on the basis of this point of view that we must reexamine the need for information that was discussed in the beginning of this article. People do not watch television in order to acquire just any kind of information. The sort of information that people need primarily deals with news about events which affect the group of which they are a part. This kind of knowledge is only a very small segment of what is taken to be information. In this context, television functions not only as a provider of news about what affects the group, but also as a generator and intensifier of facts that affect the 'we feeling.' News on television forms the nucleus of a virtual popular stampede. Their affective significance does not only derive from the facts themselves, but also from the size and scope of this virtual stampede.

What can be said about the need for information can also be said about the need for recreation. The success of soaps, game shows and films is often related to the fact that it is a matter of the consecrated events of a (virtual) community. Because they are viewed *en masse*, they are viewed even more *en masse*. There is always something or someone who succeeds in finding a tone that releases a specific emotion or appeals to a 'we feeling.' Once interest increases through increased media coverage, the trend becomes self-fulfilling, until the masses are sated. The whole process resembles what le Bon described when he discussed the suggestibility of the masses.

The link between the possibility of using the audio-visual media and the feeling of freedom becomes exceptionally clear when people are asked to imagine a life without television. It appears that they can scarcely imagine how to live a television-less life without becoming alienated from 'reality.' Television is no longer spontaneously considered a leisure activity. Leisure is associated with things like hobbies, gardening, going out, etc., while the media are considered to be on the same level as sleeping, eating, drinking and maintaining social contacts.

6. Ethical Consequences

For the purposes of this article, I do not have to go into great detail concerning the ethical consequences of the group dynamic paradigm for which I have cited evidence. It seems sufficiently clear to me that such a perspective sheds a completely different light than the consumer-producer paradigm on the success of television as a medium. Yet I would like to show in what direction ethical evaluation is pointing.

The ethical consequences opened up by the group dynamic paradigm point in two directions, a positive and a negative. From this perspective, the medium of television can be considered as a relief for old, sick and isolated people. Empirical data show, for example, that old people who watch a lot of television are more alert than those who do not. Television involves people in their community, and they feel less abandoned or excluded.

The negative aspects are closely related to the evolution of social life in general. Europe is witnessing a reduction of participation and interest in many groups. The number of active members of religious communities has declined sharply, as well as the number of active participants in political parties. Following the developments in the United States, the strength of European trade unions is waning. Similarly, membership in cultural organizations seems to be on the decline. In any case, the amount of time that people invest in this sort of social involvement is quite small compared with the number of hours spent in front of the television. A consequence of this might be that the suggestibility of the viewing public increases, by which we mean that the group dynamic generated by the media resembles that of an ephemeral mass more than that of differentiated groups that presuppose a certain initiation, engagement and active participation. If Freud is correct in saying that people owe their critical powers to the fact that they are members of various groups, thus viewing group ideals with a grain of salt, then the reduction of social participation as a result of television will have negative aspects. Already one can observe that people with insufficient social capital, who do not participate in an interactive social life, will more easily be tempted to believe what they see in sensationalistic news reports. Such an audience is more receptive to undemocratic propaganda.

At the same time, the mass media have more and more come under the control of powerful financial groups. These monopolies, combined with the increasing suggestibility of the viewing public, have resulted in a degree of power concentration that has never before been seen. The step made by media personalities into politics is a foretaste of a future in which the powers that, until now, have been separate (powers whose influence was restricted to a specific domain, for instance, the political, the legal, the commercial or the journalistic domain) will fuse. It is most doubtful that this development will improve social dialogue.

THE ECONOMIC RATIONALE BEHIND THE MASS MEDIA INDUSTRY AND MARKET TODAY: FACTS AND FIGURES

Hilde Van den Bulck

This chapter attempts to paint an economic picture of the mass media. To understand the data provided, we shall analyse the rationale behind the functioning of the mass media as an industry. The main technological, economic, political and socio-cultural factors that have made the mass media 'market' what it is today will be looked at. We shall focus on Europe with obvious and inevitable references to the US. Though the focus will be on audiovisual media, press and other media will be included.

1. Looking Back: The 'Traditional' Media Scene

Media were traditionally a 'national affair', developing within a national context, with national ownership and bound by national regulations. Newspapers by and large restricted themselves geographically to a national territory understood in terms of organisation, ownership (owned by small to medium-sized publishers, often a 'family') and target audience. The only alternatives were regional as opposed to trans- or international newspapers. Even though radio frequencies were determined internationally, their allocation was treated like a national political affair. The alleged scarcity of frequencies was used by governments to limit broadcasting rights to one central national institution. A prime example was television. Almost everywhere in Europe and in a lot of countries the world over, broadcasting was provided by national organisations, delivering a public service in a specific language within the boundaries of a nation-state. Price (1995: x), following Eli Noam, states: "The single and unified nation-state, the main unit of government around the globe, was matched and served by its national monopoly communications network, usually owned and operated by the state as a public service, like the rail-road." In this way, every nation state aimed at and established its own 'autonomous audiovisual space' its politically, economically and culturally autonomous broadcasting environment of a limited and controlable size and character. Finally, the *'new media'* were, as Mazzoleni and Palmer (1992: 37) put it, "considered a marginal territory where ectoplasmic entities would wander in a foggy landscape."

This is not to say that there were no exceptions. Public service broadcasting, for instance, was (and is) next to non-existent in the US commercial system, even though the US audiovisual sector was by and large 'national.' Moreover, the current conglomerations are not a complete novelty. Mazzoleni and Palmer (1992: 28) make clear that the discussion about the dangers of concentration was already prevalent before the first world war due to press barons like Viscount Northcliffe (1865-1922 — UK) and W.R. Hearst (1863-1952 — US). The scale and scope of concentration today though is far bigger.

2. Factors of Change

Since the early 80s, the media have undergone fundamental changes, resulting in the media scene we are confronted with today. Before turning to the data in question, we will look at some of the important factors which have helped to bring this about.

2.1. *Technology*

Although one should be careful not to take a technological determinist stance, technological innovations are having an ever increasing influence on developments in the mass media. (Ferguson, 1986; Lee & Tonghe, 1994; Murdock, 1994) Technologies perfect the ways in which the media function and contribute to the development of new media services and infrastructure. As such, the communication industries are witnessing a fundamental technological change with significant implications for their organisation.

Central to these developments is *digitalisation*, the shift from analog to digital coding. In analog systems, the shape in which information is stored and transmitted carries a certain continuous and recognizable relation to the original form (e.g., tones on a black and white negative and the play of light in the fotographed scene). Digital systems translate all information — image, text, data or sound — into a universal computer language so that everything can be reproduced in binary codes.

This digital revolution has very important consequences for the future development of communication industries. Because they used very different ways of coding information, analog systems helped to maintain the boundaries between industrial sectors. Every sector had its own technologies for information storage and transmission. Now that all information can be kept and sent in digital form, these historic barriers are being brought down, causing a *convergence* between formerly distinct communication sectors. The result is that we live in a multimedia environment in which ever more diverse symbolic data can be stored, transmitted and consulted by consumers at the same time. This process of convergence is organised around a triangular configuration of the most important communication industries that are ever more closely entwined. (cf. Murdock, 1994)

Figure 1: *The Communications Industry*

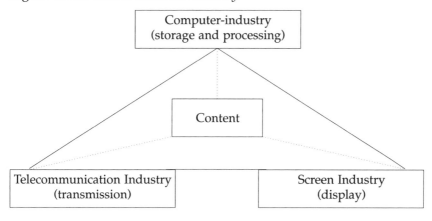

At the apex of the triangle is the computer industry providing the basic hardware and software for the storage and retrieval of digital information. The telecommunications industry is geared to the transmission of digital information. To this end, use is made of the radio spectrum, cable and satellite. As digital information occupies far less space than analog codes, the radio spectrum can carry many more channels (digital compression). Replacing copper by fibre optics, cable too can transport a lot more communication channels (broadband systems). In this way, the radio spectrum, cable and satellite lay the foundations for what is known as the new Information Super Highway — a global network of channels equipped to transport digitally coded information in large amounts at high speed, including television images to telephone conversations and video-conferences. The confrontation of the user with these new digital information services is increasingly organised around the screen, in particular around screens installed at home or in the office. They are the most important mechanisms to display information. They are the core point of delivery for a wide variety of services (television programmes, video games, shopping channels), all becoming more and more interactive. The technological convergence of computer, telecomunications and screen industries around digital coding stimulates an accelerated industrial convergence: important corporations from each corner of the triangle merge and form alliances in an attempt to gain maximum profit from these new technological ties between corporations. Yet, these systems of storage, processing, sending and display can only be useful in relation to information systems that people actually want. As a result, the main players of each corner of the triangle can be seen to form alliances with those who have access to the content of software, either text (publishers), images (film and television companies), recorded sound (record companies) or data (data banks). For example, the acquisition of Capital Cities/ABC by Walt Disney in 1996, means that a Hollywood studio (producer of content) controls a radio and television network.

2.2. *Economy*

All these technological factors have allowed new software and hardware producers to enter the media market. In markets, the structural conditions of access are very important for the functioning of the competitive process. Even though new technologies provide the means of entry, and thus serve the goal of diversity, the cost of entry and the competence of entry work towards the establishment of *integrated multinational and multimedia* corporations that can strengthen their control over the information flow. In this way, they can play to the dynamic of these markets, particularly the advantages of economies of scale and scope. Therefore, the battle over the industrial development of the old and new media is fought across boundaries and is dominated by transnational corporations. (Garnham & Locksley, 1991; Negrine & Papathannasopoulos, 1991) The growing competition between old and new media and between old and new media corporations in the information market, education and entertainment, has resulted in a growing commercialisation of both content and exploitation, in the opening up of new markets (Eastern Europe) and the search for new specific market segments (narrowcasting).

2.3. Politics

These technological innovations and economic developments have been accompanied by a changing political climate in which the role of national governments is reduced. (Blumler, 1992; Murdock, 1992) The threat to 'traditional' practices and structures was always latent, but it took the specific convergence of developments and interests under certain circumstances for these threats to become effective, leading to denationalisation, privatisation, liberalisation and de/re-regulation. In the 80s, the pressure for change became real. The 'traditional' situation was seriously challenged not only by the neo-liberal political climate with its critical attitude towards regulatory activities, but also by the growing interest in and attraction to the so-called 'information technology revolution' and the expansion of communication technologies. These factors resulted in a reverse dynamic. First, new technologies require the formulation of a new policy to control and exploit them. Second, because of convergence, changes in one sector influenced other sectors. Third, the pressure to organise (directly or indirectly) the media through liberalisation eventually resulted in the creation of an international media market.

In Europe, this process was reinforced by the growing internationalisation (Europeanisation) of political decision making. The regulatory and pro-active initiatives of the EU, particularly with regard to the audiovisual, had a profound impact on the European states both within and outside the EU. Since the 80s, the EU has been responsible for much of the shaping of the European mediascape. Even though this internationalisation is, in part, a necessary result of the internationalisation of the media through technology, these changes are definitely influenced by the changing political climate in which the role of the nation state is being rethought.

The result was a serious change in policy based on privatisation, denationalisation, liberalisation and a relaxing of regulatory programmes. (Blumler, 1991; Collins & Murroni, 1996; Mosco, 1990; Pilati, 1993) These changes in media and telecommunication policies were very 'friendly' toward all new technologies and allowed for a certain proliferation. In a deregulated and liberalised regime, media corporations are enabled to follow, both nationally and internationally, the demands of the market and they themselves become commodities. This results in a growing concentration of media power, in turn demanding the attention of national and international regulatory bodies. In this way, the changes since the 80s have resulted in a fundamental internationalisation of the sector at the levels of capital, production and policy.

3. The New Media Market

Since the 80s, a new mass media environment has developed, best described as a 'transnational oligopolistic media market,' with new central players and principles and a new problematic. (Albarran & Chan-Olmsted, 1998; Blumler, 1992, Mazzoleni & Palmer 1992, Murdock, 1992; Pilate, 1993; Van Poecke & Van den Bulck, 1994)

3.1. *The Scale of the Market: Key players*

A first indication of the size and shape of the media market can be obtained by looking at some hard data. Who are the main economic players in the field? How many of them are there? How big are they? Such data can be simple but very revealing.

To ensure internal and external validity, all basic quantitative data are taken from the same source (European Audiovisual Observatory). They are complemented by more in-depth material. Following the EAO, the nationality of a company is determined by the country in which its Head Office is located. The size of a company is indicated by the yearly turnover in USD. The total turnover represents all the activities of a company. The audiovisual turnover represents all the audiovisual activities of a company.

3.1.1. *The World's Top 20 Multimedia Companies*

Multimedia companies must be understood here as "companies or groups involved in at least two different branches: press, cinema, broadcasting, sound recording industry, video-games industry, etc." (Yearbook, 1995) This means that these companies can have subsiduairies (or even their main activity) outside the media and communication sector (for instance, General Electric/NBC). Here, the turnover figures refer only to their media and communication aspects.

Table 1: *The World's Top 20 Multimedia Companies 1993-1997*

Co	1993 Country	Turnover USD	Co	1995 Country	Turnover USD
1. Matsushita	JP	22.723	1. Time Warner	USA	14.375
2. Philips	NL	10.008	2. Bertelsmann	D	12.534
3. Bertelsmann	D	8.682	3. Viacom	USA	11.689
4. Time Warner	USA	7.963	4. Havas	FR	9.107
5. Sony	JP	7.305	5. News Corp	AU	9.028
6. News Corp	AUS	7.129	6. Sony	JP	8.619
7. Matra-Hachette	F	5.214	7. Fujisankei	JP	7.457
8. Havas	F	4.938	8. Capital C/ABC	USA	6.879
9. Capital C/ABC	USA	4.663	9. Matra Hachette	F	6.269
10. Paramount	USA	4.434	10. Walt Disney	USA	6.002
11. Times Mirror	USA	3.714	11. Polygram	NL	5.479
12. Walt Disney	USA	3.676	12. MCA (Seagram)	CA	5.325
13. FinInvest	I	3.663	13. Thorn-EMI	GB	4.556
14. CBS	USA	3.510	14. Gannett	USA	4.007
15. Thorn-EMI	GB	3.326	15. BBC	GB	3.487
16. BBC	GB	2.936	16. Times Mirror	USA	3.448
17. Fujisankei ('92)	JP	2.326	17. CLT	LU	3.093
18. CLT	L	1.994	18. FinInvest	IT	2.844
19. Tribune	USA	1.953	19. Tribune	USA	2.245
20. Pearson	GB	1.865	20. Cox Enterprises	USA	1.865

Co	1996 Country	Turnover USD	Co	1997 Country	Turnover USD
1. Bertelsmann	D	12.498	1. Walt Disney	USA	17.459
2. Walt Disney	USA	12.117	2. News Corp	AU	13.566
3. Viacom	USA	12.084	3. Viacom	USA	13.206
4. News Corp	AUS	10.619	4. Time Warner	USA	12.412

5. Time Warner	USA	9.201		5. Bertelsmann	DE	11.840
6. Sony	JP	9.087		6. Sony	JP	9.872
7. Havas	F	7.324		7. Time Warner Ent	USA	7.531
8. Time Warner Ent	USA	7.010		8. Havas	FR	6.517
9. ARD	DE	6.450		9. Matra Hachette	FR	6.448
10. Matra Hachette	FR	6.466		10. ARD	DE	6.295
11. Polygram	NL	5.628		11. Polygram	NL	5.686
12. NHK	JP	5.617		12. Seagram	CA	5.455
13. Thorn-EMI	GB	5.263		13. Gen. Elec/NBC	USA	5.153
14. Seagram/				14. NHK	JP	5.091
Universal Stud.	CA	4.876		15. Cox Enterprises	USA	4.936
15. Cox Enterprises	USA	4.600		16. Gannett	USA	4.286
16. Westinghouse/				17. Thorn EMI	GB	4.090
CBS	USA	4.125		18. CBS Corp	USA	3.808
17. Gannett	USA	4.022		19. BBC	GB	3.357
18. BBC	GB	3.558		20. Times Mirror	USA	3.319
19. Times Mirror	USA	3.400				
20. CLT	LU	2.859				

These top twenty have witnessed some significant changes over time. The ranking can differ considerably from one year to the other, due to the continuous merging and changing of ownership. Comparing the top three versus the bottom three of this ranking, it becomes obvious that even between the 20 biggest companies (that already hold a significant part of the world market), there is a serious discrepancy in turnover (in 1997 of 4 to 1). The market can thus be seen to be dominated by a few gigantic companies. The places of origin of these mega-companies are not very surprising. In 1993, the ranking included 9 European, 7 US, 3 Japanese and 1 Australian company. By 1997 the top had reversed with 9 US, 7 European, 2 Japanese, 1 Australian and 1 Canadian corporation. In 1993, the US only had 1 company in the top 5. By 1997, it dominated in terms of turnover with 3 out of 5. The 4 European companies in the top 10 seem to indicate a promising future for the continent's media industry. The fast moving aspect of this business can be illustrated by the turnover of Bertelsmann that went from 8.682 in 1993 to 12.534 USD two years later. The reason it lost its 1996 top position to the American Walt Disney Group (also the world's leading audiovisual group, *cf.* table 3) lies with the merger of its audiovisual operations with CLT (in CLT/UFA, cf. *infra*). The merger of Time Warner and America Online (January 2000) will increase its turnover dramatically, thus pushing Walt Disney from its number one position over night. On average the top 20 companies have seen a yearly increase in turnover.

Table 2: *The World's Top 20 Multimedia Companies 1997 with Sectorial Breakdown of Communication Turnover*

Rank	Company	Country	Turnover Communication	Programming Film & Radio-TV	Music & Video	Publishing/ Magazines	Books	IT	Advertising
1	Walt Disney	US	17.459	-	-	-	-		
2	News Corporation	AU	13.566	59,4		34,6	6,0		
3	Viacom	US	13.206	49,8	32,4 (1)	18,7			
4	Time Warner	US	12.412	35,7	29,7	34,6			
5	Bertelsmann	DE	11.840	38,1		25,0	36,9		
6	Sony	JP	9.872	50,7	49,3				
7	Time Warner Entertainment	US	7.531	100,0					
8	Havas	FR	6.517	42,2 (2)		28,8			28,9
9	Matra Hachette	FR	6.448	7,7		72,8	12,2		
10	ARD (radio/tv)	JP	6.295	>90%				7,3	
11	Polygram	NL	5.686	16,2	83,6				
12	Seagram	CA	5.455	71,9	28,0				
13	General Electric/NBC	US	5.153	100,0					
14	NHK (radio/tv)	JP	5.091	>90%					
15	Cox Enterprises	US	4.936	-		-			
16	Gannett	US	4.286	16,4		83,6			
17	Thorn EMI	GB	4.090		100,0				
18	CBS Corporation (radio/tv)	US	3.888	>95%					
19	BBC (radio/tv)	GB	3.357	>90%					
20	Times Mirror	US	3.319			74,3	25,7		

It is interesting to see how the multimedia companies' activities are spread over the different media sectors. Some, like Viacom or Time Warner, have spread their activities more or less evenly over different sectors whereas others are less balanced. Even though the press sector is often considered to be part of the 'old media', publishing houses represent a strong industrial power. This becomes clear from the position of companies such as Hachette or Gannett. Communication groups such as Havas may not be heavily involved in audiovisual media, yet they do have considerable interests in other media. As such, these printing and communication companies have a secure financial base and often a strong world-wide presence. These can prove to be the prerequisites to make them leading market players of the future. The distinct growth in multi-media supports (combining sound, image, print and computer software) will make the consumption of both entertainment and educational products more common and thus profitable. Again, this will influence the ranking in years to come.

3.1.2. *The Worldwide Corporate Audiovisual Market*

In both academia and the media industry, the bulk of attention in the last two decades has gone to the audiovisual market. This is not to say that press corporations have been confined to the fringe of the media market. Groups like Bertelsmann and News Corp. show otherwise. Yet, an important part of their growth and a lot of the growth in the market in general is situated at the audiovisual level. Therefore, it is worth studying the world's leading audiovisual groups.

Table 3: *Ranking by Audiovisual Turnover of the 12 Leading World Groups: 1992-1998*

Rank	Company	Country	1992	1993	1994	1995	1996	1997	1998	'97AV/T
1	Walt Disney (1)	US	4.197	5.089	6.591	8.150	14.237	17.459	17.444	78%
2	Viacom	US	1.454	2.028	5.171	8.772	9.818	9.997	12.023	82%
3	Sony	JP	6.659	7.320	7.945	8.619	9.087	9.872	-	19%
4	Time Warner (2)	US	9.975	3.334	3.986	4.196	5.084	7.892	8.977	61%
5	Time Warner Entertainment (2)	US	-	5.755	5.997	6.718	7.498	7.531	-	66%
6	News corp. (3)	AU	3.115	3.534	4.190	4.881	6.200	7.328	-	57%
7	ARD	DE	5.587	5.611	5.824	6.601	6.450	6.295	-	100%
8	PolyGram	NL	3.763	3.993	4.525	5.479	5.628	5.686	5.311	100%
9	Seagram/Universal Studios (3)	CA	-	4.606	4.744	4.876	5.417	5.455	-	100%
10	General Electric/NBC	US	3.363	3.102	3.361	3.919	5.232	5.153	-	6%
11	NHK	JP	4.437	5.254	5.744	6.043	5.617	5.091	-	100%
12	CBS Corp.	US	-	-	-	931	3.952	5.061	-	72%

The ranking of the audiovisual companies differs considerably from the top 20 multimedia companies. The exclusion of press and publishing operations changes the top 12 world rankings, with Europe losing ground to the United States. The ranking of the world audiovisual market has changed dramatically over time, and is a very good illustration of the move to a 'transnational oligopolistic media market.' In 1987, 9 of the top 12 companies were terrestrial broadcasters — the three major American networks (Capital Cities/ABC, NBC, CBS), NHK, Finnvest, the BBC and RAI. By 1995, only 4 of these companies are included in the classification. Other companies witnessed a dramatic growth. Viacom, a minor player in 1992 and only 14th in 1994, in 1995 suddenly moved up to the top position after taking over Blockbuster and Paramount. The year after, with a growing but similar turnover, it loses top place to Walt Disney. The sale of Polygram by Phillips to Seagram in December 98 will have pushed this company to the top three by the end of 1998 — although the market of video games (vital for these companies) is fickle, which makes their position unstable.

As in the multimedia ranking, there are serious and still growing discrepancies in corporate turnover of the audiovisual media. A look at the top fifty audiovisual companies confirms the disparity in corporate turnover. The ratio of the top company's audiovisual turnover to that of the fiftieth company is 1 to 13 in 1997, as against 1 to 10 in 1993.

Some holdings, particularly American groups such as Viacom, have seen spectacular growth in audiovisual turnover. In part, this can be ascribed to the numerous takeovers, acquisitions and mergers in recent years. It should be noted, however, that not all these increases result from mergers. They can also be due to internal growth within the group. News Corp. provides an interesting illustration of the latter as its growth in audiovisual turnover is due to the success with the audience of its broadcasters in the US (Fox broadcasting), Britain (BskyB) and Asia (Star TV).

There is a considerable difference in the percentage of audiovisual turnover in the total turnover of the companies in the ranking. Whereas a lot of companies have a majority stake in the audiovisual, there are companies — even though they are key players in the audiovisual market — whose main activity lies elsewhere. Good examples are Sony and General Electric/NBC: Only 19% and 6 % of their total turnover comes from audiovisual activities respectively. Time Warner's merger with America Online will redefine the percentage of total turnover generated from audiovisual activities.

Finally, though not surprisingly, it should be noted that public service television carries greater weight in Europe (ARD comes 5th) and Japan (NHK ranks 7th) than in the US.

Within the top 50, European industry is the most heavily represented with 24 companies in 1997 against 14 US, 8 Japanese and 4 other (Brazilian, Mexican, Canadian and Australian) companies. As such the future of the European industry looks quite rosy. But in terms of turnover, the picture is quite different. The average size of European companies listed in these rankings (2.367.6 million USD in 1997) is noticeably smaller than that of the American (4,795.9 million USD) and Japanese (3,585.9 million USD) and is increasingly growing at a much slower rate than that of American and Japanese companies. Compared to 1996, there was even a 0.1% drop for European while a 13.6% and 7.4 % increase for American and Japanese companies respectively.

3.1.3. *The European Audiovisual Market*

To complete the picture, let us take a look at the European audiovisual market.

Table 4: Top 50 European Audiovisual Market

Rank	Company	Country	AV turnover	Total turnover	AV turnover/ Total turnover	Growth AV turnover
1	ARD	DE	5.086,7	5.584,1	100%	9,8%
2	PolyGram	NL	4.438,3	5.024,3	100%	13,2%
3	Bertelsmann	DE	3.845,7	12.230,4	35%	11,7%
4	BBC	GB	3.097,0	3.852,0	100%	24,4%
5	Thorn EMI	GB	3.116,9	5.823,1	62%	16,4%
6	CLT-UFA	LU	2.315,0	2.828,6	91%	11,5%
7	Carlton	GB	2.099,0	2.562,6	100%	22,1%
8	RAI	IT	2.376,6	2.544,9	100%	7,1%
9	KirchGruppe	DE	2.094,0	2.244,4	100%	7,2%
10	BSkyB	GB	1.262,0	2.102,3	100%	66,6%
11	CANAL+	FR	1.634,7	2.065,6	87%	9,8%
12	Mediaset	IT	1.601,7	1.749,2	100%	9,2%
13	TF1	FR	1.492,0	1.567,0	100%	5,0%
14	RTL	DE	1.349,0	1.415,2	100%	4,9%
15	ZDF	DE	1.145,1	1.407,3	100%	22,9%
16	The Rank Group Plc	GB	762,4	2.918,8	44%	68,1%
17	Granada	GB	738,7	5.943,6	17%	33,1%
18	Pro 7	DE	761,8	952,7	98%	22,0%

19	SAT.1	DE	885,2	892,5	100%	0,8%
20	France 3	FR	839,4	836,8	100%	-0,3%
21	Channel 4	GB	638,7	803,0	100%	25,7%
22	France 2	FR	830,5	762,2	100%	-8,2%
23	Viacom International Netherlands B.V.	NL	747,0	-	-	-
24	ORF	AT	698,0	725,3	100%	3,9%
25	SSR	CH	709,0	709,8	100%	0,1%
26	United International Pictures N.V.	NL	775,0	605,0	100%	-22%
27	NOS	NL	694,0	598,0	100%	-13,8%
28	Kinnevik	SE	427,0	578,6	100%	35,5%
29	United News & Media Plc.	GB	463,1	2.863,8	20%	24,8%
30	RTVE	ES	598,5	550,1	100%	-8,1%
31	Pearson PLC	GB	251,6	3.331,5	15%	102,7%
32	Cinema International B.V.	NL	393,8	469,7	100%	19,3%
33	M6	FR	370,4	459,0	100%	23,9%
34	Time Warner Ent. Ltd	GB	441,8	-	-	-
35	Matra Hachette	FR	430,0	9.970,2	4%	1,6%
36	CANAL+ Espana	ES	441,8	429,1	100%	-2,9%
37	Radio France	FR	436,7	425,7	100%	-2,5%
38	Endemol	NL	421,9	417,1	100%	-1,1%
39	Time Warner Ent. Ltd	GB	410,5	410,5	100%	0,0%
40	Antena 3	ES	461,4	389,6	100%	-15,6%
41	Sverige Television AB	SE	405,0	387,9	100%	-4,2%
42	TVP	PL	361,8	386,5	100%	6,8%
43	Premiere	DE	306,0	376,1	100%	22,9%
44	Deutsche Welle	DE	274,1	353,9	100%	29,1%
45	Gestevision Telecinco	ES	261,4	347,0	100%	32,7%
46	DR	DK	343,6	344,9	100%	0,4%
47	YLE	FI	349,7	340,7	100%	-2,6%
48	NRK	NO	283,5	315,9	100%	11,4%
49	United Cinemas International Multiplex B.V.	NL	274,3	309,2	100%	12,7%
50	Gaumont	FR	198,7	289,9	100%	45,9%
p.m.	Yorkshire Tyne Tees PLC ('97: Granada	GB	338,0	162,4		-
p.m.	Nethold (now taken over by Canal+)	NL	234,0	-		-

In the first instance, the European audiovisual market paints a less dramatic picture of change. In 1997, 33.2% of the market was still taken in by Public Service Broadcasting (PSB) (17 out of 50 companies.) Moreover, two of the top five companies are PSB with ARD at top position and BBC coming fourth. The financial health of certain PSBs seems to be improving, with a general increase in turnover, coupled with mostly positive net income figures for 1997.

The other positions of the top five companies are taken up by three groups whose business is in music: PolyGram, Bertelsmann, Thorn-EMI. However, the positioning strategy of these three companies differs. While for Bertelsmann, music and video make up only 38% of its turnover, with Polygram these account for 84% of its turnover. Thorn-EMI is exclusively involved in the phonographic sector. These companies also score well on the world audiovisual ranking (cf. table 3), giving Europe a stronghold in the world market.

A country by country breakdown of the European audiovisual top 50 shows the importance of the German and British companies (27% of the combined turnover of the top 50 companies). Dutch companies take third place (13%). The Netherlands provides a good example of European enterprise with Endemol (a merger between JE Entertainment and De Mol) featuring in the top 50 for the second year running.) It is one of the main producers and exporters of TV programme formats in the European markets.

Yet, these optimistic remarks need to be modified. First, despite the survival of PSB, it is walking a tight rope. The public radio and television sector still carries considerable clout, with 17 out of 50 top companies, making up 33.2 % of the market. Yet its overall share in the market seems to be decreasing (34.2% in 1996) due to a slower rate of growth (9.2 % from 1996 to 1997, as against 12.3% for the 50 top companies taken as a whole). Also, several PSB still experience structural problems due to the crisis in both their public sector (TV licences) and commercial (advertising) financing. Second, several of the companies referred to are, in fact, not European but the affiliates of American companies (e,g., The Rank Group PLC Viacom International Netherlands and Time Warner Entertainment's British affiliate). PolyGram, acquired by Seagram in December 1998, no longer appeared in the rankings of 1999.

3.2. Structure and Dynamics of the Industry

As explained in the introduction, the economic battle over the industrial development of the old and new media is fought across national boundaries, and is dominated by multinational corporations. The data confirmed that the two most important trends to follow from this are concentration and transnationalisation.

First, almost the entire communication and information sector is witnessing a concentration movement leading to oligopolisation, in which the economic market, through takeovers and mergers, becomes concentrated in the hands of only a few providers. A striking example can be found with the British ITV franchises (regional network stations), where the decentralised principle is undermined. In November 1996, Carlton (already controlling Carlton Television and Central) bought Westcounty Television; in June 1997, Scottish Television acquired Grampian and took an 18% stake in Ulster (to be bought out completely in due course); and in August 1997, Granada bought Yorkshire — Tyne Tees Television. Takeovers are not limited to buying single companies though. Another European example of the intricate web that the audiovisual market has turned into can be found with CLT/UFA. This company, with one of the largest audiovisual turnovers in Europe, is the result of the merger of Bertelsmann's audiovisual activities (UFA. Film Und Fernseh CmbH & Co KG) with CLT (of Audiofina) and with Havas as a committed partner. So, as a result of these and similar ventures, only a few but very large corporations and conglomerates such as Walt Disney, Viacom, Time-Warner, Sony, News Corporation, Bertelsmann and CLT control the market. One of the more important battles, therefore, concerns the ownership structures of multimedia groups. The economic logic of digitalisation requires the formation of multi media groups that can operate in previously separate sectors and that can gain maximum advantage from technological convergence. Many of the companies in the top rankings of the audiovisual market are multimedia companies (e.g., News Corp.) or diversified companies with interest in electronic goods (eg. Sony) or in transmission and programming (production, distribution, broadcasting, cable, video and sound recording). Sony, for instance, has its main business (4.355 billion Yen in 1999) in electronics (audio equipment,video equipment, television, computers, electronic components), followed by games (consoles and software, 760 billion), music (719 billion), pictures (540 billion), insurance (339 billion), and others (credit-card businesses, satellite distribution services, internet-related businesses, etc., 81 billion.) Time Warner is involved in cable television networks through Turner Broadcasting (merged in 1996) and HBO, publishing through Time Inc and New Line Cinema, entertainment through

Warner Bros. and Warner Music Group, and cable systems through Time Warner Cable. Each of these companies themselves have several subsiduairies (e.g., Warner Bros has 18 different subdivisions).

This multimedia concentration is problematic in (at least) three different ways. First, it increases the possibility for media owners to use their control over the communication markets for political purposes (e.g., Berlusconi in Italy). Second, it leads to corporate strategies based on synergies, i.e., the exploitation of one product in as many markets as possible. The marketing of Pocahontas (and many other Disney characters) by Walt Disney (the animation film, the dolls, the books, the jigsaw puzzles, lunch boxes, etc.) is but one of many examples. The question here is whether cultural diversity is undermined by bringing onto different markets variations of one theme. Finally, it increases the structural power of the main corporations — their potential to determine the rules of the game which smaller and weaker competitors need to abide by.

These multimedia conglomerates are part of another important trend in the industrial organisation of communications systems — the strengthening of the *transnationalisation* in which the main corporations operate across the frontiers on a global scale. These conglomerates maintain that the manner in which the production, distribution and consumption processes are currently unfolding, pushes them toward a global policy. Since the initial costs of programme production make up the main investment, and since the further costs of reproduction or transmission for wider audiences are comparatively low, there has always been an expansive dynamic within the media. And since audiences are spread geographically, this dynamic has always had a geographic dimension pushing toward a wider 'audiovisual space.' What we are witnessing now is the penultimate fulfilment of this logic by organisations whose aim is to compete on world markets and whose priority lies with economies of scale that enable this. Examples abound. Rupert Murdoch is a prime example of a transnational multimedia mogul. Australian in origin, Murdoch obtained American citizenship to expand his Australian businesses with American takeovers. He used his friendship with Margaret Thatcher to effectively take control over British satellite television (set out to be British) and was quick to enter (successfully) the new market of the far East. Thus, News Corp. has dominant interests in at least three continents, and as such proves to be a typical example of current market trends.

4. Looking Forward: Hope or Despair?

By way of conclusion, one can consider the consequences these media evolutions have for individuals as well as societies. These consequences have been discussed extensively in the recent past on both academic and public fora, most often from a 'doomsday' perspective. Other contributions in this book discuss several of these matters more fully and in-depth. But we would like to draw attention to two important issues.

One area of concern is the consequence of the above-mentioned evolution on the functioning of the media in the *public sphere* and thus on civil society (for an interesting discussion, see Braman & Sreberni-Mohammadi, 1996). In Habermas' ideal of the public sphere as "that space of social life determined neither by market nor by the state in which the formation and reformation of public opinion through open debate is deemed possible" (Sreberni-Moham-madi, 1996: 9), the mass media have always been given a prominent position. Even though this public sphere in its ideal form never has been or will be realised, it has always had a strong position (implicitly or explicitly) in both media theory and practice. A central position in this was always given to the press, but PSB too was set out and has always striven to provide a forum for democratic ideas. The transnationalisation of the media as well as the growing interwovenness of different media (eg. transnational news media, news on the internet) has been heralded by some as the basis for a global mediated public sphere and thus as the bringer of worldwide political democracy and participation, a 'true' civil society. Yet, the political economy of the media provided above, should at least caution for an over-optimistic analysis. First, the media becoming an economic commodity — rather than a part of culture — seems to imply an 'economisation' of the public sphere in which ideas have to prove economically viable. Equally, access to the civil forum increasingly carries a price tag. And, finally but most importantly, one must ask who's ideas are being brought to the worldwide forum when this forum is owned by only a handful of Western companies? (see also, Verstraeten, 1996).

The second area of concern is related to *collective identities*. Here the discussion in resent years has been particularly sweeping and rife with strong but often simplistic statements. Starting point is the perceived shift in identities: As Hall states:

> The old identities which stabilized the social world for so long are in decline, giving rise to new identities and fragmenting the modern individual as a unified subject. This so-called crisis is seen as part of a wider process of change which is dislocating the central structures and processes of modern societies and undermining the frameworks which gave individuals stable anchorage in the social world. (Hall, 19992:274)

The exponential growth in international media and the mediatisation of culture in general is seen to undermine these vested identities or, in the words of Price (1994),: "[the] plethora of changing signals, floating, then raining from space, poses impressive problems of belonging, identification, nationalism and community." Terms as coca-colonisation, americanisation and the like are often used to describe the processes caused by the above-shown shifts in media structures. Concentrating the media (-content) in the hands of only a few transnational (and often American) corporations is seen to lead to homogenisation of culture with a distinct American signature, depriving people and local communities from their (national) roots. This bleak picture needs modification though. First, the main 'problem child' in this story is national cultural identity which is seen to be eroded by the internationalisation of the media. Yet, this reasoning ignores the fact that national culture is itself 'a site of contestation on which competition over definitions takes place' (Schlesinger, 1991:174) and is thus itself a power-related construct. Second, it is important to realize that, still according to Hall, identity is a matter of becoming as much as being, a continuously constructed and reconstructed category. Identity is not an essence, not fixed and unchangeable over time. The identities now under threat through internationalisation, were themselves in the past replacing older identities. Finally, even though the internationalisation is undeniable, there are also counter-forces, such as the clear localisation that seems to have accompanied the globalisation of culture. This seems to indicate that the dreaded homogenisation will not be total. This is not to argue that the economic developments in media are of no cultural consequence, on the contrary. But it does warn against a media-centric view of cultural homogenisation, implying that media in itself are strong enough to change the distinctiveness of complete regional or national cultures and identities. Collective identity formation in all its aspects is a much wider process than simply the part that is established through the media.

Literature

ALBARRAN, Alan B., Sylvia M. CHAN-OLMSTED (1998), *Global Media Economics: Commercialization, Concentration and Integration of World Media Markets*. Ames (Iowa), Iowa State University Press, pp. 194-215.

BLUMLER, Jay G. (1991), 'The New Television Market Place: Imperatives, Implications, Issues' in James CURRAN, Michael GUREVITCH (eds.), *Mass Media and Society*. London, Edward Arnold.

BLUMLER, Jay G. (ed.) (1992), *Television and the Public Interest: Vulnerable Values in West Euorpean Broadcasting*. London, Sage.

Braman, Sandra, Annabelle SREBERNI-MOHAMMADI (eds.) (1996), *Globalization, Communication and Transnational Civil Society*. Creskill, Hampton Press.

COLLINS, Richard, Catherine MURRONI (1996), *New Media, New Policies: Media and Communications Strategies for the Future*. Cambridge, Polity Press.

European Audiovisual Observatory (1995), *Statistical Yearbook: Film, Television, Video and New Media in Europe '94/95*. Strasbourg, Council of Europe.

European Audiovisual Observatory (1997), *Statistical Yearbook: Film, Television, Video and New Media in Europe '97*. Strasbourg, Council of Europe.

European Audiovisual Observatory (1998), *Statistical Yearbook: Film, Television, Video and New Media in Europe '98*. Strasbourg, Council of Europe.

European Audiovisual Observatory (1999), *Statistical Yearbook: Film, Television, Video and New Media in Europe '99*. Strasbourg, Council of Europe.

FERGUSON, Marjorie (ed.) (1986), *New Communication Technologies and the Public Interest*. London, Sage.

GARNHAM, Nicolas, Gareth LOCKSLEY (1991), 'The Economics of Broadcasting' in Jay G. BLUMLER, T.J. NOSSITER (eds.) *Broadcasting Finance in Transition: A Comparative Handbook*. Oxford, Oxford University Press, pp. 8-22.

HALL, Stuart (1992), 'The Question of Cultural Identity' in Stuart HALL, David HELD, Timothy MCGREW (eds.). *Modernity and its Features*. Cambridge, Polity Press - Open University.

LEE, Matthey, Gary TONGE (1994), 'Technology: Delivering the Goods' in Nod MILLER, Rod ALLEN (eds.) *Broadcasting Enters the Market Place*. London, John Libbey, pp. 83-97.

MAZZOLENI, Gianpietro, Michael PALMER (1992), 'The Building of Media Empires' in Karen SIUNE & Wolfgang TREUTZSCHLER (eds.), *Dynamics of Media Politics: Broadcasting and Electronic Media in Western Europe.* London, Sage, pp. 26-41.

Graham MURDOCK (1992), 'Citizens, Consumers and Public Culture' in Michael SKOVMAND, Kim C. SCHRØDER (eds.) *Media Cultures: Reappraising Transnational Media.* London, Routledge, pp. 17-41.

MURDOCK, Graham (1994), 'Communication Politics. Trends and Issues in Contemporary Europe'. Unpublished paper.

NEGRINE, Ralph, S. PAPATHANASSOPOULOS (1990), *The Internationalisation of Television.* London, Pinter, 1990.

PILATI, Antonio (ed.) (1995), *Mind: Media Industry in Europe.* London, John Libbey, 1993.

PRICE, Monroe E. (1995), *Television, the Public Sphere and National Identity.* Oxford, Clarendon Press.

SREBERNI-MAHAMMADI, Annabelle (1996), 'Globalization, Communication and Transnational Civil Society: Introduction' in Sandra BRAMAN, Annabelle SREBERNI-MOHAMMADI (eds.) *Globalization, Communication and Transnational Civil Society.* Creskil Hampton Press, 1996, pp. 1-20.

Luc VAN POECKE & Hilde VAN DEN BULCK (eds.) (1994), *Culturele Globalisering en Lokale Identiteit: Amerikanisering van de Europese Media.* Leuven, Garant.

VERSTRAETEN, Hans (1996), 'The Media and the Transformation of the Public Sphere: A Contribution for a Critical Political Economy of the Public Sphere' in *European Journal of Communication,* 11 (1996) 3.

PART III

ETHICS OF
MEDIA PROFESSIONALS

JOURNALISM ETHICS

Barbara Thomass

Ethics in journalism seeks to understand the principles of good journalistic conduct and reasons for it. The morality of human action and its legitimation are some of the main questions of practical philosophy dealt with in the field of ethics. Ethics analyses the structure of morally correct action and claims to deliver ideas on "how to act so that actions can be regarded as moral actions." (Pieper, 1991: 97, translation B.T.) Moreover, ethics describes and analyses patterns of behaviour and fundamental attitudes with respect to their moral content, recognizes moral problems and conflicts, develops propositions and solutions and examines them according to their moral consequences. The same applies to journalism ethics.

When we look at ethics in society we might discover inconsistent trends. Today, on the one hand, it would be fair to say that more and more norms are considered to be dubious and are found to be less binding. On the other hand, there is a growing demand for ethics as a social resource of guidance, as it has become increasingly evident that the market and law, as the two other big sources of regulation of society, are not working adequately. So, instead of regulation by market incentives or by juridical commandments and interdictions, steering by values and norms comes into consideration. And this is the same with journalism ethics too. Legal limits for media and journalism are rather widely drawn in pluralistic societies because it is in their interest. These limits are fiercely defended by the media in order that they may enjoy a high amount of freedom and autonomy. And the market, although the sovereignity of the audience can serve as a countering power, drives journalism toward some behaviour which is often in contradiction to its unwritten rules. So, ethics may serve to maintain a journalist's autonomy.

In practice as in theory, it is generally acceptable to speak about ethics when one discusses the actions of journalists, the quality of their products or about failures and conflicts, as when it is about the legitimation of a value judgement of such actions and their theoretical foundation. But we have to distinguish between the morality of journalists and journalism ethics, that is, the theory of moral conduct.

This article will give a short overview of the history of the foundation of ethics and its role for the conceptions of media and journalism ethics. I will also show the origins of journalism ethical debates. The article argues for embedding journalism ethics into a wider system of ethical levels which may help to assess the problems in question. This will be explored with the examples of typical journalistic ethical conflict fields.

1. The Debate on Journalism Ethics

The reasons for a journalism ethics date back to the time of differentiation of society, the development of a modern state and forming of the role of the individual in a state community. Connected to this process were ethical questions which focussed on the relationship between the individual and the society, between individual freedom and state claims. As media and the journalistic profession developed further, the aforementioned questions were also asked in their respective fields. The first ideas about journalism ethics thus stem from main philosophical ideas. There, we find the concept of the role of the freedom of the press in society, which is the background for journalism ethics because it is the specific status which is claimed for the actors of a free press that demands an adherence to certain professional principles.

Philosophers of the 18th century, while shaping the concept of the relationship between the state, society and the individual, developed a system of norms conscious of the duties and freedoms of the press and journalists. Some of those norms entered into constitutions and juridical explanations of those constitutions. Others, not that open but not less important, are part of journalists' ethos in a modern democracy. Thus, Thomas Hobbes argued that a reigning power should not be almighty and that people ought to have their own sovereignty. Hence, the fundamental idea of journalism: People should be informed, and this is why media should play a specific role in society. The 'marketplace of ideas' was a concept of John Milton, which claimed that truth will be revealed by the free exchange of ideas. The modern consequence of this concept is the idea that the media simply have to publish the facts and the audience will make up its own mind. This, in a nutshell, is the classical theory of the freedom of the press. Furthermore, we can trace back the idea of the social responsibility of the press to utilitarianism as it had been worked out by David Hume and John Stuart Mill. The categorical imperative of Immanuel Kant furnishes the foundation for the idea that the individual journalist is responsible for finding out what is good and bad about his or her professional conduct.

In modern times, the ethical debate in journalism was strongly encouraged by scholars in the USA who were in close contact with the professional development of journalism. Codes of ethics date back to 1910 in Kansas. In 1947, the Hutchins Commission of the Press pled for a social responsibility of journalism toward society. This commission, which was inaugurated because of inceasing misfunctioning of the press, claimed that an ethical journalist works in the service of mankind, and not in pursuing his or her own goals. Thus, the dominance of the concept according to which reporting pure facts is the quintessence of journalistic morality was taken over by the idea that journalism is socially and morally responsible.

Three authors have been vital in shaping the ethical debate on journalism in the USA: Wilbur Schramm, together with others, the author of the 'Four theories on the Press.' He elaborated the position of the Hutchins Commission and pled for social responsibility and social control of the media. (Siebert, Peterson, Schramm, 1956; Rivers, Schramm, Clifford, 1980)

John C. Merrill, who condemned the widespread codes of ethics in the USA was in favour of the individualistic and engaged self-responsibility of a subjective journalism (e.g., 1977). Finally, Clifford G. Christians, who viewed the professional ethos and self-regulation of journalists as not sufficient, and thought it necessary that journalism and journalism education be completed by a system of values and moral philosophy. (Christians, Covert, 1980)

Later on, the debate grew to cover the whole system of media. The relationship between journalistic conduct and credibility was questioned (Fink, 1988), the role of the development and foundation of norms was discussed and different levels of abstractions were considered in the analysis of the field between individual ethics and the ethics of the communication system. (Goodwin, 1983; Odell, 1983; Lambeth, 1986; Meyer, 1986; Cooper, 1986, 1989; Christians, Rotzoll, Fackler, 1987; Fink, 1988; Altschull, 1990; Day, 1991; Cohen, 1992; Gordon, Kittross, Reuss, 1996)

2. The Individualistic and the Functionalistic Approach

Embedded in ethical thinking is the idea that ethical choices have to be free ones because only a person who acts on his or her own can be held responsible for his or her actions. But this view is conflicting with the conditions of modern media production. This is why ethical reflection on journalism ethics in recent times has strongly been motivated by the theory of functionalist structuralism. Thus, it is commonplace in communication science that journalists do not work as single individuals who are solely responsible, but in a system of economic, technical and hierarchical structures where responsibility is difficult to spot. (Blöbaum, 1994) This problem encouraged a long ongoing debate between defendants of a position that considers it as necessary to take into account the whole system in reflecting upon ethical questions and those who insist on focusing on the individual when ethical concerns are at the fore.

The individualistic approach considers the morality of the individual as being the starting point and the final aim of any ethical reflection because it is ultimately the moral agent who is acting and who is to blame for his or her actions. "Im Journalismus gibt es eine personale Verantwortungszuweisung", Boventer states clearly. (Boventer, 1996: 64) And consequently he demands, "Von Tugenden, von Schuld, von Schuld und Gewissen muß gesprochen werden". (Ibid.: 60) Although he recognizes that journalism is integrated in structures, economic conditions and juridical regulations, he is not willing to exclude the single journalist from his or her personal responsibility. Furthermore, "Der Journalismus hat zwar die Systemzwecke zur Voraussetzung, aber in seiner Subjektivität überschreitet er die bloß technischen Zwecke auf ein Mehr hin, das Journalismus erst zu Journalismus macht". Thus the journalist becomes the adressee of normative appeals, as they are expressed in codes of ethics or codes of practice.

It is exactly the sense and utility of those ethics of appeal which are contested by the other position, namely, the functionalistic

approach, focussing on the systemic character of modern information and media production: "Nicht mehr der einzelne als 'ganzer
Mensch' macht Journalismus, sondern Journalismus wird durch
organisatorisches Handeln produziert". (Rühl, 1996: 93) To consider
journalism as a social system means to start form the point that different structures with many values, norms, roles, positions, techniques, etc. create the selection and editing of media information.
The consequence: "A... indiviuelle Wertvorstellungen, Gesinnungen
und Willensentscheidungen sind im Journalismus gegenüber organ-
isatorischen Arbeits- und Berufsprämissen zurückgetreten". (93)
Insofar as it is still possible to speak about personal accountability,
its significance has been reduced enormously. Appeals to conscience
informing as a codes of ethics, "erweisen sich als untaugliche Ver-
suche, organisatorisch und persönlich bestimmtes Entscheiden im
Journalismus global zu steuern, zu kontrollieren und zu stabil-
isieren". (96) Instead of this, Rühl pleads for a professional ethos that
starts from values of the whole socitey, which then is transferred to
journalism. The leading category for this ethos should be deference:
"Achtung (deference) ist eine besondere, im Kommunikationsprozeß
hergestellte Struktur für normatives Erleben von Mitmenschlichkeit
und damit eine, vielleicht *die* zentrale Kategorie einer ... Kommunikationsethik". (Rühl, Saxer, 1981: 487)

From both positions, the following insight might be gained. While
reproaches of the first, the normative-ontological consideration, are
made insofar as it reduces the complex dependencies in the journalistic system to appeals concerning just the single journalist, the
approach of functionalist structuralism theory is criticized for its not
being a sufficient practical aid for journalism. Nevertheless, the latter is worthwhile "weil er die Ethikdiskussion entstaubt und das
journalistische Handeln in Medienorganisationen entmythologisiert
hat." (Weischenberg, 1992: 204)

3. A Wider Framework for Journalism Ethics

The confrontation of both approaches which was played out in a
very polarized manner, had nevertheless served to focus on the
question of how far responsibility reaches and on the task of ethical
considerations to define the limits of agents, and their moral actions
and the various parts of the system.

Metaethics

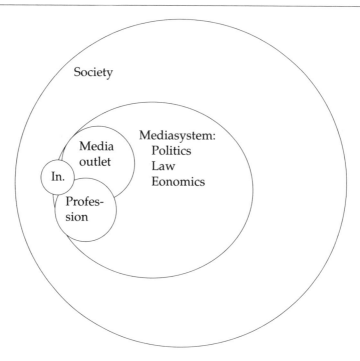

Instead of confronting the system and the individual as being the incompatible foci of ethics, a model of six levels is proposed in which areas of ethical content can be determined. (Loretan, 1994: 61)

(1) On a metaethical level, we discuss fundamental principles of media ethics in general. Freedom is such a principle of fundamental significance for journalistic ethics.
(2) On the level of politics and the political culture of society, these principles gain a certain concretion according to the historical and social background. Thus, freedom of expression and information are accepted values in pluralistic societies.
(3) The level of media politics sets the framework in which the media system is developed and in which media enterprises are organised. Here, such examples as whether freedom of information includes the right to protect one's sources or how the access to information is guaranteed are considered.
(4) On the level of the single organisation, we can observe how the different media units perform within this given framework. There,

differences, e.g., between a tabloid press or a public service broadcasting news, are to be explained.

(5) On the professional level, we can discuss the existence or normative demands for journalistic actions and their realisation.

(6) On the individual level, the focus is on the possibilities of action of the single journalist (or a member of the audience as well.)

These different levels serve also as analytical categories for fostering ethical considerations, thus trying to gain insight into the ever repeated question of who is to blame. If we discuss real actions and their consequences, we can speak within this model of six levels of graded responsibility. Hence, it would be of useless interest to try to play the one off the other, but it is necessary to consider the interdependence of different areas of responsibility, ethical conflicts and accountability.

One example may be employed to show how far the mentioned levels interrelate and influence each other. If we want to evaluate media production with regard to its performance for a democratic society, economic criteria are not appropriate. What is economically successfull is not necessarily the same for morality. At present, media success is measured only according to its economic success. Growing competition in the media market limits freedom of communication. Maintaining freedom of communication is an ethical and democratic concern. As the reason for the media market is founded in the idea of freedom of communication, ethics may ensure the survival of the market. Ethics serve individual and social orientations, and should lead to the accomplishment of ethical behaviour. As ethical theory fundamentally starts from the idea of the freedom of the individual to acknowledge moral behaviour; only voluntary behaviour can be ethical behaviour. This is why economic pressure is not appropriate for the achievement of ethical standards. In spite of that it can impede moral behaviour. Thus moral behaviour faced with economical pressure needs spaces of freedom. The answer to the question of whether a media enterprise creates such spaces for the newsrooms is — among others — dependent on the ruling production norms. Ethical reflections thus start when production norms are theoretically reflected upon and practically evaluated. This may happen within a journalist's organisation or news team whose members decide wether they stand up for the improvement of their working conditions. So, those reflections within one's argument penetrate the professional level, the organisational level and the level of media politics and may return to the individual level.

Any relevant topic of the debates within journalistic ethics can be integrated and discussed within this six-level scheme. So we can argue that the role journalists should play within society can be considered on the political and cultural level and touches the individual one. Given the longstanding heritage of ideas about the role of the media in society, a starting point for reflections about journalistic ethics is the question of which role journalists have to play and which task they should fulfil. Is it pure reporting, social responsibility, controlling the power, giving an audience orientation, being the advocate for the poor and socially handicapped, etc. The above mentioned scholarly discussion, which has developed on the metaethical level, shows how these concepts in a normative debate have changed.

It is different as well if we look closer at an empirical perspective on the self-concept of journalists in different countries, which would be a description on the individual level. Thus, we find much more in France (and Western mediterranean countries) the idea of a journalism nourished by the ideas of commenting and giving enlightenment to the audiences than in countries like Great Britain, where the Anglo-saxon model of a pure reporting and sharp investigative journalism is much more prevalent (Thomaß, 1998). In only one country is the self-image of journalists reconstructed with time and the development of the media landscape. A younger generation of journalists working in commercial audiovisual media in Germany see themselves less as 'educators' of their audiences than their elder colleagues in public service broadcasting do. (Schneider *et al.*, 1993) Thus we see how an individual perspective is influenced by the level which was described as organisational.

The self-image of journalist is primarily an individual feature and can be regarded as the (generalised) personal and action-oriented ideas of what and how a journalist should do. On that base, principles and norms are developed and discussed on the professional level, and try to give a general, ethically founded answer to the question of what a journalist should do. While ethical reflection fundamentally starts at the point that individual action has to be considered within the framework of social coexistence of people, journalistic action has to be legitimated towards two groups of individuals: those who are audiences and consumers of the journalistic production and those whom they meet while carrying out their job, including interview partners, sources, or subjects about whom they report. It is rare that the interest of one of these groups is identical with that of the other one.

But this is only one of these ethical dilemmas journalists have to confront while doing their job. Further examples include:

— The tension between demand for the new, unknown or problematic aspects in a given society and the interest in maintaining the dominant social patterns.

— The tension between the demand for 'objective' reporting and the fact that the representation of conditions in a society is always interpreted and created by the subjectivity of a reporter or editor.

— The tension between the obligation to serve society and the one to obey the financial interest of the media entrepreneur or the status aims of the profession.

— The tension between personal professional integrity and the demands of the media enterprise. (White, 1986: 47)

These dilemma are both located on one level and between different levels. They cannot be decided normatively and in a singular act. They refer to a prerequisite of any ethical problem: Ethics, if it should prove to be efficient, is an act of reflection and discourse, by which in a given situation principles are weighed and decided upon. The reason is that, in ethics, we nearly never find unmistakable or unambigous answers and solutions. Thus ethics does not facilitate the journalist's decision making process, but helps to make it more circumspect. Ethics does not deliver easy recipes, but sharpens the capacity of judgement within large spaces of discretion and freedom. The six-level-model can serve therefore as a framework to bring problems to the fore and understand the underlying structure of them.

4. Ethical 'Tools' on the Individual and Professional Level

So, journalistic ethics on the individual level is about the ability of the single journalist to identify ethical issues and dilemmata and to find his or her way through them in accordance with or by weighing different principles stemming from his or her responsibility towards his or her media enterprise, the public, the people with whom he or she had been working, etc.

But the ability to identify these problems with the help of frame-works is only one aspect of journalism ethics. Another is the ability to make decisions and to make good decisions. Therefore, more tools are needed on the individual and on the professional level, as for example, media laws can be regarded as tools on the level of media politics. A helpful tool is to ask questions about the situation where a decision is necessary. By setting up the right questions, the ethical dimension of a problem can be examined more exhaustively, so that the resulting decision will have a more sound character. The follow-ing list of such questions stems from a training booklet in the USA where a long tradition of teaching and training in journalism ethics has been developed. It provides refined material for improving deci-sion-making abilities. According to this list, a journalist facing an ethical dilemma should ask:

What do I know? What do I need to know?
What is my journalistic purpose?
What are my ethical concerns?
What organisational policies and professional guidelines should I con-sider?
How can I include other people, with different perspectives and diverse ideas, in the decision-making process?
Who are the stakeholders, i.e., those affected by my decision?
What are their motivations? Which are legitimate?
What if the roles were reversed? How would I feel if I were in the shoes of one of the stakeholders?
What are the possible consequences of my actions? Short term? Long term?
What are my alternatives to maximise my truthtelling responsibility and minimise harm?
Can I clearly and fully justify my thinking and my decision. To my colleagues? To the stakeholders? To the public?
(Society of Professional Journalists, 1995: 18)

Those or similar questioning should lead to a sound decision in dilemma situations. But they are not sufficient. Another dimension of improving journalistic ethics is the question of how far abilities are developed, to defend them even against constraints and contra-dictions. This is where the idea of the systematic character of media production has to be considered again. Because even if the journal-ists are confronted individually with many different ethical prob-lems, they are often confronted with the same sort of problems which stem from common developments in media production and the journalistic profession. Some of these conflict fields will be characterised in the following section.

5. Fields of Conflict Between
   Individualistic and Functionalistic Approach

Even among the very core actions of journalism, namely, research and investigation, where the single journalist is held responsible for his or her behaviour, the culture of the newsroom and the demands of the employer (in a wider sense the demands of competition and the challenge of the scoop) are decisive factors within the decision. How far a journalist is willing to go to get his or her information? Will he or she eavesdrop, use confidential documents without the consent of the source, uses hidden microphones or cameras, hide his or her identity as a journalist, pay for information? These seem to be individual questions, but the answers will be dependent on the newsroom culture and on the corporate identity of the media enterprise.

Furthermore, the fundamental journalistic principles of fairness and accuracy may be seemingly put into practice by the single journalist. But working conditions, the pressure of deadlines and production norms, the acceleration of news processing by digital techniques will have a decisive influence on a journalist's decisions of when a story is 'fit to print.'

As political and economic agents try to influence the media more or less and want to have convenient image representation, they develop a sophisticated system of methods for influencing journalists' attitudes and decisions. Favours of official administrations, a subtle management of access to information, the journalist's dependence on information and his or her sources, the seductive relationship to the powerful, practices of bribing and open efforts to corrupt, all these means can end up endangering the journalist's independence and lead to their possible corruption. This danger is not only prominent among those who work in rather precarious or economically challenging situations. Especially in those circles where the line between the media elite and the political elite is not well drawn, distorted and biased information may result from a lack of consciousness of the role of the journalist.

Rather near to this problem is the fact that the information industry has blurred more and more the line between journalistic information and public relations. Public relations departments are well equipped to deliver information in the appropriate form (press declarations, radio or video tapes, online messages fitting to the medium's format.) Journalists themselves are active in different fields as entrepreneurs of information, advertising, public relations and journalism, thus causing an overlap. The financial, banking and economic departments in the media especially tend to forget what and who is the purpose of their informational efforts.

The Gulf war showed a fundamental problem of journalistic ethics: The necessity to stay independent from a state's information, especially in times of war, and the growing impossibility to fulfil this demand in times when information is censored, filtered and prepared by mighty military institutions. It was not during this war that the media reflected upon their responsibilities, but afterwards when the whole disaster of information politics in this allegedly 'clean' war was to be seen. It would be an interesting question to evaluate if the media drew some consequences from these experiences, thus causing them to be more cautious in maintaining their independence during the confrontation NATO entered with Yugoslavia because of the Kosovo conflict. Initial evidence shows that there is an increasing practice of being honest about the sources in order to reflect the credibility of sources and not to follow the anticipated necessity of searching for the one truth in reporting. Rather, the audience is given bits and pieces of the complex reality, and is encouraged to construct their own pictures and evaluations of the situation. If this proves to be the major way to tackle the subject, this may already be an advancement from the times of the Falkland/Malvinas war, where the British media, for example, were often under pressure to fulfil a certain preconceived 'national' task or the aforementioned Gulf war, where the origin of information often was not obvious.

Protection of sources, which is a crucial norm for the performance of journalism and an undoubted necessity to maintain a good relationship to informants and other sources, becomes even more important in political cultures where access to information is hindered or difficult. The legal right to the protection of sources, however, by far does not exist in every democratic country. Thus it is a crucial question for a journalist to ask how far his or her employer will back him or her up, if it comes to a law suit.

Concerning the question of protection of privacy, it is, as in most areas of conflict, an important consideration to question how the cultural environment deals with questions of private morality, sexuality and individual conduct. Especially in this area, journalists all over the world could learn a lot by comparing the ways in which the Clinton-Lewinsky case, life and death of Diana, Princess of Wales, or the fact that the former French president François Mitterand had an illegitimate daughter were reported in their respective countries. In these cases, and less prominent ones as well, the way of reporting and respecting privacy is highly dependent on the expectations of the society in which the journalist finds himself or herself.

This is even more the case when it comes to ethnic minority reporting or covering ethnic conflicts. The journalist, being used to find himself or herself within a contemplative situation as an observer and a reporter of something happening outside his or her sphere, finds himself or herself in the middle of society, as he or she usually cannot avoid being part of one of the conflicting ethnic groups. Independence of judgement, willingness of giving voice to 'the other' or the others, empathy for the claims of another ethnic group, awareness for the social, economic, cultural situation of a minority, all these necessities are in conflict situations and are highly under pressure from the dominant culture. The result of the lack of the aforementioned capacities and the high involvement in the purposes of the power in the heart of one dominant ethnic group was at the origin of a media development in Yugoslavia, and not only there, which led to the phenomenon of the so-called 'hate speech.'

Conclusion

In the variety of areas of conflict, the single journalist is demanded to act and is easily to blame. Nevertheless a whole system of economic, political, cultural and technical factors and constraints influence his or her decision making process in every ethical question. Thus, it should be obvious that the individual is acting accountably within this given framework. But he or she cannot be held responsible for the conditions this framework imposes.

Hence, every functionalist reproach of the individualistic approach in journalism ethics, which criticises the neglect of the structures of journalistic production, is right because it overburdens individual responsibility. But every reproach from the individualistic approach of the functionalistic one, namely, that the acting person is becoming less apparent, is legitimate as well because structures in journalism are maintained and perpetuated by individuals. Furthermore, journalism education and further education would lose its legitimacy to demand ethical behaviour from future journalists and to train them in it. It is one of the the tasks of journalism education to prepare these beginners for a conscientious performance of the jobs within the given framework (see last chapter of this part.)

References

ALTSCHULL, H.J. (1990), *From Milton to Mc Luhan. The Ideas behind American Journalism*. New York, London.

BLÖBAUM, B. (1994), *Journalismus als soziales System: Geschichte, Ausdifferenzierung und Verselbständigung*. Opladen.

BOVENTER, Hermann (1996), 'Macht der Medien. Zum aktuellen Stand der Ethik-Debatte' in Jürgen WILKE (ed.) *Ethik der Massenmedien: Studienbücher zur Publizistik und Kommunikationswissenschaft*, Braumüller, Wien, 1996, p. 53-67.

CHRISTIANS, C.G. (1986), 'Ethical Theory in a Global Setting' in Thomas W. COOPER (ed.), *Communication Ethics and Global Change*. Philadelphia.

CHRISTIANS, C.G., C.L. COVERT (1980), *Teaching Ethics in Journalism Education*. (The Teaching of Ethics, 3). New York.

CHRISTIANS, C.G., Kim B. ROTZOLL, Mark FACKLER (1987), *Media Ethics: Cases and Moral Reasoning*. New York & London, Longman.

COHEN, Elliot T. (1992), *Philosophical Issues in Journalism*. New York & Oxford.

COOPER, T.W. (1989), *Communications Ethics and Global Change*. Philadelphia & New York.

DAY, Louis A. (1991), *Ethics in Media Communications: Cases and Controversies*. Belmont (CA).

FINK, C. C. (1988), *Media Ethics in the Newsroom and Beyond*. New York.

GOODWIN, H. Eugene (1983), *Groping for Ethics in Journalism*. Ames (IA), Iowa State University Press.

GORDON, David A., John M. KITTROSS, Carol REUSS (1996), *Controversies in Media Ethics*. White Plains (NY).

LAMBETH, Edmund B. (1986), *Committed Journalis: An Ethic for the Profession*. Bloomington, Indiana University Press; newly edited 1991.

LOWENSTEIN, Ralph Lynn, John C. MERRILL (1990), *Macromedia: Mission, Message and Morality*. New York.

MERRILL, J.C. (1977), *Existential Journalism*. New York.

MEYER, Philip (1986), *Ethical Journalism: A guide for students, practitioners and consumers*. New York & London.

ODELL, S. Jack (1983), *Philosophy and Journalism*. New York, Longman.

PIEPER, A. (1991), *Einführung in die Ethik*. Tübingen.

RÜHL, M. (1996), 'Soziale Veranwortung und persönliche Verantwortlichkeit im Journalismus' in Jürgen WILKE (ed.), pp. 89-99.

RÜHL, M., Ulrich SAXER (1981), '25 Jahre Deutscher Presserat: Ein Anlaß für Überlegungen zu einer kommunikationswissenschaftlichen Ethik des Journalismus und der Massenkommunikation' in *Publizistik*, 26(1981)81, pp. 451-503.

SCHNEIDER, Beate *et al.* (1993), 'Westdeutsche Journalisten im Vergleich: Jung, professionell und mit Spaß an der Arbeit' in *Publizistik* No. 1, pp. 5-30.

SIEBERT, Fred S., Theodore PETERSON, Wilbur SCHRAMM (1956), *Four Theories of the Press*. Chicago.

THOMAß, Barbara (1998), *Journalistische Ethik: Ein Vergleich der Diskurse in Frankreich Großbritannien und Deutschland*. Opladen.

WEISCHENBERG, S. (1992), *Journalistik: Theorie und Praxis aktueller Medienkommunikation*. 2 Bde. Bd. 1: *Mediensysteme, Medienethik, Medieninstitutionen*. Opladen.

CODES OF ETHICS

Huub Evers

"Who can bring himself to take an interest in spending the time and money needed to write down what normal people use to do anyhow and what rebels will only snap their fingers at?", an industry manager once said. (Van Luijk, 1993: 174, our transl.) More often, one can come across this type of expression in texts about codes of ethics. And when it is about media and journalism, there is sometimes added: "The more prescriptions, the less press freedom. The best press law is no press law, the best press code is no press code." Not encouraging words for advocates of ethical codes. Nevertheless, attention to this phenomenon is increasing. Indeed, the period of the large national and international codes seems to be at an end, but at the level of single companies and professional associations, ethical principles and guidelines for daily practice are increasingly being embedded in codes.

In trade and industry, much attention is being paid to 'socially responsible entrepreneurship.' Issues like human rights, environment and working conditions are getting more important for industries. More often companies are able to accept their social responsibility, self-imposed or under the pressure of public opinion. The main reason behind this is the consumer who has become an important factor. As public opinion opposes more and more the resolutions of multinationals like Shell or Heineken, people's purchasing behaviour usually forces the companies involved to embark swiftly on the course desired by the public.

The distance between government and industry is getting smaller; government must increasingly take into account the demands of the market, and industries must increasingly take into account social requirements. Entepreneurs need to get used to the fact that their actions are permanently subjects of public debate and lasting examination just as politicians actions are. And what about the media? In

this area too, single companies, newspapers and broadcasting organisations draft codes of ethics. In this chapter, after presenting a general background, attention will be paid to media ethics codes: What
are codes of ethics? What are they about? Why are they drafted? and:
What are the pros and cons? Besides a brief historical review, the
issues of professionalisation and self-regulation will be addressed.

1. General Background

A code of ethics, as Business Ethics Professor van Luijk (1993: 175,
our transl.) says, is "a collection of in-company, ethically inspired
principles, in which employees' rules of conduct are drafted and
company-policy and responsibility defined concerning interested
groups."
    First and foremost, it is important to draw some distinctions.
Which organisation is drafting a code? Is it a matter of a company-
code, a code of a certain sector of industry or the ethical code of a
certain profession? Is it primarily an internal code, addressed to
one's own members or employees, or an external one, mainly
addressed to potential clients? In most codes, attention is being paid
to both aspects. Is it a single-issue code, e.g., a code against discrimination or an environment code, or a text in which attention is being
paid to a large number of issues? It is also important, whether it is a
matter of a 'bottom line code' or a 'basic values code.' The former is
a set of minimum standards or rules under which a practitioner may
not fall or transgress. The latter is a set of articulated ideals to which
a group aspires. Most codes are a mixture of the two designs.
    As there are various kinds of codes, so too are there diverging
motives for drafting a code and diverging functions to be attributed
to a code. What kind of motives play a role in the process of drafting
and implementing a code? A code can be considered as a contribution to a new corporate identity, e.g., after a process of merger, or as
an instrument to create or improve a 'moral climate, a moral atmosphere.' A code with bottom line rules for daily practice can be seen
as a help to avoid critical situations. In times of moral stress, one can
refer to relevant passages of the code. The decision to draft a code
can be taken to improve the image of an organisation after a painful
incident to avoid a new painful performance in the public eye. A
code can be formulated as a self-regulation instrument to prevent

and to anticipate governmental regulations; it is better if one regulates oneself in co-operation with one's professional colleagues rather than trusting others to do so. Doing so oneself, one can be sure that matters progress in the correct manner.

The functions attributed to a code are closely connected with the motives underlying the decision to draft such a document. "Essentially, every (good) code is prospective self-image. The organisation defines itself for itself and its employees as for the outer world, and shapes this self-definition in a number of restrictive and positive self-accepted regulations and targets." (Van Luijk, 1993: 179, our transl.)

A function of such a process may be the improvement of the internal cohesion of a company or a sector of industry. Or to show to clients or suppliers what an organisation wants to be accountable for. Or in broader sense, to demonstrate to the outer world, that the organisation accepts and takes seriously its social responsibility. An organisation, for this reason formulating its primary principles, must naturally be able to place the code at the disposal of interested people outside the organisation. Only then can there be a question of a real ability to be accountable for people involved, including government and the public.

There are some basic conditions for a good and useful code that is effective inside and convincing outside. First of all, a code must be clear and unmistakable. It must be formulated in a clean and bright way. The articles must be substantial and useful in everyday practice. No window dressing. Second, a code must have a broad basis within the circles of professionals. It must be the result of internal debates on issues of professional ethics. Those debates among professionals may even be much more important than the document which is produced as a result of it. In a situation without loyalty to one's colleagues and a lack of integrity, drafting a code of ethics is not a solution and a guarantee for a better future. A code is not a wonderful remedy, but only an aid. Further, a code must have a good complaints procedure and provisions of sanctions. There only is a mature and professional relation with one's colleagues when everyone is willing to accept the agreed consequences of not observing the rules of the code. Moreover, observing the code must be recognised and appreciated. If integrity and loyalty to the code is punished because a staff member does not reach his target, the management of an organisation better say straight out that theirs are only commercial goals.

There are some difficulties in drafting a code of ethics. For example, the objection that the organisation can legally be held responsible for what it commits itself to in a code. Strictly and legally, this is not a valid objection, since a code does not have the force of law. Furthermore, a code can be used as a touchstone in court. It can be used in a positive way as well: The single fact of being an organisation with a code of ethics can be an argument in court in order to be granted a lighter sentence, as sometimes happens in the US.

"Nowadays an area arises of not strictly legal, voluntarily accepted obligations, laid down in codes and agreements, which are going to play an increasingly important role in social contacts and contracts," as van Luijk (1993: 184) mentions. "This involves the notion of accountability to become more open."

The next objection, sometimes raised against drafting codes of ethics, is the conviction of other than ethical considerations being in force in trade and industry. Commercial thinking and acting are incompatible with seriously considering moral principles. And where ethics play a role, it mainly is a matter of individual considerations which can not be regulated in a code. So everybody should make his or her own choice and his or her own decisions.

2. Professionalising

Do journalists have the characteristics of professionals in education and practice? In sociological literature, the subject of professionalising is studied in various ways, e.g., in the competitive examination of characteristics of various occupations. Professionalising is a dynamic process. An occupation being professionalised, gradually shows more characteristics of that ideal type. An inventory of the characteristics of professionalising processes and professional practice mentioned above has been made by Wentink (1994).

In professionalising processes, five stages are distinguished:
(1) Practitioners are employed full-time; (2) They unite in an association which regulates education and required qualifications. (3) The occupation gets its own identity, which is laid down in an exclusive name-giving. (4) The professionals and their association want to protect and socially legitimate their profession. They aspire to a legally recognised position and try to obtain an exclusive status. (5) Professional conduct is regulated by a code of ethics. Social control of the

practice is exercised by professionals themselves. A disciplinary council controls the observance of the rules of conduct.

A lot of occupations gradually attain a professional status by passing through these stages. The degree of professionalising can be evaluated with the help of a number of criteria. Sociologists usually limit the term 'professional' to 'crafts' whose practitioners meet the following nine standards: (1) They have a specific expertise acquired in a long, theoretically based and mostly specialised education. (2) They employ knowledge and skills in concrete situations and cases. (3) They have a large amount of personal and commercial freedom of decision and practice. (4) They are active at an unambiguously definable, monopolised area at which others cannot be employed. (5) They operate in a lasting tradition of practice so that an awareness of good practice has grown. (6) They have specific rules of conduct and a code of ethics which regulates the practice. (7) They do their activities from altruistic motives. Professionals serve public wealth and client's interests. (8) Clients highly trust their expertise and their moral integrity. (9) A professional organisation watches the admission to profession, draws up the conditions of entry and exercises the quality of professional practice.

Just a limited number of professionals hold an elaborated professional ethics and a code of ethics because they serve a vital and socially important value (e.g., health.) For the individual professional, these ethical codes serve mainly as a guideline for practice for the profession as a whole. Apart from that, the code certainly is an expression of a professional identity. A professional organisation can have the possibility of disciplinary regulations.

The motive to improve the collective status of professionals in society underlies processes of professionalising. Most clearly it is expressed in the personal commitment of the professional to work according to a code of ethics based on a set of professional values. "The code of ethics is only an external visible sign that the profession is collectively committed to internal regulation of its members, but, in fact, the adoption of a code of ethics is the single most important symbol of the fact that this occupation is seeking to justify itself in terms of professional norms." (White, 1995: 455)

Professionality is often characterised as an attitude in which the aspects of professional and intellectual skills, educational level and control by colleagues play an important role. The aspect of professional ethics is often seen as not being essential to that professional attitude, but as an additional requirement. In agreement with van Es and Meijlink (1995: 124), it is my opinion "that professional ethics is an outstanding matter of professional skills. Moral reflection ought to be an integral part of professional attitudes. Someone proves himself to be a professional if he or she is able to integrate moral reflections into his or her professional practice."

And what about the professionalising processes in journalism and mass media? Goodwin and Smith (1994: 34) note: "During the past 30 years, many journalists began to view themselves as members of a 'profession.' They had college degrees like other professionals and earned (...) middle-class-salaries. They believed their jobs required intelligence, creativity and independent judgement and placed demands on them that required the same level of performance expected in traditional professions like law. So, they argued, they should be looked upon as professionals and given the same kind of respect."

On the basis of his survey, Wentink draws the conclusion that journalism is not to be numbered among the category of professions. Indeed, his conclusion applies not only to journalism, but to public relations as well: Not 'professions' in the traditional sense of the word, but occupations in the process of becoming a profession. Wentink calls journalism a semi-profession. Journalism professor Lambeth thought of a compromise and called journalism "a craft with professional responsibilities." (Goodwin, Smith, 1994: 36)

3. Self-Regulation and Ethical Codes

Self-regulation is opposite to regulation by government. The profession itself defines professional norms and exercises the observance of the rules. Background consideration is the faith that putting professional practice to the test of professional ethical norms is the paramount responsibility of the profession itself, always of course within a legal framework.

A first, light way of self-regulation is the written code of ethics, a set of professional ethical norms formulated by a profession itself. Drafting and accepting a code is mostly connected with implementing a way of testing by colleagues, e.g., disciplinary regulations in order that colleagues can exercise the observance of the duties drawn up in their code and can firmly deal with offenders. People can lodge a complaint to these disciplinary councils when they hold the view that the professional involved acted negligently. The most important motive behind every self-regulatory instrument is the requirement of professionals acting in accordance with opinions and norms prevailing in professional circles.

A second motive for putting questionable practices to the test of a profession's moral standards and delivering a verdict on the cases involved is the effect of moral cohesion in professional circles and the improvement of moral judgement, which will produce a positive result on a profession's status.

Furthermore, a well functioning, self-regulatory system will prevent most government interventions. Professionals drafting for themselves rules for responsible practice is preferable to a governmental authority doing so. Besides, self-regulation is more efficient and effective than public, legal measures. It is also more efficient because alleged contraventions can be examined quicker and cheaper. There are less obstacles than there are in court. More effective since criticism of professionals hurts more than a judicial sentence.

Moreover, self-regulation is complementary to the law and the test norm is broader. That means that disciplinary councils do have more possibilities to pass judgement than courts do, e.g., they cannot only deal with illegal actions, but must also deal with legally unexceptionable, socially undesirable actions as well.

The disadvantage to self-regulation with regard to disciplinary councils or supervision committees is that of being tested by a commission consisting of colleagues, at least partly, which could suggest a (too) high degree of support and solidarity among professional colleagues. The public could get the impression of losing its hold of decision-making. Furthermore, the council could be criticised, mostly by professionals themselves, since it acts needlessly and severely. Generally, instruments of self-regulation have to contend with the disadvantage of possessing little or insufficient sanctions and of giving a rather non-committal impression.

4. History of Codes

The first codes were drawn up in the US in the early part of the twentieth century as part of professionalising processes of a number of occupations, including journalism. The very first formal code of

ethics for journalists was drafted in 1910 by the Kansas Editorial
Association. For a long period of time, journalists felt confident that
they, as professionals, ought to draft an ethical code for the profession. The American Society of Newspaper Editors, founded in 1923,
immediately drew up such a document, the 'Canons of Journalism',
in 1975, revised as the 'Statement of Principles.' Other newspaper
publishers followed, and after that associations of journalists and
publishers tried to formulate the unwritten professional rules in
obligatory texts. All these codes were based on the liberal model of
the democratic state and the notion of the important role of independent media and journalists.

But not until the 1970s were codes drafted on a large scale. The
Society of Professional Journalists, which signed the ASNE-code in
1926, drafted its own code in 1976 and revised it in 1984 and 1987.
Following the print media, other professional groups in the media
industry also started to draft professional standards, though fewer
and much later. Single news organisations too were drawing up ethical codes. In the mid-1970s, less than 10 percent of the daily newspapers had their own code. Ten years later, the percentage rose to 75.
More and more, it was a matter of one's own codes, which were
revised in cases of new developments or ethical issues coming to the
fore. (Goodwin, Smith, 1994) The large number of journalistic ethics
codes, on the basis of which ethical decisions are discussed, are characteristic of the way media ethics in the US is dealt with on a practical and scholarly level. Above all, codes are widespread in the print
media and in schools of journalism. Besides single media industries,
unions of journalists at national levels have drafted ethics codes as
guidelines for their members. These documents start from the
media's freedom and responsibility and usually hold concrete and
clear clauses and recommendations which are to provide a framework for journalist's behaviour. Leading drafters of codes of ethics
have been publishers and editors-in-chief. They are charged with
executive tasks and believe that freedom of the press could very well
be guaranteed by self-regulatory mechanisms.

In Europe, in the early part of twentieth century, codes have been
drafted first of all at national levels and then in international associations as well. At the end of the nineteenth century, the journalists
organisation in Galicia (Poland), part of the Austro-Hungarian
Empire, framed a foundation charter with a tribunal of honour and
a list of moral regulations which bound all members.

The first written code of ethics, though never formally adopted, was drafted in Sweden in 1900. In 1923, the Swedish *Publicistklubben* sanctioned a set of ethical guidelines drawn up on the occasion of a press committee. The first formally adopted code was the *'Charte des devoirs professionnels des journalistes français'* formulated in 1918 in France and accepted by the *'Syndicat national des journalistes'*. In 1931, the International Tribunal of Honour for Journalists was founded by the International Federation of Journalists and the association of journalists accredited to the League of Nations. This tribunal made its decisions on the basis of an explicit ethical code. In 1936, the League of Nations adopted the 'International Convention Concerning the Use of Broadcasting in the Cause of Peace' and the *'Union internationale des associations de presse'* set up its ethics principles. In 1939, the International Federation of Journalists drew up a code. In 1950, UNO worked at an international code which was never accepted because of the resistance of professional associations of some countries to government intervention. That was the basis of the Declaration of Principles on the Conduct of Journalists, the so-called IFJ-Code of Bordeaux. This code is a document dating from 1954 and added to in 1986, consisting of nine rather generally drafted principles. (Juusela, 1991; Laitila, 1995b; Snijders, 1995; Thomaß, 1998) Over thirty national European codes and the IFJ-code are being published at EthicNet, the Databank for European Codes of Journalism Ethics (http://www.uta.fi/ethicnet/). This collection has been started and will be periodically updated by the Department of Journalism and Mass Communication of University of Tampere, Finland. PressWise (http://www.presswise.org.uk/ethics.htm) has assembled over sixty national and international codes of journalistic ethics from around the world. These print and broadcasting codes have been explored to see how individual topics are being treated. Over thirty topics, from accuracy to plagiarism and violence, have been analysed.

Leading international PR-codes include those of the IPRA (International Public Relations Association) and CERP (*Confédération Européenne des Relations Publiques*). The 'International Code of Ethics' (Code of Athens) was drafted in 1965 by CERP, revised in 1968 and adopted by IPRA in 1965 (http://www.ipranet.org/athens.htm).

The 'European Code of Professional Conduct in Public Relations' (Code of Lisbon) is the ethical code of CERP. It was drawn up in 1978 and revised in 1989. This code was drafted to enable a better application in professional practice. It is seen as an improvement of other loosely formulated codes.

Media ethics codes have been drafted in four periods: after the first and the second World Wars, at the end of the sixties, in the course of the seventies, and finally there was a boom again at the end of the eighties and the beginning of the nineties. This last time saw revisions because of the emergence of new democracies in the former East bloc and the revision of existing codes in other countries. White (1989) notes that the process of drafting codes indeed is part of a tendency of professionalisation, but that on the other hand, the drafting of a code is always connected with a situation of 'practical needs' and outside pressure for further self-regulation. An internal and external pressure always comes up. Apart from the improvement of the level of practice and the increase of status, there are external processes of cultural, technical and socio-political changes in society at large. Such a process is often considered by journalists as a threat. McQuail (1992) says that moral principles in journalism are often expressed in the clearest way at the time of crises and at turning points in national or media history. That is the reason why, on his opinion, codes of ethics have been drafted after both World Wars. For the rest, he thinks of the rise of television, of mergers and monopolising in the world of press and the development of new technologies in broadcasting as examples of turning points. Thomaß (1998) says that the development of professional rules took place under the stress of turning away potential legal restrictions, on the one hand, and providing the profession with a positive framework of orientation, on the other hand. If public opinion requires firmer rules for the press, the press tries to ward off this danger by self-regulation. This is the background that clarifies the rise of ethical codes in the sixties.

5. Media Codes, What are They About?

On the one hand, professional rules can be imposed by a national or international government or authority. On the other hand, they can be initiated or regulated by an association of professionals. Professional ethical norms are to be found at four levels: the level of the journalist as an individual, the news organisation, the profession and society in general. In the past, representatives of a number of professions briefly and succinctly formulated the main professional duties to which they consider themselves bound in order to ensure the successful execution of their social functions. The term 'profession' is not without meaning in this context; drafting codes is an element in the professionalising process.

It should be stressed that a code of ethics does not so much have the function of establishing norms as that of confirming them. "The duties laid down in a code are not new for people involved. A code does not create norms but formulates what previously was already experienced as a binding norm. It holds, in professional circles, the extract of prevailing opinions concerning what ought to be done and avoided in professional practice. Essentially, representatives of a certain profession are not bound to the duties embodied in their code because these duties are accepted as such by their association, but because they hold the requirements for good practice. They are obliged to abide by the rules merely on account of their function. The code is only the formal confirmation of these duties" (our transl.), as Jens maintains. (1972: 27) So the meaning of a code primarily lies in stating explicitly what implicitly belongs to doing a good job.

The exact content of a code depends on the answer to the question of who has been drafting the code: a professional association, a governmental commission or a publishers association. Also important is the period of drawing up the code. "When codes of conduct are drawn up, those who draft them seldom aim to give comprehensive guidance on the full range of ethical decisions that may face those working in the profession; normally, they confine their attention to matters dealt with in previous codes, plus any new issue that is a source of public disquiet." (Harris, 1992: 73).

Anyhow, codes hold a number of clauses concerning the individual integrity of the professional. In addition, there are rules on the relationship with the public. The profession must have the image of reliability. Then, there must be an address for lodging complaints about professionals. Moreover, the relationship of the professional and his colleagues is regulated.

Snijders (1995) divides journalistic rules of conduct into three categories. First and foremost, the written and unwritten rules about how to deal with sources and subjects of publications. Here, guidelines are to be found about mentioning sources, dealing with anonymous sources, hearing both sides, protection of privacy and the publication of personal data, agreements with informants and interviewed persons, embargo agreements, confidential information and

professional secrecy. Furthermore, rules on how to deal with letters
to the editor and voluntary correction. Finally, rules on payment for
information and taking bribes. Second, the rules on how to deal with
colleagues. Journalists are not allowed to discredit the profession
and their medium. Not only a journalist's product, but his way of
acting must also be credible and reliable. That is why there are rules
about accepting free travel and gifts, about conflicts of interest,
about the tension between editorial and commercial interests and
about loyalty to one's colleagues. Finally, the rules on how to deal
with society as a whole. Here, rules are to be found about the public's right to know, about separation of facts and comment and about
objectivity in providing information. One also finds information
about weighing interests and how to deal with violence, investigative reporting and undercover journalism.

Another approach has been undertaken by Laitila (1995). After
having made a comparison of the codes of ethics collected by Ethic-
Net (http://www.uta.fi/ethicnet), she found that two-thirds of these
codes are adopted by the unions or associations of journalists. Five
codes are adopted by the journalists' and publishers' associations
jointly and another five by press councils. One code, the Danish one,
is adopted by the state and the Union of Journalists together.

A code of ethics has a two-fold function. On the one hand, an
external function "to specify accountability with regard to different
outside interests: mainly the state, the public, the sources and the
advertisers." (Self-regulation to prevent and avoid government regulation.) On the other hand an internal function "to protect the
integrity and identity of the profession itself, both from external
(state, interest groups, etc.) and internal (plagiarism, yellow press,
and so forth) pressures." From these two general functions, six more
specific ones, divided into thirteen categories, can be derived. See
Box 1. The researcher notes that, at least in principle, European journalists mainly base their professional activities on their accountability to the public and to other regulatory groups. The most common
themes in the examined codes "emphasise different aspects of truthfulness, the need to protect the integrity and independence of journalists, the responsibility of journalists in shaping public opinion,
fair means in the gathering and presentation of information, protection of the rights of sources and referents, and the freedom to
express and communicate ideas and information without hindrance." (p. 538)

Box 1

To show accountability to the public:
   Truthfulness of information.
   Clarity of information.
   Defence of public rights.
   Responsibilities as creators of public opinion.

To show accountability to the sources and referents:
   Gathering and presenting information.
   Integrity of the source.

To protect the professional integrity of journalists:
   General rights and prohibitions.
   Protection from public powers.
   Protection from employers and advertisers.

To protect the status and unity of the journalistic profession:
   Protection of the status of journalism.
   Protection of the solidarity within the profession.

To show accountability to the employers:
   Loyalty to the employer.

To show accountability to the state:
   Respect for state institutions.

In schematically presenting the main issues of PR-codes, four areas are to be distinguished (Evers, 1998: 57-58): First, the general professional duties, e.g., the obligation to practice honesty, purity, sincerity and to observe all possible carefulness in financial affairs. A public relations practitioner is not allowed to provide information or comment, knowing or supposing this information to be false or deceptive. Equally, it is not allowed to use organisations serving false interests. Public relations activities must be openly conducted and well recognised. They may not lead to deceiving other persons.

Second, the professional duties towards clients or principles, e.g., the responsibility for carrying out an assignment in a sound and informed way. The public relations practitioner must see that his independence towards the client or principle is being maintained. Furthermore, there is the duty to keep secret all confidential information of former and present principles. Information to the client may not be reducible to the source in case of potential harmful consequences for that source. Besides, a PR-code holds rules to prevent potential conflicts of interests, e.g., in case the interests of the public relations practitioner or the office may be incompatible with principal interests. Clarity is to be provided beforehand. The fee may not depend on the result. The result cannot be guaranteed, it is only a matter of the obligation to do one's utmost. No profit for one's own good may be gained from assignments.

Third, the professional duties towards mass media and public opinion. The independence and social responsibility of the mass media are to be judged as the media's right to receive information. This corresponds to the duty to provide correct information and the prohibition against deceiving public opinion or the press. In contacts with the mass media, one should observe prevailing norms and usages and exercise due caution.

Finally, the professional duties towards colleagues and the profession: The duty to refrain from dishonest competition and not to give one's opinion about colleagues in a conceited way or in such a manner as to sully a colleague's reputation.

6. Why Draft a Code of Ethics?

Professional organisations have drafted ethical codes to define moral relationships with the public, government, clients and colleagues through the channel of self-regulation, and in doing so, to improve professional practice. "Codes are efforts to lead the profession to a higher level of practice, to improve the social status of the profession and to regulate as best they can the mutual intercourse of professionals" (our transl.), as van der Meiden (1985: 41-45) states.

Generally, one could say that codes of ethics want to stimulate professionals to exercise their function in a responsible way. The profession wants to take criticism seriously and react adequately. Codes are always based on prevailing social morality: They link on to prevailing ethical considerations. Looking at codes of ethics, the underlying ethical systems are to be considered as well. "The codes commonly used today (...) spring from Judeo-Christian cultures. It is on these underlying precepts that we build our media ethics codes. The underlying precepts have an influence on what, in particular cases, we decide to call 'ethical.' One must question whether such codes will adequately serve an Islamic culture, a Confucian culture or a Buddhist culture." Then, 'press tradition' is to be considered. "Codes of ethics traditionally have been developed within the press. This was natural, but the new media environment in which we apply ethics has changed. Television rules the information environment, it is the tool of global operators and broadcasting (radio and TV) addresses the largest audience. Print and images are fundamentally different in ways that are of importance in considering journalists' ethics. The printed word is particularly adept at engaging the capacity to think and to reason. Television, on the other hand, powerfully appeals to our emotions." (Background Paper Media in Focus, 1998)

In Western democratic societies, codes do not have the function of protecting journalism from government regulation, but primarily serve as a quality guarantee for the public. With journalism drafting ethical guidelines, the public can get more insight into the way journalists do their job. Drafting and publishing these rules can be considered a gesture to the public of clarity regarding what is acceptable and what is prohibited in news production. Openness provides insight into the public's demands of various media, ranging from product quality to the newsgathering process to publishing. The mass media, seeing themselves as a watchdog of democracy, must at least be open to a continual guarding of the conditions under which news comes into being. "Under repressive regimes, a code may be a way of giving moral support to journalists who have been victimised, and of encouraging solidarity within the profession. Under more liberal regimes codes will place greater emphasis on protecting members of the public rather than journalists themselves."(Harris, 1992: 62)

Snijders (1995) mentions four good reasons for the existence of professional journalistic rules of ethics. First, it is very important for citizens, adequately functioning in a democratic society, to be well informed. So the way the mass media deliver information is important as well as the rules they observe in doing so. For citizens must be able to rely on the media. Second, in societies like ours, the media have become powerful. To avoid the abuse of power, the exercise ought to be bound by rules. Third, the media have to impose rules on themselves to prevent authorities from imposing rules on the profession. For example, European organisations like the European Parliament and the General Assembly of the Council of Europe are regularly inclined to draft codes and to move member states to use them in drawing up their national press codes. Finally, to create a good and workable relationship between the sender and receiver of information. Both groups need to be informed about journalistic rules and the differences of various media in this regard. Credibility and reliability of journalism are determined by the public's awareness of journalism observing rules.

The strongly increasing attention to ethical rules in journalism, where does it come from? Van Dijck (1995) points out the following causes; (1) Journalistic rules are to be adapted to radical changes in journalism because of technological developments. New dilemmas arise (shocking pictures, live coverage, manipulative pictures) for which the print media rules are insufficient. (2) There is a strongly increasing commercial pressure upon news organisations with affects daily practice in journalism. Speed and sensationalism can prevail over careful and balanced reporting. Strict separation of news and commercials or promotion can no longer be minutely made. (3) The decline of journalism, other social areas and professional activities urges on to further reflection on ethical rules in journalism. News and current affairs programs are increasingly going to look like entertainment, i.e., 'infotainment'. Furthermore, entertainment is presented more and more in the format of news or information. Some people take about "the newsification of culture."

These developments urge journalism to adapt explicitly its rules to both the interest of journalists themselves and the public, requiring clarity on the way news is being effectuated and wanting to know whether the public can trust journalists.

6. The Pros and Cons of a Code

Codes of ethics were drafted in a period when people put more confidence in written agreements than they do at present, as van der Meiden notes. Modern professionals think the norms in codes are too broad and too idealistic. They are aimed more at the situation than at the general norm. Nowadays, codes have a decorative function, but are not very useful in practice.

Obviously, a shift can be seen from a more deductive to a more inductive ethics: It is not the general rule that is paramount in making ethical decisions, but the demands made by concrete situations.

At most, in a series of concrete, 'situationally' defined decisions, a guideline can become visible that can be useful in future decisions. This is what van der Meiden (1994: 338-339) describes as a 'non-valid ethics,' "an ethics refraining from rules, but only attributing validity to the concretely taken decisions." (our transl.). That means privatising and individualism in ethics.

The call for journalistic codes, according to Schuijt (1995: 90), is "absolutely understandable, but questionable as well, certainly if one realises these calls as mostly coming from the political wing" (our transl.). This is understandable since the mass media in a democratic society perform important functions such that certain guarantees for good practice are considered desirable. This is questionable since the proposed rules often hold restrictions on the limits of freedom within which the media ought to work. First, there is the consensus issue. In a pluralistic society, various opinions on ethical subjects often prevail, including the media as well. And when, nevertheless, an agreement is achieved about the content of a code, it will necessarily be limited to some divergently explicable matters of course. It is wiser, particularly in ethics, to formulate open norms which leave scope for evaluation and consideration within the concrete circumstances of the case.

An objection revolves around a code becoming a legal instrument in a judge's hands. If the judge uses the code as a guideline, journalistic ethical norms are drawn into a legal framework.

As one can read in this book, Hamelink finds a professional code useful as a draft of moral accountability that a profession accepts towards the public, but unfit as an instrument for decision-making in moral dilemmas. He holds the view that rules, based on moral principles and, in journalism, mostly drawn up in codes of ethics, may provide a hold on rather clearly structured situations, but that they fail to hold up against moral dilemmas. It is just impossible to draft guidelines for all situations of moral choice that point out what moral rule is to apply in a specific dilemma, what priorities are to be established and what alternative action needs to be chosen. Goodwin and Smith (1994) state as well that codes deal primarily with cut-and-dried issues and do not come to grips with the realities of newsgathering or help reporters solve the ethical problems they frequently encounter. Certainly, there are a lot of journalists holding the view that there are better ways to deal with ethical problems than codes of ethics. They prefer frequent staff meetings to discuss

ethics and other newsroom problems. Obviously, drafting codes of
ethics isn't a matter of course, particularly in journalism. Certainly
not everyone in journalism is convinced of its sense and desirability.
A written code is found to be either too general and loose and therefore meaningless and unfit, or detailed and clear, and therefore a
danger for editorial freedom and a hindrance for journalistic behaviour.

Another argument against rules laid down in a code is that a written code could have a rigid effect on a period of continuously changing opinions. How can a profession in a morally pluralistic society
formulate a set of norms that are relevant for practice? Drafting
norms means misunderstanding the situational character of the professional ethics of journalism. Most media professionals do their job
in conformity with media organisations. "Codes of media ethics can
become an ideology and simply justify and defend the 'safe' social
status of media workers." (White, 1995: 456). Besides, codes are often
phrased in too idealistic terms. A set of well composed guidelines
easily becomes a moral alibi while, really, awareness of personal
responsibility and attitude of the professional must be decisive for
reliable and fair practice. In this context, it is observed that journalists without codes are perfectly able to make their decisions in
morally painful situations. Moreover, a limiting list of what is permitted and what prohibited could suggest that not specifically mentioned issues could be permissible. And, last but not least, constitutional freedom of expression and freedom of the press imply that
journalism cannot be a closed issue. Hence, punishing a person who
breaches the rules is difficult, if not impossible.

Another more practical disavantage is, that outsiders can refer to
such a document as well, e.g., in court. Therefore, a code needs to be
formulated in a considerably more careful way than when they are
applied only to journalism. Some media attorneys recommend
media organisations not adopt a code, since it could be used as evidence against journalists in libel and privacy suits.

These arguments are partly valid and convincing. Indeed, in a
code of ethics, not everything can be anticipated and regulated. As
all ethics, professional ethics certainly is determined to a large extent
by the situation. For every code must be in force, that adaptation to
changing opinions, circumstances and practices is needed. In doing
so, rules of conduct must be changed, if they are based on an insufficient consensus. As Star-Telegram's columnist and retired ombuds-

man Phil Record writes (http://www.startelegram.com/ colum-nist/record2.htm), "Writing a code for a news operation is not sim-ple because journalists confront new and unforeseen experiences each day. There is no way to write a code to cover every situation. Therefore, there needs to be enough breathing room in a code to pro-vide for the new, the unforeseen, the unexpected." So, the revised code of his paper reads: "No ethics code can address all possible sit-uations. The guidelines outlined in this code deal with obvious potential problems and may be used to develop approaches to situ-ations not covered and which are unforeseeable."

The change of a code could happen in a periodical 'restatement of the law'. Such a process of developing or revising a code can do as much to stimulate and develop ethical thinking as the code itself. Debating change brings focus, as appears from the Australian expe-rience. (Ethics in Journalism, 1997) Probably, the public would be more able to evaluate journalists and journalism on the basis of well-known rules accepted by the profession itself. A code simply draw-ing up what is already experienced as a binding norm, how could this be an attack on the freedom of the press? Here, the differences between ethics and law are insufficiently inspected.

The objection of a code of ethics being a legal instrument in a judge's hands is a curious one. If the judge uses the code as a guide-line, why should journalistic-ethical norms be drawn into the legal framework? Why should a judge examining the ethical code of jour-nalists and relevant verdicts of a press council be an objectionable matter?

Another argument to draw up a code, in spite of all objections, is the fear of possible intervention by a government. Therefore, it is argued that journalism and the mass media would be wise to draft a visible instrument of self-regulation on their own accord.

The reach of a code of ethics is important as well. For, a code being in force for one single news organisation needs to be drawn up in a less comprehensive way than a code with national force. Moreover, a code for one specific news organisation can be more aggravated or even more, totally attuned to the particular circumstances of the organisation involved. A written code of ethics can be applicable for a smaller number of the mass media, as it is more detailed. (Snijders, 1995) Nevertheless, here, is an important obstacle for which norms are seen by all journalists of all media as binding for their behav-iour? Moreover, journalism is not a protected profession, which raises the question of what can happen if someone is breaching the rules or, to state it more clearly, if an editorial staff declares that it does not want to have anything to do with a code.

The inclination to draft longer and more detailed codes, holds a risk. The public appears to be more protected, but the professional is exposed more to the temptation of slipping through the holes of the net. A consequence of bringing out detailed sets of regulations could be "that it fosters a loophole-seeking attitude of mind." (Harris, 1992: 67) If it is not exactly described in the code as unethical, it is therefore permitted! A brief code with some rather general principles can be more easily applied to new situations that could not be foreseen by the drafters of a code. An ample set of regulations with detailed guidelines has to be adapted to the new situation, which takes up a great deal of time.

However that may be, a code of ethics cannot eliminate the personal responsibility of journalists and does not dare to do so; it is just an aid in carefully weighing principles, arguments and circumstances. If a journalist in a concrete situation has arguments to not follow the usual rules, this can be discussed on the basis of arguments. Hence, codes of ethics hold guidelines and no rigid prescriptions. Immediate 'live' coverage of certain events is more and more put into practice. The time, inevitable at daily newspapers, of newsgathering and the editing of the story to the deadline and publication of the paper, is absent in television journalism. Often there is no time for reflection, which is vital for sound decision-making. A code of ethics could be a help.

According to van Ruler (1995), there are three key conditions of drafting codes of ethics for public relations purposes. (1) First and foremost, a PR-practicioner must have influence on the strategy of the organisation as a whole. What is the value of a PR-code when written or unwritten rules of the organisation point in another direction? Ethics of those responsible for public relations must fit into ethics of those responsible for the organisation as a whole. An organisation attaching no importance to communication with stakeholders and making light of its social responsibility, does not need PR-practitioners. Because of these considerations, it is argued for the necessity of a communications manager at the highest organisation level, so that his or her opinion is listened to (which requires authority based on knowledge and insight) and he is able to influence organisational strategy. (2) Second, there must be a theoretical framework in which the norms, drawn up in a code, become understandable and acceptable as an expression of the moral standard of a competent professional. (3) Finally, the profession must agree upon the content and essence of the profession and upon the use of a debate on this subject. Drafting a code does not make sense if there is no clear professional identity. The PR-profession must be able to indicate a profession's content with arguments. Only in doing so, is the professional recognised and acknowledged as such by others. Only if these three conditions are met, is it useful to think about drafting a code. A code must be an expression of a full-grown professional standard, not an attempt to create it.

7. Changes and Developments

Laitila (1995a, 1995b) has been able to compare thirteen codes with their previous versions to see whether and where changes have been made. These changes refer to the addition of clauses concerning banning bribes or any outside influences on journalistic work. She explains this by pointing out growing media concentration and commercialisation. At present, there are more clauses about copyright, the right to reply, presumption of innocence and prohibition of praising or inciting violence. This might refer to the sensationalism and the internationalisation and the ethical problems caused by new technologies. Some clauses have disappeared from the codes. Mostly they refer to the contribution to peace and professional secrecy.

Harris (1992) holds the view that in existing codes little attention is paid to plagiarism as a journalistic mortal sin. A reporter should not steal or rewrite another reporter's story. He explains the absence of this issue in codes of ethics by pointing out that plagiarism has not become a topic of public debate. Moreover, he does not agree with the drafters of the existing codes for not condemning chequebook journalism more broadly.

Laitila (1995a, 1995b) wonders whether in European journalism, similar rules and ideals are being shared and whether it would thus be theoretically possible to create common ethical guidelines for European journalists. In the national codes, is there enough of a basis for a European code of media ethics? Is it possible and desirable to draft a common code? Laitila examined the possibility by comparing the national codes and seeking similarities in norms, values and opinions of good journalism. From her research, she draws the conclusion that a common code should contain at least the following issues:

— Truthfulness in gathering and reporting information.
— Freedom of expression and comment, defence of these rights.
— Equality by not discriminating against anyone on the basis of his or her race, ethnicity, religion, sex, social class, profession, handicap or any other personal characteristics.
— Fairness by using only straightforward means in the gathering of information.
— Respect for the sources and referents and their integrity; for copyright and laws of citation.
— Independence/integrity by refusing bribes or any other outside influences on the work by demanding the conscience clause. (1995a: 543)

And what about the desirability of such a common code? Who is waiting for a Euro-code? Mostly, four arguments are put forward, particularly by the Council of Europe. First and foremost, the argument of public distrust: The decreasing status of journalism in the eyes of the public. The role of the media was under discussion, e.g., during the Gulf War and after the dramatic death of Diana, Princess of Wales. The speed of reporting (scoops) seems to be far more important than the reliability and quality of the information. Neither journalists nor the audience have time to reflect upon the news. Commercial pressure has become very strong. Journalistic independence, violence and sensationalism in the media are issues which the public are worried about.

Second, the argument for the continuity of the efforts made by the European Parliament. The proposal for a European press code could be considered as an outcome of a discussion which already started in 1970. It could be argued that citizens from different member states increasingly share the same media facilities in a common information area. Since Euro-standards are being developed for all kinds of products and services, why not for media products and journalism?

Third, the argument of internationalisation of the media. Compared to the increasing internationalisation of the media industry, press self-regulation on a national level is no longer sufficient.

Finally, the argument of the new democracies, especially in Central and Eastern Europe. Common media ethics guidelines are seen as a helpful model and a huge encouragement to create a basis for responsible journalism in those new democratic countries.

These arguments remain rather weak, as Laitila states. Public distrust of the media is not removed by a common code, and the new democracies can be helped by the Western media industry without a code. The argument of continuity in the work of European organisations is absolutely invalid as an argument for a code. The internationalisation of the mass media remains the most firm and relevant form of argumentation.

References

CHRISTIANS, C. (1989), 'Self-Regulation: A Critical Role for Codes of Ethics' in E. DENNIS, D. GILLMOR, Th. GLASSER, *Media Freedom and Accountability*. Westport, Greenwood Press, pp. 15vv.

COOPER, Th. (ed.) (1989), *Communication Ethics and Global Change*. White Plains (NY), Longman.

DIJCK, J. van (1995), 'Inleiding: De regels van het spel' in M. SNIJDERS (ed.), *Ethiek in de journalistiek*. Amsterdam, Otto Cramwinckel.

ES, R. van, T. MEIJLINK (1995), *Ethiek en professie*. Kampen, Kok.

Ethics in journalism : report of the Ethics Review Committee, Media Entertainment and Arts Alliance, Australian Journalists' Section (1997). Melbourne, Melbourne University Press.

EVERS, H. (1987), *Journalistiek en ethiek*. Delft, Eburon.

EVERS, H. (1994), *Media-ethiek*. Groningen, Wolters-Noordhoff.

EVERS, H. (1996), 'Niederländischer Pressekodex. Ein heikles Thema für den Journalismus' in *Agenda*, (1996)Juli-Oktober, pp. 47-49.

EVERS, H. (1998), *Communicatie-ethiek*. Tilburg, Academie voor Journalistiek en Voorlichting.

GOODWIN, G., R. SMITH (1994). *Groping for Ethics in Journalism*. 3rd ed. Ames, Iowa State University Press.

HAMELINK, C. (1997), 'De journalistiek en het vraagstuk van de morele keuze' in *Communicatie* 26(1997)1, pp. 3-19.

HARRIS, N. (1992), 'Codes of Conduct for Journalists' in A. BELSEY, R. CHADWICK (eds.), *Ethical Issues in Journalism and the Media*, London/New York, Routledge.

JENS, L. (1972), *Beroepsethiek en code van de maatschappelijk werker*. Deventer, Van Loghum Slaterus.

JUUSELA, P. (1991), *Journalistic Codes of Ethics in the CSCE Countries*. Tampere, University of Tampere.

LAITILA, T. (1995a), 'Journalistic Codes of Ethics in Europe' in *European Journal of Communication*, 10(1995)4, pp. 527-545.

LAITILA, T. (1995b), 'Codes of Ethics in Europe' in K. NORDENSTRENG (ed.). *Reports on media ethics in Europe.* Tampere, University of Tampere, pp. 23-80.

LUIJK, H. van (1993), *Om redelijk gewin. Oefeningen in bedrijfsethiek* (Exercises in business ethics). Amsterdam, Boom.

MCQUAIL, D. (1992), *Media Performance: Mass Communication and the Public Interest.* London, Sage.

MCQUAIL, D. (1994), *Mass Communication Theory. An Introduction.* London, Sage.

Media Ethics: Rights and Responsibilities of Journalists and Media Professionals (1998), Background Paper Media in Focus, European Round Table, The Hague January 1998.

MEIDEN, A. van der (1985), 'PR Nederland en de ethiek. Een meditatief-kritische analyse' in *Themanummer PR en V/Cahier,* Juni 1985, pp. 41-45.

MEIDEN, A. van der, G. FAUCONNIER (1994), *Public Relations. Profiel en Professie: Inleiding in de theorievorming.* Groningen, Martinus Nijhoff Uitgevers.

NORDENSTRENG, K. (1989), 'Professionalism in Transition: Journalistic Ethics' in Th. COOPER (ed.), *Communication Ethics and Global Change.* White Plains (NY), Longman.

SCHUIJT, G. (1995), 'Journalistieke ethiek en recht' in M. SNIJDERS (ed.). *Ethiek in de journalistiek.* Amsterdam, Otto Cramwinckel.

SNIJDERS, M. (1995), 'De schuchtere relatie tussen Nederlandse media en de ethiek' in M. SNIJDERS (ed.). *Ethiek in de journalistiek.* Amsterdam, Otto Cramwinckel.

THOMAß, B. (1998), *Journalistische Ethik. Ein Vergleich der Diskurse in Frankreich, Großbritannien und Deutschland.* Opladen, Westdeutscher Verlag.

WHITE, R. (1989), 'Social and Political Factors in the Development of Communication Ethics' in Th. COOPER (ed.), *Communication Ethics and Global Change.* White Plains (NY), Longman.

WHITE, R. (1995), 'From Codes of Ethics to Public Cultural Truth: A Systemic View of Communication Ethics' in *European Journal of Communication,* (1995), pp. 441-460.

Appendix 1
International Federation of Journalists
Declaration of Principles on the Conduct of Journalists

Adopted by the Second World Congress of the International Federation of Journalists at Bordeaux on 25-28 April 1954 and amended by the 18th IFJ World Congress in Helsingör on 2-6 June 1986. This international

Declaration is proclaimed as a standard of professional conduct for journalists engaged in gathering, transmitting, disseminating and commenting on news and information and in describing events.

1. Respect for truth and for the right of the public to truth is the first duty of the journalist.
2. In pursuance of this duty, the journalist shall at all times defend the principles of freedom in the honest collection and publication of news, and of the right of fair comment and criticism.
3. The journalist shall report only in accordance with facts of which he/she knows the origin. The journalist shall not suppress essential information or falsify documents.
4. The journalist shall use only fair methods to obtain news, photographs and documents.
5. The journalist shall do the utmost to rectify any published information which is found to be harmfully inaccurate.
6. The journalist shall observe professional secrecy regarding the source of information obtained in confidence.
7. The journalist shall be aware of the danger of discrimination being furthered by the media, and shall do the utmost to avoid facilitating such discrimination based on, among other things, race, sex, sexual orientation, language, religion, political or other opinions, and national or social origins.
8. The journalist shall regard as grave professional offences the following:
   - plagiarism
   - malicious misrepresentation
   - calumny, slander, libel, unfounded accusations
   - the acceptance of a bribe in any form in consideration of either publication or suppression.
9. Journalists worthy of that name shall deem in their duty to observe faithfully the principles stated above. Within the general law of each country the journalist shall recognize in professional matters the jurisdiction of colleagues only, to the exclusion of every kind of interference by governments or others.

Appendix 2
The Code of Athens
The International Code of Ethics of
the International Public Relations Association

The Code of Athens, which is the International Code of Ethics of PR practitioners was adopted by the International Public Relations Associ-

ation General Assembly, which was held in Athens on May 12, 1965 and
modified at Teheran on April 17, 1968.

Considering that all Member countries of the United Nations Organisation have agreed to abide by its Charter which reaffirms "its faith in
fundamental human rights, in the dignity and worth of the human person" and that having regard to the very nature of the profession, Public
Relations practitioners in these countries should undertake to ascertain
and observe the principles set out in this Charter;
   considering that, apart from 'rights', human beings have not only
physical or material needs but also intellectual, moral and social needs,
and that their rights are of real benefit to them only in so far as these
needs are essentially met;
   considering that, in the course of their professional duties and depending on how these duties are performed, Public Relations practitioners
can substantially help to meet these intellectual, moral and social needs;
   and lastly, *considering* that the use of the techniques enabling them to
come simultaneously into contact with millions of people gives Public
Relations practitioners a power that has to be restrained by the observance of a strict moral code.

On all these grounds, all members of the International Public Relations
Association agree to abide by this International Code of Ethics, and if, in
the light of evidence submitted to the Council, a member should be
found to have infringed this Code in the course of his/her professional
duties, he/she will be deemed to be guilty of serious misconduct calling
for an appropriate penalty. Accordingly, each member *shall endeavour*:
1. To contribute to the achievement of the moral and cultural conditions
   enabling human beings to reach their full stature and enjoy the inde-
   feasible rights to which they are entitled under the 'Universal Declaration of Human Rights';
2. To establish communications patterns and channels which, by fostering the free flow of essential information, will make each member of
   the group feel that he/she is being kept informed, and also give
   him/her an awareness of his/her own personal involvement and
   responsibility, and of his/her solidarity with other members;
3. To conduct himself/herself always and in all circumstances in such a
   manner as to deserve and secure the confidence of those with whom
   he/she comes into contact;
4. To bear in mind that, because of the relationship between his/her
   profession and the public, his/her conduct — even in private — will
   have an impact on the way in which the profession as a whole is
   appraised;

shall undertake

5. To observe, in the course of his/her professional duties, the moral principles and rules of the 'Universal Declaration of Human Rights';
6. To pay due regard to, and uphold, human dignity, and to recognise the right of each individual to judge for himself/herself;
7. To establish the moral, psychological and intellectual conditions for dialogue in the true sense, and to recognise the right of these parties involved to state their case and express their views;
8. To act, in all circumstances, in such a manner as to take account of the respective interests of the parties involved: both the interests of the organisation which he/she serves and the interests of the publics concerned;
9. To carry out his/her undertakings and commitments which shall always be so worded as to avoid any misunderstanding, and to show loyalty and integrity in all circumstances so as to keep the confidence of his/her clients or employers, past or present, and of all the publics that are affected by his/her actions;

shall refrain from

10. Subordinating the truth to other requirements;
11. Circulating information which is not based on established and ascertainable facts;
12. Taking part in any venture or undertaking which is unethical or dishonest or capable of impairing human dignity and integrity;
13. Using any 'manipulative' methods or techniques designed to create subconscious motivations which the individual cannot control of his/her own free will and so cannot be held accountable for the action taken on them.

SEVEN CHARACTERISTICS OF THE 'ETHICAL' PUBLIC COMMUNICATOR: PROTECTING THE QUALITY OF DEMOCRATIC COMMUNICATION

Robert A. White

The ethical norms of public communication outline our personal responsibilities for the quality of communication in our communities, whether that be our local community or a community as large as our nation. 'Public' communication often refers to the mass media — newspapers, radio, television — , but it could also be a speech or other information meant for potentially all of the citizens of given community.

All of us are familiar with the problems of the quality of our physical environment: the quality of the air we breathe the water we drink and the food we eat. If a chemical company pours pollution into the air and the water so that thousands of people are poisoned or physically deformed, then we rightly accuse the owner of that company of gross irresponsibility. If all industries are pouring pollutants into the atmosphere and this is causing a dangerous global warming, then all of us — including the owners of the corporations involved — will be affected. If a world holocaust does occur, then all of us are in some way responsible.

The quality of our informational and communication environment is no less important. If newspapers, television and other public media systematically and continually publish false information about a particular race or group of people, then this may so poison our perception of reality that the public will tolerate or even legitimate mass genocide against those people. If the media systematically accept bribes not to inform the public of massive corruption and misuse of taxpayers' money, then we must accuse these media of irresponsibility. If a country collapses because of continual misinformation, then all of us are in some way responsible. The twentieth century has witnessed major genocides and mass injustices on virtually every continent in which the media cooperated with deliberate spreading of prejudices and falsehoods. Often the media have said, "We are simply giving the people what they want". Nevertheless, the media must be accused of irresponsibility in these cases, and, even more so, the ordinary citizen should be held responsible for tolerating these media. On the other hand when the media create public awareness of human rights, injustices and personal compassion — even when these media are working underground and at the margins of society — the media can rightly be praised for their social responsibility.

The term 'ethics' comes from the Greek word meaning good personal character. Ethics do not refer primarily to professional codes or textbook explanations of professional duties, but to the personal 'characteristics' of those participating in public debate (Klaidman and Beauchamp, 1987: 5-19). Codes of professional ethics are written by members of professional associations to establish a minimum consensus on acceptable practices and maintain the good name of the profession. Before these formulas can be written down, they must exist in the ideals of outstanding professionals, in the everyday practices of news rooms and in the expectations of the public regarding the media. For example, a managing editor feels obliged to remind a young reporter that an article is potentially a violation of personal privacy because the editor knows that this article violates the public sense of 'propriety' and would cause an outcry against the newspaper... with potential loss of subscribers. The editor also knows that if the article were about her, she would feel that her human dignity would be violated. The editor can gain the support of the young journalist simply by pointing out the code, but even codes are useless if journalists do not have a habitual desire to act morally. The good or bad quality of our public communication ultimately depends on what kind of persons *we are*.

In the following pages I would like to outline seven characteristics of the ethical or 'moral' public communicator... and you might ask yourself if you are this kind of person. My sources for these descriptions are the classical discussions of the 'ethics' of public communication that go back to the training manuals of the early 'sophist' teachers of rhetoric in ancient Greece. Virtually all of the discussions of ethics of public communication go back to the Greeks and use terminology such as 'ethics' which derive from the Greek language largely because the Athenian Greeks, some six hundred years before the Christian era, were among the first to create a democratic process of community decisions that allowed all citizens to participate in the decision making process. These guidelines for good public participation have come down to us through Roman sources and the European heritage of the Romans. The modern democratic constitutions throughout the world have drawn on these sources and on philosophical-legal discussions about media related to democracy. The sources are very pluralist in that the characteristics are the holdings of thinkers locked in debate, and it is necessary to present the debate about the particular characteristics. Nevertheless, there is finally consensus that these seven characteristics are crucially important for good public communication.

1. A Person Who Demands a Democratic Public Forum

The foundation of all ethics of public communication is a habit of working to create a participatory collective decision-making process in the community (Habermas, 1991; Deetz, 1992: 145-172). Other dimensions of morality such as demand for public cultural truth and freedom of expression flow logically from a constant effort to create democratic institutions. 'Demand' may seem to be a strong word, but there is always a tendency toward concentrating power in the hands of a few and establishing or defending the right to participate inevitably faces resistance. The powerful are always fearful of citizens speaking out and always seek ways to impede free public debate.

Historically, the discussion about the characteristics of the good public communicator and communication ethics date from the time that Athenian Greeks gradually won the right to participate directly in open public debate about the affairs of their city state (Poulakos, 1995). Then, as the Athenian populace began to exercise their right to public communication, this created the need for the first 'sophist' teachers of effective public participation. Plato's attack on the sophists for teaching people how to manipulate the public regardless of the truth was based on Plato's view that the sophists were destroying Athenian democratic institutions (Poulakas, 1995) Aristotle's first manual on ethics is really a part of his training program

for public democratic political participation because he felt that
good public communication depended on being a person of generally good, ethical character (Hardie, 1968). The right of freedom of
speech in modern Europe was acquired only after hundreds of
years of insistent efforts to broaden democratic participation
(Siebert, 1965). The essential conditions of public communication
are some form of democratic guarantees. All of the seven characteristics of the good public communicator are the characteristics of
persons struggling to maintain the fragile consensus about democratic institutions.

2. A Person Who Takes the Initiative to Speak Out on Public Issues

Democracy may give citizens the right to participate, but, if the people do not exercise that right and make the effort to speak in the
public sphere, democracy collapses. A community is not just the sum
of individuals each seeking individual goals, even if they privately
work together and exchange. A community exists where there are
common services such as schools which provide equal educational
opportunities for all. The better the common good, the better the
quality of life for all. Even more important is a common culture of
justice and compassion for all, telling the truth about all, and
defending the freedom of all.

Thus the 'democratic person' is one who assumes responsibility
for the quality of life in the community and expects all other members to also assume this responsibility. Every initiative leads to
'speaking out', but also 'speaking with' others in discussion, debate
and dialogue. Above all members must have a deep sense of the
human quality of the community, a fine sense of *practices* of justice
and compassion. When failure to contribute to the common good
becomes an *ordinary practice*, then this calls for speaking out.

Journalists or other professional public communicators voluntarily assume an even greater responsibility to continually evaluate the
quality of human life in a community and make known to the public the deficiencies observed. All great journalists have been noted
for their profound sense of justice and compassion. Although all
work within media organizations, the initiative is always taken by
the individual within the organization and negotiated within the
organization.

Taking the initiative to speak out requires a certain habitual confidence in one's own ideas and a resistance to fatalistic conformity.
Even more it requires a sense of one's human dignity, one's autonomy and one's *human right* to voice one's opinion. Inevitably, taking
a position meets questioning and opposition that demands the
courage of one's own convictions. The public also has its right to
question the truthfulness, the goodness, the usefulness or the timeli-
ness of a proposal. Public statements are thus made with a strategy
of dealing with the likely reaction of the public and with a strategy
of entering into debate.

A public statement is always taken with the intention of influencing public opinion and moving the public to some kind of action
individually or collectively. A statement assumes the freedom to the
audience to accept or reject what is being said. Thus a statement
must be designed with persuasive, rhetorical art.

3. A Person with a Sense of Moral Obligation
   to Build a Communicating Community

In our contempory culture we are so deeply conscious of personal
rights and freedom that we tend to think that a person must follow
individual inclinations and ideas as long as this action does not
cause any immediate harm to anyone. We are inclined to think of
'obligations' in our actions as simply free contracts that happen to be
convenient to all concerned: "You help me achieve my individual
goals, and I will help you achieve your goals".

If, however, we think more deeply about how our actions cause
good or harm to others, we soon realized that my or other's human
rights mean nothing if others are not 'obliged' to respect them and
cooperate with them. It is also evident that if we abuse the ecological balance in nature around us, we will do harm not only to the
forests but also to the healthy environment for all human beings...
including myself. We become aware that the world of nature and
human dignity has an interdependence such that its harmony and
well-being depends on mutual respect and obligation. This interdependence in nature and among persons is not something I can arbitrarily change or ignore, but rather something I *must* learn to understand and respect as a given of human existence. If we follow our
whims and desires without thinking of this interdependence, we

begin a kind of chain of reactions that creates chaos in the world. This structure of existence that is a given for our human and cultural decisions is the basis for what we all the 'moral order', the realm of obligations in human decisions (Christians, 1997: 11-12).

A paradox of human actions is that a person is, on the one hand, *free* to decide whether to follow moral obligations or not, and, on the other hand, *conscious* of the chain of harmful results even to myself if the obligations are not respected. As conscious, free, reasoning beings, we assume moral obligations *conscious* of possible alternative actions, *free* to choose as we wish and able to *reason* our way to conclusions about the course of action that causes the greatest good and least harm. The 'punishment' for violation of what we refer to as the `laws' of moral obligation is the destruction of the quality of human life and human society which, because of the interdependence of existence, ultimately destroys the violator himself.

A further paradox is that if persons freely assume certain social and professional roles they assume obligations toward the people that come to depend on them in their professional role. If a person freely decides to become a medical doctor, that doctor assumes moral obligations toward those who put their lives in the hands of the doctor. If the doctor consciously does not do all that the medical science permits in order to save a life or health, we rightly accuse that doctor of violating a moral obligation. Likewise, if a person chooses to enter into the profession of journalism or other profession of public communication, then that person assumes the obligations that profession entails. We have defined the basic obligation of public communication in terms of promoting a democratic society measured in terms of justice and respect for human rights. If a journalist becomes aware of the violation of human rights in a society and consciously avoids the assumed duty to inform the public of these violations, then we may rightly accuse such a professional of moral negligence.

A journalist or other professional communicator is considered most 'moral' when he or she is conscious of abuses of democratic society such as the violations of clearly defined civil rights and is furthermore conscious that he or she has a moral obligation to inform and move the public to action regarding these abuses. Such decisions may be mixed with motives of promoting a career, gaining more subscribers to the newspaper or advancing the good image of the profession, but the actions of such a journalist are considered in the profession as a 'moral ideal'.

Moral decisions in newspapers or other media institutions are complex collective decisions of all persons involved, from the owners down to the young professional. The definition of media obligations can involve the whole media industry, government regulators and the general public. In this context the profession and the industry have a moral obligation to define what are key moral issues, such as invasion of privacy. They are also obliged to come to a consensus regarding the proper practical norms regarding these issues, and then to educate all members of the industry toward respecting these norms. However complex the process may be, the moral obligation is ultimately rooted in the interdependence of humans in society and the interdependence of existence. It may be difficult for a society to see the moral issues of interdependence in public communication, but if the society does not come to a state of clarity about the moral obligations, then this negligence may destroy the quality of life in that society.

The sense of moral obligation in the character of public communication is so important that it must certainly be listed as one of the basic characteristics of the good public communicator. Every moral philosopher from Plato to Habermas has considered a highly developed moral consciousness as essential to the character of the public communicator.

4. A Person with a Passion for Truthful Public Communication

The ideal held up to every young journalist is the person who seeks out the complete truth of public affairs such as the irresponsibility of public officials and then verifies every detail with objective, documented data. The most damning criticism of a newspaper is that it has made an error in reporting some public event. Every editor pores over the copy of reporters to spot possible errors or exaggerations. Yet every person who has worked in public media knows how difficult it is to discover *what is important for the public to know* and to summarize in a few paragraphs the significance of this for the public. The public wants to know the five 'w's' (who, what, why, where and when) as accurately as possible, but, above all, people want to know whether something has happened that will affect their lives, their families, their jobs and the well-being of the community as a whole.

The issue of 'truthfulness' comes to the surface as soon as citizens and professional communicators aggressively take advantage of the right and obligation to express one's views in the public forum. It is not enough to master the art of persuasion and elegant expression, as Plato argued against the sophists (1961). You may win the public to your opinion, but this may eventually bring the government and the society to ruin because it is not based on a truthful picture of reality. Nor does truth mean simply accuracy in reproducing an account of an event. The truth lies in presenting a vision of collective action in the community which will bring about the kind of community that we wish to come into existence. Truth is closer to the good, to that which *should be* rather than that which 'is' now (Pippert, 1989).

All who deal with public communication know that 'news' is not about the ordinary events, but about new opportunites for the community or about events which disturb or pose a threat to the well-being of the community. News is about 'problems' for the community to solve, and the community opens its public forum to those who may have something worthwhile to say about the good of the community. The challenge to the person who really believes that he or she has a 'true' solution for the problems of the community is to present an analysis of the causes of the problem and a path of action that is 'true' to the public's experience and knowledge.

Often members of the public do not have enough information or clarity to express just what should be done. The persuasiveness of public discourse comes not so much from a play upon emotions — desires, fears and hatreds — as from what makes reasonable sense given the complexities of the issues. One must take into consideration what the community such as a nation has historically defined as its original 'constitution', that is the values and goals of the society that the founders initially had in mind. The present problems are discussed in terms of whether this helps or hinders the realization of the original goals or whether the new crises require a changing of the fundamental goals of the community. Thus the person with a passion for truthfulness must know the history, the dreams, and the inspiring symbols that are lodged in the memory of the people. With this knowledge of the original goals and information about the present alternatives, the public communication can construct a scenario for the future that seems 'true' to members of the community.

In practice the truth emerges from a 'narrative account' which combines the 'is' and the 'ought'. The narrative dimension of truth is enshrined in the reporters' definition of preparing a statement for publishing as 'getting the story'. On the one hand the public will recognize a statement as true if the speaker can sort through the confusing mass of details and summarize for the people what the 'problem' is that is currently causing so much trouble and who in the community are 'guilty' of causing this problem. By assigning guilt and designating the villains of the story, the issue takes on a moral dimension and is linked then with the good as well as the 'is'. The 'solution' or vision of the future which the story offers is defined very concretely by naming possible protagonists in the narrative, the struggles which are necessary and the possible outcomes which the 'heroes' of the story are expected to realize. The very openness of the narrative invites the public to enter in and speculate about alternative heroes, struggles and outcomes. The 'truth' is the scenario for the future which the whole community creates according to the values and interests of the persons who participate in the public debate. The good public communicator is a person who is able to animate a discussion and debate in the community and keeps that open until the community has a satisfactory vision of the future.

Inevitably the question arises, "What are the criteria for affirming that one scenario for the future is more true than another?" The classical criterion for community action is the common good and the principles of contributive and distributive justice (each contributes according to capacity and receives from the common good according to need). The common good depends much on the needs of the society at the time, and public debate is precisely a debate about who should contribute and who has need. The truth then becomes a matter of adjudicating between a variety of moral claims. The test of the honesty and impartiality of a public communicator is the independence of the influence of the powerful who may attempt to override justice and get a decision favorable to them. The greatest test of the passion for truth is the insight to see what is the most just scenario for the future and the ability to resist all external influences to be unjust (White, 1995).

A further criterion of truthfulness is found in underlying perennial, universal values of the community. At any given moment there are many competing ideologies and interests being introduced into the public forum. Often these are the distorted conceptions of reality that the powerful are able to manipulate, at least for this period in history. Truth is found in what is enduring across the ages, in the contemplative and the philosophical, in that which is separated from the everyday world and from the centers of political-economic power.

Still another criterion of truthfulness is that consensus which emerges out of a moment of profound intercultural dialogue in which *all* moral claims — including the oppressed and the marginal — are heard and discussed. This dialogue is not without its conflicts, its challenges and accusations of dishonesty, but as long as there is a fundamental respect for the right to different cultural identities there is a possibility of forging common symbols. The truth is found in those unifying symbols in which all parties feel that finally they can find something of their identity. Truth is, thus, more likely to be found in complex, polyfacetic symbols that can be interpreted in many ways than in concepts of univocal meaning. Likewise truth is more likely to be found in poetic, dramatic and ritual discorses than in the pragmatic discourses of empirical science.

5. A Person who Seeks Freedom of Expression

One of the most striking characteristics of professionals in the media is their desire for freedom to say that they feel has to be made public. The most damning thing that can be said of a media professional is that he or she has sacrificed his or her independent judgement out of dependence on a government or any other powerful institution. The media professional is a person who is convinced that the way toward the truth is to be found, in large part, in one's own personal conscience and personal intuitions (Merrill, 1974). No social institution, no matter how sacred, is to be blindly trusted. Every statement of a public official must be questioned, tested and verified.

The ethos of free expression has been a characteristic of democratic society since ancient Greece, but the explicit formulation of the norms of freedom in philosophy, in national constitutions and in professional codes emerged in the sixteenth and seventeenth centuries. Two institutional forces for the establishment of the modern industrial nation clashed. The centralizing monarchies such as the Tudors and Stewarts in Britain and the Bourbons in France claimed that coordinated mobilization was essential. The entrepreneurial bourgeoise, on the other hand, claimed that their initiatives and inventiveness was the main source of modernization. The monarchies and their governing bureaucracies defended rationalized organization while the defenders of human liberty called for government decisions through open-ended public debate that had no central rational control (Siebert, Peterson, Schramm, 1956). The result of three centuries of debate was a compromise of constitutional government which guaranteed, in orderly legal fashion, the right to free expression in the public sphere. The culture of constitutional democracy defined the freedom of the press and the freedom of expression as a central part of modern social life.

To be truly free, however, requires a deep and habitual sensitivity to one's own intuitions regarding the truth or falseness of what is being said in the public sphere. The starting point is a strong sense of the dignity and 'sacredness' of the person. The 'sacredness' of the person means that life and other rights are considered above cultural questioning. A strong conviction about the sacredness of the person leads to a keen perception of any unjust treatment of persons and an almost instantaneous outcry regarding any violation of human rights. There is also a sense of the sacredness of one's own conscience. Because one's awareness of injustices is so esteemed, it is important to continually question dispassionately one's own ideas and continually verify the validity of first intuitions. Once there is certainty about one's convictions, then one must be courageous in expressing them in public. The person who desires to be authentic abhors double standards: thinking one thing but conforming exteriorly to the dictates of society. And because one's convictions are sacred, a person with the desire for freedom feels that the voicing of convictions in the public sphere is a moral obligation. Freedom from external coercion, from censorship or any other powerful political or economic influence must be steadfastly denounced and resisted. Even for pragmatic reasons of greater creativity and diversity of ideas in a society, it is important to keep open a space of freedom in which initiatives to speak out are protected, no matter how aberrant some opinions may seem to some people. There is always the desire to protect the public from potentially destructive ideas, but it is better to err on the side of freedom. The lone prophetic voice may be the last bastion of truth when the whole world has gone astray. In the strict libertarian tradition, there is only one opinion which must be resisted: the opinion that it is better in some contexts to have authoritarian censorship.

The sense of obligation to voice one's convictions in the public sphere is not done without some awareness that all convictions, even mine, could be mistaken. Human pride, self-interests, hatred and vindictiveness are to be found in all opinions. There is trust, however, in the public collective debate with all forms of diversity. The truth is to be found in the public debate which puts every opinion to the test. Every collective decision is, to some extent, provisional. Absolute truth is not to be found in human cultural formulations. Every formulation in human society must be left open for a further and perhaps better forumulation of the consensus. The desire for freedom to continually voice new intuitions leads to a more tentative, 'social contract' notion of society. Our social solidarity is better based on a tentative agreement about what brings the greater happiness and continual progress in society. This does not deny the absoluteness of the dignity of the person, but suggests that human dignity leads toward continual dialogue. The absolutes are to be found in human dignity not in any particular form of human cultural formulations.

Although public debate is a continually evolving process, the sacredness of the person requires a definition of the space surrounding the person as also sacred: one's personal privacy, the sacredness of the home and some minimum property, the right to one's authorship and invention, the freedom to take economic or political initiatives. The freedom of speech in the public sphere requires a general socio-cultural context of freedom: freedom of assembly, freedom of political organization, freedom of physical movement, freedom of religion, freedom to choose one's education and freedom from affective dependency, freedom from substance dependency and freedom of personal aspirations. This freedom does not mean individualism or egoism, although this is a constant danger, but the freedom to give oneself to others in community. Freedom to express oneself does not talking to one self, but the freedom to speak to the community authentically and to give one's authentic self to the community.

6. A Person Committed to the Development
   of a Democratic Society and the National Common Good

The movements toward constitutional governments provided guarantees for the equality, rights and freedom of initiatives to all persons and set the foundations of the modern nation in the nineteenth century. The nation formed a single interrelated political, economic, cultural and linguistic system, and all citizens had the right to participate in the collective decision making of this system. This meant that not just an elite ruling class but all citizens had to have access to information about the decisions to be made and had to have the channels to make their voice heard in the public sphere (Rivers, Schramm, Christians, 1980: 48-50).

An essential part of the new nation is the right to free assembly and to free organization as a source of influence in public decision making. The structure of organizations standing between the private sphere of the individual, family and cultural communities and the monopoly of coercive force in the state became the effective sphere of public debate, public policy and legislation.

One of the key steps in the transition from a society of small 'city states' to a large centrally integrated nation was a new form of interpersonal trust and solidarity based not on birth or other forms of ascriptive identity but on guarantees of technical expertise and professional service. The classical professions, such as medicine and law, had always required an oath binding the interior conscience to provide good service to all regardless of social class or other status symbols. The nineteenth century brought a professionalization of all service occupations. The universities were opened to the new professions to provide a diploma as a guarantee for potential clients of the technical expertise. The professional associations with their codes of ethics raised the status of the various professions by guaranteeing the good conduct of its members.

The press and other forms of public media often played a significant role in establishing constitutional government, and, in the new national societies, the printers and others involved in public communication were elevated into a professional 'calling' to provide the informational interconnection of all citizens and organizations. Like other professions, the profession of public communication has defined its expertise as the capacity to facilitate democratic public debate and collective decision making. Those entering into the profession of public communication increasingly have a specific university degree guaranteeing their expertise, and they form associations with a code of ethics and a form of public 'oath' analogous to the medical and other classical professions in which the person with the professional colleagues promises to use his or her 'scientific' expertise for the good of individuals and of society. The ethos of truth and

freedom characteristic of public communicators was broadened to a
freedom to exercise one's social responsibility.

Like other professionals, public communicators forswear economic gain as the principle motivation, but thereby gain a moral
prestige and influence in defining the cultural values of the society.
The university-level education and the culture of the associations
develops within professionals in public communication a series of
new moral obligations.

In the context of a democratic nation, the person working in public communication has a commitment to respond to the public's right
to know what major political, economic and cultural decisions are
being taken in the nation, what are the variety of proposals being
made by national leadership and what are the implications of these
proposals. Since the members of the public cannot speak to political
leaders or be present in the scene of a national disaster to determine
responsibility, the media professional represents the public in confronting these situations. The public communicator must maintain
the personal commitment to truth and to fidelity to his or her own
conscience, but to this is added the need to know what questions the
public are asking and to get information to answer these questions
unrelentingly. The reporter, for example, knows that the ability to get
information which is complete, objective (portrayed as if the reader,
listener or viewer is there directly present), accurate and interesting
is necessary to gain a public for a newspaper, radio or television station. In the competitive world of media, if another medium offers
better information the public will go there. The economic survival of
the newspaper or television station — and the jobs of those who
work there — depend on the *ability to respond to what the public thinks
is its right to know.* In addition, the profession, in effect, tells the public that it has assumed a moral obligation to serve democracy and to
respond to the human dignity of the person as citizen.

The formation of civil society with its proliferation of associations,
organizations and movements representing citizen interests also
means that the media professional must carry into the public sphere
the interests and cultural identities of many different sectors of society. In this context the media professional becomes the neutral common carrier of messages, but there is the added obligation of making
sure that what a given movement or organization wants to say is
honest and in the interests of the general public. The media cannot
take the position of any one movement, but must make sure that

movements and associations are forced to debate and justify their positions so that the public can decide for itself.

At the heart of democratic constitutional govenment are the mechanisms of checks and balances that prevent the concentration of social power and the systematic exclusion of large sectors of the population from participating. In the conception of democratic society, the media are given a special role as the 'watchdog' of citizen's rights, the fourth estate acting to decentralize power and the 'conscience' of the society. The media are given a 'license' attributed to no other institution to investigate abuses of power on the part of the government, but of all other public institutions such as the church, the professions, economic entrepreneurs and economic corporations. The professional commitment to a democratic society requires, first of all, that all public officials are subordinate to the legitimate laws and that their actions are known to the public so that the public can control them. The media assume a special commitment to the movements of the poor, the less powerful, the marginal. New social actors must be well represented and have the space to refashion their denigrated public image.

The democratic nation builds its solidarity around a single national culture, a single language, a single public educational system, a single national literary and artistic cultural tradition, and a national civil religion which has its roots in the major historical, institutional religions. The media are given the role of the cultural memory of a nation and providing the forum in which the national cultural heritage is 'lived', 'debated', 'reformulated', 'challenged' and 'celebrated'. For example, a basic educational system is part of the socialization of the young into the language, literature, history, economic system, health system, and basic civil religion, At its best, the media are the place where different aspects of this tradition that one has learned are really experienced. Above all, the media bring the *various* cultural and subcultural traditions into the common public sphere. The fact that so much of media is aimed at the whole public, simultaneously means that different cultural traditions are translated into a common denominator that all can understand.

The enormously challenging obligation of media professionals is to develop within their own professional ethos a sense of what is 'good quality' media. The ideologies of the democratic nation have argued that the measure of the good is 'the common man', not some artistic or other form of elite. The norm is the 'popular culture'. All professional activity depends on current research to provide an ever better professional service to the public. For example the medical profession depends on a very large applied medical research operation which, in turn, depends on a often highly theoretical research tradition. The research tradition underlying media professionals is the attempt to understand what is good media. In the cultural sphere this is more difficult because cultural options and values are being debated. Thus the increasingly dominant line of research underlying the service of the media professions is media criticism and forms of cultural studies. The media professional assumes the obligation to be in contact with this through the best trade journals and journals of media criticism which are aimed, not at other researchers, but at media professionals.

7. A Person who Facilitates Direct Citizen Participation

The history of the ethics of communication is a long process of gradually opening the public sphere to a more universal participation. In earlier periods, the limitation to higher status males excluded the great majority. The limitation of content of public statements to officially sanctioned truth systems tended to exclude many opinions from the discussions of the public sphere. The libertarian movements opened up access considerably, but still tended to restrict participation to those who had the financial resources to own a press and limited the content to the voice of the proprietor/publisher. The movement to professionalize media raised the status of media workers and gave them a greater voice within media organization, but effectively limited the right to participate to those with the capacity to use sophisticated media languages and to those who were part of heavily capitalized mass media. In all of this the voice of the ordinary citizen was rarely heard. At best, opinions of non professionals were filtered through the statements of authorities, proprietors or professionals.

The gradual extension of the vote and other forms of effective 'citizenship' to all adult persons created demands for a more direct voice in the public sphere. A crucial factor in this opening was the recognition of the right of free assembly and the right to form movements such as labor unions which created an alternative communication system. Initially, most citizens were content to let their opinion be known through official spokespersons of their organization or movement, but increasingly the right to communicate views more directly became an major social issue.

Underlying the various movements for the universal human right to communicate was a shift in the mid-twentieth century in the conception of the person stemming largely from the new human sciences and from more personalist, existentialist philosophies. The human sciences showed that communication, expressing one's ideas and goals, is essential in the proper development of the human person. Education and other forms of communication are not a matter of behaviorist imitation and learning but actively assorbing new ideas through questioning, dialogue and debate. Solidarity in groups, communities, factories, organizations and nations is not simply a matter of discipline but of allowing members to accept proposals on the basis of the expression of their own ideas. Antisocial behavior, passivity, and alienation are the result of not being allowed to participate in the collective decisions of the group. Philosophically, the essence of personhood as 'rationality' was rejected in favor of a conception of personhood as creativity, symbolic capacity and the capacity to be the subject and creator of history. For a democracy to function, it is not enough to allow citizens to approve policies and proposals that wiser and better educated experts have formulated, but all citizens should express their ideas and participate actively in public, collective decisions.

The realization of the importance of direct participation for human and social development sparked the growth of new contexts and forms of communication in small groups, local communities, and in movements. Group dynamics, non-directive animation approaches and the Freirian group-level conscious-raising methods of education were one expression of this new ethos of communication. Virtually all of the major popular political movements in contexts such as South Africa, Iran or in Latin America, because they were excluded from the large official media, learned to communicate through 'small media' that permitted easy, wide-spread access to networks (Annabelle Sreberny-Mohammadi and Ali Mohammadi, 1994). Also important is the growth of participatory approaches in media: community broadcasting, participation in all stages of radio and television broadcasting planning and production, the organization of press councils to handle the complaints of the public regarding the media, and various citizen's movements to improve the quality of media. Fan groups attempted to become significant influences in the development of media. Particularly important have been the strategies of the new movements among women, racial and ethnic minorities, life-style and subcultural movements for de-legitimating a negative public image and projecting a new image in the media. Most of these movements cast their proposals for a new society in terms of their civil rights, and they formulated their demand for access to the public sphere in terms of their 'right to communicate'.

In the face of resistance to 'citizen participation' by entrepreneurial and professional media interests, a series of forums were opened to develop an intellectual foundation for 'the right to communicate' (UNESCO, 1980: 160-174). One forum was the debate regarding the New World Information and Communication Order. The new nations of the 'Third World', emerging from a colonial background, argued that the great majority of the people in these nations had no access to the media and that it is necessary to introduce national communication policies which give much more access to people in rural areas and to the urban poor. The obstacle, in this view, is the control of information flows by transnational commercial interests both between nations and within nations in a way that favors access by urban elites. These information flows favor Western, elite cultural interests and are a negation of the cultural and communication rights in many parts of the world. Many minority regions and minority groups of the nations of the North also seek a forum for the expression of their cultural values and communication rights. Other forums are the new movements — gender-based movements, youth movements, ethnic and racial groups.

For a series of reason these contradictions emerged with particular force in the late 1960s and 1970s. The public service and social responsibility roles were questioned as inadequate. In the context of falling credibility of the 'mass' media and the threat to democracy from civil strife, the role of public communicator took on new dimensions which can best be described as the advocate and animator of the 'right to communicate', especially in favor of the new movements and new subcultures.

A first dimension of the advocate/animator role is providing a channel of access for social movements into the public sphere (White, 1991). Television journalism and documentary have proved especially effective because these bring the vivid emotional power of a protest demonstration or social problem right into the homes of the public. In an era when the welfare state pretended to have most social problems under control, investigative journalism and advocacy learned to seek out and provide a channel for leaders of civil rights and other movements. The traditional independence of the public communicator provides a position for critique of dominant ideologies, but now by giving the microphone to dissidents in the society. The mark of the truly distinguished journalist or dramatist is to help alternative movements articulate their message.

A second dimension of the advocate/animator role is to provide a forum in which the silent groups of society — the poor, the marginal, minorities suffering from prejudiced public image — can dialogue among themselves and with the larger society. In this context the public communicator is not just providing a microphone but educating silent groups on how to effectively communicate in the public sphere. The prototype is the animator in the method of group communication of the Freirian tradition who makes sure that all participate, that there is a dialogue and that all discover their cultural identity. The development of the right to communicate in this case often means a struggle with hegemonic cultural groups whose identity has been based on the subordination of other groups and who feel threatened by new minority actors coming into the public sphere at an equal level.

A third dimension of this role is to encourage the participation of all sectors of the community so that all talents, interests and subcultures are represented in the public forum (Christians, Ferré, Fackler, 1993). It also means setting up occasions for dialogue between between different interests of the community and moving toward the resolution of conflicts. Community media are staffed largely by volunteers and potentially every member of the community can become a public commnicator and express his or her right to communicate by gaining access to the media. The traditional professional has become more of a teacher on how to use the media effectively. This has blurred the line between 'professional' and 'lay' communication.

A fourth dimension of the advocate/animator role has emerged with the 'public journalism movement', namely, to actively involve the public in 'setting the agenda' of public debate (Glasser, 1999). Thus the traditional power of the proprietors and professionals (shared with leaders of hegemonic interests) for 'setting the agenda' and 'gatekeeping' is returned to the people. The role of the public communicator is to provide a forum in which the community decides what are the important issues and the community controls the narrative construction of villains and heroes that collective decision processes have a coherence from the perspective of the public. This represents a new alliance between a dissident sector of the professional communicators and the public which attempts to exclude those professionals in the employ of the powerful — the public relations specialists — who are seeking get the assent of the public without the public really understanding the causes and consequences of decisions.

A fifth dimension is the promotion of a process of public media events in which conflicting cultural groups (the protagonists of the contemporary 'culture wars') are brought into interaction and dialogue in a way which enables them to develop common symbols representing a common cultural identity. Some of the most effective forums for this cultural negotiation are the media rituals that enable all conflicting subcultures to engage in a celebration of commonalities in a popular, festive, sacred discourse removed from the everyday pragmatic power struggles. In contrast to the pragmatic moments of everyday life which use only a rationalistic, political-economic discourse excluding many forms of cultural capital, the ritual context recognizes the right of *all* subcultures to be present on an equal level and to project the importance of their culture for the community. In these rituals of public culture, formerly excluded subcultural identity symbols become part of the commonly shared myth of the community.

Conclusions

The present chapter has traced the development of the calling of the public communicator over the centuries. We have summarized the ethos or character of the communicator in terms of seven deep, habitual desires: (1) an increasingly democratic society; (2) courage to speak out on public issues; (3) a sense of moral obligation to build democratic communities; (4) truth and justice in public communication; (5) freedom of expression; (6) responsibility for the needs of citizens and (7) advocacy for the poor and marginal. The role has demanded a person who is increasingly resourceful, varied and ready to accept challenges. It is not surprising that throughout the world professional communication is attracting some of the most competent and idealistic young people. The media are at the center of modern society. Given the social importance for the quality of life today, the role of the public communicator demands an ever greater moral commitment.

The importance of the media in society also means that the media are ever closer to the centers of economic and political power. Professional communicators have never felt greater pressure to maintain their personal moral integrity within the great media enterprises of the Murdochs, the Thompsons and now the internet interests. It is perhaps important that the right to communicate is now a far more public moral claim than it has been in the past. The defense of truth, freedom, social responsiblity and advocacy in the name of democracy cannot be restricted to a few media professionals. The quest for the exercise of the right to communicate which began some two thousand five hundred years ago in the *agora* of Athens has to become a much more deeply felt need by every citizen in the society.

References

CHRISTIANS, Clifford G, John P. FERRÉ, P. Mark FACKLER (1993), *Good News: Social Ethics and the Press*. Oxford, Oxford University Press.

CHRISTIANS, Clifford (1997), 'The Ethics of Being in a Communication Context' in Clifford CHRISTIANS, Michael TRABER (eds.), *Communication Ethics and Universal Values*. London, Sage Publications, pp. 3-23.

DEETZ, Stanley (1992), *Democracy in an Age of Corporate Colonization: Developments in Communication and the Politics of Everyday Life*. Albany (NY), State University. Press of New York.

GLASSER, Theodore L. (1991), 'The Idea of Public Journalism' in Theodore GLASSER (ed.), *The Idea of Public Journalism*. New York, The Guilford Press, pp. 3-20.

HABERMAS, Jürgen (1991), *Moral Consciousness and Communicative Action*. Cambridge (MA), The MIT Press.

HARDIE, W.F.R. (1968), *Aristotle's Ethical Theory*. Oxford, Oxford University Press.

KLAIDMAN, Stephen, Tom L. BEAUCHAMP (1987), *The Virtuous Journalist*. Oxford, Oxford University Press.

LAMBETH, Edmund (1986) *Committed Journalism: An Ethic for the Profession*. Bloomington, Indiana University Press.

MERRILL, John G. (1974) *The Imperative of Freedom: A Philosophy of Journalistic Autonomy*. New York: Hastings House Publishers.

PIPPERT, Wesley G. (1989) *An Ethics of News: A Reporter's Search for Truth*. Washington, Georgetown University Press.

PLATO (1961), *Theatetetus, Sophist*. Trans H.N. FOWLER. Cambridge, MA: Harvard University Press. Cited in John POULAKAS (1995), *Sophistical Rhetoric in Classical Greece*. Columbia, University of South Carolina Press.

POULAKAS, John (1995), *Sophistical Rhetoric in Classical Greece*. Columbia: University of South Carolina Press.

RIVERS, William L., Wilbur SCHRAMM, Clifford CHRISTIANS (1980), *Responsibility in Mass Communication*, 3rd edition. San Francisco, Harper and Row.

SIEBERT, Frederick S. (1965), *Freedom of the Press in England 1476-1776*. Urbana — Chicago, University of Illinois Press.

SIEBERT, Frederick S., Theodore PETERSON, Wilbur SCHRAMM (1956), *Four Theories of the Press*. Urbana/Chicago: University of Illinois Press.

SREBERNY-MOHAMMADI, Annabelle, Ali MOHAMMADI (1994), *Small Media, Big Revolution: Communication, Culture and the Iranian Revolution*. Minneapolis, Minnesota University Press.

UNESCO (1980) *Many Voices, One World* (Report by the International Commission for the Study of Communication Problems, Sean MACBRIDE, Chairman). Paris, UNESCO.

WHITE, Robert A. (1991), 'Democratization of Communication: Normative Theory and the Sociopolitical Process' in Joy GREENBERG (ed.), *Conversations on Communication Ethics*. Norwood (NJ), Ablex Publishing Company, pp. 141-161.

WHITE, Robert A. (1995) 'From Codes of Ethics to Public Cultural Truth' in *European Journal of Communication*, 10(1995)4, pp. 441-459.

MEDIA ETHICS AND THE ISSUE OF MORAL CHOICE

Cees J. Hamelink

Media professionals are frequently confronted with complex moral choices. In the daily routine of the editorial selection process, questions are posed about the admissibility of candid cameras, illegally acquired information, undercover journalism, or payments to sources. The protection of sources is a frequently raised issue as is the violation of people's privacy or the treatment of victims of catastrophes.

In all such situations, choices will be made that are (in different degrees) based upon moral considerations of a personal or professional nature. There are always different courses of action possible in choice situations and the decision for one of them can have serious impact on individuals and institutions.

Therefore, the key issue for any professional ethics is the justification of moral decision making. In other words, how do professionals achieve justifiable decisions in moral choice situations?

1. Moral Choice

It is a common observation in most human communities that people make distinctions between forms of conduct they find morally justified (sometimes *prima facie*, sometimes after philosophical reflection) and behaviour they condemn as morally unacceptable.

There are most probably no genuinely a-moral societies and very few absolutely a-moral individuals. Usually, we find in communities and among individuals some form of collective or personal moral consciousness. It would seem a logical conclusion that most people are capable of a moral account of their acts with regard to themselves, their peers, or the collective they belong to (family, colleagues.)

The search for guidance in moral choice leads inevitably to the question whether ethical theory can provide arguments that justify choice A versus choice B in specific situations. Without conducting a comprehensive analysis of all available approaches to moral choice, even a brief survey indicates that the conventional methods cannot satisfactorily resolve how people (in this case professional journalists/editors) should come to justifiable decisions.

Conventional ethical theories are usually divided into deontological (or duty-based) and utilitarian-consequentialist (effect-based) approaches.

1.1 *The Deontological Approach to Moral Choice*

1.1.1 Act Deontology

This method is largely determined by the assumption that most people intuitively know how to choose in moral dilemmas. This implies that the crucial factor in moral choice is personal moral intuition. Journalists often claim that they instinctively knew it was right to publish a story or a picture. Their moral feeling instructed them that the use of certain materials was all right. The problem with this approach is the enormous latitude it offers for shady moral trickery which basically serves self-interest only. The method implies a large degree of arbitrariness. Moral arguments based upon intuition are difficult to justify and even more so when people define intuition in different ways.

1.1.2 Rule Deontology

The rule-deontological method takes the position that rules based upon moral principles can provide guidance in moral choices. In essence, the method searches in concrete situations of moral choice for the moral rule that applies.

For journalistic practice, such rules may be articulated in a so-called Code of Conduct. However, given the great variety of choice situations and the inevitable general nature of the rules embedded in Codes, these moral rules are not likely to provide concrete moral guidance. Moral prescriptions in codes suggest an almost universal applicability which is not realistic since actors, situations and interests differ greatly over time and place. The rules of the Code may prescribe that journalists should tell the truth, but they usually do not explain how this general principle should be applied in concrete situations. Different rules in a code may conflict with each other and the Code does not explain how choices should be made when basic moral principles clash. Neither does a code help its users to understand when justifiable exceptions to the rule can and must be made. It is relatively simple to reach a consensus about the rule that people's privacy should be respected in newsmaking, but this does not explain how in certain situations the exception to this rule is justified. Also, a problem arises when no single moral rule is valid for all the different circumstances of its application in real life.

Codes can be useful as instruments to identify an autonomous professional group. They can, by suggesting common rules for the members of a profession, contribute to the credibility and accountability of professional performance. A code of conduct tells clients what quality they may expect from the professionals.

Although codes of conduct can certainly provide a starting point for ethical inquiry and debate, they fail to provide concrete moral guidance. A grave problem with codes as instruments of the deontological method is their neglect of the consequences of moral choices.

1.2 *The Utilitarian Approach to Moral Choice*

This consequentialist (effects-based) approach has two important variants: act utilitarianism and rule utilitarianism.

1.2.1 *Act Utilitarianism*

This method is casuistic, meaning that from case to case it must be considered what type of conduct has the best consequences.

This casuistry is necessary since general rules and principles are of little use in the great variety of choice situations that real life confronts us with. However attractive this may seem, the approach has certain drawbacks. First, who defines what optimal consequences of certain choices are? Second, it is extremely difficult to establish what optimal consequences are under different conditions for different moral agents.

1.2.2 *Rule Utilitarianism*

This method assumes that one finds sufficient similarity between choice situations for general rules to be useful. In this sense this method resembles rule deontology. Both methods propose that general rules should define what moral acts are. However, because of the large variety of real choice situations rule utilitarianism is bound to fail. Moreover, like act utilitarianism, there is no unequivocal understanding of what constitutes the best consequence (effect) for the largest number of people.

An important attraction of utilitarian methods is that they take the consequences of moral choices seriously.

A complex problem however is that most of the time people cannot know the consequences of their acts. Moreover, consequentialist type approaches imply the risk that beneficial ends justify immoral means.

In journalistic practice, the best consequences of moral decision making are often identified as the effects that optimally serve the "common good." This suggests a societal consensus about the notion of "common good." In reality, this is a highly evasive concept that has many different interpretations. In all societies, opinions about what constitutes the "common good" are divided. Actually, its meaning is often defined by the most powerful groups in society and rarely coincides with the needs of the less powerful. Just like deontological methods, consequentialism is ill-suited to provide concrete moral guidance.

The application of classical moral theories of the deontological or utilitarian signature provides little or no help in the resolution of concrete moral dilemmas in real-life situations. Moral principles, in difficult choice situations, do not provide guidance to unequivocal, consensual decisions. Examples can be found in choices about euthanasia, abortion, suicide, armed conflict, social security, immigration, and drugs policy.

Concrete experiences in such fields as medical and business ethics have led "to a serious if not widespread erosion of confidence in the power of normative theory to decisively guide the resolution of real practical problems." (E.R. Winkler, J.R. Coombs, *Applied Ethics*. Oxford, Blackwell, 1993: 3) In the quest for a more adequate approach, it has been proposed to conceive of morality as "an evolving social instrument" that is part of a specific cultural context. (*Ibidem*: 3) This suggests a contextual approach to moral decision-making, which "adopts the general idea that moral problems must be resolved within the interpretive complexities of concrete circumstances, by appeal to relevant historical and cultural traditions, with reference to critical institutional and professional norms and virtues, and by relying primarily upon the method of comparative case analysis." (*Ibidem*: 4)

The contextualist approach rejects the deductive model of moral problem-solving and prefers an inductive model of moral argument. This does not imply the wholesale dumping of moral theory or moral principles, but it does position theory and principles differently in the course of reasoning.

From the contextualist perspective, a primary task in the situation of choice is the precise interpretation of the moral issue at stake. The first step is the attempt to understand in detail what the basic choice is in a concrete case. This differs from the deductive approach where one begins with a general moral theory or general moral principles and applies these to the concrete case.

The deductive approach is inadequate because, for example in many complex medical cases, it fails to make crucial distinctions such as whether the moral issue at stake is "killing" or "letting die."

The contextualist approach proposes a comparative case analysis through which resolutions to new choices are sought by reasoning from solutions that were preferred in similar situations.

In the course of the inductive moral argument, questions are asked about the institutional and cultural settings and their value orientations in which choice situations are located. In this light, questions are also asked about the consequences of choice and the interests involved. "Where does the choice lead to?" "Is this desirable?" "How are benefits versus damages of choice distributed?" "Whose interests are served with a particular choice?" And, "Who gains and who loses?"

2. How Can Ethics Contribute?

The most useful contribution ethics can make to journalistic practice consists of critical and systematic reflection on the question of how robust and transparent accountability for moral choices can be achieved. This implies that the essence of the ethical contribution is found in the development and testing of procedures for the resolution of moral choice situations. Since there are never ideal solutions for moral choices and since any moral choice is essentially contestable, the public justification of choices made has to demonstrate that the process of moral decision making was conducted in a responsible manner.

2.1 *The Responsible Procedure*

Basically, there is only one standard by which the quality of moral decision making in journalistic practice can be tested, namely, the "responsible procedure." To measure moral choices against the yardstick of due procedural care seems at the surface an easy position. Most professionals accept the notion that they should act responsibly. The Code of Conduct of the Dutch Association of Editors-in-Chief, for example, stipulates that journalists have to operate with due care. The problem is that this suggests that "due care" is a clearly defined concept, which it is not. There is little or no clarity about what precisely constitutes "due care" in journalistic professional practice. There is a general notion that "due care" would seem to imply the need for checks and balances and the establishment of the reliability of (multiple) sources. This is helpful, but only in a limited way. The idea of a "responsible procedure" goes far beyond the mere application of basic professional rules. There are at least three essential characteristics for this kind of procedure.
(1) Those involved in decision making are ready to accept public accountability for the choices they make: They can and will explain to public fora how their choices serve, beyond their narrow self-interest, a broader public interest.
(2) The procedure implies a careful reflection on the balancing of different (personal, professional and social) interests with basic moral principles (such as those adopted in human rights law.)
(3) The procedure should be transparent, institutionalised and reiterative. It should be possible to explain to outsiders how the procedure works, it should be a normal and recurrent part of institutional operations and a learning process in the sense that the participants' capacity to learn from errors is improved over time.

2.2 *The Ethical Dialogue*

In most choice situations, there are factual, conceptual and moral dimensions which need to be distinguished since the problems these dimensions pose need different solutions. In moral disputes it is not always differences of moral principle that are at stake. If we look better, we often discover that it is only a different interpretation of the facts or a different perspective that makes us disagree. Actually, the factual and conceptual dimensions of a situation sometimes cause more disagreement than moral aspects! In many situations parties can agree on some common sense moral principles such as the need to defend human rights or the wish to avoid complicity with criminal regimes or the desire to protect people against the ill-effects of toxic waste. However, the factual claim that "A" protects these principles more adequately than "B" may be fiercely contested.

There are also choice situations in which we confront a conflict between basic moral premises we hold and other pressing interests, which can be of apolitical, economic or personal nature. Even more complex are those situations that demand choices between two or more basic moral principles that are equally valid but demand different and conflicting courses of action. These are real dilemmas since any course of action violates a fundamental moral value. If we violate principle "A" by doing X, we commit a wrong. Equally if we violate principle "B" by doing Y, we commit a wrong. The dilemma challenges us to choose between two wrongs.

The ultimate choice as presented in the motion picture, "Sophie's Choice", is hardly a choice situation at all. The movie features Meryl Streep as Sophie, a mother, who in Nazi Germany faces the ultimate dilemma when a German officer gives her the choice to save either her little son or her little daughter from deportation and subsequent death. Sophie is morally obliged to save both her children. Yet, she may save only one. No ethical reflection on the lesser wrong can help Sophie. Possibly the only honest way out is by throwing the dice!

Since choice situations that are not, in fact, about moral issues can be resolved without ethical reflection and because Sophie's choice defies any rational approach, we should concentrate on those situations that represent real moral dilemmas. Situations where moral principles and pressing interests collide. It could be argued that in these situations the quintessential problems of editorial decision making must be confronted.

The key question for journalistic ethics, then, becomes, "How can procedures of due care be developed for editorial decision making?" A possible approach to the development of responsible procedures is systematic and regular ethical dialogue in the editorial room. Ethical dialogue represents methodic and critical reflection upon moral choices. For this dialogue, a method of moral argumentation needs to be designed that may not automatically lead to the only acceptable moral choice, but that renders moral choices communicative acts that are transparent for all those affected by these choices.

The proposal for an ethical dialogue assumes there are always various plausible solutions to moral choice situations. Therefore, ethical reflection should not focus on identifying the single correct solution, but rather should concentrate on the due process of the moral argumentation.

Ethical dialogue will be conducted in different modalities in different editorial rooms. Without being too dogmatic about this, it would seem that some minimal guidelines could be given.

(1) The ethical dialogue does not depart from a consensus on fundamental moral values, but seeks those solutions to moral dispute that optimally accommodate the parties' interests and principles. In the dialogue, moral choice is conceived as a reiterative and dynamic process since situations and moral standards change over time and space.

(2) The dialogue departs from the assumption that in choice situations there are always different plausible solutions.

Those involved in the decision making process accept that all moral choices are essentially contestable.

(3) It is important to conduct the ethical dialogue regularly. The capacity for dialogue needs to be learned and demands considerable practice. Moral argument is not an inherent talent and needs to be learned. Regular ethical dialogue helps to fine-tune people's capacity for and sensitivity to moral argument. Experiences in various professional situations, for example, in health care institutions, show that when people engage in this dialogue, their process of moral choice making becomes more transparent, more prudent, and more robust.

(4) It is important to take the initial moral positions of participants in the dialogue seriously. Some members of the editorial staff will have ready-made positions and know which choices they prefer. Such positions will have to be subjected to critical inquiry in the dialogue. How well-founded are the arguments for these positions? Can those who make certain moral claims justify their position with arguments that go beyond the intuitive feeling that their moral preference is the best? Arguments like "my moral intuition tells me it is all right to use this photograph" are too subjective to be useful in the exchange with other positions that may be based upon different moral intui-

tions. Usually, in exchanges on moral issues, there will be diverging positions. Arguments to support different positions need to be tested against their relative strengths and weaknesses. It is important here to distinguish between emotional-intuitive and factual arguments. In the process, the dialogue evolves from individual, subjective statements to a collective, inter-subjective understanding.

(5) It is also important that a "protocol" is established from the choice making process. This records the reasoning through which the eventual choice was reached. The protocol may in principle be accessible for all those affected by the choices made, but is primarily indispensable to the learning process of the institutions and individuals concerned.

(6) To facilitate the dialogue, it is often advisable to use for moral decision making a minimal check-list of guiding questions that address domains such as the interests that are served by different choices, the consequences of alternative options and their distribution across different agents, the limiting of harmful consequences, the reversal of roles ("what if the consequences of a choice did affect yourself?") and the reversibility of choices.

An initial checklist for a responsible procedure could contain the following questions:

(1) Which interests (social, corporate, personal) are served by choice A versus choice B?
(2) Can these interests be justified by non-subjective and non-intuitive arguments?
(3) Can it be demonstrated that the preferred choice is more in line with generally adopted professional rules than the alternative choice?
(4) For which actors (individuals, groups, institutions) does the preferred choice have important consequences?
(5) Can such expected consequences be justified?
(6) Can all consequences be reasonably foreseen? What is the degree of uncertainty? Can the uncertainty of possible important consequences be justified?
(7) Can possible harm to those affected be avoided?
(8) If harm to those affected is inevitable, can it be minimised? Can the aims of publication be achieved through alternative ways?
(9) On which grounds are alternative methods rejected? How strong are the arguments for the rejection of alternatives?

(10) What would have been the choice, if the roles had been reversed, i.e., the professionals or their loved ones had been the topic of reporting?

(11) Is the preferred choice (ir)reversible?

(12) Are those who made the choice ready to account publicly for their decision?

Concluding Observation

The professional who is willing to accept the challenge of ethical dialogue, takes his/her ability to account for professional choices seriously. Herewith, he or she lives up to the ancient Socratic insight that since professionals know what they do and why they do it, they are also capable of public accountability for their practices.

COMPUTER ETHICS

Porfirio Barroso

1. Computer Science: An Actual Social Phenomenon

In the last years the handling of information by means of computers, has practically come to invade all fields of human activity. In time, it has shown itself to be the element with the most transformative capacity in our lives and in our societies.

Since 1945, when the first digital electronic computer was created, technological advances and the spread of its applications have had an absolutely unexpected and surprising evolution. They have broadened their capacities, generalised their uses, and possibilities of interconnections in networks, intranets and webs have introduced us into what we now know as the 'computer science revolution.'

In this way, computers have come to occupy a central place in many of our activities and in almost all forms of social organisation. Our societies practically depend on information technologies for the organisation of industry and commerce, the functioning of public administration and the management of the huge public services which sustain and legitimate states and all forms of collective life. Without computers, the functioning of the majority of the institutions wherein we enact our daily lives becomes inconceivable, including the companies and educational centers where we work, the supermarkets where we obtain our basic goods or the banks whose services we employ.

Today, the handling of information by means of computers, or what we vaguely know as 'computer science,' constitutes the most significant technological innovation and the most relevant social element for understanding our times. In this way, it constitutes something like the environment in which we live, the contextual situation that takes control of the greater part of our work, activities and interactions. We are becoming more aware of its economic, social, and cultural global impact, but we have already assumed that whether in explicit forms or in more subtle and surreptitious ways, computer science is changing the condition and the texture of our lives and activities.

In terms of the repercussion of its effects, the computer can be compared to the printing press, electricity, or the steam engine, which was the heart of the industrial revolution. The recent appearance of new concepts such as 'cyberspace,' 'navigator' or 'virtual reality' serves to help us catch a glimpse of the limitless possibilities that the computer and computer science can make available for us in the immediate future.

The future of the progressive hegemony of computer science over our world permits us to expect enlightening effects and positive repercussions for the quality of our lives, but at the same time, it forces us to consider whether or not the prevailing role of computer science will not bring along perverse effects and unwanted consequences. Does the new computer science epoch imply the coming of a new age of knowledge, shared culture and a more just and participative democratic coexistence or does it merely constitute the prelude to a world full of risks for the life of individuals and societies? Will it be possible to guarantee the security of data and information stored in computers as well as the confidentiality of our interpersonal communications or is it the gateway to a world of glass houses, which would make impossible all forms of privacy and private life? Will we have guaranteed our most fundamental rights or are we on the road towards new and ever keener forms of vigilance and social control? Must norms and laws for its regulation and control be established, or must we oppose these very norms in order not to limit individual liberty or restrain creativity and the development of new possibilities of information technologies? These questions constitute a simple demonstration of the uneasiness that the new universe of computer science brings about. Like other technological innovations, it does not merely constitute a technical reality. Rather, it implies a social and human reality, and hence, our concerns cannot be limited to the technical dimension, but rather, imply political and ethical dimensions as well. Like all technological innovation, it can be changed into a liberating and humanising element or it could degenerate an open dimensions of risk and dehumanisation. Everything depends on what we would be able to make of it, and the policies that we would eventually establish for its use.

This is the context of the present need for reflection, analysis and clarity in understanding the nature and the impact of computer science, both in their repercussions and their effects: the need for an ethical discussion on computer science which makes possible its rational and humane use.

2. Ethico-Social Implications of Computer Science

Many uncertainties have been expressed regarding the social impact of computers. The 'quid' of these uncertainties is a broad but difficult question as to how the extensive use of computers is affecting the character and quality of our life. Are computers improving our life? Does it foster or corrode the most precious values that we hold? Does it impede or facilitate democracy? Does it develop the sense of security or that of risk? Does it improve the life of some at the expense of those of others? Do human beings lose control in the sense that computers take over the decision-making process?

Twenty or thirty years ago, these questions could be posed with the intention of deciding whether or not we should go forward with information systems in sectors like banking and government, or in technologies such as aviation and power plants. Today, we no longer take such a questioning stance. Instead of asking ourselves if we should go forward with computers, we nowadays ask related questions such as designing, integrating, and using information systems and look for the best way to manage software property, privacy, legal responsibility, etc.

The questions related to the social impact form a part of the ethical domain in at least two distinct ways. First, the changes that computers put into effect could affect long-held values of our society, including privacy, democracy, equality and autonomy. Second, the social effects could enter the ethical domain when the changes computers bring about create a new field that needs to be organised and delimited by rules; the rules, for their part, have to be designed in such a way as to create an atmosphere that satisfies moral requirements and serves human well-being.

3. The Social Value of the Computer and Democracy

There are two values which are extremely important in our society: autonomy and access. These values are crucial in a democratic society. In a certain way, the point of departure is the Kantian understanding of the value of human beings as ends in themselves, because this understanding serves as the foundation for valuing individual autonomy and the importance of democratic societies. In other words, this understanding of human beings needs a society in which individuals take the opportunity to follow their own plans for their lives and have a say in the governance of public institutions that directly and indirectly affect their lives. Hence, the first point focuses on the way that computers affect individual autonomy.

Second, we could focus on the question of access. That the autonomy of some would be increased or improved at the expense of the autonomy of others contradicts the value of individuals as ends in themselves. In a just society, liberties and restrictions, benefits and responsibilities are distributed in an equal manner, and all individuals have access to the opportunities for achieving their goals. In particular, this means education and the seats of power and authority. If the rules systematically distort things to give advantages to certain groups and disadvantages to others, then justice is thwarted. Of course, even if we aspire to the ideals of equal opportunity and just distribution, we do not always attain them. Hence, we have to ask ourselves not only whether or not computers are compatible with our ideals in principle, but whether or not in reality they are being utilised in a manner that leads us away or towards our ideals, and in this way, rendering lesser or greater justice.

Within a rather short period (30 to 40 years) information technology has become a fundamental part of our world. In one form or another, it has an impact on the life of every individual. At birth, information about you is entered into a database; you depend on computers when you drive a car, talk by telephone, travel by plane, transact business with banks; much depends (or will depend) on computers in your work. Nevertheless, there has been little public discussion and little national or international planning for this technology. We have allowed market forces to decide which applications to develop, how they develop, who has access, etc. Without any doubt, the market has been affected, and is being affected by privacy laws, property laws and legal responsibility, which make difficult the development of certain possibilities of a technology while facilitating the development of others. Nevertheless, these restrictions on the market have emerged in an ad hoc manner. A problem arises, and then we respond. For instance, if a problem concerning the computerised files of video rent shops arises, then we respond by approving legislation; if a problem with computer hackers comes up, we respond with the appropriate legislation. What we lack, for a change, is a general vision of what we would like computer science to do for us, and then, an active plan to manage their evolution in this direction.

Now that we understand more vis-à-vis its enormous power and potential, it would be good to invite public discussion on the future development of information technology. For example, we could consider personal information as a part of our society's infrastructure and manage these as such. We could think of information technology, in general, as an infrastructure and from there, manage its development, distribution and integration to maximise the positive effects, minimise the negative effects, and increase efficiency. This perspective could make us consider changes of the following type: change property laws so that more of the public have a good grasp of software; invest in a national, public web site; establish a public service for personal information; ensure that all citizens have access to terminals and certain databases in public libraries and post offices; and other things along this line.

4. The Security of Data

Forester's and Morrison's concerns centered on the illicit and uncontrolled use of data stored in databases for very particular ends: business, advertising and even crimes. Similarly, they referred to the chaos that could ensue, and which in fact has happened, if there were errors in or errors were introduced into some of these databases. (Forester, Morrison, 1990) Hence, for example, a respectable citizen could find himself or herself identified as a delinquent because of the erroneous entry into the computerised police record of the Social Security Number of a true delinquent; a person who one fine day could discover that he or she is classified as dead by a computer error, etc. Looking at the deliberate manipulation of government, military, or company computer data for criminal purposes, what is

certain is that our lives depend in great measure on the information
stored in computers.

We have an irrefutable example of the insecurity of data of a personal or temporary nature in the film *The Net*, when the protagonist
realises that all of her data of a personal or intimate nature stored in
computers became the public domain of the Praetorians, her adver-
saries and enemies. For Richard A. Spinello, the security of data concerns not only the necessary growth of technology for the protection
of information systems and information, but the development of
guidelines pertaining to the divulging of sensitive data as well.
(Spinello, 1995: 203)

Problems can be caused both by persons far away from the company such as hackers, and by those within the company, that is to
say, the employees or consultants themselves. The greater part of
these problems has been caused by company personnel, having dissatisfaction as a motive; these employees have manipulated the
information systems for their own benefit or simply sabotaged them.
The main objective of security is self-protection, and that the other
parts have confidence in this protection as well. Hence, companies
as well as employees have the moral obligation to protect information that has been confided to them, because the loss of this sensitive
information can cause irreparable damage.

Let us consider the ethics of computer data security from the perspective of the perpetrator. In the case of the hacker who has entered
a system illicitly, regardless of the harm caused, even if it has not
been obvious, it remains equally serious as the case when the harm
was serious because, in both cases, the respect for property rights
has been violated and some valuable resources has been wasted.

The nature of the information is another problem. Is there legal
responsibility for the replication of information without permission?
For example, although it would not be considered 'theft' in the
strictest sense of the word, it would still be a serious violation of privacy.

Another ethical problem is the need to bear in mind the right to
freedom of expression; and this poses questions such as whether or
not computer networks have to be neutral with respect to the informational contents they carry and whether or not electronic publications enjoy the same protection as publications in traditional media.

The British Computer Society's Code of Conduct of 1978, in the
section on Privacy and Private Life, Security and Integrity, deals

with the security of data of a personal or private nature in these terms.

"One of your most difficult responsibilities is to determine the value of a system in terms of what would be lost if the security system were cracked (e.g., harm to national security by leaking processed military data, personal privacy or leaks of medical information or frauds through financial information.) This notwithstanding, a review is required to help in making a decision, calculating the coverage and costs of the security system, in at least these four areas:
— Protection: preventing threats from becoming reality.
— Detection: to arrive in time to suppress the action.
— Suppression: to limit the effect.
— Recovery: to rectify [errors] and ensure that the system functions again."

5. Computers and the Quality of Life

Forester and Morrison, without ignoring the evident benefits that computers bring to our lives, have focused more on the problems and damage that excessive computerisation of work can lead to.
They focused particularly on the substitution of people by computers in various fields of labour, and they asked if this substitution was really ethical and necessary in a world where unemployment had become endemic.

Forester and Morrison also analyse the effects that working with computers have on individuals. (Forester, Morrison, 1990: 40) Far beyond what is possible to imagine, computers, despite the fact that they ease our work, generate greater stress and other complications for those who work in a computerised office. The authors quote various studies, according to which routine work (which many people who sit in front of a computer and deal with data without having to think, analyse, or arrange these, hour after hour) ends up producing stress, anxiety, depression, and even coronary diseases. All this is due to lesser satisfaction with the work, decreased relationships with co-employees, and a low appreciation of the work done. This means that computers decrease the quality of life of some workers, not to speak of those who remain unemployed. Once scene of the film The Net corroborates this assertion, when the American police asks the neighbour of the protagonist of the film and says "she does not

know her neighbour because she never comes out, she does everything through the computer, she orders a pizza delivery, buys her
groceries and does her errands through a computer."

Another dilemma that Forester and Morrison pose is the possibility of monitoring workers with computer methods: controlling, for
example, the number of phone calls from clients that they can
receive; the number of phone calls that they can make, the data that
they input into computers by day and hour? (Forester, Morrison,
1990, 40ff) For some authors, this is a practice that will end up violating the privacy of the worker. However, perhaps the most important ethical question in this sense is that computers add to the sense
of depersonalisation, and this depersonalisation of work can end up
overriding human judgement, and therefore conscience as well, thus
committing unethical acts without recognizing that these could
harm or affect other people.

6. The Moral Responsibility of a Computer Scientist

Because computer science is a relatively new field, the professionals
of computer science have not even had the time or the organisational
capacity to establish an organised aggregate of moral or ethical rules.
Other, older professions such as medicine or law already have their
own codes of ethical and professional conduct. Within computer science, a further problem exists, even as it is a very open and still
developing field, and into which many different tasks apply.

One of the problems is that computer scientists sometimes work
with processes, with very small parts of bigger projects, and their
concerns are generally very far removed from the real and social
effects of their work. The use of computers to store increasingly vital
and important information places much power in the hands of these
professionals, a power which can easily be abused by those without
scruples or those that fall into temptation.

Computer science professionals have to face all types of ethical
problems in their daily work. For example, what can a computer scientist do when he or she knows that a very simple program is being
sold by his or her company as if it were a very complex, and therefore exorbitantly priced product? Or, who is to assume responsibility
if a computer system crashes? What must a computer scientist do if
he or she sees that his or her company is clearly violating the law

concerning the intellectual property rights of another person or company? Perhaps he or she comes across the fact that his or her company uses its programs to obtain data from people in a manner that violates one's privacy and private life.

Some efforts have been made to help professionals face these types of conflict through ethical codes, notwithstanding the fact that their effectiveness has been put into question. The pressure from industry, economic or otherwise, bearing down on professionals to disregard ethics in their daily profession is enormous. Some authors criticize these codes because they are merely 'public image enhancement' tools; i.e., they are used in order for society to have a better image of the profession, but not for the profession to improve its ethical practice.

According to Duncan Langford it has been a long time since software was the product of one simple programmer. Groups of software engineers now work in the evolution of maintenance systems and the resultant complexity of software is increasingly dangerous. Some of the existing software has to be recycled many times and in the words of an old saying, 'the responsibility of all is the responsibility of none.' Consequently, who is actually responsible, if a reassembled application is utilised in circumstances not anticipated by its original authors creates problems? Who is ethically responsible if a new piece of the complex development of a software malfunctions?

Obviously, it depends on the circumstances. However, it is extremely necessary to arrive, by some way or other, at a clear definition and a delimitation of responsibility in accordance with the evolution of the problem. In particular, the manner in which a programming team structures itself is crucial. All the members, including the head of the team, must have a clear perspective on the area of their responsibilities and must be ready to accept responsibility for these. To do this, they have to be attentive to the ways in which their part of the project affects the other sectors, as well as the entire project. A project director, aside from his usual activities, needs to coordinate the specifics of the responsibilities of each member of the team. It is also important to distinguish clearly between ethical and legal responsibilities, which, although they sometimes come together, must not be assumed to be necessarily so. A good distinction to keep in mind is that the legal responsibility has to be that of the group, and that the ethical responsibility is always personal.

7. Codes of Computer Science Ethics

To draw up a certain understanding of the relation between professional duties and ethics, codes of ethics can be very helpful. They have proved to be a tool for resolving problems associated with people who work in the most diverse fields of Information and Communication Technology.

One of the purposes or goals of the codes is to enhance the understanding and the formulation of new ethical questions emergent in the new society. In this way, the codes would also boost international cooperation which, vis-à-vis concrete questions such as personal liberty and privacy and private life or in the area of security, has demonstrated its invaluable approach in the provision of general norms of ethics that up until now has been regulated only by laws.

The detractors of the Codes insisted that the codes favour a new 'corporativism' and function as a mere defense of the profession, the codes do not include ethical principles per se and that most of the time, they are a simple list of recommendations without a series of established or justified priorities. The codes, from this point of view, can be considered as consultative or advisory for the profession, but in this form, they do not really end up as being beneficial to society. From another point of view, others emphasise 'the explosion of the profession' or their already weak identity and the difficulty of defining whether or not they have this identity. Consequently, it is almost impossible to give a complete meaning of the concept of its application.

On the other hand, those that favour the codes stress that the application of the codes can be judged from an ethical perspective, viz., even if the code's principles would not be ethical per se, these otherwise give an orientation and can change the habits of conduct, particularly when the society seems to accept habits or customs that are barely ethical. Further, they insist on the flexibility of the codes, their role of anticipating the law and standing up to the imperceptible abuses that can happen across the breadth of computer science.

Codes of Computer Science primarily emerged as part of the social construction of 'professionalism' of those who dedicate their work to the processing and managing of information by computers. They constitute a declaration of constitutive principles of the culture of a profession, of the credibility, and prestige and social respect for this new profession. It is understood that in the encounter of new situations and new forms of encounter, professional practice carries with itself the practice of the great ethical principles. However, the codes will refer to the great ethical values implied in the exercise of the profession. In this sense, they attempt to be a practical ethics.

Together they compose an 'urgently needed ethical culture,' or an ethical practice which gives an orientation. A provisional ethical commitment about a field, the practice of which everyday, discovers and invents new ways and applications. In addition, every innovation will require a new effort of reflection on the ethical repercussions of its application.

The Codes of Ethics of computer science are quite young. The oldest have been around for some twenty years. They appeared in the 70s as the first associations of computer scientists emerged. Along this line, we will next present an account of the first deontological codes of computer science in chronological order:

— The first item that comes to us is the existence of a 1968 deontological code of computer science: 'Association for Computing Machinery, ACM, Code of Professional Conduct,' London, 1968.

— The Code of Conduct of the British Computer Society was proposed as such in 1970.

— In August of 1973, L. Pettiti presented, 'Rapport sur les problèmes de l'informatique juridique?' in Abidjan, at the Conference held in the World Center for Peace through the Law. He proposes the drafting of a Charter of computer science profession.

— 'Criminal Justice Information Control in Santa Clara County, Code of Ethics' Santa Clara county, California, 1971; seeks to balance the moral demands of criminal justice and the right of the individual to information that the judicial police has filed about him or her.

— Norms of computer science Deontology from CITEMA 1974.

— CDP (Code of Conduct and Good Practice for the Holders of Certificates of Data Processing. Institute for Certification of Computer Professionals) 1974.

— BCS (British Computer Society) Code of Conduct 1976.

— ICCP (Institute for Certification of Computer Professionals) Code of Ethics 1977.

— NZCS (New Zealand Computer Society) Code of Ethics and Professional Conduct 1978.

— IEEE (Institute of Electrical and Electronics Engineers) Code of Ethics 1979.

— DPMA (Data Processing Management Association) Code of Ethics, November 1981.
— CIPS (Canadian Information Processing Society) Code of Ethics and Standards of Conduct 1985.
— CSSA (Computer Society of South Africa) Code of Conduct 1988.
— IRLAND Code of Ethics 1988.
— Draft Code of Sackman 1990.
The rest of the codes of computer science ethics that we know were conceived in the 90s.

All of the codes refer to an adaptation of the universal principles of general ethics to their professional practice and aim to respond to the main ethical dilemmas that they face in such practice.

The handling of information through computers, which is the nucleus of the computer science profession, essentially carries with it a permanent conflict of interests among the most varied groups concerned (professionals, organisations, users, clients, society in general, etc.) and constantly faces ethical dilemmas. Hence, it would seem to be extremely important to find ethical regulation and commitment. In research done by Vitel and Davis involving computer science professionals at the beginning of this decade, it was found that 50% of those surveyed declared that they had many opportunities for unethical behaviour in the exercise of their profession. One fifth of these professionals indicated that they personally knew of other professionals who behaved in an unethical manner.

The necessity of ethical regulation and of deontological codes is not due only to what the professionals subjectively feel. Rather, it is also due, on the one hand, to the complexity of the development of information technologies and the diversification and possible harm and risks of their use, and on the other hand, to the moral distance that characterises the practice of computer science (with moral distance understood as the 'moving away from each other' of the act, i.e., the handling and management of information, and the responsibility or morality of such an act.) In other words, in the use of computer science.

The influential factors in this moral distancing, which makes possible incorrect behaviours are: anonymity, the physical distance between an action and its repercussions, the increase of victims and harm that can provoke a bad ethical decision, etc.

As codes of professionals of the storage, processing and use of information, they have a closeness and a narrow parallelism with the rest of the professional codes related to the management of information. In many articles, they recall the other information sciences.

The codes constitute an ethical practice, an applied ethics. They are a conjunction of rules and norms of behaviour in which a particular way of understanding the good and ethical responsibility, in relation to the objectives and function of those who professionally opt for excellence in the management of information systems, is crystallised.

The codes define an ethical culture of the profession. An ethical culture that goes beyond the relativism and the subjectivity of individual values, which is closer to the rigour and the sanction of positive legislation and carries an orientating potentiality, helps present and define the major problems, make people conscious of their responsibilities, and gives an orientation in ethical decision-making. All these things constitute the taking on of an ethical stance.

The codes also constitute a strategy for professionalisation. They contribute to the creation of a corporate culture, they reinforce the social construction of a professional image. In this way, a conscience of computer science professionals emerges, offering at the same time a social image of integrity, strictness and quality.

The codes also have an educational function. Together, they are a catalyst of an ethical stance that has been assumed by computer science professionals, and have as an end, the elevation of the level of social responsibility of the professionals of information management by means of computers.

The accelerated addition of new technological innovations and new fields and forms of application of computer science, the codes of professional ethics constitute an urgently needed ethical culture. The oldest ones have had to be revised, and every now and then, attempts to accommodate this regulation to the changes.

The codes are a necessary ethical culture, a practice-orientating ethics. A provisional ethical commitment in a field, the practice of which discovers and invents new ways and applications daily. And each innovation will require a new effort at reflection on the ethical repercussions of its application.

Certainly, computer science codes of ethics, just like the other codes of the other information sciences, have sometimes been criticised for ineffectiveness, having been reduced to general declarations of obvious principles which no one discusses, or at other times, for imperious dogmatism, by virtue of which it is not infrequent to hear some say that the codes should not be considered necessary. Nevertheless, the concern and collective ethical reflection on such an influential theme as the use of computer science in our societies are present and ward off the risks of information technologies becoming factors of dehumanisation.

References

BARROSO ASENJO, Porfirio, Jesús María VAZQUEZ (1996), *Deontología de la Informática* (Esquemas), Instituto de Sociología Aplicada, Madrid.

BERLEUR, J., K. BRUNNSTEIN, K. (1996), *Ethics of Computing: Codes, Spaces for Discussion and Law.* London, Chapman & Hall.

FORESTER, Tom, Perry MORRISON (1990), *Computer ethics. Cautionary Tales and Ethical Dilemmas in Computing.* Cambridge (Mas.), The MIT Press.

JOHNSON, Deborah G. (1996), *Ética Informática* (trans. Porfirio Barroso), Madrid, Universidad Complutense de Madrid.

KIZZA, Joseph Migga (1996), *Social and Ethical Effects of the Computer Revolution.* London, MacFarland & Company Inc.

LANGFORD, Duncan, (1995), *Practical Computer Ethics.* London, McGraw-Hill Book Company.

SPINELLO, Richard A., (1995), *Ethical Aspects of Information Technology.* Englewood Cliffs (NJ), Prentice Hall.

ZUBOFF, Shoshana (1988), *In the Age of the Smart Machine: The Future of Work and Power.* New York, Basic Books.

HYBRID FORMS IN MARKETING COMMUNICATION: THE INCREASINGLY FUZZY BOUNDARIES BETWEEN INFORMATION AND COMMERCE

Aagje Geerardyn & Guido Fauconnier

It is common knowledge that advertisers are finding it more and more difficult to make effective contact with their target group by means of the traditional modes of advertising. It is becoming increasingly difficult to reach and influence the consumer on account of the so-called 'communication and information overload', i.e., the phenomenon of consumers being confronted every day with an enormous quantity of commercial messages and the growing irritation among the public that goes together with it. As competition for the attention of consumers becomes more fierce, advertisers have to find alternative and more effective ways to spread their message. (Goodlad, 1997: 73-74; Nebenzahl, Secunda, 1993: 1; Sandler, Secunda, 1993: 73-74; Van der Gaag, 1994a: 40) This explains the growing popularity of 'non-spot-advertising.' With this term, some Dutch writers and experts (Sengers, 1997a: 22; 1997c: 46; 1997d: 5; Sengers, van Vugt, 1998: 12) are referring to all expressions of advertising which have neither the form nor content of a traditional television commercial. Here, one can think of the meteoric rise of event marketing or what one would call the marriage between advertising and entertainment. (Sengers, 1997b: 46-51) More and more advertisers organise their own events (e.g., a music festival like The Heineken Night of the Proms or Marlboro concert tours), and hope to reach their target group in a more effective, playful way. The term 'non-spot-advertising' also covers the increasingly close working relationship between the media and advertisers. This cooperative relationship takes different forms. First, there is simple sponsoring. 'Bartering' involves a transaction in which the advertiser supplies a completed production (e.g., a television program) or other goods in exchange for advertising time and space. (de Langen, 1998: 48; Kassaye, Vaccaro, 1993: 40) For its part, the media greet these and other forms of cooperation with the advertising world with open arms, for economic reasons. As production costs steadily increase, advertising forms a welcome source of income.

This cooperative relationship raises no (ethical) problem in itself. According to Lipman (in Sandler and Secunda, 1993: 74), however, reductions in advertising revenues are making the media more and more prepared to "throw basic journalistic rules out the window, crashing through the wall that is supposed to separate advertising from editorial coverage." In this article, we want to examine this specific, far-reaching form of interaction between advertisers and the media, where the border between advertising and editorial coverage becomes blurred. Modes of advertising emerge out of this interaction which seem to involve hybridization between promotional messages and editorial content. We will discuss the following hybrid forms successively: (a) advertorials, (b) sponsored magazines, (c) infomercials, (d) product placement and (e) free publicity.

We believe that these hybrids raise two important ethical questions. First, in the light of the far-reaching cooperation between the media and advertisers, it is hard to ignore the question of the influence of commercialism on the freedom of the media. And, what about the credibility of both the media and advertisers when they merge (too closely) together? The second question is about the possibility of misleading the consumer. We find it hard to shake the impression that these hybrid forms of advertising, at least, sow the seeds of confusion. After every discussion of these hybrid forms, we will steadily delve deeper into these questions.

1. Advertorials

The term 'advertorial' is a contraction of the words 'advertisement' and 'editorial.' The term says it itself: a combination of editorial material and a commercial message. There seems to be no univocal definition of the term 'advertorial' in the available literature. Different authors give divergent definitions of this form of advertising. However, all the definitions we have found in the literature have the following in common: an advertorial is essentially a printed advertising message, but has the look and the content of an ordinary newspaper or magazine article. Some authors add that the message is paid for (Goodlad, 1997: 78; Rossiter, Percy, 1997: 340; Van de Gaag, Jong, 1996: 12) or that the word 'advertisement' is mentioned in an advertorial. (Sandler, Secunda, 1993: 74; Soeterbroek, Vanderhoek, 1981) We will stick to the common definition, because we believe there are advertisements which fail to meet the supplementary conditions, but still can be regarded as advertorials.

In creating an advertorial, the editorial form of the medium is taken into account as far as possible. This can include anything from editorial style to the choice of the font. Secondly, due to its informative approach, also the content of an advertorial resembles that of an ordinary article. All advertisements aim to persuade, but advertorials do not primarily express a suggestive-emotive approach, unlike the case of normal advertising (Fauconnier, 1992: 193), but rather a more rational-factual approach. For this reason, the language employed is not directly persuasive, but more oriented at conveying information. The emphasis, therefore, is on providing information about the product.

1.1 *Editorial Freedom/Credibility of the Medium and Advertising?*

According to a survey of a number of large businesses in the Netherlands, advertisers and advertising agencies believe that using advertorials holds many advantages: one can convey a great deal of information, the text can be easily tailored to the readers of every magazine or newspaper, it forms an alternative to aggressive and/or irritating advertising, advertorials have a good attention value, and so on. (Oeseburg, 1995) Another advantage of advertorials consists in the fact that they "enable advertisers to 'borrow' the goodwill and credibility associated with the host publication." (Mazur, in Goodlad, 1997: 75) The reader regards advertorials as approved, as it were, by the medium in which they appear. (Van der Gaag, 1994a: 41) Doesn't this mean that intermingling of editorial material with advertising, as is obviously the case with advertorials, poses a threat to the credibility and objectivity of the medium? Hemels (1998: 147) claims that the more journalism comes under the influence of commercialisation by way of advertising, the more vulnerable it will become to public criticism. The results of a study by Admedia (the advertising core of the VNU magazine group) supports this view. The majority of consumers think that too much sponsored information leads to doubts about editorial objectivity. (s.n., 1996: 1) The media itself are concerned about such questions. Interviews with representatives from editorial departments indicate that advertorials are primarily seen as a way of bringing in extra income, and some even talk of 'commercial blackmail' and 'a necessary evil.' Their main concern is "the need to maintain an acceptable balance between advertorial and editorial content." (Goodlad, 1997: 80-81)

A number of organisations have created guidelines to address this issue. According to the guidelines of the Periodical Publishers Association (PPA), not too many advertorials may appear in a single edition. The scope and number of special advertising spots in any edition must not be disproportionate to the scope and nature of the medium. (Goodlad, 1997: 75; s.n., 1993: 8) The VNU expresses this numerically: The number of advertorials in weekly magazines is restricted to two an edition, and four for monthly magazines. Furthermore, the advertiser may not make use of the authority of the (title of) the medium by mentioning it once more in the advertorial itself. Nor can there be advertorials about a certain product when the medium gives that product away to its readers for free in a special offer. (Van der Gaag, 1994a: 41)

Advertorials could also pose a threat to advertising itself. The study by Sandler, Secunda (1993: 73, 77) indicates that those working in the field believe that advertorials can damage both the credibility of the medium and the consumer's trust in advertising. When editorial material loses its integrity by becoming too closely integrated with commercial messages, then advertising itself, and not just the medium, becomes less trustworthy.

1.2 Misleading Advertising?

Advertorials, as a mode of advertising, clearly have an intention to persuade. But because they resemble ordinary articles, in both form and content, they look as though they are intended to spread knowledge. This leads us to the question whether advertorials, on account of their ambiguous nature, can mislead the public. Is it clear (enough) to consumers that they are dealing with an advertising message intended to persuade, but where is the intention to spread information as the focal point of attention?

One question that we can ask is whether it is clear to consumers that they are indeed dealing with an advertisement. According to the

Belgian advertising code (article 11), advertisements must be recognizable as such, particularly in media with editorial content. (Fauconnier, Van der Meiden, 1993: 143) To prevent possible deception, guidelines have been set by the Periodical Publishers Association (PPA), the Advertising Standards Authority (ASA), and the Institute in Public Relations (IPR) among others (Goodlad, 1997: 75; s.n., 1994: 7) and the powerful publisher VNU magazine group in the Netherlands (Van der Gaag, 1994a: 41; Van der Gaag, de Jong, 1996: 12). For the VNU, an advertorial must be made recognizable by placing words like 'advertisement', 'advertising,' advertorial,' or 'sale' at the top or bottom of the advertising page. In addition, the identity of who is behind the advertorial must be made clear by including the logo or pack-shot in the publication. It is prohibited to use the same typographie font for the advertorial that is used in the medium itself. (The font, however, must resemble that of the rest of the medium in order to disturb the rhythm of the publication as little as possible.)

Such regulations make it possible for consumers to recognize an advertorial as an advertorial. However, not all media take these guidelines into account. There has also been next to no research about whether these guidelines are effective or how their application is governed in practice. Goodlad (1997: 76) refers to a study (Cameron and Haley) conducted by senior editors and advertising managers of US publications that indicates that "most publications were proactive in their handling of advertorials; most respondents had some policy in place, though typically unwritten." Goodlad conducted his own study (Goodlad, 1997: 79), and it also indicated (for example) that labeling practices are variable. Not all advertisements that possess the characteristics of an advertorial are marked with a label such that consumers can recognize it as an advertorial.

This also raises the question whether consumers recognize an advertorial even when it has been 'labeled' in the above-mentioned manner. According to Sandler, Secunda (1993: 74), the success of advertorials can be explained by the fact that, even when there is a discernible difference with the editorial pages, the readers only vaguely perceive the difference. The results of the study by Dekker (Van der Gaag, 1994b: 42) also point in this direction. After having been told what an 'advertorial' is, almost a quarter of the respondents did not seem to recognize the advertorials presented to them. The fact that advertorials look like editorial material apparently has a very strong effect, even when the advertorial has been made conspicuous in one way or another.

1.3 *The Need for Clear, Unambiguous Regulations and More Research*

There is much confusion about what is allowed and what is not. There is certainly a need for clarity about what is permitted in regard to advertorials. In our view, the blurring of the boundaries between editorial and commercial material leads to a demand for unambiguous regulations. We support Kurver (in Van der Gaag, 1994a: 41) and Sandler, Secunda (1993: 77) in their call for the establishment of clear rules regarding standards for labeling, appearance, and recognizability of advertorials, and for the preservation of the credibility of the media and advertising. The advertising world itself does not seem adverse to such regulations. According to those in the field, however, this should be a matter of self-regulation, motivated by the fear that the government will otherwise impose very strict and inflexible laws in the future, and thereby threaten freedom of expression. (Sandler, Secunda, 1993: 77-78; Van der Gaag, 1994a: 40-41)

We cannot, or dare not, make any statements about how these regulations should actually be formulated. The research field surrounding advertorials is still mostly uncharted territory. Much of what is written and said about advertorials, and how they operate, is based on a combination of intuition and anecdotal evidence. (Goodlad, 1997: 76) We need further research into the use and operation of advertorials, and how they are perceived by the consumer, and this research can in turn contribute to the formation of good regulations. As far as the definition of an advertorial is concerned (what sort of advertisement would fall under the regulations), we advocate a broad interpretation. We have defined an advertorial as 'every printed message that essentially has a commercial intention to persuade, but resembles an ordinary editorial article in appearance and content.' In our view, this includes cases where the product is not promoted in the editorial text itself, but the link with an advertisement nevertheless cannot be ignored. A striking example: A magazine interviews a soap opera star about a miraculous wrist bracelet, and the interview contains a reference to an advertisement (with a coupon for the bracelet) a page further on. (Van der Gaag, de Jong, 1996: 12) The reference does not even have to be this explicit. Take for example those articles that typically appear in health magazines, often available for free in pharmacies. The article takes the form of a testimonial in which someone bears witness to the healing powers of a certain vitamin. In such articles, the brand name of the product is sometimes mentioned, almost in passing, but in other cases there is no word about the product to be found. However, next to the article, on the same page, there appears an advertisement for a product which contains that same vitamin. This is certainly no coincidence. Even though the article itself in such cases does not have an openly commercial message, is not the link with the advertisement strong enough — or the chance that the consumer regards the advertisement and the article as a whole high enough — to regard the article as an advertorial?

In connection with this issue, we would also like to point out that this hybrid phenomenon can be found on the Internet, in the form of websites that look like ordinary sites but are, in fact, advertisements. What we said about advertorials can also be applied to them. These sites should be subject to the same regulations as advertorials.

2. Sponsored Magazines

There is also no clear definition for the term 'sponsored magazine.' However, on the basis of the common elements in the various and diverse definitions in the literature (Aerts, 1989: 2; Schuttel, 1988: 7, 11; Souterboek and Vanderhoek, 1981; Knecht, Stoelinga, 1988: 89; Suer, in Winnebust, 1990: 7), we can offer the following general definition. A sponsored magazine, originally called a 'corporate sponsored magazine,' is a (usually) unsolicited and freely distributed printed publication which is financed by one or more organisations, and strongly resembles a magazine. According to the definition of Schuttel (1988: 11), the points of resemblance are, for example, the inclusion of clearly-defined editorial articles, a minimum length of sixteen pages and periodic publication.

Sponsored magazines share these general, common attributes, but they can also be distinguished from one another on the basis of a number of specific characteristics. We give here only the most relevant characteristics, in anticipation of our later discussion of ethical questions. First, we can distinguish sponsored magazines by the number of clients (i.e., organisations) and/or advertisers, that is, they must have one or more of these. When there is more than one client, the sponsored magazine is usually organised around a certain theme or a certain domain which contains the interests of the various clients (e.g., gardening or health.) As far as the number of different advertisers is concerned, sponsored magazines are in principle accessible to third parties, on the condition that these are not in competition with the sponsors. (Schuttel, 1988: 11; Knecht, Stoelinga, 1988: 89; Suer, in Winnebust, 1990: 7)

Furthermore, sponsored magazines can also differ from one another according to the aim of the client. There are many reasons why an organisation opts for a sponsored magazine. We can make a global distinction between public relations aims and marketing aims. By PR-aims, we mean the creation of goodwill and sympathy, corporate image building or promotion of the organisation's reputation, and the creation, advancement or maintenance of relations with the customer. (Hieselaar, 1990: 386; Schuttel, 1988: 37) There are also sponsored magazines with a commercial, sales-promoting function. (Hieselaar, 1990: 386; Schuttel, 1988: 7) Here, the emphasis is on conveying information, creating brand-name recognition and generating sales. (Schuttel, 1988: 37) In this context, there are what are called 'free gift magazines,' 'catazines' (a contraction of catalogue and magazine) and magalogues (magazine — catalogue.) These are the most commercially oriented sponsored magazines, whose primary goal is to draw the consumer's attention to a certain product amid the editorial material. (Hieselaar, 1990: 384) On the basis of these different functions, sponsored magazines are grouped into three categories: public relations magazines, information magazines and sales magazines. Many sponsored magazines, however, fulfill a combination of these functions. (Schuttel, 1988: 38-39)

Finally, we can distinguish sponsored magazines according to the content of the editorial articles. The content of some articles restrict themselves to the products, services or brand-names of the client(s). Others go further and deal with the organisation itself (e.g., which charities the organisation supports). Still others include subjects that have an indirect or even no connection with the advertiser at all, but try to connect with the broader interests of the target group (D'Ieteren Magazine is a good example. Along with advertisements for Volkswagen and Audi, one can find very general pieces about sport, culture and holidays.)

2.1 *Editorial Freedom?*

The question of editorial freedom is irrelevant in this context. A sponsored magazine is commissioned by one or more organisations and is also produced by the editors according to the wishes of the client(s). There is, therefore, no question of an ethically questionable influence being exercised by the advertising world on editorial freedom and objectivity.

2.2 *Misleading the Customer?*

In our view, sponsored magazines can mislead, or at least confuse, the customer in two ways. The first possibility concerns the medium as a whole. Independent of its specific form, content or aim, every sponsored magazine looks like a magazine. For this reason, we can also wonder whether a sponsored magazine is adequately recognizable. Is it clear to consumers that they are not dealing with an independent magazine, but rather a magazine financed by advertisers which ultimately intends to persuade them? We will not consider here the question of precisely how the advertiser hopes to influence the consumer. The question of whether the sponsored magazine aims at enhancing the reputation of the organisation (PR aim) or at stimulating the sales of products or services (marketing aim) can only be answered by examining each specific magazine. Moreover, all the above-mentioned aims of sponsored magazines can be considered valuable from both PR and marketing perspectives, which shows that sponsored magazines are located in a borderline area. (Hieselaar, 1990: 383-385) Whether it is about PR or marketing, the ultimate goal is to influence the consumer. Is this intention not (too much) concealed, in this case behind the outward appearance of an ordinary magazine?

In some sponsored magazines, one can indeed find hints that one is dealing with a sponsored medium. The fact that the magazine is distributed free of charge is already one indication. In sponsored magazines financed by one client, that client's name is often mentioned in the title (e.g., BMW Magazine.) Nevertheless, such indicators are not sufficient to make a sponsored magazine recognizable as a sponsored magazine. It is often not obvious from a magazine's title which organisation is responsible for its publication (Knecht, Stoelinga, 1988: 89), especially when there are several clients involved and the content of the magazine revolves around a certain theme. In addition, some sponsored magazines make themselves look even more like ordinary magazines by means of certain features. Advertisements from third parties can give the sponsored magazine the aura and feel of an ordinary, popular magazine. (VNU, 1990: 65) To treat subjects that in themselves have nothing to do with the advertiser or his product (e.g., the above-mentioned d'Ieteren Magazine) reinforces the resemblance with an independent magazine. Whatever the aim or content of a sponsored magazine is, is this not again a case of camouflaging the intention to persuade the customer on the part of the client(s), this time behind something that looks like an independent magazine that provides information or entertains the consumer? Does not the whole medium of sponsored magazines in itself operate in a misleading way?

But it is not just the medium itself that can work in a misleading way. We see a second, additional danger for deception in the content of so-called editorial articles. We find it hard not to regard sponsored magazines, in many cases, as a protracted series of advertorials. (In the section about advertorials we already referred to the example of sponsored health magazines.) As far as the possible deception of the consumer is concerned, we can ask the questions we already raised about advertorials. Would it not be appropriate to subject articles in sponsored magazines that clearly contain a commercial message to the same regulations as advertorials? Or is it sufficient that a sponsored magazine as a whole makes its own nature conspicuous to the reader (for example, by a statement on the front page)?

3. Infomercials

The term 'infomercial' is a contraction of the words 'information' and 'commercial.' There is no clear definition of this term, and it is also difficult to formulate a definition because the term 'infomercial' covers a lot of ground. In general, one can say that infomercials are longer than ordinary commercials (1 to 60 minutes) (Belch, Belch, 1995: 465; Dresmé, Krützman, 1994: 2.14-15) and that they have the same significance for the audio-visual sector as advertorials have for printed media. Like advertorials, infomercials involve a blurring of the boundary between editorial matter and advertising. An infomercial is essentially a commercial, but looks, to a lesser or greater extent, due to its form and content, like an ordinary informative and/or amusing television program.

To determine in what degree the different forms of infomercials look like ordinary programs, we can situate them along two axes. The first axis concerns form, the second content. (Smets, 1997: 23-28)

Along the form axis, we situate infomercials according to their concrete program form. On one end of the axis, we place independent television broadcasts, and on the other end, the infomercials that constitute an item in an existing television program.

When an infomercial is an independent television broadcast, the content is completely determined by the advertiser. In this form, infomercials are not part of normal television programming, with the result that they do not appear in television schedules and are usually broadcast outside of prime time. The advertiser must therefore provide its own publicity. A clear example of this form of infomercials is 'The Apple Movie' of the computer business Apple. This 24-minute-long infomercial, whose aim was to promote the Apple Power Book and to enhance the corporate image of Apple, was a self-contained and non-repeated television broadcast. (Dresmé, Krützman, 1994: 6.19-20)

On the other extreme of the form axis, we find infomercials that fall within regular television programming because they contribute to a television program. We can make a further distinction here between two forms. On the one hand, there are teleshopping programs, such as the well-known 'Amazing Discoveries' or 'TV Boetiek' in Flanders, which are in fact composed of a series of infomercials. On the other hand, one can also find infomercials in ordinary television shows. For example, a Becel infomercial was included in each broadcast of 'Koffietijd', the service program for housewives produced by the Dutch commercial station RTL4. In this part of the show, a Becel consultant discussed some aspect of nutrition which could be related to a product in the Becel line. (de Graaff, 1995: 55-56)

Intermediate forms on this axis are infomercials that are part of an ordinary commercial break, or ones whose content is related to a program but do not make up part of it. For example, during the Dutch Tros series "t Zal je maar gebeuren' ('It Could Happen to You'), where emergency situations are reconstructed, there were infomercials for the insurance company Centraal Beheer. (s.n., 1998: 6)

On the content axis, we can place infomercials that are theme-oriented at one end, and those that are action-oriented at the other. Theme advertising is information-oriented: the advertiser attempts to tell the public something about his product or brand name. This kind of advertisement is, however, oriented more towards influencing the knowledge and attitudes of the consumer, and less concerned with buying behaviour. With action advertisements, the converse is true: the primary aim is to encourage the consumer to act, i.e., to buy (or test) the product. (Fauconnier, Van der Meiden, 1993: 53; Floor en Van Raaij, 1989: 14)

An example of extreme theme-oriented infomercials are the 'Ford Today' spots. These short (one minute) infomercials were regularly placed at the start of a block of commercials on the commercial Flemish station VTM. Each successive infomercial went deeper into general questions by car drivers, such as how an airbag works, what is ABS, how the 'Car of the Year' is chosen, and so on. The brand name Ford was never predominantly present in them. (Grosemans, 1994: 24) Another example are the above-mentioned Becel infomercials. Viewers of 'Koffietijd' were offered the chance to send questions to the Becel consultant, which could be discussed in a later broadcast. (de Graaff, 1995: 55-56)

Infomercials are never purely action-oriented. The main difference with ordinary commercials is, after all, that they give a more detailed description of the product or brand name. The informative angle is essential. Infomercials, therefore, always aim to spread knowledge and influence consumers. Besides this, however, they can also create clearly action-oriented effects by providing the consumer with an opportunity to respond. This can take the form, for example, of a telephone number viewers can call in case they want more information or if they want to order the product immediately. Teleshopping programs, with their direct response infomercials, are the clearest example of this type. After and during a thorough description and demonstration of the product, the consumer is presented with all sorts of buying information (price, special offers, etc.) and finally a telephone number to order directly. The consumer here is clearly being urged to buy the product.

If we combine the two axes, we end up with the following coordinate system in which every infomercial can be located according to form and content. (Smets, 1997: 28)

Figure 1

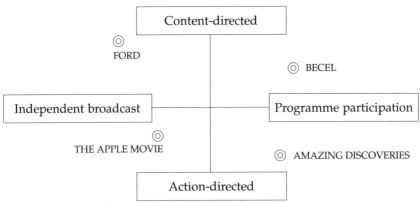

3.1 *Credibility and Objectivity of the Medium?*

As far as the possibly negative effect of infomercials on the credibility of the medium in which they appear is concerned, the same remarks raised with advertorials are applicable here. Infomercials which make up part of a television program take advantage of the credibility of the host program in which they appear. Like advertorials, in the eye of the viewer they are (as it were) approved by the producers of the program. This is not, or not directly, the case with self-contained infomercials. Nevertheless, one can claim that self-contained (especially program length) infomercials indirectly take advantage of the credibility of ordinary television programs by resembling them. Doesn't this mixture of ordinary television material with advertising pose a threat to the credibility and objectivity of both the program in which they appear and the medium of television as a whole, just like advertorials do?

To avoid this danger, or at least to reduce the risk of it, we believe that regulations can be created like those covering advertorials, e.g., regulations concerning the number of infomercials permitted in programs and on television as a whole. European legislation, for example, already stipulates a daily maximum of one hour for home shopping programs such as 'TV Boetiek.' (Van der Gaag, 1994c: 31)

3.2 *Independent Productions?*

We believe that infomercials that are part of an ordinary television show raise a second problem, namely, the question of the independence of the producers of the 'host program.' This form of infomercial is created by the producers of the program together with the advertiser. The threat that the producers thereby lose their independence ultimately depends on how much power the advertiser has. In the Becel infomercial, the content is determined by the producers of the program 'Koffietijd' and not the Becel consultant. However, the consultant can give advice during the process of discussing how items should appear on the show. (de Graaff, 1995: 55) As long as the producers are those who decide what subjects appear in the program and which products or brand names are suitable for it, in our view, the independence of the producers seems largely secure. However, when the creative choices behind the show are in function of the product or brand name, and thus the advertiser is allowed to interfere to a large extent, does not the influence of commerce on the freedom and independence of the producers go too far?

3.3 *Misleading the Consumer?*

Similar questions to those we raised about the possibility of misleading consumers in regard to advertorials are also relevant here. As a form of advertising with an intention to persuade consumers, infomercials look as though they have an informative and/or entertainment function due to their (greater or lesser) resemblance to, or appearance in, an ordinary television program. Here, the question again is whether the consumer is really aware that infomercials are commercials disguised as (a part of) an independent television program. For reasons like those given in our argument about the need to ensure that the advertorials are recognizable to the reader, we believe that infomercials should be subject to similar regulations. The Federal Trade Commission (FTC) and the National Infomercial Marketing Association (NIMA) have already done so in regard to program length direct response infomercials. They prohibit infomercials that can mislead the 'reasonable thinking consumer' by (for example) leading the consumer to believe that he is watching a news program or a show that is presented by a disinterested party with the pure aim of informing or entertaining the viewer, and not a sponsored commercial. In addition, any such program must state the following: "The program you are watching is a paid advertisement for (name of product or service)." The script must include that disclosure within thirty seconds of the program's beginning, and again before each reiteration of instructions for ordering the advertised product. When advertisers break these rules, they are fined by the FTC, or the advertiser loses its membership with the NIMA. (Belch, Belch, 1995: 465; Preston, 1994: 76)

Such regulations, like those covering advertorials, can indeed ensure that the viewer recognizes an infomercial for what it is. In our view, it would be advisable to subject all forms of infomercials to such regulations, including those that are not action-oriented. We tend to think that the risk of confusing the consumer is higher with purely theme-oriented infomercials. The intention to persuade the consumer is conspicuous in direct response infomercials, because there is information about buying the product and the appeal to buy it. This intention remains concealed in the case of theme-oriented infomercials.

We therefore disagree with Graaff (1995: 55) when he claims that there is no question of theme-oriented infomercials being illicit commercials because these are not properly speaking commercials at all, seeing as the product is just a subject of conversation, commentary, or discussion, rather than being promoted. There are indeed some infomercials that apparently do only provide information about the product or brand name, and even about subjects which only form part of the same general field as the product or brand name (as is the case, for example, with the Ford infomercial.) And the consumer is indeed not openly encouraged to buy the product. Nevertheless, the product or brand name is put in a favorable light and the ultimate intention behind doing so is to positively influence the consumer, if not directly via his buying behaviour, then indirectly via his attitudes and knowledge. (And we believe that a positive influence on the knowledge or attitude of the consumer towards the product or brand name can only have a positive, albeit indirect, effect on buying behaviour.)

We also believe that the extent to which infomercials can be misleading also depends on the kind of station the infomercial appears on. On a commercial station, the influence of advertising is expected, and therefore more easily 'suspected.' On public stations, one does not expect such practices to take place, and the illicit aspect of infomercials is therefore greater.

One form of infomercial, therefore, has more potential to mislead than another. Leaving these differences between different forms of infomercials aside, all the forms mentioned raise the ethical question whether in infomercials, the underlying intention to persuade consumers is hidden (too much) behind the intention to provide information. Like with advertorials, this area of study is mostly uncharted, and we believe these sorts of questions should be more thoroughly investigated.

4. Product Placement

Product placement is the inclusion of a brand name product, service, package, signage, or other trademark merchandise within a motion picture, television program or music video, in return for cash fees or reciprocal promotional exposure for the motion picture, television program or music video in marketers' advertising programs. (Babin, Carder, 1996: 140; Nebenzahl, Secunda, 1993: 1; Sandler, Secunda, 1993: 75) The well-known Bond films, in which a large number of different commercial brand names make an appearance, are a very striking example of this. (Dheedene, 1996; Wijman, 1997: 36-38) There are examples of product placement in television shows such as, for example, the fact that all detectives in the BRTN series 'Heterdaad' drive Ford cars (Dheedene, 1996) or the successful program 'De Mol' where all participants use Mercedes cars to carry out their assignments.

Product placement is described in different definitions as a practice within audio-visual media. However, one can find product placement in printed media as well. For example, in the well-known comic strip 'Suske en Wiske', the main protagonists always fly with KLM. That the producer and the advertiser are working together becomes obvious when one notices the wide variety of 'Suske en Wiskes' that are available on every KLM flight. (Dheedene, 1996)

4.1 *Independent Productions?*

Sometimes a brand name receives a surplus (emotional) value by being linked with a story. In the film, Top Gun, for example, the main character downs a can of a certain brand of beer after a violent battle, and the brand of beer thereby gains an extra value of masculinity and toughness. In this case, the advertiser had no influence on the scenario. (Fowles, 1996: 144) However, it is possible that advertisers in other cases may well make demands in regard to how their products appear. Some advertisers, for example, want their product to appear in the proximity of, or be mentioned by, a famous film star (but they must pay extra for this.) (Nebenzahl, Secunda, 1993: 1) In the older but still popular film, Some like it Hot, the film-maker has Marilyn Monroe telling another character (Tony Curtis) that she will think of him every time she sees a shell (the logo of Shell Oil.) Advertisers count on the fact that the public identifies with film stars, and therefore will buy the products that they see the stars using. Sometimes this goes so far that in a film all the 'good guys' drink Coca-Cola and all the 'bad guys' drink Pepsi. (Dheedene, 1996) In such cases, the advertiser is definitely taking something away from the independence of the producer. Product placement can influence the original intention of the screenwriter. (Nebenzahl, Secunda, 1993: 10) In the United States, there are agencies that try to get their hands on the newest film scripts as soon as possible in order to find out which products will fit in the film. (Dheedene, 1996) In our view, however, this is a rather restricted and harmless form of product placement because the advertiser ultimately has very little influence, and it ultimately changes little about the story.

4.2 *Misleading the Consumer?*

"Critics claim that the audience is unsuspectingly influenced by this uniquely insidious and deceitful form of advertising." (Babin, Carder, 1996: 150; Nebenzahl, Secunda, 1993, p. 1) Some take their criticisms further and claim that "product placements work as sub-liminal inducements because their context is ostensibly a movie, but not an ad, so that each of them comes sidling towards us, dressed up as non-advertising." (Nebenzahl, Secunda, 1993: 2; Sandler, Secunda, 1993: 78) Subliminal advertising is defined as commercial messages aimed at the subconscious. (Goleman, in Nebenzahl, Secunda, 1993: 1) They contain messages that lie under the perceptual threshold, and therefore, are not consciously perceived by the consumer. (Fau-connier, Van der Meiden, 1993: 58)

The criticism that product placement operates subliminally is, in our view, exaggerated. A study by Babin and Carder (1996) suggests, to the contrary, that viewers "are able to correctly recognize brands placed in a movie, while correctly distinguishing among those brands that did not appear the film they viewed." Perhaps the viewer does not realize that advertising is involved, but he at least knows that there is a message. With subliminal advertising, however, the consumer is not even aware that there is a message. (Pieters, Van Raaij, 1992: 112)

On the other hand, product placement can be misleading, considering that the advertisers' interest and intention to influence the viewer is concealed behind something else, in this case, the context of the story. When viewers are not aware of the practice of product placement, then we can speak about an illicit activity.

The study by Nebenzahl, Secunda (1993) on the attitude of the film audience shows that viewers are generally positive about product placement. The majority of those interviewed even preferred product placement over other forms of on-the-screen promotional activities because it was unobtrusively integrated into the film. "The small minority who object do so on ethical grounds. They perceive product placement as a clandestine approach which deludes the consumer," and they believe this practice should be forbidden.

5. Free Publicity

'Free publicity' occurs when a medium places an organisation, its products or its brand names in a positive light. The factor which determines whether an organisation, product or brand name can be the subject matter of an article is the news value that it has for the reader or viewer. The term itself reveals an important characteristic of free publicity: The advertisement is free, the advertiser does not need to do anything in return in order to have its product publicised. (Marck, in Smets, 1997: 39-40; Van der Gaag, de Jong, 1996: 12)

5.1 Ethical Questions

Although (free) publicity is one of the recognized tools in the classic communication repertoire, there are still some questions to be raised here. Strictly speaking, free publicity in our view does not mislead the customer, nor does it undermine the independence of editors or producers. The advertiser has in principle no control over the content of what is publicised. The medium wants to inform the consumer about the existence of (often new) products, brand names or organisations, and decides itself about what it discusses and whether its reports are positive or not.

Nevertheless, we believe that this system can lead to an ethically questionable form of influence due to the (increasing) pressures of commercial interests. For example, it is possible that an organisation or company decides not to make information about its (new) products available to a certain medium because its products have been negatively reviewed by that medium in the past, thereby taking away the medium's possibility to inform its readers or viewers in the future; or the organisation decides not to advertise in that medium anymore because of negative criticism, and thereby eliminates a source of advertising revenue. This (very real) danger will make journalists careful about making remarks that are too negative. In this way, the advertiser imposes a form of self-censorship on editors or journalists. It is not at all inconceivable that an advertiser would reward a reporter with various benefits (e.g., a holiday or another gift.)

As far as the possibility of misleading the consumer is concerned, we can make the following remarks. When (in certain cases) the above-mentioned implicit influence by the advertiser is present, which makes the medium feel obligated (as it were) to put the organisation, its products, or brand names in a positive light, is the consumer not being misled to a certain extent? Are commercial interests not being concealed behind what looks to be purely editorial material? And does this not pose a threat to the consumer's confidence in the editorial content itself?

Moreover the study by Admedia (the advertising core of the VNU magazine group) indicates that the consumer does not perceive free publicity as free publicity when watching features on shopping. Reports or features on shopping are a special form of free publicity where magazines or (lifestyle) programs display new products without adding much in the way of editorial commentary. These generally revolve around a certain theme (e.g., new fashion collections or watches, a report about a certain shopping street). Often consumers think that these are paid advertisements. (Van der Gaag, de Jong, 1996: 12; s.n., 1996: 1) Due to the fact that the boundaries between editorial material and advertising are becoming more and more fuzzy, the consumer is often unsure whether media coverage of commercial matters is sponsored or not. In our view, this means it is necessary to establish clear regulations concerning free publicity. With advertorials and infomercials, it should be made clear that we are dealing with paid advertising. Can we not similarly convey to the consumer in one way or another that free publicity is not sponsored by the advertiser?

6. Conclusion

6.1 *Ethical Questions*

Aside from what has been said in this article, everyday life seems to be more and more pervaded by an often inconspicuous intermingling of culture and commerce. This is most apparent in what is offered in tourism, entertainment, popular culture and in the media in general. This intermingling even occurs in the educational context: Advertising in school agendas, on the bulletin boards of universities, in cultural and scientific publications, and even in scientific conferences. It is possible that in our society, a latent process of cultivation has taken place with the result that the average Westerner places an exceptionally high value on an almost unrestricted consumption of a vast and increasingly varied number of consumer products without being aware of doing so. All sorts of philosophical and political questions, which we did not deal with, could be raised here. However, both the remarks we just made about the intermingling between culture and commerce, as well as the questions surrounding it, form a good background for the general conclusions of this article. There are some specific ethical questions arising from whether one actively promotes, or passively permits, the existence of a twilight zone between editorial material and marketing, and hybrid forms between information and advertising. We would like to set out these questions in what follows.

Due to the need for additional advertising revenue, more and more is being written in function of commercial interests. We have already shown in our discussion of different hybrid forms that an overly intimate working relationship between the media and advertisers poses a threat to editorial freedom.

The credibility of both the media and advertising itself can be undermined when they work too closely together. When the boundary between editorial material and advertising becomes too blurred, this constitutes an attack on the credibility of these inseparable but distinguishable fields of communication. (Hemels, 1998: 156) We have also applied this standpoint to hybrid forms where there is no question of an intermingling of commercial and editorial elements, namely, product placement and the medium of the sponsored magazine. Does the (too extensive) incorporation of commercial messages (in product placement) and the resemblance between sponsored magazines and ordinary magazines also possibly endanger the credibility of these media, e.g., film and magazine?

We would like to go somewhat deeper into the question of whether the hybrid forms we discussed can be regarded as misleading advertising. All the hybrid forms examined above are covered by the definition of advertising according to Floor, Van Raaij. (1989: 18) They define advertising as 'persuasive information about products, services and companies, where use is made of the mass-media and whose aim is to influence the knowledge, attitude and possibly the behaviour of the target group in a way favorable to the advertiser.' When examining each of the hybrid forms, we repeatedly raised the question whether they, as modes of advertising, conceal (too much) their ultimate intention to influence, and therefore, operate misleadingly or, at least, confuse consumers. Can we speak here of 'covert communication' or, more specifically, illicit advertising? Tanaka (1999: 41) defines covert communication as "a case of communication where the intention of the speaker is to alter the cognitive environment of the hearer, i.e., to make a set of assumptions more manifest to him, without making this intention mutually manifest." Illicit advertising is advertising that attempts to hide its message and tries to disguise itself as a message from an independent source. This technique can involve the content as well as the form. (Fauconnier, Van der Meiden, 1993: 57)

In making these claims, we realize that we have to be careful not to indulge in excessive suspicion. But we cannot shake the impression that there is something ethically questionable about each of the hybrid forms discussed. More concretely, we are concerned that the advertising message as such is disguised. The disguise can take place in various ways. In this context, we refer to the distinction made by Fauconnier (1995: 206) between the primary or main intention and the secondary intention of a communication message. According to Fauconnier, when analyzing concrete messages it is often difficult to find out what the precise relationship between primary and secondary intention is. In some cases, the secondary intention is nothing more than a technique to help bring about the desired result. In the hybrid forms we discussed, we believe such a technique is being employed. Is the apparently primary, but actually secondary, intention to inform (in advertorials, infomercials, and some sponsored magazines) or intention to entertain (in some forms of sponsored magazines and infomercials) not subordinated to the ultimate primary intention to influence the consumer? And of crucial importance in this context: Is the primary intention to influence not disguised behind the secondary intention? With product placement and the medium of the sponsored magazine, the intention to influence is not disguised behind another intention, but (respectively) in the context of the story (e.g., a film) or behind the outward appearance of an ordinary magazine. The intention to influence is essential to advertising. When it tries to disguise this, it also conceals its identity. According to Tanaka (1999: 43), we can indeed regard this as covert communication: "The advertiser tries to make the addressee forget that he is trying to sell something." On account of its hidden character, we believe this can be regarded as illicit advertising. An advertising message whose sender (the advertiser) intends to influence recipients (consumers), but where the identity of the message cannot be discerned by the average recipient, can be considered 'hidden' or 'disguised' from the standpoint of the consumer, and in this sense can be labeled as illicit advertising. (Fauconnier, 1973: 2)

According to Fauconnier (1992: 199), all techniques that aim to conceal the identity of the mode of communication are ethically unacceptable. On the other hand, in making an ethical judgment, one must consider whether the technique is being intentionally employed. In our view, this is indeed an intentional technique. The intention to persuade is covered up, the identity of the advertising message is concealed. This is part of a carefully planned strategy. On the one hand, one tries to hold the consumer's attention by preventing him or her from mentally or literally tuning out when he or she sees an advertising message. "This is a way of seducing readers into paying attention to advertisements which they otherwise selectively avoid." (Myers, in Tanaka, 1999: 43) On the other hand, the advertising message is camouflaged in order to give it more credibility, i.e., it is understood by the consumer as coming from a neutral source. In this way, the advertiser can conceal his or her self-interest in an illicit manner. The message is always presented as something different than a standard advertising message, and therefore in our view,

advertorials, sponsored magazines, infomercials and product placement (and in certain cases, free publicity) can be regarded as forms
of advertising which have, at least in part, an illicit character.

However, the above point must be qualified somewhat. The subtle
distinction Fauconnier (1973: 2) makes regarding infomercials and
advertorials can be extended to cover all the hybrid forms we have
discussed above. When these hybrid forms are subjected to guidelines (e.g., the announcement that the message is sponsored) that
make their commercial intention to persuade conspicuous to the customer, they become more 'open.' The advertising message is then in
principle not hidden from the customer, and he or she can recognize
its identity. Nevertheless, the discourse and approach of hybrid
forms retain an element of dissimulation. A tendency to conceal the
intention to persuade the customer persists, be it behind an informative discourse, an entertainment discourse and/or the context of the
medium or the story. Even though these hybrid forms rarely constitute illicit advertising, in our view they should be characterised as
quasi-open or quasi-concealed.

6.2 Postmodern Advertising Techniques?

On the one hand, the use of hybrid forms in advertising can be
explained by reference to the consciously chosen marketing communication strategy that lies behind it. On the other hand, some writers
point to another possible explanation. Advertorials, sponsored magazines, infomercials, product placement (and in a certain sense, free
publicity) could be considered postmodern advertising techniques.
This explanation is interesting, but it should be treated with a certain
amount of reservation. In our view, in many philosophical texts,
postmodernism is too easily put forward as an explanation for all
possible social changes.

The relationship with postmodernism can be drawn in two ways.
On the one hand, we could explain hybrid forms as the advertising
world's response to consumer behavior. The postmodern consumer
would (more than before) distrust the motives of businesses and
advertising campaigns. The consumer no longer lets himself get
taken in by slick advertising messages. The postmodern consumer
does not believe everything he sees and hears, but wants to know
the truth, to be informed in order not to end up buying a lemon.
(Popcorn, Marigold, 1996: 313) Modes of advertising characterised

by an informative aspect (infomercials, advertorials, sponsored magazines, and free publicity) would, in this view, be understood as a way of meeting the consumer's growing need for information, especially when the products in question are the kind that are desired more for their functional qualities rather than their surplus emotional or psychological values.

On the other hand, one may wonder whether the intermingling we are discussing can be explained as a typically postmodern phenomenon. With postmodern culture, we are no longer dealing with a mass culture, but a so-called mosaic culture. Various styles exist alongside one another, and the elimination or blurring of boundaries is a characteristic feature here. (Antonides, Van Raaij, 1994: 83; Fauconnier, Van der Meiden, 1993: 89) In mass communication, different genres are mixed together in all sorts of ways. Besides the aforementioned blurring of the boundaries between advertisement and information and/or entertainment, there are combinations of information and entertainment (infotainment), education and entertainment (edutainment), ... (Fauconnier, 1995: 205)

References

AERTS, Ria (1998), 'Sponsored media: journalistiek met commercieel oogmerk' in Guido FAUCONNIER (ed.), *Mediagids*. Antwerpen, Kluwer, pp. 1-7.

ANTONIDES, Gerrit, W. Fred VAN RAAIJ (1994), *Consumentengedrag: een sociaal-wetenschappelijke benadering*. Utrecht, Lemma.

BABIN, Laurie A., Sheri Thompson CARDER, (1996), 'Viewers' Recognition of Brands Placed Within a Film' in *International Journal of Advertising*, 15(1996)2, pp. 140-151.

BELCH, George E., Michael A. BELCH, (1995), *Introduction to Advertising and Promotion: An Integrated Marketing Communications Perspective*. Homewood, Irwin.

DE GRAAFF, Willy (1995), 'Infomercials op gespannen voet met merkuitstraling' in *Adformatie*, 23(1995)13, pp. 55-56.

DE LANGEN, Ruud (1998), 'Adverteerders worden ondernemers' in *Adformatie*, 26(1998)6, p. 48.

DHEEDENE, Henk (1996), 'Zichtbaar verborgen verleiders: Waarom Suske en Wiske altijd met KLM vliegen' in *Het Nieuwsblad*, 12 juli 1996, http://www.vum.be/nbifvverlei.html.

DRESME, Peter B., Jos A.M. KRÜTZMANN, (1994), *Direct response televisie: Het eerste Nederlandse boek over DRTV*. Amsterdam, De Bijenkorf.

FAUCONNIER, Guido (1973), 'Het verschijnsel sluikreclame' in *Informatiebulletin Centrum voor Communicatie Wetenschappen*, 3(1973)2, pp. 2-5.

FAUCONNIER, Guido (1992), *Mens en media: Een introductie tot de massacommunicatie*. Leuven/Apeldoorn, Garant.

FAUCONNIER, Guido, Anne VAN DER MEIDEN (1993), *Reclame: een andere kijk op een merkwaardig maatschappelijk fenomeen*. Bussum, Coutinho.

FAUCONNIER, Guido (1995), 'Over infotainment, infomercials, advertorials en andere 'vreemdsoortige' mengfenomenen in de massacommunicatie' in Ed HOLLANDER, James STAPPERS (eds.), *Communication Culture Community: Liber Amicorum James Stappers*. Houten, Van Loghum, pp. 201-207.

FLOOR, Ko, Fred VAN RAAIJ (1989), *Marketing-communicatiestrategie*. Leiden/Antwerpen, Stenfert Kroese.

FOWLES, Jib (1996), *Advertising and Popular Culture*. California, Sage.

GOODLAD, Neil, Douglas R. EADIE, Heather KINNIN, Martin RAYMOND (1997), 'Advertorial: Creative Solution or Last Resort?' in *International Journal of Advertising*, 16(1997)2, pp. 73-84.

GROSEMANS, André (1994), 'Een TV-magazine als reclame' in *PUB. Media, marketing, reklame*, 19(1994)1, p. 24.

HEMELS, Joan (1998), 'Reclame en journalistiek: Tussen verlokken en verlakken' in *Adformatie*, 26(1998)38, pp. 147-156.

HIESELAAR, A.G. (1990), 'Extern gerichte periodieken' in J.N.A. GROENENDIJK, G.A.Th. HAZEKAMP, J. MASTENBROEK (eds.), *Public relations en Voorlichting: Beleid, organisatie en uitvoering*. Alphen aan den Rijn/Deurne, Samson, pp. 383-391.

KASSAYE, W. Wossen, Joseph P. VACCARO (1993), 'TV stations' use of barter to finance programs and advertisements' in *Journal of Advertising Research*, 33(1993)3, pp. 40-48.

KNECHT, John, Bonny STOELINGA (1988), *Communicatie Begrippenlijst*. Deventer, Kluwer, 1988.

D. NEBENZAHL, Israel, Eugene SECUNDA (1993), 'Consumers' Attitudes toward Product Placement in Movies' in *International Journal of Advertising*, 12(1993)1, pp. 1-11.

OESEBURG, Liesbeth (1995), *Advertorials*. Tilburg, Academie voor Journalistiek en Voorlichting (afstudeerscriptie).

PIETERS, Rik, Fred VAN RAAIJ (1992), *Reclamewerking*. Leiden/Antwerpen, Stenfert Kroese.

POPCORN, Faith, Lys MARIGOLD (1996), *Clicking! Strategieën voor een nieuwe life-style*. Amsterdam/Antwerpen, Contact.

PRESTON, L. Ivan (1994), *The Tangled Web they Weave: Truth, Falsity & Advertisers*. Madison, University of Wisconsin Press.

ROSSITER, R. John, Larry PERCY, (1997), *Advertising Communications & Promotion Management*. New York, MacGraw-Hill.

ANDLER, M. Dennis, Eugene SECUNDA (1993), 'Point of View: Blurred Boundaries — Where Does Editorial End and Advertising Begin?' in *Journal of Advertising Research*, 33(1993)3, pp. 73-80.

SCHUTTEL, Petra (1988), *Sponsored magazines: een terreiverkenning. Onderzoek naar de waarde van een marketing-communicatie instrument.* Amsterdam, Universiteit van Amsterdam (doctoraalscriptie voor de Vakgroep Communicatiewetenschap, Faculteit der Politieke en Sociaal-culturele Wetenschappen).

SENGERS, Fred (1997a), 'Adverteerder wordt hoorndol van non spot advertising' in *Adformatie*, 25(1997)12, p. 22.

SENGERS, Fred (1997b), 'Verloofd: marketing en entertainment' in *Adformatie*, 25(1997)38, pp. 49-51.

SENGERS, Fred (1997c), 'Hoeveel non-spot kan een mens verdragen?' in *Adformatie*, 25(1997)47, pp. 46-48.

SENGERS, Fred (1997d), 'Regime Mediawet is echt niet het einde van nonspotprogramma's' in *Adformatie*, 25(1997)49, p. 5.

SENGERS, Fred, Theo VAN VUGT (1998), 'Zeg nooit nooit tegen non spot' in *Adformatie*, 26(1998)6, p. 12.

SMETS, Hans (1997), *Advertorials en infomercials. Postmoderne advertentietechnieken.* Leuven, K.U. Leuven Departement Communicatiewetenschap (eindverhandeling).

SOETERBOEK, Louis, Jan Wolter VANDERHOEK, (1981), *Encyclopedie voor reclame en marketing.* Deventer, Kluwer.

TANAKA, Keiko (1999), *Advertising language: A pragmatic approach to advertisements in Britain and Japan.* London/New York, Routhledge.

VAN DER GAAG, Arjo (1994a), 'Grijs gebied tussen redactie en commercie breidt zich uit' in *Adformatie*, 22(1994)10, pp. 40-41.

VAN DER GAAG, Arjo (1994b), 'Advertorials: kan het de lezer eigenlijk wat schelen?' in *Adformatie*, 22(1994)10, p. 42.

VAN DER GAAG, Arjo (1994c), 'Teleshoppers zoeken juiste format voor kritisch publiek' in *Adformatie*, 22(1994)27/28, p. 31-32.

VAN DER GAAG, Arjo, Ton DE JONG, (1996), 'Grensoverschrijding redactie en commercie houdt niet op bij advertorial' in *Adformatie*, 24 (1996) 23, pp. 12-13.

VNU Media Partners & Multi Media International (1990), *Sponsored magazines: een mediumtype doorgelicht.* Amstelveen, VNU Media Partners/Multi Media International.

WIJMAN, Erwin (1997), 'De Bond van adverteerders' in *Adformatie*, 25(1997)50, pp. 36-38.

WINNEBUST, G. (1990), 'Het sponsored magazine: Van wildwest tot serieuze propositie' in *Sponsored magazines*. Bijlage bij Nieuwstribune, 7(1990)38, pp. 6-11.

S.n., (1993), 'Britten leggen advertorial aan banden' in *Adformatie*, 21(1993)11, p. 8.

S.n., (1994), 'Uitgevers verscherpen advertorial-richtlijn' in *Adformatie*, 22(1994)1, p. 7.

S.n., (1996), 'VNU herziet advertorial-beleid' in *Adformatie*, 24(1996)22, p. 1.

S.n., (1998), 'Centraal Beheer komt met infomercials van drie minuten' in *Adformatie*, 26(1998)5, p. 6.

JOURNALISTIC LIBERTY AND THE INVASION OF PRIVACY

Marcel Becker

The practice of journalism as a profession has many facets that have an ethical dimension. The way journalists deal with these problems is often condemned. They are regularly blamed because they violate essential moral values. This sometimes leads to resignation. Famous statements about journalistic ethics are: "Talking with a journalist about ethics is like talking with the director of a distillery about total abstinence (of alcohol.)" (Evers, 1987: 251) and "Journalists do not need to be bribed to behave unethically." (Belsey, Chadwick, 1992: 1) In these statements, we witness an interpretation of the relation between ethics and the work of journalists that is not only clearly negative, but even mutually exclusive: In doing their work, journalists are impeded by ethical considerations. This implies that the best journalist is the one who takes no notice of the aforementioned kinds of consideration.

However, there are signs that the relation between journalistic work and morality is not generally experienced as negative and mutually exclusive. A first sign is implied in the reaction to so-called moral mistakes of journalists. Often, this is a reaction of indignation. Such a reaction not only makes clear that the action is seen as wrong but there is also regret and anger. Clearly these reactions stem from disappointment. And is disappointment not caused by the expectation that someone should have acted otherwise? If this is the case, indignation ultimately originates in the conviction that a journalist has done things a good journalist finds unworthy.

The indignation gives rise to a growing number of debates about the ethical dimension of journalistic work. In these debates, key concepts of our moral vocabulary ('integrity,' 'freedom,' 'responsibility') play an important role. Although they are viewed as being self-evident, often debates are confused because their precise meaning is unclear. Only in-depth knowledge about the key concepts provides a responsible use of the vocabulary to judge and articulate the merits and wrongs of journalistic work. Besides, the relation between the values at stake and the meaning of journalistic work for society must be elaborated. In debates about ethical matters, there is seldom an explicit reference to the task of journalists and the significance of their work. (Lambeth, 1992: 167) Often it is surpassed by other points of view (for instance, the economic one.)

For this reason, we shall take a case and show how the moral questions the case involves can be treated in terms of fundamental moral reflection. One of the topics that regularly gives rise to moral indignation is the invasion of privacy. In order to get the news, journalists penetrate into the personal lives of people. Often these actions are considered morally questionable. The public debates about these cases have international dimensions. For instance, in the Clinton-Lewinsky case, there was wide spread indignation about the role of the media. Some of the media were condemned for being preoccupied with details of sexual behaviour. Where does this indignation come from? What is exactly wrong with the invasion of privacy? Which image of good journalistic behaviour is implicitly present in condemnations? These questions make clear that we restrict ourselves to the problem of the media publishing details from celebrities' personal lives. We are not interested in privacy problems relating to data-storage.

In order to answer our questions, we first shall present an exploration of the concept of privacy (1). Afterwards, we will elaborate a view of the deeper meaning of journalistic activity. This elaboration is realised by discussing a core value that is often used to justify the invasion of privacy, i.e., the notion of 'liberty' (2). Finally, we will say something about the conditions under which the invasion of privacy is justified (3).

1. Privacy

In speaking about privacy, we face at least two kinds of problems. These problems are mutually related, but discussions are often confused because their difference is neglected. First, there is lack of unanimity about the content of the concept 'privacy.' Privacy and the invasion of privacy not only indicate a physical proximity, but also a knowledge about a person. (Gavison, 1984: 347) In the case of the latter, there is the question of whether the invasion of privacy merely points to the amount of knowledge about a person or points to the control of access to information. (Wasserstrom, 1984: 316-331). Because we are not interested in data-storage, the latter is not important to us.

Second, there are discussions about the normative value of privacy. Often, privacy is described as a right that anyone can claim. It is even mentioned in the 12th article of the *Universal Declaration of Human rights*: "No one shall be subjected to arbitrary interference with his privacy, family, home or correspondence, nor to attacks upon his honour and reputation. Everyone has the right to the protection of the law against such interference or attacks." The formulation of privacy as a right furnishes an explanation of the moral indignation that occurs in cases of the invasion of privacy. Journalists should, as every citizen, respect the rights of other citizens. But what is the moral standing of this right? Does it prevail under all conditions or must it be considered as a *prima facie* right? The latter seems to be the case. Regularly, maintenance of this right results in moral wrongs. For instance there is the possibility that the concept of privacy impedes discussions about moral behaviour. When we allow individuals to do in private what we would have good reasons for not wanting them to do at all, we are inconsistent and hypocritical. In this case, it is better to reduce privacy and facilitate moral discussion. (Gavison, 1984: 367) Sometimes the concept is clearly misused, for instance, when it serves as a guide to hide moral evil. Hence, there are regular situations in which the right is overruled. But what criteria must be used? In order to make good judgement in such situations, we need to know on what normative conviction the right of privacy is based. What is good about privacy and why should it be respected?

To answer these questions, first, a few remarks about the content of privacy will be made. Afterwards, the moral dimension of the concept will be discussed.

The concept of privacy is derived from 'privare', the Latin ancestor of 'to deprive.' It is a negative concept. The emergence of the public-private distinction is a characteristic feature of modern times. As Berlin says, "the sense of privacy itself, of the area of personal relationships as something sacred in its own right, derives from a conception of freedom which (...) is scarcely older, in its developed state, than the Renaissance or the Reformation." (Berlin, 1969). Indeed, privacy is closely connected with the modern idea that a human being has a right to live his or her own life and create his or her own personality. (Reiman, 1984: 300-316) Various enlightenment thinkers such as Kant, Locke and Rousseau stressed, each in his own way, that an individual has to consider his existence primarily as his own existence and has a right to control it as far as possible. It should not be forgotten that they had strong normative reasons to grant this right to individuals: It enabled the individual to reach personal growth. In our so-called 'individualistic era,' the significance of privacy is often stressed. In a situation of privacy, a human being feels free; there is no strong pressure to fulfil expectations. Because the direction of this learning process is not influenced by public morality, privacy contributes to learning in creativity. It insulates the individual against ridicule and censure at early stages of groping and experimentation, and in this way stimulates diversity and heterogeneity. (Gavison, 1984: 361)

However, privacy should not be restricted to situations in which individuals have spectacular and unique experiences, in which they distinguish themselves from public morality. The core of the concept of privacy is not people's desire to have a private morality that differs from public morality. In this case, privacy should be related to those actions that are deviant from public morality. But it is not the content of the action that makes something belong to the sphere of privacy. A wide range of actions can be exercised in the private domain. Think about lovers saying the most trivial words to each other. It would be an offense to suggest to them to make their corny expressions public because of the triviality of what they are saying. The most banal, commonplace actions, for instance, walking with one's children in the park can be 'private,' as is shown by the indignation of public persons about obtrusive photographers who take pictures of them while they are doing things we all do. Hence, there is a close relation between privacy and negative freedom: In this respect the moral substance of the action is not important. As Warren and Brandeis state in their classic article, the right to privacy can be contrasted with property-rights regarding literary artistic products. (Warren, Brandeis, 1890: 79)

To the persons involved, what happens in situations of privacy is very important. The most trivial words and actions reflect a deep dedication and intense relationship. This implies a specific relation between people in situations of privacy. In one of its first descriptions, the English jurist and philosopher Stephens described the core of privacy as "observation which is sympathetic." (Schoeman, 1984: 10-11) 'Sympathetic' stems from the Greek 'sym-pathein', which means 'being involved with the same.' Indeed, in privacy situations people experience the same things as important. This can take place in diverse situations and several locations. Privacy is not located at a fixed place for instance the home, it concerns behaviour, inward emotions and convictions that can be shown and experienced in several places. Sometimes, these locations are accessible to everyone (as for instance, the park). So, privacy should be distinguished from secrecy. The core of secrecy is intentional concealment, but privacy often relates to ordinary events and experiences of everyday life that are not intentionally concealed. Sometimes private concerns are secret, sometimes they are not. (Belsey, 1992: 81). In spite of this close relation between private and public life, we immediately recognise a situation of privacy that ought to be respected. This becomes clear in those events of public life where suddenly privacy becomes important. For instance, in the turmoil around car accidents or events in hospitals, restraint is asked from bystanders.

The emphasis on privacy in the middle of public life makes clear an essential characteristic of privacy. A small, clearly distinguished domain is created; what happens only should be shared by those who directly participate in the event. They are tied together in undergoing common experiences. They have an immediate relation to what is at stake; in this relationship they are deeply engrossed. This involves an implicit agreement that unless there are clear indications otherwise, those things that happen only matter to those who are present. It implies a trust in interhuman relations, that what happens will not automatically be made public. Intrusive photographers violate this trust. Intrusion of privacy is committed by someone who does not sympathise with the other persons; he or she does not share the meaning of what is going on and is not directly involved. He or she is an outsider. Even worse, they perpetuate the moment so that many people that have no relation to the meaning of what is happening can act as witnesses.

What is disturbing about the invasion of privacy can be made clear when we compare privacy-relations with more deviant modes. First, there is a difference between occasionally being noticed and being eavesdropped upon. In eavesdropping, someone participates in an indirect and corrupted way in what is going on. Indirect, because he or she gets knowledge without participating directly in what is going on. The matters at stake are not his or her matters. Corrupted because he or she is not genuinely interested. He or she sees the other person not primarily as a subject with his or her own sensibilities, goals and aspirations, but as an object of his own curiosity. (Benn, 1984) Another deviant mode is observation. In observation, there is a larger distance between subject and object. The absence of direct involvement makes it probable that only the surface of the action is seen. In the eyes of an observer, a religious ceremony is reduced to a picturesque scene. In the invasion of privacy, these two perspectives face one other. Someone who is involved in something he or she estimates to be important is observed by someone else who is not directly involved and should be excluded. When he or she is aware of the other person, he or she sees himself through his or her eyes. The agent who discovers that he or she is witnessed loses spontaneity. There is no direct involvement any longer in the meaning that is at stake. The motivation for observation aggravates this problem. Curiosity, the desire to exploit knowledge by taking pictures that can be sold, these are all motivations that are far removed from the motivations of the people they observe.

After this description, we can turn to the question of under which circumstances the invasion of privacy by the media can be justified. We shall first discuss a key concept in the discussions about the invasion of privacy, namely, the notion of freedom (which will be used interchangeably with liberty.) This notion often serves as a justification of the aggressive actions of journalists, who reveal public details about private lives. It is said journalists are free to write what they want, people are free to read (or not read) what they want. In order to know whether this is done justly, we have to investigate how freedom relates to the mission and task of the media, and what the notion of 'freedom' means in this context.

2. The Concept of 'Freedom' and the Proper Task of Journalists

Compared to codes of conduct, there are, presently, only few elaborated statements of the proper task of journalists and justifications of journalistic freedom. (Lambeth, 1992: 17) Over the past 20 years, many universities have started mass communication studies, but fundamental reflections on the task of the media are scarce. There is a gap that is not yet filled by (ethical) literature. However, we can turn to a literature that is somewhat older: From earlier times, in the twenties and thirties of this century and even before, when the social landscape was changed dramatically by the emergence of the new media, one can find several positive statements of this kind. These statements are elaborations of enlightenment philosophy. In fact, from the beginning of the enlightenment there has been continuous reflection on the advantages, modalities and possibilities of spreading information.

The enlightenment philosophers were convinced that the growing possibilities of spreading information should be used to cultivate people. Under the concept of 'public opinion,' they maintained that people from different factions should meet each other in a common space, where they could exchange information, discuss and debate. In the open exchange of opinions, there is continuity and progress. The same 'public discussion' is the subject of today's debates, tomorrow's conversations and the day after tomorrow's newspaper articles. (Taylor, 1995) Sometimes, there emerges a consensus and common understanding about vital matters. Discussion and exchange of information make people change their opinion.

The relation between public opinion and political power was full of tension. The enlightenment thinkers considered themselves part of a community in which differences of opinion were solved by discussion. The people would have been able to participate in political decisions. In the end, they believed reason shared by all people, was able to domesticate power. The political equivalent of this line of argument was democracy.

In this process, the emerging media were of vital importance. In the beginning of the 19th century, the press was characterised by partisanship, invective and unrestraint. But behind the negative and sometimes destructive statements, there was a positive conviction. Government was the chief foe of liberty, and the press should be free to serve as a guard against governmental encroachments on liberty. Information could, against the suppression of absolute monarchs, help in uncovering the truth. The social function of the press consisted in making clear and transparent matters that are of common interest. This is clear in the German word for 'public', '*Öffentlichkeit*', which means 'openness.' Taken literally, it concerns the principle of communication without borders. (Pöttker, 1997; Habermas, 1962)

However, this should not be taken too literally. It does not point to an immoderate or superfluous amount of information. A principle of journalistic civic mindedness is not to 'publish whatever you want to publish.' There *is* a normative, guiding conviction underlying the enlightenment pleas for openness. Journalists should be oriented to the participation of the public in making decisions that are important to society. This does not mean that journalists should moralise. It is only a direct consequence of the recognition that if not all can be published, inevitably a selection must be made, and that the most important criteria must be relevance for society and the possible contribution to democracy.

The close relation between people's level of cultivation and political participation continued to be a central topic in the 20th century. In the beginning of this century, the enlightenment heritage was explicitly manifest in key documents such as Walter Lippmanns' *Public Opinion* (1922). Lippmann saw in the media possibilities for 'civic enlightenment,' which had an intrinsic value and stimulated political participation. In the (scarce) positive statements outlining the tasks of the media we witness today, we recognise as underlying the conviction that discussion of information concerning the major problems the world and its people face is necessary to both democratic understanding and democratic action. A truly democratic society is not a society where votes are counted once every four years; democracy is an institution in which public debate and public conversation are very important. Democracy is a forum in which informed citizens rationally debate about those issues which face them. In this institution, the media are one of the important mechanisms stimulating the process in which the choices are made. Journalists advance the public interest by publishing facts and opinions without which a democratic electorate cannot make good decisions. (O'Neill, 1992: 21) This makes them, in large measure, responsible for the quality of the democratic process. In current statements about the tasks of the media, this can be recognised. For instance, those who say that the media should stimulate discussion in a pluralist society point, implicitly or explicitly, to this task. And all that counts as important functions of the media can be reduced to this task. The media bring the news, i.e., they tell us what important things are going on and which things should be objects of discussion and debate. They also present a broader framework and introduce topics of discussion. In large measure, they set the stage and agenda. Journalists do not say what we think, but they have an important voice in determining what we think about. Moreover, the media are a forum for critique and commentary. (Lambeth, 1992: 38) In presenting different voices that can be commonplace or challenging the media contribute to the forming of opinion. Of course, the different ways in which the media fulfil their task cannot be separated clearly. We daily witness how they are interconnected.

In the description of these processes, the notion of 'freedom' has played an important role. A free press supplies access to information that a citizen requires in order to act in a democratic, responsible manner. The enlightenment philosophers stressed the importance of the free flow of opinions. In current descriptions of journalistic activity, this is related to the value freedom in several ways. To gather important facts and trace abuses, the journalist should be free to move. He or she should be free in the sense of being independent; he or she should not accept gifts or be dependent. Moreover, to present the news and express the viewpoints, he or she should be free to express and articulate his or her views. Only when these conditions are fulfilled, is there a true freedom of the press, which causes diversity of opinion and stimulates discussion.

To investigate further the close relation between freedom and the task of journalism, we shall study two key documents employed to justify the freedom of the press: *Areopagitica* of the poet John Milton (1644) and *On Liberty* of the philosopher and member of parliament, John Stuart Mill (1859). Milton wrote *Areopagitica* at the beginning of the English revolution when parliament tried to restrict the freedom of publication. The pamphlet is a vigorous plea for freedom of opinion, in which the writer rises far above the politics of the day. Inspired by *Logos Areopagitikos* (the speech to the democratic assembly) of the Athenian orator Isocrates, he asks for the lifting of censorship. Freedom is a central concept in his argument, but Milton's use of the concept is ingeniously embedded in a broader framework. He was convinced that freedom would contribute to discovering truth. If all ideas were widely known, the best idea would gain most support. Hence, Milton was confident that truth was definite and demonstrable and that it had unique powers of survival when permitted to assert itself in an honest and free contest between opinions. Censorship obstructs this process.

In explaining this process he attaches much importance to reason, but he describes it in a specific way. He uses a vocabulary that suggests that reason is not only a human faculty but also a human transcending principle to which mankind has to listen. Milton speaks of the 'breath of reason,' and says that the person who prevents a book being published kills 'reason itself.' Human rationality is the capability to listen to 'the voice of reason.' Ultimately, reason is a principle that stems from God. This becomes clear when Milton presents an explanation of the power of reason in a religious vocabulary. A religious framework determines Milton's argument in several ways. Sometimes he refers to the Bible. Citations from this infallible source of knowledge should prove the truth of what he is saying. For instance, he supports his argument by pointing to St. Paul who thought the insertion of sentences of Greek poets into Holy Scripture was not blasphemous. And he quotes St. Paul's, "Prove all things, hold fast what is good." More indirectly but also qualifying the religious framework, Milton professes his trust in a truth that will emerge sooner or later. God will guarantee this emergence of truth. In an incomprehensible way, God accompanies the history of humankind, but ultimately, He will bring humankind to know better times. A clear sign of God's intention is that He enables humans to participate in reason, which will ultimately lead them to truth.

It is clear that underlying Milton's argument is a conviction that is not rationally justified. He presents it as being clear to those that are listening. His opponents in parliament have to recognise this truth because of their shared religious convictions. Ultimately, *Areopagitica* is more an appeal than a rational argument.

More than two-hundred years later, John Stuart Mill wrote, *On Liberty*. He fears not so much the power of authorities, rather, he is more frightened by the intolerance of mass opinion and its uniformising tendencies. He describes *On Liberty* as a book with one truth: "The importance, to man and society, of a large variety in types of character, and of giving full freedom to human nature to expand itself in innumerable and conflicting directions." (Mill, 1873: 259). The defence of freedom is based on two arguments. First, the person who rejects an opinion presupposes his own infallibility. However, facing the abundance of different and divergent opinions in history, we must conclude that the human being is fallible. Fortunately, it is also a human quality that mistakes can be corrected. Hence, ongoing discussion is absolutely necessary. The second argument is based on Mill's conviction of what it means to hold 'an opinion' and to be free. To hold an opinion means having a real sense for the meaning of an opinion. This requires discussion with divergent opinions. "...[N]o one's opinions deserve the name of knowledge, except so far as he has either had forced upon him by others or gone through of himself the same mental process which would have been required of him in carrying on an active controversy with opponents." (Mill, 1859: 252) The only way to reach knowledge of a matter consists in correcting and completing an opinion by collating it with those of others. If there is no intense public debate, there are only 'empty words' that have lost their meaning. So a conflicting opinion always has some importance: It can defy and challenge one to articulate an opinion. Behind this thought lies the conviction that people always improve when they are opposed. Mill points to dialectical methods as developed in Platonic dialogues and medieval scholasticism. His concept of freedom is directly derived from this conviction. Only an opinion that is come into being through struggle with other opinions can count as 'free opinion.' True freedom is accompanied by diversity of opinions and ongoing debate.

Mill's view on discussion and debate is based on a set of convictions about human development. As an heir of the enlightenment tradition, Mill supposes that humanity is in the process of progress. More and more people hold stronger and better opinions. However, this progress is not assured, it has to be continued by ongoing rational investigation, debate and discussion. "When an opinion is true, it may be extinguished once, twice or many times, but in the course of ages there will generally be found persons to rediscover it." (Mill, 1859: 240) In defending the value of liberty, Mill intends to contribute to this. Only when let free human beings can develop their capacities, improve themselves and advance humankind. This pre-occupation with individual growth and human progress presupposes that a distinction can be made between good and bad development. His words imply the presence of moral keystones. Indeed, in describing this process, Mill sometimes gives evidence of possessing some normative assumptions. He regularly makes clear that some forms of life should be more appreciated than others. For instance, he says that people should act in such a way that the 'higher parts of our nature' be developed. (Mill, 1873: 173) He even states that some cultures are further on 'the road to perfection' than others; they are happier, nobler and wiser. (Robson, 1998: 349) However, Mill does not elaborate a clear picture of the desired future because perhaps he fears it would contradict his plea for open discussion (we shall not discuss whether such a fear is correct.) It is most probable that he appeals to common understanding about moral ideals. In that case, there is a similarity with Milton. Both appeal to standards that they do not make explicit because they are commonly shared.

Of course, there are many differences between Milton and Mill. Milton protests against the (mis)use of power by political authorities, whereas Mill protests against the devastating influence of public opinion. Milton grounds his defence of freedom in firmly held religious belief; in *On Liberty*, the normative assumptions are more hidden. But there is a striking similarity in the structure and presuppositions of the arguments. Both Mill and Milton are convinced that deep in their heart, human beings desire to know the truth, and mankind is on the way to reaching the truth. (Siebert, 1956: 43) It is self-evident to them. They do not make it explicit nor do they explain it. This self-evident thesis is the groundwork of their quest for free competition of opinion. Freedom is not a goal in itself that can be used to justify whatever action, it is a means to find truth. So there is in both the *Areopagitica* and *On Liberty* a tension between defence of freedom and open discussion, on the one hand, and implicit normativity, on the other. There might be fruitful ways to deal with the tension when normativity is made more explicit. However, this is not our main point of interest here. Important is the conclusion that the defence of freedom is part of a larger project, both for one of the first and one of the later spokesmen of the enlightenment tradition. In this respect, the difference between these liberal thinkers and pre-modern thinkers is mitigated. There is still an individual-transcending truth to be reached. The difference is that the truth is not monopolised any longer by church or state authorities. The opposition from which liberalism is born is *not* primarily the 'truth of the church' versus 'truth of the individual,' but 'the individual as medium to discover truth' versus 'church authority to discover truth.' This applies equally to so-called negative *and* positive forms of liberty. In positive liberty (freedom for) it is more explicit where the use of freedom aims, and means are offered to reach the goal. In negative liberty ('freedom from restraint') it is more hidden, but nevertheless very important.

When we make the implicit normative expectations of liberal tradition more explicit, we come to the paradoxical statement that freedom carries concomitant obligations. (Schramm, 1956: 73-104) It is a right claimed for the good of society. Anything done in the name of freedom must have some relation to the common good. This has severe consequences for the practical applications of the concept. Freedom cannot be arbitrarily used to justify any action whatsoever. Neither does it justify actions motivated by pure self-interest. And, freedom always must be balanced against the private rights of others and vital social interests. (Schramm, 1956: 96-97). Applied to the invasion of privacy, this means: Those justifying it only by saying that journalists are free to write what they want use the central concept of the enlightenment, but they do not do justice to the tradition.

Of course this does not mean that any use of freedom to justify the invasion of privacy is false. When freedom is embedded in a larger framework it is possible that, in terms of this framework, the invasion of privacy can be described as morally just. In the next section, we will examine this possibility.

3. The Conditions under which the Invasion of Privacy is Justified

A comparison of privacy and journalistic activity makes clear that these two phenomena have significance in different contexts. Journalists are working in public life and so, by definition, do not have anything to do with private life. A soon as something is labelled as a 'private affair,' it is not apt to be made public. However, this only holds when something *really* is a private affair, i.e., when only a small circle of people are involved in the meaning that is at stake. As soon as it reaches further, other people have a right to know. The general interest is involved and an appeal to privacy is without sense. Hence, discussions about the invasion of privacy by journalists should deal with the question of whether the events have significance for more people than those directly involved. If such is the case, it should be known in wider circles.

The sphere of personal attitudes, feelings and thoughts is very small for people that hold important positions in society. In their case, behaviour that otherwise counts as personal has public import. We consider journalists, in some measure, justified in examining their lives closely, searching for concealed evils. For instance, they control whether these people have public recourse to public goals.

We praise journalists who reveal the misuse of public means. In order to do this, they need an 'aggressive attitude' that can imply the invasion of privacy. But how far can one go? It is commonly agreed that people with an important social position have a relatively large influence on people's moral behaviour. Many people watch their behaviour and emulate them. A large part of this influence is unconscious, but we all recognise it when we say that public people, willing or not, serve as (moral) examples. This gets confirmed when we see how moral education works. To a large extent, morality is shaped by emulating examples set by others. This starts at home. A golden rule for educating children is: Give a good example. Also, in public life, people serve, consciously or unconsciously, as examples. We need not go into the details of this process. For now, it is important to realise that people who stand high on the social register have a large influence on others. This influence gives them some responsibility. Parallel to their *functional* responsibility, these people have *moral* responsibility. This counts more when people work in politics or public administration. As servers of public interest, they must be of good moral standing. To function well in their work, moral integrity is required. Literally, integrity means 'wholeness.' In this case, it points to the impossibility of separating one's public role from one's private life. This is especially important in communication processes. Public officials and politicians must convince people, which is only possible when the arguments are not only sound but also when a personality is convincing. As Aristotle already made clear in *The Rhetoric*, the credibility of the speaker depends on large part upon his or her moral character. The perception of the content of the words is influenced by (the perception of) the speaker's character. In times of elections, politicians are aware of this. Their message is supported or defeated by their personality.

So there are clear signs that the concept of privacy presupposes a distinction that cannot be maintained with regards to those who occupy prominent positions. It justifies judging these people more critically. However, this course of reasoning goes against important presuppositions of modern times. Modern western people are said to be, and pretend to be, capable of rational and autonomous decision making. That image falls away when people are judged by their personal characteristics which vaguely influence emotions. It opens the door for easy manipulation. Should we not restrict as much as possible the practice of attaching importance to the behaviour of important people?

So there seem to be two apparently contradicting positions. In the first, the modern view of autonomous individuals is adjusted and put into perspective. In the second, the modern ideal is maintained, and any involvement of personal characteristics in a discussion must be rejected. As extreme positions, they are both unattractive. In the first case, a cultural ideal is neglected, and in the second case, a clear phenomenon that is visible to anyone, and is supported by legitimate moral considerations, is denied. However, if we take them not as extreme positions, there are possibilities of reconciliation. The mechanisms by which personal lives of important persons have wide influence should be acknowledged openly. When we are conscious of the fact that the personal characteristics of the politician are of some importance, we handle it in a healthier way. We know the real source of our interest in politicians' personal life; we focus on the relevant matters and do not pay attention to trivial and vulgar details. The discussions of matters of privacy will be reduced to important matters. If we do not, it reduces to a lower morality in which important questions are neglected. In this case, social and legal tolerance for the public exposure of private lives can corrupt a society by encouraging the diversion of attention to such matters away from important economic and political issues. The enlightenment ideal can be helpful by making visible the possibilities of inauthentic dealings with the matter. Faithfulness to the enlightenment ideal will help one acknowledge commercial motives, the thirst for sensationalism and help in morally questioning these developments. It reminds us that a culture that is faithful to its roots of individualism should not be merged into trivial accounts of its celebrities.

Prudent dealing with situations implies careful consideration of every situation. There is no absolute boundary where general interest starts and privacy ends. To support this consideration, some general guidelines can be given. First, privacy must be distinguished from the 'personal.' The 'personal' points to someone's characteristics and convictions. These can have a direct influence on one's actions in the public sphere. Sometimes we say that a public official 'has a strong personality,' and this has important consequences for his public work. But this opinion or personality can be a consequence of private experiences that no one needs to know. (Although this sphere is described as 'personal;' in this case, the word personal is used differently, which makes the distinction more difficult.) One's personal characteristics do not necessarily justify the invasion of one's privacy.

A second consideration concerns the person who judges the situation. Who decides the range of privacy that public people can enjoy? It is clear that these people themselves should not determine where privacy starts. It would make someone the judge of his or her own case. An appeal to privacy has often been misused to hide important information. The privacy of these people is always liable to be under scrutiny. Strictly speaking, these people do not have privacy; they do not have an assurance that can be assured as 'private' under all circumstances. (Belsey, 1992: 86) However, this is not a plea for an intensive examination of the private lives of politicians. It must be understood as an indication that journalists have serious responsibilities. It is for them to resist the temptation of less than ethical motives. They should deal with the freedom that is given to them in a responsible way.

Journalistic activity is guided by principles and not by the curiosity of the people. This is denied by those journalists who equate the fact that people want to see something with the public's right to know something. This is a mistake. The slogan 'the people's right to know' can refer to:

1. The fact that the public is interested out of vulgar, idle curiosity. In that case, the public does not have the right to know. No right exists which assures the satisfaction of idle and morbid curiosity.

2. A matter that is clearly and directly related to public interest. In such matters, the public has a right to know. The journalist has a duty to present his or her view.

References

BELSEY, Andrew (1992), 'Privacy, Publicity and Politics', in Andrew BELSEY, Ruth CHADWICK (eds.), *Ethical Issues in Journalism and the Media*. London/New York, Routledge, pp. 77-92.

BELSEY, Andrew, Ruth CHADWICK (1992), 'Ethics and Politics of the Media: The Quest for Quality' in Andrew BELSEY, Ruth CHADWICK (eds.), *Ethical Issues in Journalism and the Media*, pp. 1-14.

BERLIN, Isaiah (1969), 'Two Concepts of Liberty' in *Four Essays on Liberty*. London, Oxford University Press, pp. 118-172.

EVERS, Huub J. (1987), *Journalistiek en ethiek. Een onderzoek naar Regelgeving in de Uitspraken van de Raad voor de Journalistiek 1960-1985*. Delft, Eburon.

GAVISON, Ruth (1984), 'Privacy and the Limits of Law' in Ferdinand A. SCHOEMAN (ed.) *Philosophical Dimensions of Privacy: An Anthology*, Cambridge, Cambridge University Press, pp. 347-402.

HABERMAS, Jürgen (1962), *Strukturwandel der Öffentlichkeit: Untersuchungen zu einer Kategorie der Bürgerlichen Gesellschaft*. Suhrkampf, Frankfurt am Main, 1992 (1962).

LAMBETH, Edmund B. (1992), *Committed Journalism: An Ethic for the Profession*. Bloomington, Indiana University Press.

LIPPMANN, Walter (1965), *Public Opinion*. New York (NY), Macmillian.

MILL, John S. (1859), 'On Liberty' in *Collected Works*, pp. 213-311.

MILL, John S. (1873), 'Autobiography' in John M. ROBSON *et al.* (eds.) *Collected Works of J.S. Mill*, Routledge & Kegan Paul, Toronto, 1977-1991, pp. 1-291.

PÖTTKER, Horst (1997), 'Öffentlichkeit als Gesellschaftlicher Auftrag. Zum Verhältnis von Berufsethos und Universaler Moral im Journalismus' in Arnulf KUTSCH, Horst PÖTTKER (eds.), *Kommunikationswissenschaft - autobiographisch: zur Entwicklung einer Wissenschaft in Deutschland*. Wiesbaden, Westdeutscher Verl., 1997, pp. 211-231.

REIMAN, Jeffrey (1984), 'Privacy, Intimacy and Personhood' in SCHOEMAN (ed.), *Philosophical Dimensions*, pp. 300-316.

ROBSON, John (1998), 'Civilization and Culture as Moral Weapons' in John SKORUPSKI (ed.), *The Cambridge Companion to Mill*. Cambridge, Cambridge University Press, pp. 338-371.

SCHOEMAN, Ferdinand (1984), 'Privacy, Philosophical Dimensions of the Literature', in SCHOEMAN (ed.), *Philosophical Dimensions*, pp. 1-33.

SCHRAMM, Wilbur (1956) 'The Social Responsibility Theory' in Fred S. SIEBERT *et al.*, *Four Theories of the Press*. pp. 73-104.

SIEBERT, Fred S. (1956), 'The Libertarian Theory' in Fred S. SIEBERT, Th. PETERSON & Wilbur SCHRAMM, *Four Theories of the Press*. Urbana, University of Illinois Press, pp. 39-72.

TAYLOR, Charles (1995), *Philosophical Arguments*. Cambridge (MA), Harvard University Press.

WARREN, Samuel D., Louis D. BRANDEIS (1980), 'The Right to Privacy — The Implicit Made Explicit', repr. in SCHOEMAN (ed.), *Philosophical Dimensions*, pp. 75-103.

WASSERSTROM, Richard (1984), 'Privacy, Some Arguments and Assumptions' in SCHOEMAN (ed.), *Philosophical Dimensions*, pp. 316-331.

HOW JOURNALISM ETHICS IS TAUGHT AROUND EUROPE: THREE EXAMPLES

Barbara Thomass

In journalism and its decision processes, ethical reflection and the resulting arguments are just one aspect beside other legitimate arguments arising from technical, legal, hierarchical or market-driven considerations. But they have to find their place, if the journalist wishes to fulfil his or her role in society. To be efficient ethics needs an act of reflection. The professional ethics debate needs places in order to be developed, it needs education and training within the areas of professional socialisation as well as in everyday professional discourse. If we wish to raise awareness about journalism ethics and the quality or nature of ethical behaviour, journalism schools and other institutes of journalism education play an important role, as they claim to have the possibilities of providing young journalists with a concept and an ethos of their profession that is adequate for their importance in society. The question of whether or not they fulfil this obligation is the focus of the following article.

After giving an overview of the institutional settings, different school systems and methods of journalism in the countries of the European Union, this article summarises the results of a survey which was done in three countries, namely, France, Britain and Germany. French, British and German representatives of journalism teaching bodies were interviewed as experts about their opinions and ways of teaching ethics.

1. Journalism Education in Europe

In general, we find four types of journalism education all over Europe: on-the-job training, which is often combined with supplementary courses; a full university study programme, including the various aspects of communication studies; schools of journalism; and advanced journalism training or postgraduate studies for people who already hold an academic degree.

The underlying thinking of on-the-job training is the idea that learning by doing is the best way to introduce a novice to the skills and necessities of the job. By allowing the neophyte to work with an experienced collegue who can show him or her the tricks of the trade, the more experienced worker can help improve the practical knowledge of the recruit by correcting his or her daily work. Ethical considerations and the acquisition of a code of practice would accompany the apprentice into his or her introduction to the world of the newsroom. This was the prevailing journalism education pattern in Europe until the end of the Second World War, although a systematic training in schools or universities had already been designed decades before in the United States of America.

With the growing complexitiy of society that the journalist has to cover and the growing knowledge of the communication process of mass media, the aforementioned way of training journalists is no longer considered to be the one and only method of training. But in many European countries on-the-job training is still the only or main way to enter a career in journalism. This is the case in Portugal and in Luxemburg. In Britain, France, and the Netherlands, the number of journalists who enter the job with no special professional training is still considerable but decreasing (Stephenson, Mory, 1990: 9.)

In some countries, for example Germany, it was felt that there should be more systematic education outside of the on-the-job training approach. There, journalists' associations, publishers' and radio and television associations agreed on a curriculum of theoretical courses which were to be followed in addition to the learning by doing method. Such theoretical courses had been optional for years and had been written into a tariff agreement in the beginning of the nineties. We also find, for example in Belgium, institutes for journalism training which are managed by journalists' and publishers' associations. All these models draw on the idea that some fundamental knowledge and insights cannot be taught solely by on-the- job training.

The advent of more theoretically oriented courses gave rise to the academisation of the profession, which led to the establishment of a wide range of journalism and communication studies programmes. Faculties dedicated to the analysis of information in society are much older. *Zeitungswissenschaft*, the study of newspapers, was already established in Germany by the beginning of the last century; 1937 saw the establishment of the Institute for the Science of the Press at the Sorbonne in Paris (Stephenson, Mory, 1990: 10.) But the majority of western European universities established these new programmes during the seventies. The titles of these new programmes varied greatly and reflected the different approaches which combined a practice-orientated education with a theoretical scientific basis: Social communication we find, for example, in Portugal and Belgium, mass communication and media studies in Britain, communication science in the Netherlands and Belgium, information science in Spain, information and communication techniques or information and communication sciences and techniques in France, journalism and communication science in Germany and so forth.

In general, these study programmes consist of a three to five year programme and lead to an officially recognised academic degree. Often, it is demanded that applicants follow a practical training of several weeks before or while following their studies. Sometimes these studies are combined with another programme. For example, economics or political sciences. The advantage of such combinations is that one will be able to bring more expertise of a particular field to one's journalism studies programme, thereby refining one's journalistic acumen.

In the beginning, study-work programmes were not well perceived by the industry, as it was argued that the vocational training would not be sufficient due to the lack of professional equipment within the universities. But the more the faculties of social science, where most of these programmes were located, made efforts to obtain, for example, digital publishing software, audio and video equipment, and limited the enrolment of these study programmes, the more academic journalism education became accepted by employers in the media.

Now, these vocational courses, which lie within programmes often taught by external professional journalists, are combined with traditional social science studies in the field of communication, focusing on universities' traditional strengths: critical analysis and an intellectual foundation which takes into account the social responsibility of the profession. This is why ethics, as a vital part of education, is mostly found and profoundly treated within the journalism programmes of universities.

But schools of journalism are catching up to their university counterparts in this field. They exist more in northern than in southern Europe. They are often founded through private initiatives, as for example, the Journalists' Training Centre in Paris (1924) or the Institute of Higher Studies in Mass Communications in Brussels (1937), or they are initiated by authorities as the Journalists' Training Centre in Lisbon, where the journalistic profession played a role in the efforts to found a private training institute.

Usually the programmes of these schools are shorter than the university ones. Generally, they are three or four years in length (Oporto in Portugal, Aarhus in Denmark), but five year programmes also exist (Cologne, Germany.) It is a common feature of all journalism schools to put stress on vocational training, mostly with the help of a well equipped simulated newsroom. Moreover, general knowledge and analyses are less important or less represented in course syllabi. While universities often offer specialised courses in journalism ethics, these schools tend to integrate the subject into their vocational training programmes.

Recently, the media industry took the initiative to found journalism schools through which they feed their staff needs for their media conglomerates. This is the case, for example, with the Henry-Nannen-School of the German publishing house Gruner & Jahr or the Axel-Springer-Journalism-School. These schools admit, in general, only a very limited number of students who have to pay for their courses and who are admitted only after a special admission screening process.

Postgraduate studies for students already holding an academic degree is the fourth way of journalism education offered in Europe. It is mostly universities which are active in training courses that involve intense vocational training of one or two years. The students have either followed communications-orientated studies during their primary studies or they may have been working as a free-lance journalist and are chosen through a highly competitive procedure. Although these programmes really focus on vocational, even technical training, as the success of the admission offers is dependent on how smooth the candidates enter into the job market, they try to keep the balance between the social and cultural aspects of the profession and the reflections on such aspects. Postgraduate studies are to be found in France, Britain, the Netherlands, Italy, Spain and Sweden. Other countries are involved in developing similar programmes, and this proves that such postgraduate programmes are well regarded within the industry (Stephenson, Mory, 1990: 20.) Ethical considerations are integrated more or less into the whole programme, as the dense syllabi of one or two years do not seem to allow for a deeper treatment of special questions in communication studies and journalism.

2. The Survey

In the following section, we shall investigate the methods of training journalists and the role teaching ethics plays within these various forms of training. We shall focus on three European countries. In France, the recognition of schools of journalism by the profession is important. This importance is affirmed in a national tariff agreement between journalists' organisations and employers. At the time of the survey, this document named eight schools, three of which were private (another private one has applied for official recognition,) three based at universities and three institutes of a university (Rémond 1994, 144.). Academic journalism study programmes and journalism schools require students to complete a two year study programme. All these recognized bodies are decisively oriented to vocational practice. From these nine bodies, five were chosen for the survey, and among those, two based at a university, the other four being private ones. Thus, the sample can be regarded as a representative one. In the United Kingdom, there are two recognizing bodies: the *National Council for the Training of Journalists (NCTJ)* and the *National Council for the Training of Broadcast Journalists (NCTBJ.)* From 18 colleges and universities which offer *NCTJ* recognized journalism programmes four were chosen, representing five programmes. The other interview partners came from *NCTBJ* recognized colleges, and thus were concerned with training broadcast journalists. Furthermore, one academic programme not recognized by either agency was included. Usually these programmes are a year in length and are geared to postgraduates. In Germany, a similar recognising agency does not exist. Therefore, a mixture of relevant journalism education programmes was chosen: two full time study programmes (usually of four years minimum,) one postgraduate programme, one secondary subject programme and two journalism schools.

With the representatives of each of these agencies or regulatory bodies, expert interviews were carried out based on a questionnaire frame of 15 topics. This procedure was chosen because expert interviews and their interpretation allow for the elaboration of the common and non-individual, representative topics, shared structures of relevance, constructions of reality and of meanings (Meuser, Nagel, 1991: 452.) A comparative analysis was employed to investigate the results of the interviews.

2.1 The Significance of Ethical Reflection within Education

Let us begin by examining the significance which is given to ethics in journalism education. Are ethical components inherent to the study aims of the programmes described? In France, journalism education focuses on expertise in journalism and mainly its instrumental competences. Ethical components are to be found only sporadically, as for example, by the demand to *"faire des journalistes compétents, conscients"*. In such a case, the humanistic character of the general education which is given by the programme is underlined. It is expected of young journalists to consider their responsibility when they reconstruct reality. Moreover, in Germany, ethical components are only occasionally to be found in the description of the study goals, for example, competences in conveyance and reflection are aspired to, or like one expert stated, an interiorisation of a moral-ethical framework should be achieved in addition to the perfect mastery of the craft. In the United Kingdom, study aims mainly at the capacities of the students to be fit for the demands of the labour market. One finds, for example, statements like it is necessary "to prepare people to be fully effective working professionals", "to teach them how to be journalists and how to operate as journalists, certainly to start with the provincial newspapers", or "to enable students to be equipped to be employed in the broadcast industry."

During the interviews, the experts made more statements about the relevance and significance they attach to the treatment of ethics during their programmes. The criteria evaluated, therefore, were: (1) The representation of ethics in syllabi. (2) The relevance of ethics as a topic for examination. (3) Projected or desired changes in the curricula. (4) Cooperative efforts with other persons or outside bodies concerning a topic.

Similar results were found for the French and the German programmes concerning the weight ethics should have in journalism education and the efforts to put this into practice. In the United Kingdom, the answers of the experts signal a fundamental change in the sense that more importance should be given to the topic. But most of the experts seem to feel isolated in these efforts because they think their colleagues have not yet recognized the need for it.

Counterdistinguished from the above-mentioned similarities, the aims pursued in the teaching of ethics are very different from country to country. In Germany, those aims are oriented to fundamental principles — "deference toward human beings" seems to be a fundamental principle or a certain aspect in the behaviour of the single journalist. In France, principles are not that important. Here, statements which underline the intellectual capacity of journalists are more important. While in Germany characteristics such as "having a backbone," being able to resist, maintaining an upright position or conflict abilities are regarded as being important aims of dealing with ethics. French experts focus on intellectual qualities: the ability to think about problems, the capacity to reflect and argue in the field of ethics. Their colleagues from the United Kingdom give precedence in their teaching to sound reflection and action, especially in crisis situations.

2.2 Content of Teaching Ethics

Among the answers concerning contents of ethics seminars or aspects of journalism ethics which are dealt with, there were many hints about fundamental ideas in the minds of the interviewed persons that can be referred to as concepts of ethics in journalism. They are important for teaching as they deliver the background from which these experts teach.

Hence, two dimensions are specific within the concepts found in Germany: concentration on the individual and accentuation of responsibility. In nearly all interviews, quotations can be found which consider, in both dimensions, the responsibility of the individual to be postulated and which demand that such responsibility should be fulfilled, even against constraints and even if the responsibility of the individual is put into question because of negative conditions. But, as educators are strongly motivated by the task to educate journalists for their future profession, the focus of attention within the ethical debate is on the individual. The accentuation of individual responsibility is the dominating characteristic feature of nearly every answer in France as well. Individual responsibility is stressed when statements are made about a general professional ethos, the realization of which in practical actions, is regarded nevertheless as incumbent on the individual. The postulation, however, of individual responsibility is strongly relativised. Thus, there are statements which account for a bigger amount of responsibility falling to editors-in-chief. These statements underline the collective process of decision-making concerning ethical questions or they stress the interdependency and interaction of individual and collective responsibility in the newsroom. Most of the British experts have a concept of a graduated responsibility, according to which the conditions of the newsroom, the media enterprise, market mechanisms and the media system have to be taken into account, as they determine the space of free action for the individual (see chapter on journalism ethics.)

Ethical norms in journalism are based on ethical theories either of philosophical origin or stemming from communication science. It may deepen the comprehension of foundation and legitimation of professional norms, if students know about them, and thus may be reasonable ingredients of those parts of the curricula which deal with ethics. But only the full time study programmes in Germany consider this necessary, and teach history of ethics in philosophy where normative aspects of journalism are embedded. The experts from the other bodies absolutely reject this approach or reduce it to a discussion of contributions from communication science.

The strongly vocational character of the French education programmes gives reason to the supposition that they do not treat ethics in a theoretical way by referring to philosophy. And this is true. All experts clearly refuse to present such texts to their students.

Likewise, the British experts do not treat ethics in a theoretical way. They argue that there is not enough time for this approach, that education has to be oriented to future professional life in a practical way and that students would not comprehend these ideas.

2.3 Ethical Problems in Professional Practice

A substantial amount of those parts of the curricula dealing with ethics is dedicated to ethical problems of the practice of professional life. Therefore, the interviews had questions concerning the significance of such practical problems within the contexts of lecturing and teaching. The significance of the problem of corruption and corruptibility, for example, is considered in Germany to range from being central to being marginal. Furthermore, the standards the experts demand in this field from future journalists are also very different. The majority of the statements agree that it is necessary to define the point where corruption begins, and this with the help of real cases. While corruptibility has been a huge topic within the debate of the scientific community in France, which had damaged the credibility of journalism severely, it is not a real topic within education. The prevalent pattern in the statements is that it is up to one's inividual judgement to decide whether or not a journalist is being bribed or corrupted by accepting gifts. Thus, the issue remains on an unreflective, subjective level. British as well as German experts do not agree upon whether or not the corruptibility of journalists is an important issue to be discussed with students. There are some who consider it to be a marginal problem within British journalism, and thus not very important as a topic of journalism education; others see a danger emerging from strategies involving journalists in biased projects, and consequently treat this topic within journalism education.

Statements about the protection of privacy in France are much more central, an issue that is considered as representative of public life. The interviewed persons defend the French unwritten rule that the private life of politicians should not be reported. German responses raise once again the problem of setting limits. For example, which sphere of private life should be protected? And again the range of opinions varies widely from the defence of the principle that private life should be taboo for journalists to the idea that the concept of a private life is in a state of dissolution. The relevance of the issue is acknowledged for both persons of public life and for unknown citizens. All experts consider it an important issue for journalism education. In the United Kingdom, discussions about a law for the protection of privacy have witnessed a long standing public debate. But this is not being reflected in the statements of the experts. On the contrary, there is rather an approach of relativisation. For example, there is the push to connect the issue to the question of access to information, access being rather restricted in the UK , or some wish to leave it up to the individual to decide how far he or she wants to intrude on a person's privacy.

Questioned about methods of research and investigation, experts in Germany wanted to achieve the highest standard possible in so far as they wanted to find as much information as possible in a given amount of time by fair means. But opinions differed on how to find criteria for this standard. It was rare that the experts outright refused methods like eavesdropping or the methods of the paparazzi. But more often than not they pled for a careful consideration of the methods of investigation at one's disposal. This approach is of no relevance in those schools where practical hints for investigative journalism are at the fore. Besides the justification of investigative methods, experts gave comparable importance to the question of whether or not there is any investigating involved at all and whether or not young journalists can achieve a certain competence in this field.

British experts likewise judge this issue as important, but they differ according to the depth at which the issue is treated. Rather pragmatically, it is dealt with when the question of the further relationship with the source is at the fore. As investigative reporting in British journalism has a high reputation, it is in the opinion of the experts very important to make students aware of the ethical implications of such proceedings. The ruthless behaviour which is favoured and demanded in some parts of the British press, especially the tabloid papers, has obviously sensitised the experts. They dedicate a considerable part of their teaching to it, and want to develop criteria which might serve as guidelines for professional behaviour.

The majority of the French experts are convinced that ethical problems concerning investigative methods are best dealt with during practical journalistic exercises. Concomitantly, they state that a journalist who is well acquainted with professional rules will not be in danger of ethical misconduct. In particular, checking facts and the treatment of reality are considered dimensions which are easily dealt with in practical exercises where it is important to raise awareness and sensibility. Furthermore, some schools present investigative methods with which students are not yet confronted during their education, but which are nonetheless relevant. For example, ways to obtain documents in an unauthorized or deceitful way. But none of the experts is willingly to deliver guidelines for these problems. As well, one expert states that one should be allowed to ignore the guidelines given by the French journalists' charter, if such a decision is well balanced and has been made in conjunction with his/her colleagues in the newsroom.

In view of the difficulty of accessing official information in France, one could assume that protections of sources plays a significant role in professional life and in journalists' education as well. But this is not the case. Although they concede that it is an important issue and that they present it in their teaching, French experts tend to be satisfied simply to inform the students about the legal prescriptions in that field. In Germany, however, opinions about protection of sources are very heterogeneous. For some experts, it is a primary precept, and thus must be presented to students with a high priority. Others believe that this issue is not at all important for teaching. In the United Kingdom, experts are well aware that there exists no law for the protection of sources such that they have to raise awareness among students that students could come into conflict with the law, if they follow this journalistic rule. But there are also views that it is difficult to treat the issue within a practical education.

Codes of ethics or practice may serve as the guidelines the experts were looking for according to several responses. But the *Principles of the German Press Council* do not play a very important role in German journalism schools. The university study programmes deal with them in any case, although they are judged as ranging from "unalterable, but not sufficient" to a slight "we refer to it." In the United Kingdom, there are several codes. The *Code of Practice* of the *Press Council* does not have a reputation comparable to the German text, as it is perceived as being too influenced by the industry. The competing codes of the journalists' organisations are not that widely spread. Thus, British experts are rather sceptical about their professional codes. Their answers range from "better that than to have none" and "useless." French experts have the symbolic character of codes in mind. The answers give the impression that they regard the presentation of these text as an obligation, but that they are not very convinced theses codes could be effective or legitimate.

2.4 *Methods of Teaching Ethics*

"You cannot teach ethics." This opinion was to be found several times in the French interviews. If we consider the widely found conviction that dealing with ethics during journalism education is necessary, it is of special interest. Hence the question of which methods are to be used to present ethical questions and norms. As ethical decisions are dependent on an enormous amount of real circum-

stances, ethical reflection has to be embedded in practical considerations — this is the prevailing idea. In French journalism schools,
methods of dealing with ethics are completely directed to practical
and experience-based treatment and to the discussion of current
examples and case studies. Besides practical exercises, which com-
prise in any given programme a great amount of time, students have
to report on their practical training in a real newsroom which is a
part of the programme as well. And this is another forum where ethical questions based on their new experiences are discussed.

British experts generally refused a systematic approach to the
teaching of ethics and favoured a practical approach. The majority of
the answers show that students are confronted with prepared case
studies presenting a specific ethical problem about which the students have to discuss or write. The experts prefer this method
because it allows for a clear input, and offers students a glance at the
real problems of professional life. Moreover, it is also regarded as a
disadvantage, as the experiences of students are not taken into consideration. This is why some experts prefer to focus on problems students face during their practical exercises, preferring to explore ethical dimensions with the help of such problems.

In Germany, only some study programmes offer specific courses
about journalism ethics and only some experts consider this to be
reasonable. Prevailing is the agreement that the issue has to be integrated into the whole curriculum. Dependent on the character of the
programme, the focus lies on treating ethics mainly within practical
exercises or within course work. The greatest variety is presented by
one expert who uses as methods lecturing, elaborating ethical topics
within theoretical course work, discussing case studies and explor-
ing ethical dimensions in the journalistic output of the students.
Journalism schools which refuse to offer seminars with theoretical
input prefer exercises in developing journalistic skills and discussions
with experienced journalists to deal with the question of ethics. All
experts agree on the importance of a case- oriented approach to
ethics, whereas they differ in how they treat the cases. Another
method of dealing with ethics is the already mentioned form of letting students report on their experiences during a stay in a real newsroom or to organise debates about those experiences.

Considering the variety of possibilities of dealing with journalism
ethics in education as, for example, practiced in many programmes
in the United States, the amount of methods used in these three

European countries is rather modest. According to a study of the *Accrediting Council on Education in Journalism and Mass Communication (ACEJMC)*, the offering of specific ethics courses is combined with the integration of ethical issues in the whole programme. And a list of methods shows many possibilities:

> Ethical decision making case studies...
> Lectures...
> Explanations of principles...
> Short, periodic written assignments...
> Research papers...
> Small group discussions...
> Lectures by outside professionals...
> Students' presentations of topics...
> Role playing...
> In-depth study of selected issues...
> Panels of opposing viewpoints...
> Simulation games...
> Students report interviews with professionals...
> Lectures by academics from other departments...
> Novels or plays... (Lambeth *et al.* 1994, 24.)

3. Conclusion

Looking at the comparative study of how ethics is taught in three Western European countries, some generalizations may show the following results. Differences are not that big as may have been assumed.

French as well as German bodies give comparable weight to ethics in journalism education and show a similar effort to put this into practice, whereas in the United Kingdom, the situation is changing from a rather marginal dealing with the issue to a greater consideration. But there are differences concerning the aims of studies: In Germany, they are oriented to a certain attitude such as "showing backbone", defending an upright position, and to fundamental principles. In France, intellectual abilities are regarded as more important. British experts maintain as study aims the competence to reflect about ethical problems, taking into account the given circumstances of the media system.

If we compare the contents of teaching of ethics, a generalisation can be made with regard to two dimensions: While French experts are rather willing to leave decisions of professional ethical problems up to the individual, their German colleagues repeatedly try to find criteria for defining limits, thereby giving an objective foundation to decisions. In the United Kingdom, there is a tendency to offer help for decision-making in those fields where a problem is already well known and discussed (protection of sources, methods of investigation,) whereas problems in other fields are left to the individual to decide.

French teachers in journalism concentrate on intellectual abilities, and thus rely on having created the preconditions for such individual decision making. In German journalism education, the experts try to provide objective norms, and thus give a reliable foundation for their demand of a consequentialist behaviour. In the United Kingdom, the relationship between the guideline-oriented approach and individual discretion within journalistic, ethical decision-making is not clearly defined yet, as the treatment of the topic is evidently in considerable flux. When no evident problem arises where norms are developed and desired, the decision is left up to the individual.

Comparing the statements about the content of the teaching of ethics, a second result can be seen: There is a wider range of judgements concerning the mentioned conflicts in Germany and the United Kingdom, whereas French experts are more in agreement concerning these problems. Protection of privacy, protection of sources or the possibility of the corruption of journalists, the opinion about the relevance of these subjects is more polarized in these two countries.

Comparing the methods French, British and German experts use in teaching ethics, a greater variety was found in Germany, but this is due to the more heterogeneous character of the chosen bodies. Furthermore, the greater importance French and British journalism schools give to experience-oriented methods in comparison to the German ones has to be seen within the context of their homogeneity. In Germany, a systematic-theoretical approach is more important, and this is because of the weight of academic programmes.

Nevertheless, an inverse outcome seems to be plausible: The acceptance of greater individual discretion coincides with an approach based on experience. A systematic theoretical approach allows for the development of a foundation and objectivation of ethical decisions. National specificities that led to greater differences in perceiving ethical problems and ideas about their solutions (see, Thomaß, 1998) were not that important in the field of teaching ethics in journalism education.

References

LAMBETH, Edward *et al.* (1994), 'Role of the Media Ethics Course in the Education of Journalists' in *Journalism Educator* (1994) Autumn, pp. 20-26.

MEUSER, Michael, Ulrike NAGEL (1991), 'Expert Inneninterviews — vielfach erprobt, wenig bedacht. Ein Beitrag zur qualitativen Methodendiskussion' in Detlef GARZ, Klaus KRAIMER (eds.), *Qualitativ-empirische Sozialforschung. Konzepte, Methoden, Analysen.* Opladen.

RÉMOND, Edith (1991), 'À propos de la formation des journalistes' in *Le supplément: Revue d'éthique et théologie morale* 90(1991), pp. 143-146.

STEPHENSON, Hugh, Pierre MORY (1990), *Journalism Training in Europe*, (ed.) European Journalism Training Association and Commission of the European Communities.

THOMAß, Barbara (1998), *Journalistische Ethik. Ein Vergleich der Diskurse in Frankreich, Großbritannien und Deutschland.* Opladen.

PART IV

ETHICS OF
MEDIA USERS

ETHICS FOR MEDIA USERS

Cees J. Hamelink

Most work in the field of media ethics focuses on media producers. From such early classics as Merrill and Barney (1975) to more recent studies by Christians, Ferré, and Fackler (1993), most books on media ethics deal with the resolution of moral dilemmas media producers face in the execution of their profession. The existing codes of professional ethics address the rights and wrongs of professional producers. Explorations of media morality (such as reported in the *Journal of Mass Media Ethics*) almost exclusively deal with the moral problems of the messengers and their messages. Many journalists' bodies have adopted codes of ethics for the self-regulation of professional conduct. Press councils around the world deliberate and judge the standards by which producers should behave. A key concern of this producer-centred activity in media ethics is the quest for professional freedom, quality, and responsibility in media performance. Freedom specifically refers, in this context, to efforts to maximise editorial independence and minimise external interference. Quality refers to completeness, diversity, reliability, independence, and impartiality of media reporting. Responsibility refers to professional attitudes towards colleagues, sources, and clients. It also refers to the assumption of accountability for media products. This quest is inspired by the unprecedented capacity and reach of the mass media and people's reliance on them. The insight that media performance is critical to the degree of democratic participation in societies produces a strong incentive to protect media freedom, to maintain high quality standards and to ensure responsible professional attitudes.

However laudable all the efforts in the field of professional ethics may be, they leave the issues of freedom, quality and responsibility the sole concern of the professional. This is odd since professions necessarily imply relationships between professionals and clients.

In most professional codes, there are provisions that deal with this relationship. Professionals are expected to respect the autonomy of their clients, to avoid abuse of the vulnerable position of the client, to inform the client fully and honestly, to maintain the confidentiality of the communication, and to act with expertise and carefulness. The client is present in the prescriptions for professional conduct since (as in most journalistic codes) the obligations of the professional are based upon the rights to which the clients are entitled. A perspective shared by many professional codes is that since clients have the right to receive opinions, information and ideas, they should be properly informed about matters of public interest. This relation with the clients has also been resoundingly endorsed by several decisions of the European Court of Human Rights.

All this attention paid to the client is, however, still a rather one-sided approach to the relationship. It would seem more accurate to perceive of the professional-client relation as an interactive process which depends upon a mutual commitment. This also implies that the client actively contributes to the professional performance. Some thirty years ago, Wilbur Schramm addressed this in a chapter on responsibilities of the government, the media, and the public. Schramm pointed to a shared responsibility for the quality of mass communication by public regulatory bodies, the media themselves, and the general public. "The listening, viewing, reading public underestimates its power" (Rivers, Schramm, 1969: 249), Schramm wrote, and he suggested the need for alert and discriminating audiences.

Many years later, in a book written from the practitioner's experience, Mort Rosenblum took up the notion of shared responsibility for the quality of international reporting. Current world news leaves us with enormous gaps in our knowledge about the world, and Rosenblum blames this on media managers who are obsessed with ratings and earnings and who prefer entertainment over information. But, he also blames the correspondents who distort the facts and fall victim to the pollsters and the PR firms. Rosenblum provides many illustrations of how the professionals fail. However, he also includes the general public in his analysis of the problem: "If the suppliers have not done better, it is because consumers have not demanded it... If surgeons or plumbers foul up, they are sued. But who asks about the people who presume to be covering the world? Customers howl when a merchant does them wrong. Why do newspeople get off so easily?" (Rosenblum, 1993: 287)

If one accepts the interactive character of the professional-client relationship, it follows that media ethics cannot be limited to the rights and wrongs of the producers only. It should also be an ethics for media users. The case for user ethics can be defended by demonstrating that not only producers but also users face moral choices in connection with media freedom, quality and responsibility. Such choices come about when users are faced with situations in which alternative paths of action are available that represent different values. Actually, moral choices imply preferences for a type of action that is awarded a higher value than a possible alternative.

Users and Freedom

Restrictions on media freedom are often the combined efforts of censors, collaborative media producers and consenting users.

During the Gulf War, people were kept ignorant but many also preferred to remain ignorant. As Ronald Dworkin observed, "Truth may be the first casualty of war, but some people's desire to be told the truth is a close second." (Dworkin, 1991: 2) This could be supported by the finding that nearly eight out of ten Americans supported the Pentagon restrictions on the press and six said that the military should exert more control. Eight out of ten said the press did an excellent job and over 60% thought the press coverage was accurate. [1] The war demonstrated that official censorship, journalistic self-censorship, and the users' refusal to be informed reinforced each other. The complicity of users was an essential component in the reduction of freedom of the media performance.

In cases such as war reporting, users can actively or passively support censorship or act against it by monitoring mainstream media, raise censorship issues in local media, join anti-censorship groups, start anti-censorship campaigns, or boycott products from censors.[2]

The widespread practice of governmental and corporate secrecy provides yet another illustration of possible user complicity in reducing access to information. This can be very harmful as it ham-

---

[1] Reported in the *International Herald Tribune* of February 1, 1991.

[2] A similar experience occurred in a more recent war, the NATO war against the Federal Republic of Yugoslavia in 1999. Once again, most international media functioned in highly biased, selective and partisan ways and little did most audiences care.

pers people's understanding and blocks the knowledge of alternatives. If consumers condone the withholding of information about matters that affect their well-being, they themselves fail in their duty to inquire about what governments and major corporations (for example in nuclear technology, automobile manufacturing, or chemical waste production) are doing. Most people who want access to this type of information have to rely upon the mass media as professional intermediaries. This implies that they have to monitor whether the media indeed fulfil this mediating role. They also have to contribute to the necessary conditions for the mass media to do so, for example, by providing popular support for the protection of editorial independence.

When users feel very strongly about certain moral issues and expect the professionals to confirm their preferences, they may be tempted to exercise pressure on editorial policies. This can easily lead to populist censorship that interferes with editorial independence. Users have to decide whether their occasional moral panic about media's anti social contents is justified. They have to question whether harmful acts result from these contents and whether the perceived harm is so serious that it warrants the attempt at censorship.

Users and Quality

We can observe across the world that ordinary people have begun to take responsibility for the quality of their primary, natural environment. The ecological movement demonstrates this quite convincingly. This active concern about human conduct in relation to all forms of non-human life is a moral choice people make. Largely in response to their primary, natural environment, human beings create a secondary environment. This is the human-made cultural environment in which the mass media are crucial tools.
One could also argue that the degree of concern *vis-à-vis* this secondary environment is a matter of moral choice. If people withdraw from this concern, they make the choice not to take responsibility for its quality.

In most societies, people are, at present, not overly concerned about the quality of the cultural environment. By and large, people are more worried about the killing of whales than about the killing of minority TV-programmes. However, since the cultural environment is as essential to our common future as the natural environment, one may well argue that people's movements should begin to focus on the production and distribution of information. If people refuse to be silenced and do not want to live with a massive choreography of televised violence, they cannot trust states and markets to accommodate their communication needs. They will have to take action themselves. If people do not want to be surrounded by electronic surveillance, political propaganda, or by the incessant appeal to consumerism, they cannot be complacent about existing communication structures. It could well be that the degree of people's concern about the cultural environment represents one of the most critical moral questions of our civilisation.

Users and Responsibility

In a variety of situations, media users can become important sources of media reporting. This raises questions for the way they behave. Users can provide honest or deceptive accounts. They can act as unreliable sources who confidently make claims about areas about which they have no knowledge or who over dramatise the events they have witnessed. Users can offer their information for free or they can try to make a profit and accept payment for an exclusive story. The latter practice of "chequebook journalism' is currently on the rise. People may be offered a good deal of money, if they reveal personal secrets.

The practice whereby the highest bidder acquires exclusive rights to a story, violates the principle of the freedom to gather information. It also raises serious questions about protection of privacy since the information offered often concerns other people's private lives.

An irresponsible practice, such as the distribution of deceptive information, is an issue for both the deceiver and the deceived. Being deceived implies disempowerment and loss of autonomy. This is however not the sole responsibility of the messenger.

Autonomy is not an ideal located somewhere outside us and dependent upon whether or not an external agent grants it.

Rephrasing a statement by Paolo Freire, we could say that it is the task of the deceived to liberate themselves and their deceivers. (Freire, 1972: 21)

In more and more countries media users have the legal possibility to use the right of reply. This right has also been incorporated into the Council of Europe's Convention on Transborder Television. Users will have to question to what extent this right should be used. There are examples of where this right has been deployed to take up large portions of media space/time for self-serving purposes. Users should question whether this is a responsible attitude.

Responsibility also implies that media users actively demand accountability from media producers. This confronts them with the choice of being for or against active participation in citizen organisations that monitor media performance or in representative policy making bodies in the media.

Media-Consumer Initiatives

There is presently an increasing number of initiatives around the world through which ordinary people are beginning to express a concern about mass media performance. Examples include such initiatives as

The Friends of Canadian Broadcasting, which, since 1985, is a constituency of advocates for public broadcasting representing over 36,000 families.

The Charter of Rights of Television Viewers, drawn up by the French Association of Television Viewers in 1991.

The Charter of Television Viewer's Rights, proposed by the Japanese Forum for Citizen's TV in 1992.

The Communication, Information and Networking Alternative Treaty, which was signed by non-governmental organisations during the 1992 UNCED in Rio de Janeiro and which stipulated, among other provisions, the right of all people to communicate, to collect, to disseminate and to exchange all information they choose.

The Charter for the Reader, adopted by the International Book Committee in 1992.

The Voice of the Listener and Viewer Society, which held an international conference in London in April 1993 attended by 125 representatives from 40 countries.

The Declaration entitled, *Responsibility in a Media-based Society* which was adopted by a working group of the European Television and Film Forum in January 1994 at Düsseldorf. This TV consumer's declaration was drawn up as an expression of the needs and interests of viewers and addresses the more active role of consumers in relation to TV.

The Declaration on New Technologies and the Democratisation of Audiovisual Communication, adopted by the participants of the 1994 International Symposium convened by Vidéazimut and CENDIT in New Delhi, India.

The US-based Cultural Environment Movement, which is a non-profit corporation that builds a broad constituency and takes lessons from the environmental movement in creating a freer, fairer and more diverse cultural environment. The movement forms a coalition of media, professional, labour, religious, environmental, health-related, and women's and minority groups working for liberation on the cultural front.

The Initiative to launch a *People's Communication Charter*. This is the beginning of the creation of a broad international movement of alert and demanding media users. The People's Communication Charter is an initiative that originated in 1991 with the Third World Network (Penang, Malaysia), the Centre for Communication & Human Rights (Amsterdam, the Netherlands), the Cultural Environment Movement (USA), the World Association of Community Radio Broadcasters (AMARC) and the World Association for Christian Communication. The Charter provides the common framework for all those who share the belief that people should be active and critical participants in their social reality and that people are capable of governing themselves. The People's Communication Charter could be a first step in the development of a permanent movement concerned with the quality of the communication/cultural environment.

Most present attempts to mobilise media users mainly address what governments and broadcasting organisations should do and what rights consumers have. This is, undoubtedly, very important in the process of raising awareness about the need for active participation of audiences in the improvement of media quality and the democratisation of media programme policy and management.

However, claims of the representation of viewers' needs and interests in TV broadcasting and to the representation of television consumers' interests in processes of media legislation could be self-defeating, if they do not recognise the implications for the conduct of the users.

Media consumption should be viewed, like professional media performance, as a social practice which implies moral choices and the assumption of accountability for these choices.

Conclusion

The concern for mass media performance concerns not only media producers. It also involves client communities. The interactive relation between professionals and clients also implies that media users have moral choices to make and have to assume accountability for these choices. The design of user ethics should be inspired by ethical inquiry and not be limited to moralistic rules of conduct. Such rules fail to address the core problem of moral decision-making. Media users cannot obviously be coerced into the exercise of ethical inquiry. This is a voluntary project, and it be could asked why one would expect users to actually care about moral choice in connection with media use. A provisional answer points to three considerations.

First, it can be argued that for many people who are already committed to a concern about media performance, it may be a relatively small step from their current narrow focus on other agents to include their own role as well.

Second, it may well be that a growing number of media users have a latent concern about media performance, for example, parents about incessant volumes of violence, but they have not yet found a concrete articulation or platforms of expression.

Third, it would not seem unrealistic to expect, based upon experiences in other areas of life, that this latent concern can be used to generate an active interest in user ethics among numerous civil groups and individuals.

It should also be stressed that media ethics is part of the broader moral inquiry into the state of the human being. In recent years, it has acquired a particular urgency since the mass media are in the forefront of confronting us with the historical reality of dehumanization on a grand scale, and therefore, with the question about the possibility of humanisation. In this quandary two positions offer themselves as obvious and convenient solutions. The cynical position makes all moral reasoning meaningless because it views dehumanisation as the only historical reality. This position borders on moral indifference. The fundamentalist position accepts only one mould of humanity and elevates its particularist moral bias to a universal principle. This position borders on moral terror.

The challenge to avoid both extreme positions needs the joint effort of media producers and media users. For this effort, a contextual and communicative media ethics is needed that engages both professionals and clients in an open-ended, public and free inquiry into some of the most crucial moral choices of our time.

References

CHRISTIANS, C.G., J.P. FERRÉ, P.M. FACKLER (1993), *Good News: Social ethics & the Press.* New York, Oxford University Press.

DWORKIN, R. (1991), *Index on Censorship.* Nos 4 & 5.

FREIRE, P. (1972), *Pedagogy of the Oppressed.* Harmondsworth, Penguin.

HABERMAS, J. (1993), *Moral Consciousness and Communicative Action.* Cambridge (MA), The MIT Press.

MERRILL, J.C., R.D. BARNEY (1975), *Ethics and the Press. Readings in Mass Media Morality.* New York, Hastings House.

RIVERS, W.L., W. SCHRAMM (1969), *Responsibility in Mass Communication.* New York, Harper & Row.

ROSENBLUM, M. (1993), *Who Stole the News?* New York, John Wiley & Sons.

FUNDAMENTAL QUESTIONS OF AUDIENCE ETHICS

Rüdiger Funiok

Although they are the addressees and the target group of media products, the 'purchasers' of these products are usually neglected in the questions of media ethics as Hamelink has put it in the previous chapter. Reference is quickly made to the professional ethics of journalists, which are relatively clearly formalised in codes of behaviour; furthermore, the professional practice of journalists and others working in the communications sector is regulated by media laws. Moreover, there are no formalised codes of behaviour in audience ethics; the only legal regulation taken into consideration is the passing of laws for the protection of (one's own) children.

The question of which principles should be valid in a democratic media system is a pertinent subject of discussion in media ethics. Is it just the market forces, the competition of commercial services that are to play a role, or should societal notions about the cultural and democratic importance of media offerings be taken into account as well? As technical developments lead to a convergence of formerly distinct media divisions and necessitate a unified media order, these communitarian principles may and should be newly formulated and asserted now. Demands are not predominantly made on national parliaments and European bodies, but on the media industry, whose task it is to be sensitive to the claims of every audience group, including the socially underprivileged.[1] Yet, universal, uniform regularisation will not be possible, for, although there is a uniform worldwide market, cultures and societies are too heterogeneous to allow a single code of behaviour for media producers or a single nettiquette for the internet. A persistent plurality and non-controllability increasingly involves the users' media literacy, which in most cases is strongly

---

[1] Cf. for example Matthias KARMASIN, *Medienökonomie: Medienökonomie als Theorie (massen-)medialer Kommunikation.* Graz/Wien, Nausner & Nausner, 1998.

emphasised only verbally, whereas there is no mention made of the fact that media literacy needs to be supported through carefully directed educational processes and measures in media politics.

A similar silence reigns when it comes to the foundations of media literacy in an 'ethos of the audience.' What does the audience's responsibility consist in? A closer elaboration of this point is the task of audience ethics. Although the focus of this chapter will be on the issue of the audience's responsibility, reference will be made throughout to the necessary contributions of educational and political measures in order to avoid restricting the discussion to an ethics of individual duties.

1. The Question of Adequate Terminology

One of the difficulties of this subdivision of media ethics is posed by its irregular terminology. The different possible terms, including recipient, consumer, audience, user, are by no means equivalent; rather, they express divergent notions about the activity of media use.

The advantage of the term 'recipient' lies in its comprehensive applicability across the range of different media: Although people reading print media, listening to radio broadcasts and watching television use different media for different reasons in different social and individual situations, they may all be called 'recipients.' The drawback of this term lies in its being connotated with the notion of a passive reception of informative and entertaining offerings suggested by its etymology (Latin recipere: 'receive'). The concept of an *active* recipient is found in educators formulating a normative ideal or educational aim, and there are similar approaches in a descriptive science of communication which regard the reception of informations as an active, problem-solving process.[2]

The term 'consumer' emphasises the acquisitive consumption of media offerings as well as the economic aspect of the communication process. Media offerings are regarded as and reduced to com-

---

[2] Cf. Christoph NEUBERGER, 'Was das Publikum wollen könnte. Autonome und repräsentative Bewertung journalistischer Leistungen' in Hartmut WESSLER et. al. (eds.), *Perspektiven der Medienkritik: Die gesellschaftliche Auseinandersetzung mit öffentlicher Kommunikation in der Mediengesellschaft. Dieter Roß zum 50. Geburtstag.* Opladen/Wiesbaden, Westdeutscher Verlag, 1997, pp. 171-184, esp. pp. 174-179.

modities or commercial services, which leads to a lack of attention towards the far-reaching functions and achievements of mass media within the public communication of a society.

A democratic society requires the formation of public opinion through comprehensive, informative mass media, responsible for publishing and making accessible to their audience all politically relevant information. It is the audience's responsibility to welcome this information, as a part of the bulk of entertaining media offerings, with interest and critical ability. Thus, the term 'audience ethics' carries an indispensable political connotation.

Finally, there is the (active and selective) 'media user.' This fourth term stresses individual activity and the possibility of selection. Selectivity is possible and permanently required not only in the new media (interactivity) but also in the traditional mass media whose offers are received and digested through a form of internal activity.

This point is emphasised by more recent approaches within the science of communication, which regard media users no longer merely as objects of mass communication, but as subjects imparting subjective meaning to and interpretatively assimilating the offered contents. This perspective is manifest in the increasing appreciation of qualitative methods used, especially in educationally motivated recipient research, to investigate the subjective processes of selection and assimilation. According to Wolfgang Wunden, this 'Copernican turn' towards the subject underpins the basic assumption of all audience ethics, namely, the media users' activity. "Ethics can only be meaningful where actions are taken by individuals who are responsible for what they do or for what happens in a situation or a process which they have contributed to through their attitudes and actions."[3] To Wunden, the late 'discovery' of the importance of media users in the areas of media history and communication theory is one of the reasons that within the framework of media ethics, questions of audience ethics have been discussed only within the last 15 years.

---

[3] "Ethik kann ja nur einen Sinn haben, wo Personen handeln, die verantwortlich sind für etwas, was sie tun, oder für etwas, was in einer Situation oder in einem Prozeß sich ereignet, zu der bzw. zu dem sie durch ihre Haltung und ihre Handlungen beitragen." Wolfgang WUNDEN, 'Vom Ethos des Rezipienten' in *Communicatio Socialis*, 14(1981), pp. 15-22, here p. 16f.

2. Responsibility as Point of Departure

When in everyday life and everyday language the question of morally right or good action and inaction is posed, in most cases the term 'responsibility' is referred to. In specialised philosophical discussions, too, the concept of responsibility serves as a widely accepted key category. Although there are also attempts to conceive of morality in terms of justice (Rawls), the term 'responsibility' is undoubtedly used more frequently.

Following the philosophers of ethics in technology, C. Hubig[4] and G. Ropohl[5], B. Debatin[6] points out six elements or relations of responsibility: Who — What (action) — Before whom — Before what — What for — Why. To me, what seems especially relevant is his distinction between individual and collective action with regard to the 'What' of responsibility. Although strictly speaking, only individuals can be responsible subjects, action (e.g., that of journalists) takes place within a corporative context (the editorial department) and social conditions. They are responsible for their professional actions before their individual conscience and the group ethos, but also before the public.

The audience, or the audiences, constitute social quantities. The use of television frequently takes place, especially in the learning phase of childhood, within the social framework of the family. But even where there is an individual who listens to the radio, reads the papers, watches TV or uses a computer, this individual will introduce the information gained in this way into conversations with others. The audience, however, lacks social organisation. Effective action requires the activity of individuals (writing letters to the editor, sending programme reviews to broadcasting stations and to internet providers) or the initiative of TV monitoring circles or similar media watchdogs.

---

[4] Christoph HUBIG, *Technik- und Wissenschaftsethik. Ein Leitfaden.* Berlin/Heidelberg/New York, Springer, 1993.

[5] Günter ROPOHL, 'Neue Wege, die Technik zu verantworten' in Hans LENK, Günter ROPOHL (eds.), *Technik und Ethik.* Stuttgart, Reclam, 1993, pp. 149-176.

[6] Bernhard DEBATIN, 'Medienethik als Steuerungsinstrument? Zum Verhältnis von individueller und korporativer Verantwortung in der Massenkommunikation' in Hartmut WEßLER *et al.* (eds.), *Perspektiven der Medienkritik: Die gesellschaftliche Auseinandersetzung mit der öffentlichen Kommunikation in der Mediengesellschaft. Dieter Roß zum 60. Geburtstag.* Opladen/Wiesbaden, Westdeutscher Verlag, 1997, pp. 287-303.

2.1 *The Three Areas of Responsibility*

Regarding the 'What for' of responsibility, three fundamental problems or clusters of duties may be distinguished.[7] In all their actions
and inactions human beings are responsible:

1. For themselves, with respect to the chances and possibilities of
their personal development as individuals and with respect to securing their personal liberty.

2. For their social environment, with respect to the chances of the
personal development of others; here, the central problem is that of
the equitable togetherness of human beings and, consequently, the
realisation of social claims and rights.

3. For their natural environment, with respect to its preservation
as the foundation of life for themselves and future generations.

These three areas are correlated to the fundamental questions of
individual acceptability, social acceptability and environmental
acceptability.

These fundamental questions may now be applied to the use of
media within leisure time. Thus, audience ethics asks the questions:
What does self-responsible choice of media mean? What does self-
determined use of media in the service of personal development
mean? How does the use of media become individually acceptable
and non-acceptable? Certainly, we have to begin with the motives
and needs (information and knowledge, but also entertainment,)
and in this area everyone is free to set their own priorities. Still,
audience ethics asks: By which manners of media use is personal
development and individual liberty promoted, by which is it
impeded?

Furthermore, what does socially acceptable use of media mean?
How is my reading the paper, my use of radio and TV or my online-
communication changed by my not only satisfying my individual
needs, but equally respecting the rights of others? Is it not my duty
to consider the political role of the media and the conditions for
truthful information and lucid commentaries?

And finally, what could an environmentally acceptable use of
media look like? How can user behaviour contribute to limiting the
paper consumption of print media, or at least the consumption of
new paper? How can the consumption of electricity in electronic

---

[7] Cf. Stephan FELDHAUS, *Verantwortbare Wege in eine mobile Zukunft: Grundzüge
einer Ethik des Verkehrs.* Hamburg, Abera Verlag Meyer & Co., 1998, pp. 282-308.

media be minimised? How can users contribute to an increased re-usability of component parts?

2.3 *Individual Responsibility and Political Support*

Calls for ethics in the media are usually raised on a concrete occasion, which makes the present state of things appear as a state of crisis or inhumanity, as an 'out of order' state of affairs. Complaints set in: 'That can't be done, that's immoral!' Ethics attempts to investigate what the immorality consists in and to give the reasons why this sort of behaviour is not individually, socially or environmentally acceptable. Complaints based on cultural criticism (e.g., against too much TV) are, however committed they may be, not ethically relevant arguments. Neither is it satisfying to refer to the loss of validity of cultural habits, possessions or quasi-religious expectation[8]; rather, it remains to be shown *in what ways* personal and human dignity are offended.

Difficulties are posed by moral demands regarding one's own use of the media. What appears above all as a problem is other people's use of media, e.g., watching too much TV or downloading child pornography from the internet. The outrage over those willing to cruelly abuse children for the satisfaction of their sexual desires is extensive and (unlike other aspects of pornography) requires no further validation. Demands are made for internationally unified laws and carefully directed activities of law enforcement agencies, and the campaigns of individuals to keep criminal activities out of public networks are universally welcome.

Moreover, one's own use of the media is hardly ever discussed, and its wrongs or its inappropriateness rank as a negligible minor detail, which leads to a lack of clear awareness of the problem. Only on certain rare occasions does a newspaper article make one aware of journalists merely reproducing politicians' words and staging strategies without making them transparent and rendering them open to criticism. Hence, the question arises: How can *I* contribute towards a more transparent, more independent coverage? But can I really do something?

---

[8] Werner FAULSTICH, '"Jetzt geht die Welt zugrunde..." Kulturschock und Medien-Geschichte: Vom antiken Theater bis zu Multimedia' in Peter LUDES, Andreas WERNER (eds.), *Multimedia-Kommunikation: Theorien, Trends und Praxis*. Opladen/Wiesbaden, Westdeutscher Verlag, 1997, pp. 13-35.

Although the development and elaboration of an audience ethics is, therefore, difficult, it can refer to an existing media literacy and to the willingness to raise publicly objections concerning important matters. Thus, what is important here is the acceptance of individual self-responsibility and the willingness to make moral demands not only on others, but on oneself, and take to the initiative in this respect.

2.4 *What Does 'Responsible Media Use' Mean?*

Here, I shall list some demands or duties, and at the same time point out their limits. First, there is the conscious choice of media based on individual interests and needs, implying *limitation* and, consequently, a partial renunciation. As Hermann Lübbe[9] emphasises, without moderation, we founder in the profusion of information and entertainment offerings; immoderate consumption of the media has a destructive effect and renders the individual incapable of freedom.

Responsible media use implies attention to quality based on individual interests and biographies. The consumers have the modest but real power to demand high quality and vote out low quality. Although there is at all times only a small part of the audience participating in the rejection of low-quality or morally questionable offers or in boycotts of products presented in a problematic context (e.g., in programmes containing violence shown during children's normal TV watching times,) the small number of participants does not invalidate the ethical significance of these purposeful campaigns.

Finally, responsible use of the media implies attention towards the democratic role of political information, embracing the demand for and the support of an independent and investigative journalism. Cees J. Hamelink points out that, "This implies that the client also actively contributes to the professional performance."[10] Irresponsible publication of deceptive information, as in the Gulf War coverage but also in many cases of political staging, involves both sides,

---

[9] Hermann Lübbe, 'Mediennutzungsethik: Medienkonsum als moralische Herausforderung' in Hilmar Hoffman (ed.), *Gestern begann die Zukunft*. Darmstadt, Wissenschaftliche Buchgesellschaft, 1994, pp. 313-318.

[10] Cees J. Hamelink, 'Ethics for Media Users' in *European Journal of Communication* 10(1995), pp. 497-511, here p. 499.

namely, those deceiving others and those allowing themselves to be deceived.

In most countries media users are granted the legal right to reply; by demanding merely the realisation of individual preferences or by pressuring for high quality journalism, they decide to what extent and with what aims this right is made use of. Hamelink refers to the importance of groups and organisations monitoring media performance, and concludes that, "Media consumption should be viewed, like professional media performance, as a social practice which implies moral choices and the assumption of accountability for these choices." Elsewhere he summarises his demands on the audience in 'Ten Commandments for Media Consumers':[11]

> Thou shalt be an alert and discriminating media consumer.
> Thou shalt actively fight all forms of censorship.
> Thou shalt not unduly interfere with editorial independence.
> Thou shalt guard against racist and sexist stereotyping in the media.
> Thou shalt seek alternative sources of information.
> Thou shalt demand a pluralist supply of information.
> Thou shalt protect thine own privacy.
> Thou shalt be a reliable source of information.
> Thou shalt not participate in chequebook journalism.
> Thou shalt demand accountability from media producers.

Qualitative shortcomings of media contents cannot, however, be rectified merely through an adequate, critically-minded attitude and activity within the audience; a rectification also requires political regulations, which is the duty of media ethics to demand. As important as the ethics of media use is, it must not be assigned the sole responsibility in the media sector. If, for example, an excess of violence in the media leads to an increase of real violence...; the cause of this development, according to this line of reasoning, is the media consumer watching violence since he, not being morally sound, has been watching it. This relieves the producer, the actor, the programme director as well as the media politician and the media lawyer of their responsibility. Such a line of reasoning, which one occasionally encounters, assigns responsibility unilaterally. The ethics of individual media use constitutes only one side; the other side is made up of political, environmental and legal regulations which will, e.g., make questionable contents inaccessible to children.

[11] *Ibid.*, p. 505.

3. Responsible Media Use as a Part of Media Literacy

There is much talk at present of media literacy as a key qualification in an information society. Media literacy is a comprehensive objective to be reached through different pedagogical, educational and individual processes of development. Dieter Baacke differentiates four sectors of literacy.[12] (1) The ability to understand and critically scrutinise social developments informing the development of media ('media criticism.'); (2) The necessary knowledge in areas ranging from hardware to the policies of the great media organisations ('media knowledge.'); (3) The ability to receptively and interactively use media; (4) The ability to 'create' media, e.g., in designing one's own homepage or in actively working with videos.

Questions of ethics play a role in all four sectors of media literacy, not only in the first sector of media criticism, where personal standards are involved as much as the political creation of basic conditions for the freedom and the plurality of media. They are also relevant in the fourth sector, where the media user turns into a media designer and should be not only aesthetically creative, but also act responsibly.

3.1 *The Ethical Point of View as a Part of Critical Reflection*

According to Baacke[13], an understanding of developments in the media requires a 'critical reflection' containing three aspects: (1) *Analytically*, problematic social developments, e.g., economic concentration and monopolisation, should be adequately comprehended; (2) *Reflectively*, everyone should be capable of applying their analytically gained knowledge to themselves and their actions; (3) The *ethic* aspect harmonises and defines analytical thought and self-reflexivity within the context of social responsibility.[14]

---

[12] Dieter BAACKE, 'Medienkompetenz — Begrifflichkeit und sozialer Wandel' in Antje von REIN (ed.), *Medienkompetenz als Schlüsselbegriff*. Bad Heilbrunn, Klinkhardt, 1996, pp. 112-124. Also in Dieter BAACKE, *Medienpädagogik*. Tübingen, Niemeyer, 1997, pp. 98ff.

[13] Dieter BAACKE, *Medienpädagogik*. Tübingen, Niemeyer, 1997, pp. 98f.

[14] "(a) *Analytisch* sollten problematische gesellschaftliche Prozesse (z.B. Konzentrationsbewegungen) angemessen erfaßt werden können; (b) *reflexiv* sollte jeder Mensch in der Lage sein, das analytische Wissen auf sich selbst und sein Handeln anzuwenden zu können; (3) *ethisch* ist die Dimension, die analytisches Denken und reflexiven Rückbezug als sozialverantwortet abstimmt und definiert." BAACKE, *Medienpädagogik*, p. 98f.

Bernd Schorb points out that, formerly, media ethics was seen as a part of reflexivity, whereas today it has to be incorporated into the discussion as an approach in its own right. According to Schorb, in the past, human thought and action had always been accorded social relevance and carried social responsibility. In a time characterized by increasing individualisation, individualised media consumption and reciprocal network communication, developments in media do not fall under the domain of social responsibility as a matter of course. Today, the ethical point of view has to be emphasised and presented as a part of media literacy.[15]

The sociocritical patterns of thought of the generation of 1968 have indeed lost their cogency, and there are attempts to found morals on aesthetics.[16] This state of things poses the task of developing an audience ethics in a 'postmodern' way, basing this ethics on the subjective demand for an authentic life-style.

3.2 *Socially Responsible Media Use in Everyday Life*

Social responsibility becomes immediately more obvious in everyday family life. Most of us are again and again involved in discussions with children and adolescents on the media. As parents, educators or teachers, we are co-responsible for the development of the children and adolescents entrusted to our care. Small children should never be left alone in front of the TV for longer periods of time without having access to guidance and explanation of difficult or particularly fascinating programmes. Increasingly, young people digest difficult media experiences within a group of their peers, but that does not relieve parents of their responsibilities.

Parental responsibility originates with an awareness of the problems and deficits of children and adolescents in coping with media intake. Parents should, of course, offer and realise alternative leisure time activities to facilitate the realisation of their responsibility. Suggestions given to parents concerning media education should show a positive approach based not on cultural pessimism or undue moral-

---

[15] Bernd SCHORB, 'Vermittlung von Medienkompetenz als Aufgabe der Medienpädagogik' in *Medienkompetenz im Informationszeitalter/Enquete-Kommission 'Zukunft der Medien in Wirtschaft und Gesellschaft. Deutschlands Wege in die Informationsgesellschaft'*. Ed. Deutscher Bundestag, Bonn, ZV Zeitungs-Verlag Service, 1997, pp. 63-75, here p. 67f.

[16] Cf. e.g. Josef FRÜCHTL, *Ästhetische Erfahrung und moralisches Urteil: Eine Rehabilitierung*. Frankfurt a.M., Suhrkamp, 1996.

ising. Parents should be involved in discussions of the objectives as well as the realistic means of TV education. What is important is not only the parents' awareness of problems and responsibilities but also the attention given to the childrens' existing media literacy and their problems in digesting media intake. Only where both these aspects are taken into account will there be a media education which is based on ethical values *and* does justice to childrens' enjoyment of media.

Empirical studies of media consumption and media education within the family can make an important contribution to the definition and realisation of educational objectives, avoiding excessive demands and subsequent resignation and making discussions of media literacy less abstract and speculative.

In her educational conclusions, Bettina Hurrelmann[17] points out that TV consumption and TV education are always to be viewed within the context of the family structure (one parent families, two parent families with one child, families with two children, families with three or more children) and its chances and disadvantages. Problems of TV education are anchored in families structural problems, so that media literacy is, to a large extent, the ability to cope with everyday life. Although most parents consider TV education their responsibility (and expect support through schools and pre-schools,) watching TV is hardly ever seen in its relation to comprehensive media literacy, where more attention is given to the computer and its use in professional life.

One thing has become clear from these hints: Media education as well as audience ethics depend on empirical research for a complete picture and description of the situation. Defining basic objectives and setting forth the exemplary blueprint for responsible media use remain the task of a philosophy of education and of media ethics. Questions to be discussed include: How are self-determination and creative development of personal identity possible in a world dominated and determined by media? How can 'media socialisation' be organised in a way that allows for individuation and personal development? How can a certain power of resistance to media offerings be developed and preserved in order to contribute to autonomous media use?

---

[17] Bettina HURRELMANN, Michael MAMMER, Klaus STELBERG, *Familienmitglied Fernsehen: Fernsehgebrauch und Probleme der Fernseherziehung in verschiedenen Familienformen.* Opladen, Leske — Budrich, 1996, pp. 257 ff.

3.3 *Development of Personality as a Precondition*

Mettler-von Meibom[18] points out preconditions for self-determination and freedom. Basing her argument on the philosopher Michel Foucault, who called the culture of self-care 'technologies of the self,' she holds that freedom cannot be realised without the conscious practicing of self-care. This self-care includes consciously dealing with time, being able to deny something to oneself (*askesis*), turning towards the inner self and turning attention towards the emotions of the soul 'to activate the truths required for oneself.' Such elements of distancing and tranquil reflection are necessary in a situation where certain media offerings are able to fascinate us to such a degree that our media use assumes, at least temporarily, addictive traits. To Mettler-von Meibom the search for demanding ways of personality formation is part of the advancement of media literacy in private everyday life.

The philosopher Hermann Lübbe points us in the same direction, recommending one to orient media user ethics towards the traditional virtue of moderation. Immoderate media consumption has a destructive effect and renders the individual incapable of freedom; this applies not only to predominantly entertaining programmes, but also to news programmes.[19] As development of personality is the grand aim of education and self-education, the relation between media education and media ethics, especially audience ethics, shall now be looked at more closely.

3.4 *Safeguarding Media Literacy Through Media (Self-) Education*

Of the factual objectives of a governmental media policy, a high degree of importance is accorded to the promotion of trade and industry benefiting domestic media enterprises and improving infrastructure. At the same time, demands are made, at least in speeches, for comprehensive media literacy in professional areas as well as in leisure time activities. But literacy does not come out of nothing. In addition to the importance of casual learning, the knowledge of structures and the critical ability with respect to media offerings requires purposeful learning processes. There is, however, no

---

[18] Barbara METTLER-VON MEIBOM, 'Spiel — Unterhaltung — Sucht: Die Frage nach den Grenzüberschreitungen' in *Aus Politik und Zeitgeschichte. Beilage zur Wochenzeitung Das Parlament*. 19-20/97 (2. May 1997), pp. 34-46.

[19] LÜBBE, *Art. cit.*

effective promotion of these processes. As Otto B. Roegele established already in 1970,

> Obviously, the citizen is credited with an outstanding natural aptitude for dealing with the media, so that there is no need for a special instruction in this field. ... What is to become of mass media in the future, if those for whom they were developed and towards whom they address their statements do not know how to properly deal with them? ... We do not know nearly enough about the organisation, the peculiarities and the modes of operation of communication media. There remains a long way to go towards a scientifically established, practically usable theory of media operation.[20]

Competent and critical media audiences are responsible for the safeguarding of the democratic function of media as well as media producers, journalists and media institutions. Audience ethics refers not to an exclusive responsibility, but a *co*-responsibility for the successful communication between people and peoples through media, for the stimulation, maintenance and strengthening of individual and collective identities through media offerings and for the understanding and enjoyment of knowledge, art and entertaining narratives. "Responsibility for successful communication rests not only with the active communicator, but also with the recipient. This responsibility applies not only in the sphere of primary communication and in primary social relationships, but also, which is not as familiar a notion, in the sphere of mass communication."[21]

An audience or user ethics of this description, thus, shows a natural affinity to media education or, in adulthood , to media self-education. As a part of overall education, i.e., the organised growing

---

[20] "traut man dem Staatsbürger offenbar eine eminente natürliche Begabung zu, mit den Medien umzugehen, so daß man darauf verzichten kann, ihn darin eigens auszubilden. ... Was soll aus den Massenmedien in der Zukunft werden, wenn die Menschen, für die sie geschaffen wurden und an die sie ihre Aussagen richten, mit ihnen nichts Rechtes anzufangen wissen? ... Wir wissen noch längst nicht genug über Aufbau, Eigenheiten und Wirkungsweise der Kommunikationsmitetl. Der Weg zu einer wissenschaftlich gesicherten, in der Praxis brauchbaren Funktionslehre der Medien ist noch weit." Otto B. ROEGELE, *Die Zukunft der Massenmedien*. Osnabrück, Fromm, 1970, pp. 50 f.

[21] "Nicht nur der Kommunikator, sondern auch der Rezipient ist dafür verantwortlich, daß Kommunikation gelingt. Er ist dafür nicht nur verantwortlich im Bereich primärer Kommunikation und in primären sozialen Beziehungen, sondern auch im Bereich der Massenkommunikation, was nicht so geläufig ist." WUNDEN, *Art. cit.*, pp. 17 f.

into a culture, media (self-) education tries to promote active exploration of and selection from media offerings in orienting people towards educational objectives and values. To contemporary media educators, the media are not things which human beings are to be kept away and protected from; rather, they pursue discriminate media criticism and emphasise the active digesting of media offerings within the framework of acquired knowledge and the willingness to gain new experience.

Thus, the passive audience is a myth of the cultural pessimism still present and valid among disturbed intellectuals. *Kinder* können *fernsehen* ('*Children* can *Watch TV*') is the title of a book by Jan-Uwe Rogge.[22] Moreover, I defended my doctoral thesis, *Fernsehen lernen — eine Herausforderung an die Pädagogik* ('*Learning to Watch TV — a Challenge to Pedagogy.*') Both views are correct in different respects. We *already are* media literate due to our intellectual abilities and our having grown into a culture in which all of us are endowed with some critical ability. But we have to become media literate in the full sense of the word. We:

— Can and must continue acquiring knowledge of media selection and media use in the fields of entertainment, information, playing, learning, problem-solving and decision-making, especially in view of the changes in media offerings, e.g., in multimedia and on the internet.

— Can gain more experience in understanding media languages, genres, real and virtual worlds as well as in using the hardware and software allowing us access to all this;

— Should be able to analyse media and media products within their basic economic, political, technical and aesthetic conditions and to intervene if necessary;

— Should also be aware of the media's impact on our own emotions, notions and behaviour patterns as well as those of others. Certainly there is no direct and linear causal relation here, but we should make an issue of our imparting subjective meaning to media offerings;

— Should be willing to accept responsibility for the contents we offer (e.g., on the internet) — this is an important element of media ethics in media literacy.

---

[22] Jan-Uwe ROGGE, *Kinder können fernsehen: Vom sinnvollen Umgang mit dem Medium*. Reinbek, Rowohlt, 1990.

4. Anthropological Foundations of Audience Ethics

The demands of user ethics are addressed primarily towards the individual, taking into account the individual's media selection, media digesting, reply and active media use, always asking the question of responsibility in media use.

Audience ethics has to offer concrete and effective guidelines for media use. However, in establishing moral demands it has to be asked whether there is a focal point of convergence and deduction of moral maxims or at least criteria. Such a focal point is provided by general propositions about human existence as offered in philosophical anthropology. These propositions accord a central role to humankind, as he or she is a free being capable of reason whose basic ability is that of self-determination and autonomy, and is a person and a subject whose basic need is the fulfillment of his or her potential. Following the tradition of enlightenment thought, political participation in a democratic state is an integral part of this line of reasoning.

In attempting to arrive at further anthropological propositions relevant to media use and having normative status, different anthropological concepts may be made use of.[23]

Here, I shall just enumerate some questions posed to user ethics from an anthropological perspective:

— What manners and methods of media use and what minimum of media resources make life in a culture extensively dominated by the media a *good* life?
— What forms of media literacy should the individual, with the help of others, develop?
— When does the individual have the right to be spared certain media contents (e.g., in childhood and adolescence)?
— When and where is the individual summoned to develop critical distance and selective taste?
— What steps of practical reason and strategy of living are required to use media autonomously and adequately?

---

[23] Cf. Rainald MERKERT, *Medien und Erziehung: Einführung in pädagogische Fragen des Medienzeitalters*. Darmstadt, Wissenschaftliche Buchgesellschaft, 1992, pp. 56 — 61; also Christian DOELKER, 'Der archaische Mensch im Medienkonsumenten von heute' in Marianne GREWE-PARTSCH, Jo GROEBEL (eds.), *Mensch und Medien. Zu Ehren von Hertha Sturm*. München, Saur, 1987, pp.. 110-121; also Christian DOELKER, *Kulturtechnik Fernsehen: Analyse eines Mediums*. Stuttgart, Klett-Cotta, 1989, pp. 101 — 110.

— Which organisations and political initiatives help the audience to protect their rights of participation?

5. Responsibility in Media Users' Roles

Following this anthropological foundation of responsible media use, I shall consider, as a summary and partial recapitulation, the audience's duties in the three typical roles which constitute the abstract role of the media user: (1) our role as *citizens*, (2) our role as *organisers of our own leisure time* and (3) the role of educators, which most of us assume at least from time to time.[24]

5.1 *Civic Responsibility for the Media*

At first sight, media use appears as a private, individual action. However, it is at the same time publicly valid and relevant, as media users participate in the sphere of the media-mediated public. Belonging to the audience (measured e.g. in programme ratings) is a form of social existence and action. As citizens, we are co-responsible for the working of democratic institutions and, consequently, the media order. Broadcasting committees control the implementation of the services' obligations, especially the provision of information at a high level of quality, on our behalf, and the constitutionally guaranteed liberty of 'commercial' media like the press, private broadcasting or TV stations is not a boundless financial freedom, but a liberty exercised in the service of the audience.

We should not entirely leave it to our representatives to control whether the media operate in accordance with this constitutional understanding. We should, as it is demanded by the ethos of active citizenship, acknowledge, reject or subscribe to at least the most important decisions, failures or praiseworthy achievements in media politics; we have the opportunity to become active through consciously seeking relevant information and developing an independent opinion, and also occasionally through outward-oriented action like the writing of letters. Participation in community radio or TV

---

[24] Cf. Rüdiger FUNIOK, 'Grundfragen einer Publikumsethik' in Rüdiger FUNIOK (ed.), *Grundfragen der Kommunikationsethik.* Konstanz, UVK, 1996, pp. 107-122, here pp. 112-119; in the same volume Wolfgang WUNDEN, 'Auch das Publikum trägt Verantwortung', pp. 123-132, here pp. 125-128.

will depend on a special interest and the amount of leisure time; participation in TV monitoring circles will bring together parents concerned about programmes suitable for children.

To emphasise the civic responsibiliy of the audience for the public media order, Clifford Christians writes of a 'communal responsibility' of the audience.[25]

5.2 *Responsibility for Oneself and One's Own Leisure Time*

The bulk of media use takes place in our leisure time in which we are responsible solely for ourselves, the planning of our time, our willingness to learn, our choice of contents we use to entertain and stimulate us. To avoid becoming excessively 'moral,' we have to adopt a fundamentally positive view of media use in leisure time without neglecting the danger of passivity and banishing the obligation of conscious living. This encompasses the individual's ability and willingness to:

— Make conscious selections from media offerings, which are constantly increasing in a rapidly expanding information society.

— Critically judge information and entertainment offerings during and/or after using them according to genre-specific and objectively adequate criteria, especially in political coverage or advertisement and where democratic values are suppressed or endangered.

— Orient media choices towards one's needs in order to develop personal identity, individual experiences and a conscious lifestyle through media use.

As our leisure time is limited, a conscious choice of programmes requires a partial renunciation of the media and programmes. The decision to read a paper or a magazine, to listen to radio programmes or to watch TV is always made within the context of and in competition with other leisure time activities, social contacts, domestic tasks; failure to limit media use leads to a misuse of time with this specific leisure time activity.

An important criterion for a responsible choice of media is that of an individually determined equilibrium between interpersonal, social communication, on the one hand, and mediated, 'virtual' communication, on the other. This communicative balance is especially

---

[25] Clifford B. CHRISTIANS, 'Can the Public be held accountable?' in *Journal of Mass Media Ethics* 3(1988)1, pp. 50-58; in German in Wolfgang WUNDEN (ed.), *Medien zwischen Markt und Moral*. Stuttgart, Steinkopf, 1989, pp. 195-213.

threatened in cases of social or psychological deprivation. What is at issue here is a "media ecology'[26] avoiding psychological pollution through undigested experiential waste. Referring to a balanced human being, Wolfgang Wunden writes:

> "He appreciates his own inner world and its experiential space as origin of and substantial precondition for his communication with his environment, and he is able to deal with exterior reality, be it through immediate experience or through media experience."[27]

Of course, audience ethics must not be based merely on the assumption of a 'sublime' use of informative and educational offerings, but has to take into account the (quantitatively superior) use of entertainment offerings (including music) without adopting an attitude of cultural pessimism. A positive view of the audience is especially important with respect to entertaining media offerings. Human life is not based on reason alone: Where the media fulfill our wishes to gain new experience individually or with others, to make travels of the mind or to be told thrilling stories, they will fascinate us. The question of whether and when such a use of entertaining media hinders freedom and rationality cannot be decided once and for all and from the outside. A 'humane' theory of media use will not only regard information-seeking and education, but also games and entertainment as fundamentally positive.[28]

There is, however, also an uncritical consumption of entertaining or (politically) manipulating media offerings. This is why safeguarding our liberty demands guidance and educational support when we are children, self-discipline and self-education when we are adults. The period of National Socialism or a look at our political illusions (e.g., that of Socialism as an alternative to a market economy)

---

[26] Cf. Kurt LÜSCHER, Michael WEHRSPAUN, 'Medienökologie: Der Anteil der Medien an unserer Gestaltung der Lebenswelten' in *Zeitschrift für Sozialisationsforschung und Erziehungssoziologie* 5(1985), pp. 187-204; Matthias DONATH, Barbara von METTLER-MEIBOM, *Kommunikationsökologie: Systematische und historische Aspekte.* Münster, LIT, 1998.

[27] "Er versteht seine eigene innere Welt und deren Erfahrungsraum als Ursprung und inhaltliche Grundbedingung für seine Kommunikation mit der Umwelt, und es vermag mit der Wirklichkeit außer sich umzugehen, sei es auf dem Weg unmittelbarer Erfahrung oder auf dem Weg über Medienerfahrung." WUNDEN, *Art. cit.* p. 21.

[28] Cf. Thomas HAUSMANNINGER, *Kritik der medienethischen Vernunft.* München, Fink, 1993, pp. 553-563; Thomas HAUSMANNINGER, 'Grundlinien einer Ethik medialer Unterhaltung' in Werner WOLBERT (ed.), *Moral in einer Kultur der Massenmedien.* Friburg, Universitäts Verlag/Freiburg, Herder, 1994, pp. 77-96.

demonstrate the ability of the media to manipulate. In his *Brave New World*, Aldous Huxley shows how rationality is 'darkened' through an excess of shallow entertainment and a lack of critical detachment.[29] It is only through working on our personal development that we remain media literate; without media (self-)education there is no substantial audience ethos.

5.3 *Responsibility for Adolescents*

The third role relevant in media use is that of parents or educators in kindergarten or school. Most of us are again and again involved in discussions on media with children and adolescents. As parents or professional educators, we are responsible for the growth and development of the children and adolescents in our care, and have to take into account the important role of media in this educational process. In individual cases, it may be sensible to keep adolescents away from problematic media offerings; in these cases, organising alternative activities in common will be preferable to straightforward prohibition. In discussing media and media use with our children, the objective should be the promotion of their media literacy, e.g., by reflecting on critical criteria and the possibilities of adopting a critical detachment from difficult media offerings.

In youth protection acts, society comes to parents' aid by restricting access of children and adolescents to problematic media offerings. These limitations will, however, be more difficult to control and enforce in the world of international media with its different time zones. Besides, the seduction of material goods exerted through continuous advertising and the possibility of teleshopping seems to be at least as problematic as harmful movies and computer games. Although there are social groups in which TV programmes 'justify' and reinforce violence in a dangerous way, normal children and adolescents tend to take violent content less seriously than adults, and especially, professional youth workers.

What is increasingly more important, even in healthy families, is the need for parents to point out to their children that, contrary to what the media represents, one cannot have everything, that being content and living harmoniously does not depend on certain real or virtual toys, stimulants or travels. Further support to parents is

---

[29] Cf. Herwig BÜCHELE, *SehnSucht nach der Schönen neuen Welt*. Thaur, Kulturverlag, 1993.

given by society through media education in schools, the assistance accorded to self-determined media productions in youth centres and similar activities.

When one writes about Audience Ethics, one should talk about the duties and tasks which appear in this area. Therefore this article tried to list and justify the duties of a responsible media-user. But it is also important to conclude with a mention of some of the available resources. Perhaps the most important resource consists of people who are expert users of media, people who are media-literate. For young people, peers are usually more important than parents. When media are analysed in the classroom, the criteria for judging the quality of media can be sharpened. And parents can get help from booklets that advice which TV programs are suitable for children.[30] All these resources are available; knowing and using them is an important part of Audience Ethics.

---

[30] The tri-annual program guide *Flimmo - Fersehen mit Kinderaugen* (publ. and ed. by "Programmberatung für Eltern e.V. bei der Bayereschen Landeszentrale für neue Medien, München) is based on the results of qualitative research into chirdren's experience of media. These guides explain which programs children (in three age groups: 3-6, 7-10, 11-13) would enjoy, which programs they might need some help with, and which programs would be hard for them to take.

PRINTED ON PERMANENT PAPER • IMPRIME SUR PAPIER PERMANENT • GEDRUKT OP DUURZAAM PAPIER - ISO 9706

ORIENTALISTE, KLEIN DALENSTRAAT 42, B-3020 HERENT